AMERICA'S MUSICAL
PULSE

Recent Titles in
Contributions to the Study of Popular Culture

AMERICA'S MUSICAL PULSE

Popular Music in Twentieth-Century Society

Edited by
KENNETH J. BINDAS

PRAEGER

Westport, Connecticut
London

Library of Congress Cataloging-in-Publication Data

America's musical pulse : popular music in twentieth-century society /
   edited by Kenneth J. Bindas.
       p.   cm.
   Includes bibliographical references and index.
   ISBN 0–275–94306–2 (pbk.)
       1. Popular music—United States—History and criticism.
   I. Bindas, Kenneth J.
   ML3477.A48   1992b
   781.64'0973'0904—dc20   92–893

British Library Cataloguing in Publication Data is available.

A hardcover edition of *America's Musical Pulse* is available
from the Greenwood Press imprint of Greenwood
Publishing Group, Inc. (Contributions to the Study of
Popular Culture, Number 33; ISBN 0–313–27465–7).

Library of Congress Catalog Card Number: 92–893
ISBN: 0–275–94306–2

First published in 1992

Praeger Publishers, 88 Post Road West, Westport, CT 06881
An imprint of Greenwood Publishing Group, Inc.

Printed in the United States of America

The paper used in this book complies with the
Permanent Paper Standard issued by the National
Information Standards Organization (Z39.48–1984).

10 9 8 7 6 5 4 3 2 1

Copyright Acknowledgments

"Keep Your Hands Off Her," words and music by Huddie Ledbetter, copyright 1963 (renewed)
and 1965 Folkways Music Publishers, Inc., New York, NY. Used by permission.

Every reasonable effort has been made to trace the owners of copyright materials in this book,
but in some cases this has proven impossible. The author and publisher will be glad to receive
information leading to more complete acknowledgments in subsequent printings of the book
and in the meantime extend their apologies for any omissions.

Contents

PART V. GENDER

PART VI. SOCIAL CONTEXT

Preface

A short time ago, as I was lecturing to freshman-level American history students on class, race, and politics during the early twentieth century, I noticed that much of what I was saying was not hitting home. The students had difficulty grasping the concept that American society was restrictive concerning these issues, and they were particularly unaware of any present-day divisions. In desperation, I began talking about their preferences in popular music. Some preferred rock, others rap, and still others country, easy listening, or jazz, but all of them had an opinion concerning the music of their choice. When I asked them why there were so many different kinds of popular music, they said "to meet the people's needs." When I asked why and how these needs were created or what part history, economics, or racism played in the process, there was silence. After a few questions and a short discussion on the development of rock music, we returned to the original topic regarding the barriers between race, class, and politics and how jazz, country, blues, and swing helped both to perpetuate and destroy these divisions.

America's Musical Pulse: Popular Music in Twentieth Century Society is a result of that lecture transition. The book contains twenty-eight chapters from educators and scholars in history, communications, media, music, sociology, political science, and English, as well as a few professional writers. The topics chosen do not represent the only significant aspects of popular music but examine those topics that traditionally have received the most attention. The focus of these essays, as diverse and at times contradictory as they are, is to nudge readers to think of the more complex issues behind the popular sound. Too often popular music is ignored by teaching professionals, because many view the music as base or not a proper cultural pursuit, but I suggest that such views stem from lack of understanding; therefore, *America's Musical Pulse* is as much for teachers as for students.

The selections included deal with various aspects of popular music in this century and are divided among six parts—politics, class, economics, race, gender, and social context—revealing the interconnection of popular music forms with a particular era or generation's attitudes. Therefore, the book is organized both thematically and chronologically and can be used in either context. The Introduction seeks to place music within the larger learning framework, and the concluding chapter places the impact of popular music into perspective.

Since the chapters were written by different people, some of their assessments agree, and others do not; but all try to forge a link between what the students spend so much time concerned with—their music—and the issues of history, culture, and society. *America's Musical Pulse* documents the American experience as recorded in American popular song. In examining and analyzing these primary sources, perhaps a better understanding of our American society will emerge.

Introduction: The Importance of Music to People

Rudolf E. Radocy

Music, patterns of organized sound and silence in time, is important to people, evidenced by the presence of some form of music in virtually every culture. Not every person cares about any one particular piece of music, but almost every person cares about something musical. A person's level of musical involvement may vary from passionate commitment and authoritative knowledge to a vague comfort experienced when activity occurs along with background music. Several years ago, Avram Goldstein's research indicated that in the self-reports of 250 people regarding what was thrilling for them, 96 percent reported thrills came from musical passages. Just 70 percent of reported thrills were for sexual activity, and only 52 percent were for particular moments in sporting events. Clearly, music is prominent in people's lives in a variety of ways.

The origins of music are lost in the origins of human creations and behaviors. Drawing on various theories and conjectures of anthropologists and psychologists, Rudolf E. Radocy and J. David Boyle outline nine theories concerning why music might have developed:

1. Music originated in mating calls (sometimes called a "Darwinian" theory).
2. Music grew from the persistent rhythmic movements of dance.
3. Work songs that assisted "primitive" people in coordinating group efforts evolved into music.
4. People imitated bird songs.
5. Music evolved from prolonged speech uttered in emotional contexts.
6. Music evolved from accents and tonal inflections that occur naturally in speech.
7. Melodic patterns occurring naturally in young children ("lalling") served as prototypical models.

8. Sounds with relatively fixed pitches and varying loudness levels were useful in communication across relatively long distances.
9. People felt that music facilitated communication with supernatural beings.

All of the theories and conjectures have drawbacks and inadequacies. A theory attributed to the anthropologist and ethnomusicologist Bruno Nettl regarding an evolving distinction between speech and music may make some sense, although there is no way to test it adequately, at least without the benefit of time travel. According to Nettl's view, human's initial communications with each other were neither speech nor music but a combination of sounds that featured varying accent, duration, and pitch. Gradually, the sounds evolved into two classes, one of which became speech and the other of which became music. Over the eons, the speech class developed into diverse human languages, and the music class developed into diverse musical styles. E. Thayer Gaston sees music as a natural result of the development of the family and other social structures, particularly the mother-child relationship. In addition, he views it as something with which an increasingly complex brain could occupy itself. More recently, John Sloboda has viewed music as a natural outcome of evolution, which supplied a "motivation" for music. W. Jay Dowling and D. L. Harwood suggest that music has a biological adaptive value because it facilitates group activities and social solidarity. As part of a theory of multiple human intelligences, Howard Gardner offers evidence for a separate musical intelligence, characterized by the equivalence of genius and retardation, and subject to its own principles of development.

Whatever the "real" origin of music, its importance is quite evident when one considers the functions that it serves in societies, historically and today. Consideration of A. P. Merriam's functions of music is virtually mandatory in any discussion of music's roles in people's lives. While they are not necessarily exhaustive and certainly are not mutually exclusive, Merriam's ten functions, developed from an anthropological perspective, provide a solid basis for considering music's pervasive influences and importance.

One function is *emotional expression.* People may employ music to express thoughts more dramatically or passionately than they might in speech. In the 1960s, many Americans, particularly older teenagers and people in their twenties, expressed their anti–Vietnam War sentiments with songs such as "Give Peace a Chance," "Where Have All the Flowers Gone," and "Fixin' to Die Rag." Other Americans protested the actions of war protesters with "Okie from Muskogee." "We Shall Overcome" was and is an unofficial anthem of the civil rights movement, and when Soviet troops invaded Czechoslovakia in 1968 to crush the Czechs' protest movement, television news clips showed Czech citizens singing "We Shall Overcome" in their language. In the Beijing demonstrations for democracy in 1989, songs were prominent. On a more personal level, many songs express love in some way. Donald

Horton identified a five-stage adolescent love cycle (prologue, courtship, a honeymoon period, a downward course, an abandoned lonely stage) in popular music of the mid–1950s. People can find songs to express grief, joy, reverie, fright, and virtually any feeling that may be deemed emotion.

Another of Merriam's functions of music is *aesthetic enjoyment*. People may engage in esoteric arguments about the "real" meaning of *aesthetic*, but an aesthetic experience essentially involves seriously contemplating some object or event for its beauty and power to invoke an emotional experience. Music obviously may be involved in profound aesthetic experiences. One goal of music education is to provide students with the sensitivity to understand musical structures and the ability to express their sensitivities in increasingly sophisticated ways. Sometimes music is dichotomized into settings where the music itself is the main focus, as in a concert, and settings where the music is incidental to something else, as in using music to entertain people who are on hold while waiting for a telephone connection. Presumably an aesthetic experience is more likely when music is the main focus, but there may be exceptions.

Music as entertainment is a third function. Music may amuse; one may listen to it without any profound contemplation of its meaning or sensitivity to all of the nuances of musical performance. Popular music often exemplifies music as entertainment, although it also may serve other functions. (From the standpoint of many performers and the recording industry, its major function is to make money.) The entertainment function is also exemplified by situations where music accompanies other entertainment activities, such as dancing, athletic events, or songs to express grief, joy, reverie, fright, and virtually any feeling that may be deemed as emotion.

Merriam's fourth function of music is *communication*. Music cannot communicate with the precision of spoken or written language, but research has shown that people who have a shared experience with a particular musical style commonly identify it within the style, particularly for instrumental music. Music is not a universal language, but within a culture, stereotypical associations for particular sounds exist. These may be rather specific, as in the battle section from Rossini's "Overture" to *William Tell* signaling the Lone Ranger to generations of American radio listeners and television viewers. They may be more general, as when the music accompanying a movie or television drama enhances a narration. As Anne Rosenfeld points out, the experience of seeing something live for the first time, such as the Grand Canyon, might be disappointing due to the lack of music for someone who is accustomed to multimedia presentations. In Western art music, the tradition of program music (e.g., Prokofiev's *Peter and the Wolf*, Strauss's *Don Quixote*, and Dukas's *Sorcerer's Apprentice*) represents a rather specific attempt to tell a story through music. The possibility exists, of course, that the message that a listener constructs from the music is not the one the composer and/or performer meant to send; one could then argue about what sort of communication occurs. In any event, music clearly does communicate, as evidenced by the associations people make with particular sounds.

Symbolic representation, the next function, may share some similarities with communication. The music symbolizes or represents something of a nonmusical nature—perhaps a cultural value, some affective meaning, or other group or individual value. A national anthem may symbolize traditions of the nation. In addition to its function as emotional expression and communication, a loving couple's "our song" may represent some aspect of their mutual love.

Physical response, the sixth of Merriam's functions, is linked to dance and other overt rhythmic activity, as well as music's ability to accelerate or retard people's movements. Music may affect the rate at which people work, finish meals, leave a public building, or move through a store.

Enforcing conformity to social norms is evident when the music contains some expression of a societal expectancy or a warning against deviant behavior. In the 1950s, a country-western song entitled "Rusty Old Halo" warned people to be careful and righteous while they were alive, or when they died, their eternal reward would be a rusty halo, a scrawny cloud, underdeveloped wings, and a scratchy and irritating robe. Later, imaginary adolescent males were warned to stay away from a particularly macho figure's girl and avoid his turf. More positively, the Beach Boys implored youngsters to "be true to your school," and patriotic songs urge feelings of national pride.

An eighth and closely related function is *validation of social and religious rituals*. Liturgical music obviously fits here, and some of the examples already noted, such as national anthems, might be considered as well. A fraternal organization's traditional songs and college or university "fight" songs and alma maters are further examples.

Music may *contribute to the continuity and stability of culture* as it communicates and enforces expectancies and rituals. For forty years, American adolescent subculture has had various forms of music identified with it, music that teenagers could claim as their own. Folk songs from the old country may provide immigrants and their descendants with a cultural link to the past. In addition to their religious and entertainment functions, traditional Christmas carols and Hannukah songs provide a cross-generational stability.

Merriam's final function is the *contribution to the integration of society*. Music may bring diverse people together to share a common experience. Friendships may form as a result of participating in a musical ensemble. People from differing sociocultural, religious, political, occupational, and musical backgrounds may find mutual interest in particular music.

In considering the importance of music to people, one must recognize that music may not always be important as music; rather, its importance may be in terms of some catalytic function. Among Merriam's ten functions, only in aesthetic expression is the focus necessarily on the music as music. In the other areas, music fulfills its various roles by enhancing some other environmental aspect.

Music is used effectively in sales and marketing—evident not only in singing commercials but in the use of background music to create or enhance a mood. Ruth Milliman showed that customers tend to move through a supermarket more slowly and spend more money in the store when the background music is slow than when it is fast or when there is no music. When asked about the music upon leaving the store, few people were aware of it.

For over half a century, the Muzak Corporation has provided background music for commercial and industrial applications. (Despite the generic use of *Muzak* to refer to any background music, just as people may refer to any facial tissue as Kleenex, *Muzak* is a brand name. There are other background music suppliers.) While many musicians may consider Muzak as a derogatory or pejorative term (referring to it as "elevator music"), the provision of background music is a commercial success. Muzak employs the concepts of stimulus value and stimulus progression. A Muzak segment's stimulus value depends on tempo, rhythm pattern, and the types and number of instruments used in the recording. The stimulus progression unfolds as the musical segments increase in stimulus value, particularly in tempo and instrumentation. Each progression includes about five or six excerpts, with a total length of about fifteen minutes. While the results of the limited systematic research on Muzak's effects on worker output and morale as well as sales are not conclusive, many business people are sufficiently convinced of its value to allocate resources to background music.

The value of background music may be in terms of entertainment, but, perhaps paradoxically, if listeners give too much attention to it, the music is no longer in the background. Background music is defined as music that people are supposed to hear but not listen to attentively while they are primarily engaged in some activity other than listening to music. Presumably even without conscious attention, the music's presence enlivens or enhances the environment. Background music also may function as a masking sound to cover up less desirable background sounds, such as nearby conversations and machinery noise.

Music's importance to people is illustrated further by its use in therapeutic situations. This is done informally—for example, by mentally unwinding while listening to favorite music at the end of the workday—and formally, by professional music therapists who plan musical activities to meet specific goals for specific clients. Gaston, occasionally deemed the Father of Modern Music Therapy, suggests that music therapy is rooted in three principles. One exploits music's social possibilities to establish or reestablish interpersonal relationships. Music and music making may facilitate social contact.

A second principle is that music may enhance self-esteem through self-actualization, which is a reduction of the psychological distance between how a person sees himself or herself and how that person would like to be. Musical performance or listening to music with greater understanding may build a person's self-confidence and move him or her along a mental path toward a more ideal self. Gaston's third principle exploits the powerful potential of rhythm to energize people and give them a sense of order. Music is a time-dependent art form. Sounds and silences within the sounds occur for definite durations; the listener is not free to proceed through the music at his or her own pace. One needs to accept the order imposed by the rhythm. Somewhat more succinctly, Donald Michel indicated that music therapists use music's basic power to soothe or stimulate and also use it as a socializing and an expressive medium. While music therapy never cures any ailment, the use of music to help people in diverse areas of human need, such as alleviating speech impediments, making physical therapy more pleasant, assisting women in giving birth, reducing antisocial behavior, grief counseling, and focusing attention in mentally retarded people, continues to grow.

In the context of religion, the importance of music for people is obvious, whether in the sense of the role of music in worship or in the sense of what is and is not permissible in accordance with the religion's traditions. Music is an integral part of many worship ceremonies and rites, whether as a formal part of liturgy or a means of congregational participation. Arnold Perris extensively examined musical roles in Judaism, Christianity, Islam, and Hinduism and identified six major considerations for using music in worship: (1) any words must be comprehensible to the congregation; (2) performances must maintain traditional melodic and other musical practices; (3) musical instruments must be acceptable, morally and socially; (4) any music must occur at proper places in ceremonies for proper purposes; (5) music must not be misused or detract from the religious aspect of the ceremonies; and (6) artistic considerations of composers or performers should not subjugate theological and doctrinal considerations. (Arnold Perris suggests that artistic emphases at the expense of theological emphases occasiona"y have been of major concern in the tradition of Western religious music.)

Contemporary developments regarding artistic freedom versus proper public display illustrate the importance people attach to music as a potential negative influence. The rap group 2 Live Crew had certain of its recordings banned in parts of Florida in 1990 for "obscene" lyrics. Parental groups succeeded in attaching warning labels to recordings that contain sexually explicit lyrics. A court case ensued because parents alleged that a recording abetted their son's suicide. Controversy over the National Endowment for the Arts' funding of "obscene" projects, while primarily related to the visual arts, may have implications for music. Belief that certain rock music contains satanic and other antisocial messages, which may be revealed if the tape is played backward with proper equipment ("backmasking"), persists.

There is no question that music may harm people. Research and clinical evidence shows clearly that persistent exposure to music at a high loudness level may cause temporary and, eventually, permanent hearing loss by desensitizing or destroying delicate neural fibers in the inner ear. Under conditions of social pressure, loud music may increase irritation and frustration and make people more aggressive toward others; soothing music may make them less aggressive. More speculatively, John Fuller attributes the tragedy at Cincinnati in 1979 where people were crushed to death while awaiting a concert by the Who to a type of hypnotic state due to anticipation.

Music's importance is exemplified by the variety of functions it serves. It may arouse hostility or soothe; it may bring an uplifting experience or cause depression. Music is readily available in some form to almost everyone, and that its very availability is part of an interesting paradox: Music is everywhere, but musical knowledge, skill, and appreciation often are grossly undervalued, possibly because almost everyone has some musical ability and can participate in music at some level. Music education's struggle to survive in formal education and the general lack of concern for music (and for the other arts) in calls for educational reform may be related to the availability/low value paradox. If people reflect on music's unique qualities, which come from its base in organized sound and its importance in human life, their explicit values for music perhaps may increase.

BIBLIOGRAPHY

Dowling, W. J., and D. L. Harwood. *Music Cognition.* Orlando, Fla.: Academic Press, 1986.

Fuller, J. G. *Are the Kids All Right?* New York: Time Books, 1981.

Gardner, H. *Frames of Mind.* New York: Basic Books, 1983.

Gaston, E. T. "Man and Music." In E. T. Gaston, ed., *Music in Therapy,* pp. 7–29. New York: Macmillan, 1968.

Goldstein, A. "Thrills in Response to Music and Other Stimuli." *Physiological Psychology* 8 (1980): 126–29.

Horton, D. "The Dialogue of Courtship in Popular Songs." *American Journal of Sociology* 62 (1957): 569–78.

Merriam, A. P. *The Anthropology of Music.* Evanston, Ill.: Northwestern University Press, 1964.

Michel, D. E. *Music Therapy: An Introduction, including Music in Special Education.* 2d ed. Springfield, Ill.: Charles C. Thomas, 1985.

Milliman, R. E. "Using Background Music to Affect the Behavior of Supermarket Shoppers." *Journal of Marketing* 46 (3) (1985): 86–91.

Nettl, Bruno. *Music in Primitive Culture.* Cambridge, Mass.: Harvard University Press, 1956.

Perris, A. *Music as Propaganda: Art to Persuade, Art to Control*. Westport, Conn.: Greenwood Press, 1985.

Radocy, R. E., and J. D. Boyle. *Psychological Foundations of Musical Behavior*. 2d ed. Springfield, Ill.: Charles C. Thomas, 1988.

Rosenfeld, A. H. "Music, the Beautiful Disturber." *Psychology Today* 19 (12) (1985): 48–56.

Sloboda, J. *The Musical Mind: The Cognitive Psychology of Music*. New York: Oxford University Press, 1985.

Part I

Politics

1

Popular Music as Politics and Protest

JEROME RODNITZKY

When asked to define a folk song, folksinger Pete Seeger replied: "If folks sing them, they're folksongs."[1] He might have added: "If folks have political views, the music they create and perform is political." Topical and political music have always been with us, although it is natural to overlook them. Past problems are quickly forgotten, and yesterday's political song becomes increasingly irrelevant. There are classic rock songs but no classic political songs. By definition political songs are custom made for a particular time and place. Past political songs are nowhere because they were everywhere and sprang from forgotten social and political issues.

Americans sing about politics, wars, heroes, bad men, and misery in a very personal way. In contrast to contemporary protest songs, earlier songs lacked social goals. Traditional folk songs vented emotions and made people feel good but were seldom connected to any social or political movements. The same might be said about most popular music today.

Political music took a distinctly modern turn with the rise of the International Workers of the World (IWW) early in the twentieth century. Better known as the Wobblies, this militant labor group, which organized in Chicago in 1904, included socialists, anarchists, and syndicalists. They planned to organize as many workers as possible in a single union and then call a general strike to decide who would run the world—workers or bosses. To help reach this goal, the Wobblies published its *Little Red Songbook* in 1909 and handed a copy out to members with their union card. Each red cover bore the words: "To Fan the Flames of Discontent." Many *Red Songbook* ballads were written by Joe Hill, the Wobblies' most famous organizer. His labor songs were direct, bawdy, and topical. Their tunes were borrowed from religious hymns and popular music and combined with lyrics based on Hill's own view of class struggle. For example, he changed the popular "Casey Jones" ballad into a timely protest song by substituting the

Southern Pacific Railroad for the Illinois Central line and turning Casey from a heroic engineer into a strike-breaking scab.

When the IWW was discredited by its opposition to World War I, both protest songs and militant unionism hibernated during the prosperous and raucous 1920s. However, when the Great Depression hit in the 1930s, protest music and unions revived under the stimulus of hard times. New unions such as the Congress of Industrial Organizations and the United Auto Workers sang on the picket lines. For many newly organized workers, unionism was a joyous event to be celebrated in song.

Militant unionism, however, became irrelevant during the World War II crusade. More important, anticommunist hysteria during the postwar cold war drove radicals out of labor unions and, with them, the protest song tradition. Except for some recently organized workers, such as farmworkers, unions are no longer singing movements. Yet the union protest song deeply influenced many, including Woody Guthrie, and through Guthrie eventually crossed over into popular music.

Guthrie, a restless folksinger from Oklahoma, roamed through America in the 1930s, writing as he traveled. His traditional songs subtly captured the poor, other America he experienced first hand. Guthrie was bawdy, erratic, and a somewhat naive captive of the American Left, but his songs rang true and captured America's shame as well as glory. Guthrie made up songs telling what he "thought was wrong and how to make it right." He sang about the plight of migrant workers and America's natural beauty, and his optimism fired the imagination of generations of topical singers who would seek a new world.

Just before World War II, Guthrie settled in New York City. Along with a few rural folksinger friends, he planted his folk music in this liberal urban setting. This cross-fertilization would produce the many urban folksingers who mixed traditional folk songs with their own contemporary topical protest songs. It also firmly connected folk music to the political Left.

After the war, Guthrie, his young apprentice, Pete Seeger, and other folksingers and activists tirelessly worked to use folk-protest music for specific unions and political movements. Their organization, People's Songs, became involved in enough dubious left-wing ventures to ruin the reputation of a hundred groups in cold war America. Embraced by the far Left and deserted by unions, People's Songs folded in 1949 with patriotic groups snapping at its heels.

Illness forced Guthrie out of protest music in the early 1950s, and his activist friends went underground in that decade. However, a new magazine, *Sing Out*, gave them a means of national identity and communication. During the anticommunist hysteria of the 1950s, many leftist folksingers were investigated by Congress, and some were blacklisted. Even when folk music regained popularity early in the 1960s, older performers, such as Pete Seeger, continued to be blacklisted.

Guthrie and Seeger's optimism and their enthusiasm for organizing are still the most striking differences between the earlier protest singers and the more cynical youthful singers of the 1960s. The close connection to the unions probably oversimplified the struggle for the older writers. The youth culture was interested not in organizing but in freeing itself from organizational restraints. In an age of generation gaps, an obvious gulf developed between the earlier protest singers and their musical heirs.

A primary difference was the tendency of younger writers to base their songs on secondary social perceptions, usually from mass media. For older singers such as Seeger, songs were weapons to be used in a struggle they had already joined. In contrast, some younger singers like Bob Dylan simply pointed to social ills without taking part in their cure. These subtle changes took place slowly between 1955 and 1965, a period that saw a steady rise in the popularity of radical political music.

The cultural isolation of the 1950s gave folksingers a chance to perfect their art. They stepped back from overtly political music and focused on traditional folk music. Obviously, protest songs were an integral part of this tradition, but linking them to the American heritage gave them a wholesome image. In this guise, folksingers quietly invaded the musical vacuum on college campuses in the late 1950s. While jazz had become increasingly complex and abstract and rock and roll had become more nonsensical and meaningless, folk songs were filled with meaning and integrity.

The 1960s brought events that called folk guitarists to arms; the civil rights movement was the catalyst. Martin Luther King's movement was clearly a sing-in as well as a sit-in campaign. While black southern activists wrote new songs and "We Shall Overcome" became the civil rights anthem, northern folksingers developed leaders and anthems of their own. Performer-composers such as Bob Dylan and Phil Ochs released both general and specific songs against discrimination, the arms race, and the military-industrial establishment. Song titles such as "I Ain't Marchin' Anymore" and "Talking World War Three Blues" suggest the specific concerns. More general songs such as "Blowin' in the Wind" and "If I Had a Hammer" protested almost everything.

Such gifted singers as Joan Baez and Judy Collins reached out for an even wider audience. Pleasant melodic groups such as the Kingston Trio and the Brothers Four popularized folk-protest even more. As the commercial success increased, the protest characteristics were diluted, but they remained a vivid element of popular music. The syrupy, apolitical Kingston Trio was challenged by the more political Chad Mitchell Trio, and by 1964 both groups were passed in popularity by the aggressively political trio, Peter, Paul, and Mary.

Protest music conquered the campus but failed at first to dent television. In 1963 when the ABC network launched a musical show, "Hootenanny," featuring top new folksingers, it blacklisted Seeger. Many of the more militant and by now more popular folk artists rushed to Seeger's defense. Joan Baez dedicated a song to him at each of her concerts. Bob Dylan and Baez told "Hootenanny:" "No Seeger, no Dylan or Baez," and Peter, Paul, and Mary, among others, took the same stand.

By 1965 the tide had turned. The merger of rock and roll with folk-style songs, which the recording industry called folk-rock, brought political music to high school students and the best-selling record charts. Suddenly there was a media vogue for thoughtful pacifist songs such as "Universal Soldier." Political lyrics became part of the atmosphere. Roger McGuinn, lead singer of the Byrds, who had previously seldom noticed social problems, found that he was "trying to get a political message into almost everything" he wrote because there was a "left-wing thing" in the air.[2] The new stress on lyrics affected popular music in general. A decade earlier, record companies consciously made songs a little unintelligible; now clear lyrics were crucial.

In 1964 Bob Dylan had pioneered the move from acoustic to amplified folk music. This allowed record companies to merge the high school and college markets. The younger children grew up on rock in the late 1950s and were used to a heavy beat. Throughout the 1960s, folk-rock became heavier and more electric, and those who supported it as teenagers remained faithful as collegians. Youth of all ages were soon dancing to pacifist and integrationist tunes with a big beat. Message songs seemed to be everywhere triumphant. But what kind of triumph was it?

As the 1960's cultural revolution went on, the mood song replaced the message song. Increasingly, the music radiated general discontent and a vague antiestablishment mood, as opposed to focusing on specific evils. The political flavor was still there—if anything the fervor had increased—but the lyrics were no longer as important, and they could seldom be heard over the music. The new psychedelic music registered a protest of form rather than substance. The music was sexual, highly creative, nonconformist, and clearly in protest of white middle-class America.

Jazz lost many fans as it became too intellectual. Folk-rock, however, became increasingly anti-intellectual. The stress on the music rather than the lyric message reflected the new view that truth must be felt rather than rationally understood. Whereas Woody Guthrie and Pete Seeger usually deliberately played below their instrumental ability so that the musical background would not detract from the lyrics, folk-rock artists often feared that the words might divert attention from the music.

The increasingly existential mood of folk-rock threatened the effectiveness of protest songs, but the tendency of leading folksingers to cut topical songs from their repertory was even more harmful. However, the continuation of topical music magazines, such as *Broadside* and *Sing Out*, and the continued success of topical singers such as Pete Seeger and Phil Ochs were signs that protest music was far from dead at the end of the 1960s. But the declining response showed that it had been pushed to the fringes of popular music.

Nevertheless, as protest music became hazier and more closely identified with youthful life-styles, right-wing critics feared it even more. They saw protest songs as the editorials, instruments, and weapons of an alien doctrine—all the more potent because of their popular appeal and youthful idiom. For example, in 1966, Reverend David Noebel of the Christian Crusade, in a long, overdocumented book, *Rhythm, Riots, and Revolution*, and a short pamphlet, *Communism, Hypnotism and the Beatles*, charged that protest songs in particular and folk and rock music in general, were part of a communist plot to subvert America's youth. Noebel's specific charges were usually comic, but as a frightened professional patriot, he was one of the few individuals, besides singers themselves, who seemed to understand the immense persuasive power of the musical idiom. Singers were seldom modest about their influence. In 1964, Peter Yarrow of Peter, Paul, and Mary claimed that his trio could "mobilize the youth of America . . . in a way that nobody else could"—perhaps even sway an election by traveling with a presidential candidate. He added, however, that they were not going to use this power. It was enough to know that they had it.[3]

Political power and political music eventually became burdensome to some singers. In 1965, Bob Dylan felt his art had been stifled by ideology, and he declared his independence. Thereafter, his songs were intensely personal. He made his artistic break with politics crystal clear in a remarkable song title "My Back Pages." Dylan proclaimed that he had oversimplified right and wrong in his earlier songs and become what he hated most—a preacher. One line noted that he had fooled himself into believing freedom was nothing more than "equality in school." After each scathing verse, Dylan explained that he was much older then but that he was considerably younger now. Similarly, in 1969, Judy Collins gave up singing protest songs because she no longer wanted to "be a political agitator" with her music, constantly facing an audience she recognized from the last rally. Collins decided that protest songs were "like hittin' people over the head" and "finger pointing," and that the result was "not a statement of emotional depth, but of unity in the face of an . . . enemy or idea which does not agree with you."[4] She felt that protest music divided people instead of uniting them. Arlo Guthrie agreed, noting, "You don't accomplish very much singing songs to people who agree with you."[5]

Possibly singers such as Dylan and Collins flee a world that seeks to use them as symbols. While attempting to make society recognize social evils, protest writers can find themselves threatened by a new, demanding establishment. The active moral minority creates a new threat to personal identity, and the artist may escape the mob by looking inward at his or her world instead of outward at theirs. Singers edging away from overtly political music sometimes describe themselves as performers of "contemporary art songs." In the late 1960s Joni Mitchell fit this category, as did Leonard Cohen and Donovan Leitch. In 1969 Donovan, a popular British folk star, wrote that the best songwriters had "evolved to the point" where they "left protest behind and beauty" crept in.[6] Perhaps a 1970 *New Yorker* magazine cartoon summed up the new attitude best. It pictured a young female singer, guitar in hand, about to begin her performance at a coffeehouse. Before starting, she advised her audience that her songs had no "social or political significance," but she assured them that she was opposed to the Vietnamese War and in favor of legalizing marijuana, boycotting California grapes, and federal control of the economy.

There is a more practical reason that popular singers hesitate to become too political. They often know very little about politics. In *The Best and the Brightest*, David Halberstam pointed out how power and confidence led many of John Kennedy's advisers to indulge their arrogance and assume expertise in areas foreign to their specialties. Fortunately, most popular music stars are uneasy as experts on political issues. They would not discuss music in the glib, superficial way their fans often expect them to discuss ecology, racism, and other social issues. In any case, the real purpose of political music was to get people interested in issues, not to supply solutions.

Whether overtly political or not, the new folk, rock, or folk-rock music of the 1960s had political effect. Even where lyrics were not explicit, the music had an indirect radical influence by showing contempt for social mores in sexual behavior, obscenity, and drug use. Since radical cultural changes are often more shocking than political challenges, drug songs, for example, were more distasteful to the radio audience than political songs. By 1970 drug lyrics in popular music had become a national issue. In 1969 television personality Art Linkletter asserted that half of the most popular records were "concerned with secret messages" urging listeners to drop out and use drugs. Similarly, in 1970, Vice-President Spiro Agnew charged that much of rock music "glorified drug usage." It was, however, natural for drugs to be a topic of rock music, since the songs reflected youth culture. Whether or not the young took them, drugs were a clear part of their culture, just as alcohol was a major ingredient of the adult world.

The question is not whether music has social and political effects but what those long- and short-term effects are and how they can be measured. Some suggest that song lyrics have a subliminal effect and act as a catalyst for alienation and/or political action. Others feel that protest songs usually serve as a symbolic substitute for political involvement. After all, it is perhaps too easy to feel that you are moving society when all you are doing is listening to records or singing along.

The increasing profitability of the new music concerned some observers and delighted others. Simon Kunen, a student radical in the 1960s, felt that capitalism had "a self-destruct mechanism." He argued that the corporate media sought only profit, and if radical, revolutionary materials are profitable, corporations would disseminate radicalism and revolution. Most radicals were far more pessimistic and felt that the mass media usually co-opt radicalism by diluting its content and dulling its fervor. For example, in 1964 when President Lyndon Johnson proclaimed "We Shall Overcome," the song and slogan lost much of its meaning. In 1965 while the pacifist ballad, "Universal Soldier" became a nationwide hit, the Vietnamese War accelerated. More ironically, Glen Campbell, who recorded "Universal Soldier," supported the war.

In 1969, Irwin Silber, a topical song advocate, concluded that popular music's "cultural revolution" was a threat to radical reform. He argued that the American working class instinctually sensed that electric folk-rock was "basically a middle-class trip." Although Silber felt the new music reflected youthful alienation, he also believed that "doing your own thing" was a middle-class trait on which capitalism was based. He charged that the"groovy life-styles" suggested that people ignore the system that oppressed them rather than fight to change it.[7]

Most attacks against political music came from the Right; however, music can also have conservative sentiments. The preponderance of left-wing music has perpetuated the idea that political music always involves humanitarian attacks against the status quo. Historically, this has not always been the case. The Ku Klux Klan, for example, used songs to further its movement. And through the 1950s and 1960s, conservative and patriotic country and western songs made popular music an ideological battleground. The conservative songs were fewer in number, but ballads such as Merle Haggard's "The Fightin' Side of Me" and "Okie from Muskogee," as well as Guy Drake's "Welfare Cadillac," were clearly protest songs.

In the 1970s and 1980s, political songs were a much smaller part of popular music but far from obsolete. They remained a powerful American art form and played a role in America's contemporary social struggles. Although protest songs largely disappeared from the Top 10 chart, the women's movement, the black movement, the gay movement, the anti–nuclear weapons movement, and the peace movement continued to turn out topical music for their supporters. Even when protest songs have been used by very militant groups, however, they have remained peculiarly American. America's most effective protest ballads have been subtle rather than militant, poetic rather than merely idiomatic, and their orientation has been universal rather than nationalistic. American protest music has invariably sought to make individuals feel guilty for being too comfortable, too unaware, or too inactive.

The serious political singers and writers have usually been on the fringes of mass culture, but their influence had a multiplier effect. The small audiences they garnered were often activists who radicalized many others. Radical songwriters subtly influenced more popular fellow artists through artful, topical lyrics and their own personal commitment. Thus, the question is not just whether political music is alive and well commercially. Its influence cannot be measured statistically, for the few it affects may be particularly vigorous and influential. The real problem is that since 1970, political music has been increasingly fragmented by its commercial success, cultural acceptance, and artistic diversity. The most gifted topical writers and singers have moved in several directions for personal reasons.

Yet there are signs everywhere that we may be on the verge of another era of political music. The last half of the 1980s witnessed a resurgence in both student activism and folk and topical music. The success of writers and singers such as Suzanne Vega and Michelle Shocked suggests a new audience for folk music. The topical slant of Jackson Browne and Billy Joel, among others, shows more political influence and so does some rap music. The No Nukes, Live Aid, and Farm Aid benefit concerts and the "We Are the World" benefit record show even clearer connections between politics and music.

The surest sign that political music remains potentially powerful is rock culture. Led by rock superstars such as U2 and Bruce Springsteen, contemporary musicians are rediscovering social conscience. In the 1990s, rock music still has the same mesmerizing effect on youth that it had in 1970. What rock singer Frank Zappa noted in 1969 is still true. Many youths are "not loyal to flag, country, or doctrine, but only to music."[8] If there ever has been a political or social counterculture in America, surely it lived between the microgrooves.

With their special connection to youth, rock singers remain a cultural, distant-early-warning system. They can suggest emerging trends. As the number of political benefit concerts have grown and popular song lyrics have become more meaningful, they may be flashing a signal. At the same time, there is a move back to liberal arts by college students. Maybe these trends represent only style or coincidence, but maybe they mean the times "They Are a Changin" again.

NOTES

1. Pete Seeger, "Why Folk Music," *International Musician* 16 (May 1965): 9.

2. "Interview with Roger McGuinn of the Byrds," *Sing Out* 18 (December 1968): 11.

3. Alfred Aronowitz and Marshall Blonsky, "Three's Company," *Saturday Evening Post*, May 30, 1964, p. 32.

4. "An Interview with Judy Collins," *Life*, May 2, 1969, pp. 45–46.

5. Arlo Guthrie, quoted in "Woody's Boy," *Newsweek*, May 23, 1966, p. 110.

6. Donovan, quoted in UPI Dispatch, *Forth Worth Press*, November 2, 1969, p. 6.

7. Irwin Silber, "The Cultural Retreat," *Guardian*, December 6, 1969, p. 17.

8. Frank Kofsky, "Frank Zappa Interview," in *The Age of Rock*, ed. Jonathan Eisen (New York: Random House 1969), p. 256.

BIBLIOGRAPHY

Cooper, B. Lee. *Images of America in Popular Music.* Chicago: Nelson-Hall, 1982.
Denisoff, R. Serge. *Great Day Coming: Folk Music and the American Left.* Urbana: University of Illinois Press, 1972.
———. *Sing a Song of Social Significance.* Bowling Green, Ohio: Bowling Green University Popular Press, 1983.
Dunaway, David King. *How Can I Keep from Singing: Pete Seeger.* New York: McGraw-Hill, 1981.
Greenway, John. *American Folksongs of Protest.* Philadelphia: University of Pennsylvania Press, 1983.
Orman, John. *The Politics of Rock.* Chicago: Nelson-Hall, 1984.
Perris, Arnold. *Music as Propaganda: Art to Persuade, Art to Control.* Westport, Conn.: Greenwood Press, 1985.
Pichaske, David R. *A Generation in Motion: Popular Music and Culture in the Sixties.* New York: Random House, 1979.
Rodnitzky, Jerome L. *Minstrels of the Dawn: The Folk-Protest Singer as a Cultural Hero.* Chicago: Nelson-Hall, 1976.

2

"Blues What I Am": Blues Consciousness and Social Protest

FRED J. HAY

Blues music was a post-Reconstruction development in African-American musical and poetic history. For the first time black Americans—outside of maroon (fugitive slave) communities—were forced to create both a community and a culture of their own. The blues were part of this culture creation process. Born in the late nineteenth century (during a time that witnessed the virulent spread of jim crow legislation), blues evolved well into the 1950s and declined with the heyday of the civil rights movement in the 1960s. Only with the formation of an African-American community and its blues culture, as Leroi Jones (Amiri Baraka) observed, did the exiled-African, former slaves, become truly American. It is in the poetic realization of this newly evolved community of African Americans that the social meaning of the blues is to be found.

Those who have written on the blues have recognized the obvious; they are blatant songs of protest. Lawrence Gellert's 1936 publication, *Negro Songs of Protest*, includes brutally frank lyrics protesting the cruelty of a malevolent social order:

> Your head tain't no apple for dangling from a tree (repeat)
> Your body no carcass for barbecuing on a spree.
>
> Stand on your feet, club gripped 'tween your hands (repeat)
> Spill their blood too, show them you is a man.

Many other blues songs are also obviously protests—for example, "Bourgeois Blues," Leadbelly's composition about discrimination in the nation's capital; J. B. Lenior's "Eisenhower Blues," which Parrot Records was forced, by the White House, to withdraw from the market; and Julia Moody's frequently quoted "Mad Mama's Blues," which depicts in coldly detached, naturalistic, terms (a style used by novelist Richard Wright in his portrait of the homicidal Bigger Thomas) the anger of alienation:

> Want to set this world on fire, that is my mad desire (x2)
> I'm the devil in disguise, got murder in my eyes
>
> Now if I could see blood running through the streets (x2)
> Could see everybody lying dead right at my feet.
>
> Give me gunpowder, give me dynamite (x2)
> Yes, I'm going to wreck this city, going to blow it up tonight.

Others, like Howlin' Wolf's minstrel show parody/political manifesto, "Coon on the Moon," or the King Biscuit Boys' performance of comedy skits in blackface "with all that white, chalky stuff all 'round their mouths" caricatured white folks caricaturing black folks. The "blues experts" have correctly observed that these protest songs represent only a small minority of the total surviving blues lyrics. What they have not recognized is the more subtle and typical protest embodied in blues consciousness's rejection of white culture. In fact, they have too often denied this more fundamental protest.

These authorities have been oblivious to the radical poetics of the blues because they have made their examination of the blues, and discussed its meaning (or perceived lack of meaning), without regard for its natural social context. This has led them to make the false assertion that the blues song is not one of social protest but rather a mindless, escapist entertainment whose primary function was a psychic and emotional diversion from the despair of an oppressed community. The intention of this observation is not to deny the considerable cathartic potential of a blues performance but to reject that axiom of racist ideology that sees a passive, nonreactive African American, who, mired in the pathological consequences of poverty, has been unable to take positive action or to create viable, profound, and universally relevant cultural institutions.

Before the blues, there was the plantocracy—a society ruled by those who violently enslaved their fellow humans. Plantation society was destructured by emancipation, and a new African-American society was born in the segregated South. This new society was the source of the blues, and blues consciousness was the superstructure—the rationalization of its social structure. Blues culture began its decline following changes in the social organization of racism. African-American society changed greatly in the post–World War II era, especially after the rise of the civil rights movement, when blues was replaced by a new, more optimistic music, soul. Soul music more adequately reflected the social (and ideological) changes that occurred. Blues survived as the people's music longest in those pockets that were most isolated (either physically or psychically) from the current trends in African-American society.

What were the characteristics of the nascent society that produced the blues? It was comprised of ex-slaves—black and mostly illiterate—who were primarily agricultural workers and manual laborers. This society was composed of a group of individuals who were terrorized by the dominant white culture and therefore, individually and collectively, had to secrete their own hostility, their opposition to the dominant social group who oppressed them. The secrecy was made easier by the oppressor's, in the words of anthropologist Clyde Kluckhohn, "hostility to nuance"—to that subtlety that is an esteemed quality in African and African diaspora cultures.

This society was organized around distinctly different principles from the dominant white society. In fact, African-American society was organized in opposition to white society, and African-American culture reflects this counterorganization in its opposition to racism, puritanism, and a narrow rationalism. If blacks were to live in a different and materially impoverished society, they would do so with a vital worldview that allowed them the emotional dignity and psychic comforts denied them by white America. Blues culture was formed not just in opposition and conflict to the values of white society but was also an affirmation of individual worth and of African aesthetic and social values. It was an early populist expression of what would appear several decades later in the intellectualist, pan-African/African-American movement known as Negritude.

Blues consciousness was only one ideology present in the new African-American society. Other ideologies included those associated with the black middle class, the reform movements such as the National Association for the Advancement of Colored People, the popular Garveyism movement, and, especially significant, the ideology of African-American Christianity. The slaves' acceptance of their masters' religion was an assimilationist strategy, which persisted even after emancipation. Both whites and blacks understood this fact, made evident by the whites' immediate acceptance (though mostly as entertainment) of the African-American spiritual and their rejection of the blues and its moral and aesthetic values.

Blues ideology was neither assimilationist nor escapist but coldly realistic (some have erroneously called it fatalistic) about African-America's current situation and its future prospects. Blues was a denial of white America's view of blacks, Africa, and the rest of the world, as well as a rejection of the culture founded on such views. Blues was, in fact, a celebration of those cultural characteristics that were most different from and appalling to white American culture. The following extracts from blues songs illustrate some of the cultural values of white America negated by blues consciousness.

The blues song satirized the assimilationists among African Americans and appropriated their religious symbols for profane use:

> There was one ole Brother by the name of Mose, got so happy he pulled
> off all his clothes. Why?

Nobody knows what the good Deacon's doing, I declare when the lights go
 out.
—Willie "Hambone" Newbern, "Nobody Knows What the Good Deacon
 Does" (1929)

Some folks say a preacher won't steal but I caught three in my cornfield,
One had a yellow, one had a brown, looked over yonder and one was
 getting down.
—Kansas Joe McCoy, "Preachers Blues" (1931)

You got River Jordan movement in your hips, mama,
And Daddy's screaming to be baptized.
—J. D. Short, "She Got Jordan River in Her Hips" (1931)

Blues consciousness flaunted white America's sexual repression by its
expression of the erotic and its exploration of varieties of sexual experience:

Red hot mama, meat shaking on her bones,
Think about your loving when I leave town,
I got ants in my pants, baby, for you.
—Bo Carter, "Ants in My Pants" (1931)

I wear my skirt up to my knees,
And whip that jelly with who I please.
—Clara Smith, "Whip It to a Jelly" (1926)

There were other ways of copulating than the male-dominant, missionary
position:

I mean you can snatch it, you can break it, hang it on the stinking wall,
Throw it out the window women, if you catch it before it fall.
—Louise Johnson, "On the Wall" (1930)

Copulation was not the only means to sexual gratification:

Bring your yo-yo, wind the string around my tongue,
Mama knows just how to make your yo-yo hum.
—Hattie Hart and the Memphis Jug Band, "Memphis
 Yo-Yo Blues" (1929)

Well, the first woman I had, she made me get on my knees
And had the nerve to ask me, ooh, well, if I liked limburger cheese.
—Peetie Wheatstraw, "The First Shall Be Last and the Last Shall Be First"
 (1936)

And homosexuality, although its actual occurrence was less prevalent
than in white America, was freely discussed rather than hushed:

Some are young, some are old,
My man says sissy's got good jelly roll.

My man got a sissy, his name is "Miss Kate,"
He shook that thing like jelly on a plate.
—Ma Rainey, "Sissy Blues" (1926)

Have you ever left her going out jitterbugging, smelling like a rose.
Come back about 5 o'clock in the morning with a fish scent all in her
   clothes.

You know women is loving each other, and they don't think about a man,
They don't play it with no secret no more, they playing it a wide open
   hand.
—Willie Borum, "Bad Girl Blues," (1961)

The blues serves as a virtual catalog of African magico-religious beliefs:

I'm going sprinkle a little goofer dust all around your nappy head (x2)
You'll wake up one of these mornings and one dead.
—Charlie Spand, "Big Fat Mama Blues" (1930)

To dream of muddy water, trouble's knocking at your door (x2)
Your man is sure to leave you and never return no more.
—Ida Cox, "Fogyism" (1928)

Pan-African aesthetic values are apparent in certain musical predilections,
such as a preference for polyrhythms as well as in lyrical terms:

She's a heavy-hipted mama, she's got great big legs, (x3)
Walking like she's walking on soft-boiled eggs.
—Leadbelly, "Keep Your Hands Off Her" (first recorded between 1942
   and 1949; copyright 1962)

The blues people never blinked at admitting their community's use of mind-
altering substances—

I love to fuss and fight,
Lord, and get sloppy drunk offa bottle and bond,
And walk the streets all night.
—Charlie Patton, "Elder Greene Blues" (1929)

Just give me one more sniffle, another sniffle of that dope (x2)
I'll catch a cow like a cowboy, throw a bull without a rope.
—Victoria Spivey, "Dope Head Blues" (1927)

—or of the reality and necessity of crime and vice. Delta bluesman Tommy
McClennan, in "It's Hard to Be Lonesome" (1941), bragged that he did

not want any of these women who had not learned to rob and steal because they would spend their lives working for nothing in some farmer's field.

> Times done got hard, money's done got scarce,
> Stealing and robbing is going to take place.
> Because tricks ain't walking, tricks ain't walking no more (x2),
> And I'm going to rob somebody if I don't make me some dough.
> —Bessie Jackson, "Tricks Ain't Walking No More" (1930)

Blues consciousness resisted the oppression of puritan culture with humor:

> There's 25 women in this hotel with me, you and your brother. What time
>   would it be?
> That's very easy, mama, be 25 after 3.
> —Barbecue Bob, "Good Time Rounder" (1929)

> Oh, they accused me of forgery and I can't even write my name.
> —Texas Alexander, "Levee Camp Moan Blues" (1927)

While white America frequently described African Americans as animals— less than human—blues consciousness characterized African Americans in animal terms but with a difference. Flaunting and parodying the imagery of white racism, it expressed the antiwhite values of blues culture. The identification with animals was not only in the blues song, but also in the names by which blues people were known: Howlin' Wolf, Bo Weevil Jackson, Robert Nighthawk, Hound Dog Taylor, Mule, Bumble Bee Slim, and others.

> Umm, better find my mama soon, better find my mama soon,
> I woke up this morning, black snake was making such a ruckus in my
>   room.
> —Blind Lemon Jefferson, "Black Snake Moan" (1927)

The animal-human metaphor was extended to include the plant kingdom, such as the following lyric I heard in the Mississippi Delta:

> I got a Kudzu Mama, spread out anywhere you set her down (x2),
> Up against the side of a tree or flat upon the ground.

The blues delighted in reveling in what white culture considered "bad taste." This tendency led sociologists Howard Odum and Guy Johnson to describe blues lyrics as the "superlative of repulsive":

> My baby so fat and greasy, till I put ashes in my bed,
> And if I forget the ashes, then I'll slip out up on my head.
> —Robert Peeples, "Fat Greasy Baby" (1930)

Without an understanding of the societal basis of these lyrics, they might appear trivial, as they often do when performed, out of context, by rock 'n' roll bands. Examined in its proper social context, the blues song's meaning as social protest and negation is undeniable.

In all societies, the moral order is reinforced by other cultural mechanisms: religious and magic belief, group ritual and performance. Blues consciousness is manifested not only in its magico-religious traditions. Blues people not only sang about hoodoo, but many were actively involved. Robert Johnson was remembered by those who knew him as "two-headed" or a hoodoo; Tommy Johnson claimed to have made a pact with the devil in a graveyard at midnight; and Peetie Wheatstraw billed himself as the "Devil's Son-in-Law." It was not without reason that the African-American church branded the blues as the "Devil's Music." (In Julio Finn's book, *The Bluesmen,* the only book about the blues by a bluesman, the legacy of African worldview in the blues is more fully discussed.)

It is primarily the power of blues consciousness that can be truly seen and felt. The blues performance was a communal affirmation and celebration of the group's culture, and because this group's culture was created in opposition to white culture, it was a ritual of negation as well. In the shabby roadhouses, taverns, and cafés of the rural South and the urban ghetto, African Americans gathered to reaffirm their allegiance to blues consciousness. In large part, these rituals were directed by the blues musicians, who were in great demand. (The fact that blues performances often attracted large numbers of African Americans from both near and far did not escape the attention of the white owners of black jukes. Sonny Boy Williamson and Joe Willie Wilkins, two very popular Delta blues musicians, were kept for two weeks, on no legitimate charge, in the Tupelo, Mississippi, jail so that they could be forced to perform at a local white-owned juke each night. The owner realized the financial draw of the blues drama but undoubtedly was oblivious to its revolutionary meaning.)

Blues performances were often imbued with religious tone and ritual demeanor, including loud vocal prompting, signifying, and the ritual dance. One of the specialized rites of blues consciousness was the "battle of the blues" (known as "bucking" by the New Orleans street bands). One such battle, an account of which follows, was remembered decades later by those present and has become part of the Delta's blues mythology. This scene represents a personification and dramatization of white sociologists' "superlative of the repulsive."

In the early 1960s, Joe Willie Wilkins, Robert Nighthawk, and Nathaniel Armstrong were temporarily residing in the Delta town of Hughes, Arkansas, and playing at night at a local café. Unaware of their presence in Hughes, three other musicians—Houston Stackhouse, James Peck Curtis, and James Starkey—traveled to Hughes on a Saturday, looking for a gig.

Stackhouse and Nighthawk were cousins. Both were famed slide guitarists playing in a similar style; Stackhouse had been Nighthawk's teacher. Night-hawk had long been absent from the Delta, leaving Stackhouse the lone master of their slide style in the area. Now that Nighthawk had returned, it was inevitable there would be a feeling of competition between the two musicians.

Harp blower Nat Armstrong was the first to spot the newly arrived musicians as they approached the front stoop of the café where the others had been performing. Armstrong warned Stackhouse: "You'd better be careful Stack; the Hawk's inside." Stackhouse, not to be daunted by his cousin's ability or his fame as a recording artist and defenseless against the trickster Armstrong, replied, "Tell Hawk to move out of the way; the Buzzard has arrived."

Word of the impending conflict spread rapidly throughout the rural com-munity surrounding Hughes, and by nightfall, the little café was overflowing. The original night's entertainment under Wilkins's leadership was larger than usual for a small-town café. It was composed of Wilkins, Stackhouse, and Nighthawk playing guitars, Starkey on piano, Armstrong on harmonica, and Curtis on drums. Cotton fields stretched across the broad, flat expanses of the Delta, right to the café's doors. As night approached, people working in the fields would leave their work and go directly to the café. Hot, dirty, and sweaty, they danced in frankly erotic fashion in the crowded café; they ate pounds of barbecue and drank freely. Typically a crap game was ongoing in the back room, lovers were outside in the dark.

It did not take long, especially considering their fellow musicians' and the audience's prompting, for the Stackhouse/Nighthawk guitar rivalry to surface. Accompanied by Starkey's fluid piano work, the Hawk and the Buzzard battled throughout the night, neither leaving his post for a minute. After hours of playing, they became too tired to stand, and sat on the floor. By dawn, both musicians, unwilling to let up their defenses for even a minute, were sitting in pools of their own urine, still playing, still battling. The crowd, scarcely diminished, continued to perform.

Clearly this performance does not conform to white ideals of entertain-ment or religious observance. Yet celebrations of this sort have, served both purposes (and others) in the past for the African-American community. The blues ritual—"an ethnohistoric rite as basic as blood," by LeRoi Jones's (Amiri Baraka) account—is the ultimate expression of a culture born in protest to American society.

In the 1960s, blues lost its popularity with the African-American audience, replaced by another form of black music, soul. Soul—a true hybrid of blues, gospel, and rock and roll—was the music of the civil rights movement. It was, quite literally, the soul of African-American society. The African-Amer-ican community—idealized as a family composed of soul brothers and soul sisters—assumed a compelling resemblance to the African-American church in design and emotional association. For all practical purposes, the once living and vital blues is quickly disappearing, even in the most isolated and remote locations. A worldview cannot exist without its constituent community, and the community that created the blues no longer exists. Without that social basis, the blues can be denatured, made safe for white America. This process was already underway in the 1950s when white rockabilly musicians began to record "covers" (copies of songs done by other than the original singer or songwriter) of blues songs. The pace of this devitalization increased dramatically by the 1960s, when rebellious youths from around the world began to play blues songs and label themselves (and to be marketed as) blues musicians. In 1989, when Lee Atwater, director of a presidential campaign that many in the black community denounced as racist, played the "blues" at a Republican party fund raiser, it became sadly apparent that the blues had been made safe, respectable, and spurious.

As a people's music, blues may be dead, but blues consciousness continues to live in new musics that have risen to serve similar social functions: funk and rap. It is also alive, as a primary component of jazz innovation, in the jazz that is most revolutionary or, as Paul Garon described it, "audacious." The influence of the blues on literature, criticism, philosophy, and the arts continues to grow.

Blues was never solely protest. It was many things—catharsis, life-style, recreation, art, to name a few—some of which may even seem contradictory. It is no more possible to define blues consciousness precisely than it has been for Euro-American rationalism to define neatly and succinctly the blues as musical form. Blues defies such narrow conceptualization. It was a true cultural legacy of Africa that the blues were flexible, elastic, innovative, amorphous (like the Kudzu Mama), and not susceptible to empiricist characterization. Non-Western yet American, the blues were beautiful, operative, and profound. Gellert's anonymous Bluesman sang: "Jes' passin' through, didn't intend to stay. Me and white folks don't think de same way."

BIBLIOGRAPHY

Calt, Stephen, and Gayle Wardlow. *King of the Delta Blues: The Life and Music of Charlie Patton.* Newton, N.J.: Rock Chapel Press, 1988.

Finn, Julio. *The Bluesman: The Musical Heritage of Black Men and Women in the Americas.* London: Quartet Books, 1986.

Garon, Paul. *Blues and the Poetic Spirit.* London: Eddison Press, 1975.

Gellert, Lawrence. *Negro Songs of Protest.* New York: American Music League, 1936.

Hay, Fred J. "The Sacred/Profane Dialectic in Delta Blues: The Life and Lyrics of Sonny Boy Williamson." *Phylon* 48 (4) (1987): 317–26.

Jones, LeRoi. *Blues People: The Negro Experience in White America and the Music That Developed from It.* New York: William Morrow and Co., 1963.

Joseph, "Cousin Joe" Pleasant, and Harriet J. Ottenheimer. *Cousin Joe: Blues from New Orleans.* Chicago: University of Chicago Press, 1987.

Oliver, Paul. *The Meaning of the Blues.* New York: Collier Books, 1963.

3

Proud to Be an American: Patriotism in Country Music

MELTON A. McLAURIN

Since the rise of modern nationalism in the nineteenth century, patriotism has been a theme found in practically all music designed for secular audiences. This is true of both popular and classical music. The great romantic composers of the nineteenth century, for example, frequently employed patriotic themes in a deliberate attempt to enhance nationalistic feelings. Tchaikovsky's famous "1812 Overture," a musical account of Napoleon's defeat by Russian armies, is perhaps the best-known example of a patriotic theme in a classical work. In the United States, songwriters such as Stephen Foster had introduced patriotic themes to commercial popular music well before the Civil War, a conflict that inspired hundreds of popular patriotic tunes in both the North and the South. Northerners sang such well-known songs as "The Battle Hymn of the Republic," "The Battle Cry of Freedom," and "John Brown's Body," and southerners responded with "The Bonnie Blue Flag," "Maryland, My Maryland," and several versions of the prewar minstrel tune that became the region's unofficial national anthem, "Dixie's Land." It is hardly surprising that patriotism is a central theme in commercial country music.

The manner in which patriotism is expressed in country music is strongly influenced by the music's southern origins. In its infancy, commercial country music was a regional music produced for a regional audience: the white working class of the American South. Its first major stars came from the region and grew up playing the traditional folk songs and ballads that formed the basis for the development of the music. Although the music has outgrown its regional appeal, cultivating national and international audiences, the majority of those who perform and compose country music still call the South home. Most country music continues to be produced in

Nashville, the capital city of a former Confederate state. Much of what is not produced in Nashville is produced in other southern cities, among them Austin, Texas, and Muscle Shoals, Alabama.

Given its history, it is to be expected that expressions of patriotism in commercial country music continue to have a distinctly southern accent. This "southernness" that is so evident in country music results in some fundamental differences in the manner in which patriotism is expressed in country music from the way it is expressed in other forms of American popular music. One of the most striking differences is the emphasis on physical bravery. The patriotic heroes of country music are fighters, not talkers. They are courageous, they engage and kill the enemy, and they glory in death on the battlefield. These are common themes in the southern experience, themes reinforced by an article of faith with most southerners, that the Confederate troops, though ultimately defeated by superior numbers, were among the bravest, most ferocious ever to bear arms. Southerners can, and do, point with pride to a long line of fighting men, including such legendary fighters as Daniel Boone, Davy Crockett, and Andrew Jackson, and a long line of wartime heroes. Richard Pearson of Alabama led a party that, in face of fearsome cannon fire, attempted to bottle up the Spanish fleet in Santiago Harbor, thus becoming the first hero of the Spanish-American War. Sergeant Alvin York of Tennessee became the official hero of World War I because of his proficiency at killing Germans. World War II saw Audie Murphy, a Texan and the most decorated soldier of that conflict, become the nation's foremost front-line hero.

Crockett, Boone, Jackson, Pearson, York, and Murphy all had a common trait: legendary bravery under fire. This bravery, this willingness to engage the enemy directly and personally, despite mortal risk, is a central theme in patriotic country music, whether the songs are about wars past or present.

The product of the radio and the phonograph, commercial country music did not develop until the 1920s, well after World War I. By the outbreak of World War II, the music was firmly established, and its songwriters and performers extolled the bravery of American servicemen in that conflict. One of the more popular country songs recorded during the war was Red Foley's rendition of "Smoke on the Water," which provides an apocalyptic, and accurate, view of what would happen once U.S. forces engaged the Axis enemy. The great American war machine, the song predicts, would crush its foes, leaving their bodies for the vultures. The most popular patriotic country song of the World War II era, Elton Britt's "There's a Star Spangled Banner Waving Somewhere," also stresses personal bravery. Ironically, the song is narrated from the perspective of a crippled youth, who recites a list of America's fighting heroes and declares his willingness to die to protect the freedoms of his country. He begs Uncle Sam for the opportunity to fight, not to have his courage judged by his handicap. He yearns for the opportunity to perform great deeds, to become a hero, to die on the battlefield, and thus enter that special place in heaven reserved for the nation's bravest.

America's reasons for entering World War II were obvious to all; they were less clear cut in the Korean conflict. Country music songs, nevertheless, remained strongly supportive of the war effort and generally portrayed the conflict as part of the price to be paid to prevent the communist menace from conquering the world. Once again country music recounted American soldiers' willingness to perform on the battlefield in such songs as "Korea, Here We Come." Gallantry on the battlefield, country music acknowledged, inevitably resulted in casualties. Two popular tunes of the Korean War era by Ernest Tubbs, "Missing in Action" and "A Heartsick Soldier on Heartbreak Ridge," made the point that battlefield deaths were to be expected, and accepted.

The Vietnam War plunged the country into a state of political and social turmoil. The domestic violence of the Vietnam era and the rancor it produced, however, failed to alter country music's appreciation of battlefield bravery. While popular music counseled Johnny not to be a hero, country music reiterated its expectations that he live up to the martial standards of his ancestors. Perhaps the song that best expressed country music's continuing commitment to battlefield heroics was Staff Sergeant Barry Sadler's recording, "The Ballad of the Green Berets," which in 1966 reached the second spot on the country charts. Portrayed as the pride of American manhood, Green Berets were fearless, tough, trained to kill in hand-to-hand combat, and prepared to die. Not only were Green Berets prepared to die, they urged their widows, if need be, to raise their sons to follow in their footsteps. Other Vietnam-era tunes that praised the battlefield heroics of the American soldier include Sadler's "The A Team," about a group of twelve men, strong and true, prepared to go anywhere in defense of freedom; Marty Robbins's "Private Wilson White," which narrates the exploits of a soldier killed while single-handedly destroying four enemy machine gun emplacements; and Ernest Tubbs's "It's for God Country and You Mom (and the Girl I Left Behind)," which tells the story of a soldier's death in the arms of his buddy.

Patriotic country music is intense. This aspect of the music was less evident in the songs of World War II, since there was little debate about the need for or the nature of the country's involvement in that conflict. The United States had been attacked and was in a war to the death against powerful adversaries. The cold war that followed and the Korean and Vietnam conflicts presented Americans with more complex realities, which elicited more complex responses. But country music, with its strong southern heritage, continued to view the cold war as it had more traditional conflicts—in terms of black and white rather than in shades of gray. Country music also frequently questioned the patriotism of those who saw the cold war in more ambiguous terms or questioned the appropriateness of government policies. This tendency to disparage the motives of those who questioned U.S. foreign policy was evident in such Korean War–era country songs as Elton Britt's "The Red That We Want Is the Red We've Got (in the Old Red White and Blue)." It became a consistent theme in country music with the onset of social and political conflict over the Vietnam War. By the end of the 1960s, songs critical of those protesting American involvement in Vietnam essentially had replaced on country hit charts the earlier prowar songs that praised the courage of the American soldier. Typical of such songs were two hits released by Merle Haggard in 1970, both of which rose to number 1 on the country charts. In "Okie from Muskogee," Haggard decried hippies, draft card burners, and men who wore "sissy" sandals rather than boots. In "The Fightin' Side of Me," Haggard was even more explicit in his criticism of those opposed to the Vietnam War. Such people, Haggard sang, loved America's advantages but were unwilling to fight for the country. Their actions mocked the sacrifices of the nation's past heroes, and Haggard invited protesters to love America or leave it. A year later Terry Nelson and C Company expressed the same sentiments in "The Battle Hymn of Lt. Calley," a paean to the battlefield exploits of William Calley, who was court-martialed for committing atrocities against Vietnamese civilians. It also castigated those Americans who, safe at home, criticized Calley's actions. In "The Minute Men Are Turning in Their Graves," Stonewall Jackson, whose stage name proclaimed his allegiance to the warriors of the Confederacy, wailed that such founding fathers as Washington and Jefferson (both southerners) would shed tears of shame at the sight of those who protested America's actions in Vietnam. Jackson prayed that such craven souls, unwilling to defend hearth and home, would never obtain positions of power in the nation's capital. Other Vietnam era songs that condemned opponents of the war include "What We're Fighting For," written by Tom T. Hall and recorded by Dave Dudley; Bobby Bare's "God Bless America Again"; and Johnny Sea's "Day of Decision."

So strong was the country music industry's support of the war that writers and performers who had reservations about U.S. involvement in Vietnam found it difficult to express their sentiments. In 1971, Nashville songwriter John D. Loudermilk observed that it was almost impossible for an antiwar country tune to receive airtime. "If a strong anti-war song hits the charts," he said, "it would be taken off the air. They [the country music establishment] think an anti-war song is Communist, written by a man who is afraid, or doesn't want to fight."[1] This was a bit of an overstatement, for some country songs, especially those recorded after 1970, questioned the wisdom of continuing the conflict. Among them were Johnny Cash's "What Is Truth," Skeeter Davis's "When You Gonna Bring Our Soldiers Home," and Arlene Harden's "Congratulations, You Sure Made a Man Out of Him," a scathing attack on the image of the superpatriot and the only country song explicitly to criticize American involvement in Vietnam and make the country charts. On the whole, however, Loudermilk's charge accurately reflects country music's overwhelming support of the war.

The absence of prolonged conflict since the end of the Vietnam War has not diminished country music's penchant for patriotic songs. During the 1980s, country performers released a variety of patriotic recordings. Many were topical, responses to perceived threats to the American way of life. The Oak Ridge Boys, for example, reached the country charts with "My Girl Is American Made." The song, despite its use of double entendre, is a protest against the Japanese invasion of the American electronic, automobile, and optical industries. The song's heroine, unlike the products described, is American made and practically the only thing of significance of American origin in the life of the narrator. Charlie Daniels outlined the differences he perceived between America and communist nations in "In America," a song that denounces the nation's critics, foreign and domestic. The Statler Brothers recalled the sacrifice of American servicemen in Vietnam in the 1990 hit, "More Than Just a Name upon a Wall." This poignant ballad, perhaps the only popular song written and recorded about the Vietnam War Memorial, reminds listeners that the names etched in stone on the wall represent personal losses to millions of Americans. By far the most popular patriotic song of the 1980s, however, was Lee Greenwood's "God Bless the U.S.A." This song, which has become an anthem among country music fans and was a successful crossover record (one that sells in more than one market), emphatically expresses a pride in being American, an appreciation for the freedoms of American life, and a willingness to proclaim pride in country. Like many other patriotic country tunes, it also acknowledges the sacrifices of those who fought to maintain American freedoms.

Although some believe the patriotism expressed in country music is simplistic, with its proponents unaware of or unconcerned with the costs of war, the lyrics of patriotic country songs do not support such a position. Rather, country music makes it all too clear that the cost of war is death and destruction, the crippling of the human body and spirit, the bearing of grief for a loved one lost. Songs of the World War II era that underscored the human sacrifice that conflict required include Tex Ritter's "Gold Star in the Window," Ernest Tubbs's "The Soldier's Last Letter," and Bob Wills's "White Cross on Okinawa." Significantly, the songs of both Tubbs and Ritter take the perspective of the mother who loses a son.

The sacrifices of women, mothers, and wives is also a theme in songs of the Vietnam era. Loretta Lynn's "Dear Uncle Sam" expresses the anguish of a woman whose husband was killed in Vietnam. The song contains no hint of protest; the loss, though painful, is accepted as necessary. Bonnie Guitar's poignant "The Tallest Tree" is a ballad about a mother who loses sons in World War II and the Korean conflict, only to see her youngest son killed in Vietnam. "My Son," written and recorded by Jan Howard, on the surface seems to be just another sentimental war song, recalling the critical stages in a son's life and expressing the mother's desire that he be careful and return safely. The sincerity of the song that saves it from the surface sentimentality of many such tunes results from the experience of Howard, who lost a son in Vietnam.

Other songs that indicate an awareness of and a willingness to accept the human sacrifices required by war are related from a male point of view. "Ruby, Don't Take Your Love to Town," a hit for both Johnny Darnel and Kenny Rogers, relates the story of a crippled Vietnam veteran trying to retain the affections of his wife. The Wilburn Brothers recorded the popular "Little Johnny from down the Street," a sentimental tale of a youngster who failed to return from Vietnam. George Kent's recording of Tom T. Hall's song, "Mama, Bake a Pie," is the tale of an embittered, crippled veteran's homecoming. The veteran, however, feels his personal sacrifice for the country was justified.

That commercial country music is written and performed primarily by southerners who have a long and honored military tradition only partially explains the fervent patriotism encountered in country songs. Ironically, country music is intensely patriotic because at one time southerners were not. While the battlefield heroics of Confederate forces served to enhance the reputation of southerners as gallant fighters, the Civil War also branded southerners as disloyal Americans. Since the Civil War and Reconstruction, southerners have struggled to remove that stigma and prove themselves truly loyal Americans. The nation's domestic problems afforded southerners little opportunity to demonstrate their restored patriotism, as the South remained outside the national mainstream in the areas of economic development, education, and race relations. War, however, presented the former rebels with a unique opportunity to assert their loyalty, to prove that they once again belonged, to demonstrate to the nation that because of their willingness, even eagerness, to fight for it, they were rebels no longer but its most patriotic citizens.

The eagerness of southerners to fight for their country, however, never erased their sense of being southern, of retaining an identity apart from, and in some respects antithetical to, their national identity. Southerners remain both southern and American, loyal to and proud of Thomas Jefferson and John C. Calhoun, George Washington and Robert E. Lee. This dual allegiance to both the region and the nation, so much a part of the southern character, is a central theme in commercial country music, evident not only in the issues the music chooses to address but in those that it does not.

Race relations, for example, is not a prominent theme in commercial country music. It is not, and has never been, because in the area of race relations, historically the South does not adhere to national norms. Segregation in the South was both custom and law, and well into the 1970s, southerners struggled to maintain a racially segregated society, often in open defiance of federal legislation and court decisions designed to put an end to legalized segregation. Southern whites who performed and wrote country songs, and the southern country music audience, also overwhelmingly white, chose to ignore the region's, and the nation's, racial problems. Blacks have been essentially unrepresented in country music (Charlie Pride remains a noted exception) and unable to explore racial themes. Thus country music, although heavily influenced by black music, especially rhythm and blues, remains a music of and for whites.

Yet country music has never been blatantly racist or supportive of the efforts of whites who continue to resist integration. In fact, some country songs address the issue of race relations in a positive manner. Among them is one of Kenny Rogers's earliest hits, "Ruben James," a ballad that told the tale of a hard-working black farmer who raised an orphaned white child. Other country songs with racial themes that achieved some degree of popularity include "In the Ghetto," a 1960s song recorded by both Elvis Presley and Dolly Parton, which deplores the social and economic deprivations experienced by ghetto children, and Tanya Tucker's 1976 release, "The South's Gonna Rise Again," envisioning a South in which racial harmony prevails. Direct condemnations of those who hold and act upon racial prejudice, however, are rarely encountered in country song lyrics, and songs containing such condemnations rarely make the country charts. Tom T. Hall's "The Man Who Hated Freckles," a 1960s fable that condemned racial bigots in no uncertain terms, is an exception, but it was never released as a single. Such exceptions only prove the rule that race has never been a significant theme in country music.

The South, on the other hand, has been a consistent theme in country music. Although the image of the South encountered in country song lyrics has changed over the years, it has remained essentially an image of the white South, the South of the people who write and perform the music. The image of the South in popular music, of course, antedates the rise of commercial country music. The South was an established theme in the popular music of the mid-nineteenth century and was an especially popular theme in tunes written for minstrel shows. After the Civil War, American popular music helped to maintain the image of the gracious life-style of the plantation South. The rise of commercial country music would result in an alteration of the image of the South, although the image continued to be a positive one.

The South that emerges from the lyrics of commercial country music is not that of the planter and the plantation but of working-class whites, whether farmers or factory hands. It is a region peopled by decent, hard-working people beset with almost overwhelming economic difficulties. It is also a region in which traditional values are respected, religious teachings and the church are important, and the bounty and beauty of nature are appreciated. This image of the South contains in equal parts elements of myth, nostalgia, and reality and remains one of the most significant themes in commercial country music. Its continued popularity indicates that southerners who create the music, and those who listen to it, continue to identify with the South and to hold a cultural identity as white southerners.

This southern identity is expressed in many ways. In the late 1940s and early 1950s, a number of popular country songs portrayed the South as quaint and colorful, if somewhat backward economically. Among these tunes were Red Foley's "Tennessee Saturday Night," "Birmingham Bounce," and "Alabama Jubilee." Other songs of this genre include Hank Williams's "Jambalaya," Tennessee Ernie Ford's "Smokie Mountain Boogie," and Eddie Arnold's "Bundle of Southern Sunshine."

The 1960s saw a change in the image of the South as it was portrayed in country song lyrics. Many songs of this era were written from the perspective of a former southerner forced northward in search of economic prosperity. In exile, the southerner looks homeward and remembers his cultural connections to the land of his birth. Bobby Bare's "Detroit City" relates the story of a displaced southerner employed as an autoworker. Although he is employed, the worker yearns for the South and wants to return, if only he could afford to do so. Dolly Parton's "Appalachian Memories," Don Williams's "Tulsa Time," and another Bobby Bare release, "500 Miles away from Home," all develop the same theme. Parton's "Appalachian Memories" is especially direct in identifying the economic woes of the region that forced many of its residents to move northward, however reluctantly.

In the 1970s, with the rise of the sunbelt economy and the election of a southern president, Jimmy Carter, country music artists began to express openly their pride in the region. The trend began with Loretta Lynn's "Coal Miner's Daughter," released in 1970. Lynn sings of growing up in the coal fields of Kentucky and informs her listeners that she is proud of her heritage. Charlie Daniels of North Carolina recorded a number of "southern pride" songs during the 1970s, the most popular of which was "The South's Gonna Do It Again," in which Daniels implores his listeners to be proud of the South and assures them that the region will regain its former glory. Alabama, one of country music's most popular male groups, recorded several tunes praising southern life. Among them were "My Home Is in Alabama," in which the singers, all Alabama natives, pledge allegiance to their cultural heritage, and "Dixieland Delight," a song praising the South's natural beauty and casual life-style. During the 1970s and 1980s Hank Williams, Jr., practically made a career of performing pro-South songs. In many of these songs, Williams compares northern and southern life-styles and customs, to the detriment of the North. The North, according to Williams, is a land of unfriendly, uptight people who do not hunt, drink Jack Daniels whiskey, or appreciate the song "Dixie." Other country music artists who recorded songs praising the southern life-style during this time include the Statler Brothers, Merle Haggard, David Allan Coe, and Jerry Reed.

Some scholars contend that the image of the South and the loyalty to the region encountered in country music are merely the result of talented writers' and performers' crafting a product that appeals to their audience—in fact, that country musicians have no personal allegiance to the South. Published interviews of country music performers, autobiographies by country musicians, and other sources reveal a different story, however. Most country music writers and performers live in the South, certainly in part because the music is recorded in the region and Nashville is the capital of the industry. But they also enjoy living in the South. They feel comfortable there and ill at ease in other parts of the country, especially the large urban areas of the North. Joe Stampley, one of country music's best-known honky-tonk-style singers, explaining why he found even Nashville too crowded, said, "We just came back [to Spring Hill, Louisiana]. It just feels laid back here. . . . I can go hunting and fishing with the kids."[2] Charlie Daniels expressed his need to live in the South even more forcefully. Even if given a million dollars a year, tax free, to live in a big city, he would refuse: "I'd be selling my soul to do it. I don't make any bones about it—I'm proud of being from the South."[3]

This preference for the South is a conscious choice on their part, for most have lived in other regions of the United States, and many have performed extensively in Europe and, to a lesser extent, in such distant lands as Australia and Japan. They are not ignorant of other regions and cultures; they simply prefer one they consider their own. Until a much larger percentage of those who write and perform country music come from outside the South, the music will continue to express a strong sense of loyalty to the region. Ironically, it is also likely to continue to express an equally strong sense of patriotism, especially an almost unquestioning support of the nation at war. To the southerners who create country music, patriotism is neither the last refuge of the scoundrel nor the fulfillment of an obligation imposed. Rather, it is a duty embraced, a heritage honored, and, ultimately, an unqualified commitment to the ideals of American society.

NOTES

1. Christopher Wren, "Country Music," *Look*, July 13, 1971, pp. 11–16.
2. Bob Millard, "Joe Stampley," *Country Music* 7 (June 1979): 53–57.
3. Michael Bane, "Good Time Charlie," *Carolina Lifestyle* 1 (August 1982): 44–49.

BIBLIOGRAPHY

Books

Gaillard, Frye. *Watermelon Wine: The Spirit of Country Music*. New York: St. Martin's Press, 1978.

Horstman, Dorothy. *Sing Your Heart Out, Country Boy.* Rev. ed. Nashville: Country Music Foundation, 1986.

Malone, Bill. *Country Music, U.S.A.* Austin: University of Texas Press, 1968.

Malone, Bill, and Judith McCulloh. *Stars of Country Music.* Urbana: University of Illinois Press, 1975.

Rogers, Jimmie N. *The Country Music Message: Revised.* Fayetteville: University of Arkansas Press, 1989.

Articles

Buckley, John. "Country Music, American Values." *Popular Music and Society* 6 (Fall 1979): 293–301.

Dickson, Paul. "Singing to Silent America." *Nation,* February 23, 1970, pp. 211–13.

McLaurin, Melton A. "Country Music and the Vietnam War." In *Perspectives on the American South,* vol. 3. Edited by James Cobb and Charles Wilson. New York: Gordon and Breach, Publishers, 1985.

Marsh, Ben. "A Rose Colored Map." *Harper's Magazine* 255 (July 1977): 80–82.

4

"Still Boy-Meets-Girl Stuff": Popular Music and War

Jeffrey C. Livingston

Although war has overshadowed much of American public life in the twentieth century, it has had a limited impact on the lyrical themes and sales of the nation's popular music. Except for the Vietnam era, when the development of a strong peace movement made antiwar music profitable, the music industry peddled war songs that generally contained banal, politically safe lyrics. Americans displayed at best a middling interest in war songs, for, even during wartime, pop tunes about romantic love dominated sheet music, radio, concert halls, and television.

Only in World War I did the number of war songs approximate those about love. At the war's outset in 1914, the vast majority of Americans, including President Woodrow Wilson, pledged U.S. neutrality. New York City's Tin Pan Alley, the era's center of popular music composition, shared this isolationism. In 1915, vaudeville star Norah Bayes popularized "I Didn't Raise My Boy to Be a Soldier." Bayes also congratulated the president for keeping the country out of war in her successful "We Take Our Hats Off to You Mr. Wilson," written by teenager Blanche Merrill.

Gradually, however, the public mood shifted. By 1916 German assaults on U.S. shipping and American economic and cultural ties with Britain and France made neutrality increasingly difficult. Former president Theodore Roosevelt, who ridiculed "I Didn't Raise My Boy"—and ironically would lose a son in World War I—led growing numbers of Americans in urging military preparedness. Tin Pan Alley chimed in with "Wake Up America!" and "In Time of Peace Prepare for War."

With Woodrow Wilson promising to make the world safe for democracy, the United States declared war against the Central Powers in April 1917. The general public rallied behind the president, and Tin Pan Alley helped lead the way with scores of songs supporting the war. Between April 1917 and November 1918, when the war ended, Tin Pan Alley produced more songs than any other comparable period in its history.

Many songwriters were first- and second-generation immigrants who used prowar songs, like "Let's All Be Americans Now," by Jewish-Russian immigrant Irving Berlin, to demonstrate their loyalty. Alleymen also responded to governmental encouragement. The official propaganda agency, the Committee on Public Information (CPI), pressed for composition of war tunes and dispatched song leaders to theaters around the country. The military distributed songbooks in camps and commissioned special officers to lead singing. Despite paper rationing, music publishers continued to receive an adequate supply, though they reduced the size of sheet music.

There was no radio or television to bring battlefield horrors into the living room, and Americans in 1917–1918 still held to an old-fashioned, romantic view of war. A number of World War I songs were martial in spirit. Representative was the war's biggest hit, George M. Cohan's jaunty "Over There." Written the day after Wilson signed the declaration of war, the catchy ditty warned that America was on its way. The tune sold over 1 million records and 2 million copies of sheet music. Norah Bayes plugged "Over There," musically personifying the American public's turn from neutralism to war fever.

The classic "Mademoiselle from Armentieres (Parley-Vous)" (also known as "Hinky Dinky, Parley-Voo") was popular in the armed forces, while on the home front many tunes portrayed the life of the common soldier. They were often humorous, such as "If He Can Fight Like He Can Love Goodnight Germany." Irving Berlin's smash all-soldier musical revue, *Yip Yip Yaphank*, viewed the war through doughboy eyes. The million-copy selling "Oh How I Hate to Get Up in the Morning" came out of the show and went on to become an American standard.

The somber side of war could not be avoided entirely. The most popular ballad, "Till We Meet Again," sold several million copies of sheet music. Woodrow Wilson liked singing "There's a Long, Long Trail" with his family after dinner. Many songs were maudlin, like the tearjerker "Hello, Central, Give Me No Man's Land," the saga of a little girl trying to reach her soldier father by telephone.

Government strictures and broad public backing of the war limited circulation of peace songs to labor radicals and to African Americans. The period's most radical labor union, the Industrial Workers of the World, included antiwar folk tunes, like a parody of "Onward Christian Soldiers," in its *Little Red Songbook*. Black singers complained about the war as late as 1929 (Bessie Smith, "Poor Man's Blues"). A good soldier, Tin Pan Alley avoided antiwar themes, although censors did ban "I Don't Want to Get Well—I'm in Love with a Beautiful Nurse," "There'll Be a Hot Time for the Old Men When the Young Men Go to War," and a few other ribald ditties on the grounds that they encouraged draft dodging and desertion.

Overall, the government could not have asked for a better performance from popular music. Prowar songs comprised part of a broad governmental campaign that by mid–1918 nearly wiped out all organized opposition to the war. But once the shooting stopped, most Alleymen and their fellow Americans were eager to forget about the conflict. The flood of war compositions dropped to a trickle. Sensing that public musical preferences had already shifted, vaudeville house managers in 1919 tacked up signs prohibiting war songs.

At the postwar Versailles Conference, vengeful Allied leaders shocked Americans when they sneered at Woodrow Wilson's dreams of a new world order. Americans in the 1920s, reveling in normalcy, jazz, and bathtub gin, recalled their wartime idealism with embarrassment and sadness. "My Buddy" and "That Old Gang of Mine" mourned fallen comrades. A cynical Billy Rose wondered in "Unknown Soldier" if the Great War had satisfied politicians and profiteering businessmen.

This disillusionment made many Americans wary when Europe again plunged into war in September 1939. They polarized into opposing camps as a large isolationist movement battled President Franklin D. Roosevelt's efforts to inch the nation toward intervention in World War II against Nazi Germany. It took Japan's December 1941 attack on Pearl Harbor to galvanize national unity.

Before Pearl Harbor, popular music was also divided. Oddly, although their audience was small, leftist urban folksingers typified American ambivalence. With loose ties to the Communist party (CP), the folksingers hoped to use songs as ideological weapons. The best known were the Almanac Singers, whose shifting membership included Woody Guthrie and Pete Seeger. In spring 1941 the Almanacs released the album *Songs for John Doe*. The record toed the party's antiwar line, containing tunes like "Plow Under" (every fourth American boy), which militantly opposed intervention. Apart from leftists, however, few Americans heard the record.

After Germany's invasion of the Soviet Union in June 1941, the CP reversed itself and called for an antifascist "people's war." Somewhat bewildered for a few months, the Almanacs eventually followed. In their 1942 album *Dear Mr. President*, they apologized to Roosevelt for *John Doe* and urged full efforts to win World War II. With Woody Guthrie strumming a guitar that had "This Machine Kills Fascists" carved into it, the group appeared on CBS national radio broadcasts several times in 1942. The Almanacs also sang on shortwave radio broadcasts beamed overseas to American servicemen by the Office of War Information (OWI), the government's wartime propaganda agency.

Foreshadowing the McCarthy era, a series of red-baiting articles in New York City newspapers highlighted the group's leftist politics. The OWI fired them, and the Almanacs entered the military or other war-related work. Their "Round and Round Hitler's Grave" was played on the last program of CBS's War in Europe series in 1945.

By contrast, Tin Pan Alley, still the mainstream bulwark of popular music, threw its support behind both President Roosevelt and intervention early on and never wavered. Irving Berlin took the lead. When singer Kate Smith requested a patriotic song from Berlin to use for her radio show in 1939, he dusted off a twenty-year-old tune, "God Bless America." Recorded by Smith, the song reached the Top 10 in 1940 and became an unofficial wartime national anthem.

After the United States declared war, the federal government from the president down encouraged the music industry to mobilize. Berlin wrote two songs, "Any Bonds Today"—actually composed before Pearl Harbor— and "I Paid My Income Taxes Today," at the request of Treasury Secretary Henry Morgenthau, Jr. Whether these lame tunes, which scarcely rank as Berlin's best, swayed citizens is unclear.

Presumably the OWI anticipated better results when it called for tough-minded songs outlining war realities. The initial response was encouraging. Don Reid and Sammy Kaye composed the popular "Remember Pearl Harbor" within days of the attack. The first big-selling war song was Frank Loesser's 1942 "Praise the Lord and Pass the Ammunition," recorded by both the Merry Macs and Kay Kyser. Written to an irresistible folk melody, the song became so popular, despite clergy complaints about juxtaposing God and weaponry, that the federal government asked radio stations not to play it more than once every four hours.

Country and western (C&W) also made key contributions. Originating in the 1920s, C&W boomed during World War II. Southern whites brought the music with them as they migrated northward and westward to work in war industries, and Dixie servicemen carried it around the world. Government-sponsored tours and the Camel Caravan, financed by R. J. Reynolds Company and the Grand Ole Opry, dispatched country artists to military bases throughout the United States and Europe.

Rooted in the English folk ballad tradition, which featured topical broadsides, C&W generated dozens of war songs. The most famous was Bob Miller's maudlin, "There's a Star-Spangled Banner Waving Somewhere," recorded by both Elton Britt and Hank Snow. The story of a crippled mountain boy who wanted to serve his country, the tune was a huge seller. American racism and war fever were evident in anti-Japanese songs, such as "We're Gonna Have to Slap the Dirty Little Jap," released by some country artists. The most popular of this type was Red Foley's militant "Smoke on the Water," which anticipated turning all of Japan into a graveyard.

The German kaiser had been a favorite song topic during World War I. Tin Pan Alley avoided Adolf Hitler and the Germans for unclear reasons, but C&W songs addressed the Nazis. One, Spike Jones's wacky "Der Fuehrer's Face," utilized the Bronx cheer when Hitler's name was mentioned and was a major crossover hit in 1942.

The OWI felt that, after a strong start in 1942, popular music fizzled out.

The problem was not antiwar songs. The only artists to question the conflict were a few blues singers who noted at the end of the war, in tunes such as Big Bill Broonzy's "When Will I Get to Be Called a Man?" and "Fighting for Dear Old Sam" by J. D. Short, that black contributions to the war effort did not weaken racial segregation. Rather, too many war tunes, complained an OWI official, "were just love songs with a once-over-lightly war background." "It was still boy-meets-girl stuff" (Woll, 1975). Desperate for good war songs, the OWI singled out Spike Jones's "Der Fuehrer's Face" for praise. One can only speculate on how this zany novelty song, notable for Donald Duck–type voicings, improved on the romance tunes.

The OWI had a point, though. The music industry never quite caught fire as it had in 1917–1918. The public seemed uninterested in war songs, and after 1943, their numbers on the charts dropped sharply. The enthusiasm of World War I songs was missing; World War II had no "Over There." A few bouncy tunes like the vapid "Don't Sit under the Apple Tree (with Anyone Else but Me)" appeared, but more songs were sad. "I Left My Heart at the Stage Door Canteen," by Irving Berlin, "When the Lights Go on Again (All over the World)," and Frank Loesser's "Rodger Young," a folk ballad about a twenty-five-year-old soldier killed in the Solomon Islands, focused on wartime tragedy and disrupted relationships. While not specifically about the war, Berlin's huge-selling "White Christmas" evoked memories of home for servicemen deployed in foreign lands. Often emotional, C&W produced such weepers as the sappy "Comin' in on a Wing and a Prayer," which reached number 1 on the general popularity charts in 1943.

An OWI spokesman blamed the popular foxtrot and swing beats for the lack of high-quality war songs, arguing that the new rhythms were less conducive to stirring martial tunes than the one- and two-steps of the 1910s. The agency also noted that radio had become the primary transmitter of music, overshadowing dances, theaters, and concerts; love songs already prevailed on the airwaves. Other developments might be added. Graphic radio, newsreel, and magazine reports made the naive exuberance of 1917–1918 impossible. A strike by the Musicians' Union in 1943 hindered instrumental recording. Unlike the World War I era, Tin Pan Alley, though still huge, was no longer the sole source of white, mainstream popular music. Weakened by a fight between the American Society of Composers, Authors, and Performers (ASCAP) and the upstart Broadcast Music Incorporated (BMI) over song licensing, and competing with swing, folk, and country, the Alleymen could not flood the market with war songs.

The devastation at Hiroshima and Nagasaki in August 1945 sparked a surge of C&W "atomic bomb" songs. Then, for about fifteen years, war songs appeared on the pop charts in regular but tiny numbers. Regarded as necessary but unwelcome, the early cold war struggle, including the conflict in Korea between 1950 and 1953, inspired neither the public nor mainstream songwriters. Tellingly, "Dear John Letter," the tale of a soldier's lost love, was one of the more popular mainstream Korean War songs.

In the 1950s country and western took up the musical standard for conservative, right-wing values. With their audience continuing to expand beyond the South, country artists defended intervention in Korea, cold war militancy, and atomic diplomacy. Covered by Ralph Flanagan, Elton Britt's "The Red That We Want Is the Red That We Got (in the Old Red, White, and Blue)" made *Billboard*'s Top 100 in 1950. In "Advice to Joe," Roy Acuff warned Soviet leader Josef Stalin that atomic bombs would check communist expansion. Jimmie Osborne was moved in 1953 to "Thank God for Victory in Korea."

Yet in retrospect, the number of C&W tunes on Korea and the cold war is small. The American anticommunist consensus was strong and needed no musical reinforcement. Although war, especially nuclear, seemed imminent, Americans wanted few reminders in song. The Chordettes reached the charts in 1956 with their innocuous "Lay Down Your Arms." Frank Chacksfield's "On the Beach," the theme song from the 1959 film based on Nevil Shute's novel about nuclear holocaust, charted well. Just a handful of marginal white urban folk and black singers dared to protest the arms race and war. McCarthyism shut down dissent in all forms, including musical.

A large portion of 1950s war songs were patriotic recollections of America's past conflicts. Songs spoke of the Civil War ("Johnny Reb"), the War of 1812 (Johnny Horton's hit "The Battle of New Orleans"), World War II ("The Guns of Navarone"), a frontier fighter ("The Ballad of Davy Crockett"), and even the Texas Revolution ("Ballad of the Alamo"). During a highly nationalistic era, popular songwriters celebrated the country's military triumphs.

The Vietnam War was the only twentieth-century U.S. conflict to catalyze a significant number of popular antiwar songs. In direct and indirect ways, folk music was responsible. Folksingers, often with leftist leanings, gained popularity on college campuses in the late 1950s and early 1960s. Activist youth of the Kennedy era listened to, played, and wrote protest folk songs. Most touched on civil rights but some also condemned war and the arms race, such as Buffy Sainte-Marie's "Universal Soldier" and Bob Dylan's "Masters of War." After 1963 prominent folksingers like Phil Ochs and Tom Paxton protested growing U.S. involvement in Vietnam with "I Ain't A-Marchin' Anymore," "Lyndon Johnson Told the Nation," and other tunes.

Artists led by the Byrds and Bob Dylan merged folk with rock and roll to create folk rock in 1965. They brought the protest song to rock. Since rock and roll commanded a wider audience, rock protest eventually became more important than folk. Barry McGuire, former member of the folk group, the Christy Minstrels, scored the first hit with a rock protest song, "Eve of

Destruction" (1965). Written by nineteen-year-old P. J. Sloan, the tune cat-aloged a series of political and social ills, including military conflict in Asia. A number of radio stations banned the record.

The reference to war in "Eve of Destruction" was exceptional. Although rock adopted the protest song, it was slow to criticize the Vietnam War because of the controversial nature of antiwar songs. Until the late 1960s, a majority of Americans supported involvement in Vietnam. Rock depended far more than folk on market sales, and record companies and artists feared offending potential customers. Up to 1968 just a handful of antiwar rock songs appeared. Donovan's cover of "Universal Soldier" reached number 45 on the rock charts in 1965. Others, like Country Joe and the Fish's "The I'm-Fixin'-to-Die-Rag" and the Fugs's "Kill for Peace," were cult favorites that received little airplay.

The year 1968 marked a turning point. Polls showed a decline in public backing of the war, and growing numbers of young people, especially college students, regarded political radicalism as acceptable. It became fashionable and profitable for rock musicians to record antiwar songs. Four reached the Top 100 in 1968. In the next six years, twenty-six antiwar songs cracked the Top 100. Among the most successful were black singer Edwin Starr's powerful "War," which held the number 1 position in the summer of 1970, John Lennon's utopian "Imagine," which topped the charts for several weeks in 1971, and the spooky "Run through the Jungle," by Creedence Clearwater Revival. Although not huge sellers, Crosby, Stills, Nash, and Young's "Ohio," an outcry against the Kent State murders of 1970, and Lennon's "Give Peace a Chance" became anthems for the antiwar move-ment.

Many young radicals argued in the 1960s that rock protest music was a powerful tool for raising consciousness. Antiwar songs were indeed trendy, but they preached to the converted. Audiences admitted they listened more closely to beat and melody than to lyrics. Despite the changed political climate, rock songwriters remained cautious. Most declined to mention Vietnam by name, preferring allusion or condemning war in general.

By the early seventies, increasingly watered-down lyrics allowed antiwar songs to become mainstream. "Whitebread" pop-rock songs like Coven's "One Tin Soldier" and Cat Stevens's "Peace Train" carried vague antiwar messages. Always on top of trends and with an eye for profits, Motown, the "General Motors of rock," cashed in. Black artists Freda Payne, with "Bring the Boys Home," and Marvin Gaye, with his brilliant "What's Goin' On?" joined labelmate Edwin Starr in scoring hits that protested the war.

CBS censored Pete Seeger's "Waist Deep in the Big Muddy" when the veteran folkie sang the antiwar song on the "Smothers Brothers" show in 1967. Infuriated, Tom and Dick Smothers invited Seeger back, and he sang the tune, this time without network interference. The federal government made no overt moves to censor antiwar songs. Vice-President Spiro Agnew and other right-wing politicians denounced the music as un-American. The FBI maintained files on artists who criticized the war. Many people suspected that the Nixon administration's efforts to deport John Lennon in the 1970s were due more to the ex-Beatle's political songs than to his 1968 drug bust, as the White House claimed. On the whole, the government moved more aggressively against songs with drug references than those with political content.

Country and western, however, responded to antiwar songs with a vengeance. Country by the 1960s commanded a national audience. Conservative politicians such as President Richard Nixon endorsed C&W as the music of the patriotic silent majority. In 1966 country artists released about 120 prowar tunes and dedicated two albums to prowar music. A dozen war songs made the Top 100 on the year's country charts. Three of the more popular were Stonewall Jackson's angry "The Minute Men Are Turning in Their Graves," in which he curiously labeled draft resisters who opted for prison as unprincipled, and two songs covered by Dave Dudley, "Viet Nam Blues," written by a young Kris Kristofferson, and "What We're Fighting For," composed by Tom T. Hall.

Three of the biggest prowar songs were not country but had large C&W audiences. Sergeant Barry Sadler's 1966 "Ballad of the Green Berets" sold 7 million copies. Victor Lundberg's 1967 "Open Letter to My Teenage Son" spent seven weeks on *Cash Box*'s singles chart. In a spoken voice over music, Lundberg vowed to disown his son if he burned his draft card. In Pat Boone's bitter crossover tune, "Wish You Were Here, Buddy," an American soldier promised to retaliate against an antiwar protester upon returning home. It charted in *Cash Box* for two months in 1966.

After a lull, C&W outrage peaked at the turn of the decade. Merle Haggard registered giant hits with "Okie from Muskogee" and "The Fightin' Side of Me." Haggard at first regarded "Okie" as tongue in cheek, but the populist diatribe against peaceniks and hippies found a huge audience. "Fightin' Side of Me" reached number 1 on the country chart in 1970. Terry Nelson and C Company's "The Battle Hymn of Lieutenant Calley" praised the villain of the My Lai massacre. The 1971 song proved so controversial that it was banned on scores of radio stations, including the American Armed Forces Radio Network in Vietnam. Nonetheless, the song sold millions and was a large jukebox hit.

Illustrating how acrid the Vietnam issue became, even C&W musicians released a handful of lukewarm antiwar songs. Loretta Lynn informed "Dear Uncle Sam" that he needed her man less than she did. Johnny Cash recorded several songs in which he tried to bridge generational and cultural gaps. Kenny Rogers and the First Edition had a hit with "Ruby Don't Take Your Love to Town." The song's smooth country-rock melody and beat contrasted with its story of a sexually disabled Vietnam veteran.

Overall, popular music divided by genre during the Vietnam War. Rock and folk opposed the war; country and, to a lesser extent, mainstream pop backed intervention. These musical battle lines reflected the divisions within American society at large. Nevertheless, the number of Vietnam War songs should not be exaggerated. Even during C&W's outpouring in 1966, love songs continued to dominate the charts of all popular idioms.

As was the case after other American wars, following U.S. withdrawal from Vietnam, the number of high-selling war songs plummeted. In the 1980s Bruce Springsteen's "Born in the USA," Billy Joel's "Goodnight Saigon," and "Still in Saigon" by the Charlie Daniels Band dealt with Vietnam veterans. Peter Gabriel's "Games without Frontiers," XTC's "Generals and Majors," and a series of releases by the Irish band U2 condemned war in general. A few rock artists, including the Clash, Don Henley, and in particular Jackson Browne, criticized U.S. policy in Central America. Probably because these songs and artists represented exceptions, no musical backlash developed.

The historical record offers little hope to those who would use popular music as a force for social change and peace. War songs in twentieth-century popular music reinforced the status quo. After 1900 only the Vietnam War, which underwent significant questioning by Americans, catalyzed an important number of antiwar songs. During the other three major wars, popular music supported or at least did not question American military involvement. Even Vietnam antiwar music was rarely explicit and made few converts to the cause.

The staying power of romantic love songs during times of national crisis is remarkable. In every war after World War I, love themes prevailed. Americans preferred that their music, no less than other forms of popular culture such as television, film, and paperback novels, allow them to ignore, rather than to confront, reality.

BIBLIOGRAPHY

Anderson, Terry H. "American Popular Music and the War in Vietnam." *Peace and Change* 11 (July 1986): 51–65.

Bindas, Kenneth J., and Craig Houston. " 'Takin' Care of Business": Rock Music, Vietnam and the Protest Myth." *Historian* 52 (1989): 1–23.

Chinn, Jennie A. "There's a Star-Spangled Banner Waving Somewhere: Country and Western Songs of World War II." *John Edward Memorial Foundation Quarterly* 16 (1980): 74–80.

Denisoff, R. Serge. *Sing a Song of Social Significance.* 2d ed. Bowling Green, Ohio: Bowling Green State University Press, 1983.

Denisoff, R. Serge, and Richard A. Peterson, eds. *The Sounds of Social Change.* Chicago: Rand McNally, 1972.

Ellison, Mary. "War—It's Nothing But a Heartbreak: Attitudes towards War in Black Lyrics." *Popular Music and Society* 10 (1986): 29–42.

Ewen, David. *All the Years of American Popular Music: A Comprehensive History.* Englewood Cliffs, N.J.: Prentice-Hall, 1974.

Hesbacher, Peter, and Les Waffen. "War Recordings: Incidence and Change, 1940–1980." *Popular Music and Society* 8 (1982): 77–101.

Lieberman, Robbie. *"My Song Is My Weapon": People's Songs, American Communism, and the Politics of Culture, 1930–1950.* Urbana: University of Illinois Press, 1989.

Lund, Jens. "Country Music Goes to War: Songs for the Red-Blooded American." *Popular Music and Society* 1 (Summer 1972): 210–30.

Malone, Bill C. "Country Music, the South, and Americanism." *Mississippi Folklore Register* 10 (Spring 1976): 54–66.

Orman, John. *The Politics of Rock.* Chicago: Nelson-Hall, 1984.

Rodnitzky, Jerome L. *Minstrels of the Dawn: The Folk-Protest Singer as a Cultural Hero.* Chicago: Nelson-Hall, 1976.

Whitcomb, Ian. *After the Ball.* London: Penguin Press, 1972.

Wolfe, Charles. "Nuclear Country: The Atomic Bomb in Country Music." *Journal of Country Music* 7 (1978): 4–21.

Woll, Allen L. "From Blues in the Night to Accentuate the Positive: Film Music Goes to War, 1939–45." *Popular Music and Society* 4 (1975): 66–76.

Part II

Class

5

Social and Geographic Characteristics of Country Music

James E. Akenson

Country music stands as one of the major forms of popular music in American culture. Like any other musical or artistic form, country music exhibits many variants or substyles. Bluegrass, Cajun, cowboy, western swing, rockabilly, honky-tonk, crossover, and new traditionalist are but some of the terms that describe country music styles.

The eighteenth and nineteenth centuries saw an exodus from the British Isles; many of these immigrants to America settled in the Appalachian ridges and valleys and fanned out throughout the South. These humble Anglo-Americans brought with them musical instruments such as the fiddle and musical forms from which commercial country music would evolve. Ballad singing that emphasized linear stories about everyday life served as the model from which stories would be heard in modern country music. Such music fulfilled an important niche in the lives of low-status mountaineers, small farm operators, craftspeople, and laborers.

A complex process of adapting Anglo-American musical forms to the new world created the basis for the modern cultural form known as country music. The Anglo-American music received an infusion from African Americans and other sources with the introduction of instruments such as the banjo, varied performance styles, and content. Beginning in the 1920s this folk music mixture of low-status southern whites resulted in a commercial product distributed to a mass market through the technologies of radio and records. Radio stations such as WSB in Atlanta, Georgia, discovered a substantial audience for country music. The rise of country music as a commercial product provided white southerners with career opportunities other than farming or blue-collar factory employment.

During the 1920s record companies began to realize the potential market for the music of poor, southern whites. In June 1922 Texan Eck Roberson and Oklahoman Henry Gilliland walked into Victor studios in New York

City and convinced Victor executives to record several tunes. During 1923 Fiddlin' John Carson recorded "The Little Old Cabin in the Lane" and "The Old Hen Cackled and the Rooster's Going to Crow" for Okeh records; the sales surprised recording executives and made them aware of an unexpected market. August 4, 1927, witnessed a landmark event on the Tennessee side of State Street in Bristol, Tennessee-Virginia, when Ralph Peer recorded Jimmie Rodgers and the Carter Family for the Victor company. Rodgers and the Carter Family went on to sell millions of records and confirm the large market for so-called hillbilly music.

Jimmie Rodgers, the Father of Country Music, grew up in Meridian, Mississippi, and the surrounding region. He came from humble circumstances; his father worked for the railroad and failed in his attempts to farm. Young Rodgers often lived with relatives and worked as a waterboy for the railroad. As an adult, Rodgers failed to hold a wide variety of blue-collar jobs and found only sporadic employment as a railroad brakeman. He was a likable working-class failure until he managed to convince Ralph Peer of Victor to record him. Similarly early country music artists such as the Carter Family from southwest Virginia, the Delmore Brothers from Alabama, and Sam McGee from Tennessee came from humble, rural origins in the South. The country music audience was made up of poor white southerners, as were the artists who performed it.

The gradual development of commercial country music has resulted in a national and global audience. A combination of concert performances, recordings, television appearances, and sophisticated marketing bear little resemblance to the initial commercial efforts in the 1920s. In the late twentieth century, country music accounts for 10 to 15 percent of the recorded music purchased in the United States and generates annual revenues in excess of $1 billion for a variety of related goods and services. Even rock and roll, the dominant form of contemporary popular music, has roots in country music. Elvis Presley began his career appearing on country music package tours and was billed as "The Hillbilly Cat." Despite the humble origins and apparently low cultural status of country music, demographic studies suggest that a surprisingly wide range of Americans admit to liking it. Presidents Jimmy Carter and George Bush made it clear that country music even had White House approval. Like the blues, rhythm and blues, gospel, and rock, country music emerged from specific geographic and socioeconomic origins. Deep roots in the southern culture of rural tenant farmers, sharecroppers, and blue-collar workers fostered a form of popular music that today claims an international audience, from Japan to Eastern Europe.

The southern roots of country music are evident in a variety of sources— for example, song titles and content. Songs display southern-oriented content in numerous ways. Hank Williams, Jr., frequently articulates strong southern sentiments in songs such as "Dixie on My Mind," "If Heaven Ain't a Lot Like Dixie I Don't Want to Go," "The South's Gonna Rattle

Again," and "If the South Woulda Won." In "Dixie on My Mind," he bemoans the fact that he is stuck in New York City while he wishes he could be back in Alabama enjoying the southern out-of-doors. He mentions Spartanburg, South Carolina, as well as Houston, Texas, Lake Okechobee in Florida, and Jack Daniels whiskey from Tennessee. In "If Heaven Ain't a Lot Like Dixie I Don't Want to Go," he claims he would choose to go to hell—or New York City—if heaven does not have a Grand Ole Opry like in Nashville, Tennessee. He generated controversy with "If the South Woulda Won" in which he indicates that he would place the Supreme Court in Texas and the southern capital in Alabama. He also mentions Miami, Florida, Tupelo, Mississippi, Virginia fiddles, the Carolinas as a site for manufacturing automobiles, Kentucky horses, Arkansas wine, Tennessee whiskey, and Georgia as a site to train southern women to talk and smile.

Other country songs mention the South without the strident tone of Hank Williams, Jr. The group Alabama consistently mentions southern themes without being negative about other regions of the United States. Content typical of Alabama's positive yet mild tone may be found in their album, *Southern Star*. The title cut, "Song of the South," discusses hard times during the depression and alludes to the Civil War but looks to better times initiated by the Tennessee Valley Authority and states that people should not look back. Alabama tells that the author's father was a Southern Democrat—the party of poor whites. Other *Southern Star* songs with southern content are "Dixie Fire," "Pete's Music City," " 'Ole Baugh Road," "High Cotton," "Down on the River," and "The Borderline." Growing up southern and playing music comes across strongly in "Pete's Music City," with its references to northern Georgia and U.S. highway 41. The apparent Dalton, Georgia, setting refers to carpet mills and the fascination with playing music in an idyllic, carefree life-style. "The Borderline" offers a Texas cowboy drama set near the Mexican border south of San Antonio.

" 'Ole Baugh Road" offers a contrast to the prosouthern, antinorthern stance of Hank Williams, Jr. It provides evidence of Alabama's strong sense of place and connection to their southern roots, as well as their acceptance of people and places outside the South. Alabama's lead singer and song-writer, Randy Owen, speaks fondly of Baugh Road from his childhood and the decision of many others like him to stay close to it. However, Owen offers that there may be a Baugh Road in everyone's childhood, no matter where in the United States one might have grown up. The autobiographical nature of " 'Ole Baugh Road" may be seen in the 1989–1990 Fort Payne, Alabama, telephone directory. Randy Owen's polled Hereford cattle business is listed in the directory as being located on Baugh Road. The Hereford operation is titled "Tennessee River Music, Incorporated" in honor of an early Randy Owen composition, "Tennessee River." Completing the sense of the South illustrated in *Southern Star* and other Alabama songs stands the actual commitment of Alabama to Fort Payne. All four members of

Alabama—Randy Owen, Jeff Cook, Teddy Gentry, and Mark Herndon—
make their homes in Fort Payne and hold an annual June Jam concert to
raise funds for local charity.

Hank Williams, Jr., and Alabama reflect the frequent southern idea in
contemporary country music. Early commercial country music reveals that
southern references constitute a long-running tradition that celebrates a
sense of place and allegiance to the South. Mississippian Jimmie Rodgers
recorded from 1927 until his death from tuberculosis in 1933. Rodgers's
first major hit, "Blue Yodel Number 1," is more commonly known as "T
for Texas (T for Tennessee)" and also makes reference to Atlanta, Georgia.
Rodgers recorded some 110 songs for RCA Victor, which included southern-
oriented content in "Miss the Mississippi and You," "Mississippi Delta
Blues," "Daddy and Home," and "Peach Pickin' Time down in Georgia."
The lyrics of "Peach Pickin' Time down in Georgia" provide a tour of the
South, ranging from cattle roundup time in Texas to apples in Tennessee,
the Ozark Mountains in Arkansas, Kentucky bluegrass, and dancing in
Virginia. Rodgers also recorded songs with cowboy themes, including "The
Yodeling Ranger" and "The Cowhand's Last Ride."

The geographic origins of country music performers reflect strong southern roots. Researchers consistently find that the South is the cradle of country
music. Some 85 percent of country music artists born before 1910 and 73
percent of those born since 1940 came from the South. Texas leads the
South in the absolute number of country musicians, but Kentucky and
Tennessee lead when the size of their white populations is taken into account.
Kentucky and Tennessee produced 4.5 and 6.0 times the expected number
of country music performers given their respective white populations. All
of the southern states, however, exceeded the number of country musicians
expected on the basis of their respective white populations. Clearly, country
music stands deeply rooted in southern soil despite its national and international popularity.

Country music reflects not only southern roots but a specific location in
the hierarchy of socioeconomic status. The country music message reflects
on numerous themes, including rural, small-town southern images, love of
family and country, a longing to go back home to one's southern home,
and working-class images derived from urban life. Merle Haggard provides
a case in point. He offers a broad repertoire, which includes songs such as
"Grandma Harp," "Working Man Blues," "If We Make It through December," "Okie from Muskogee," and "Amber Waves of Grain." In "Working
Man Blues" Haggard tells of the difficulties of working at modest wages to
support a wife and family and informs the listener that he drinks beer in a
tavern. "If We Make It through December" tells of a family man who has
been laid off from his factory job, dreads being unable to give his young
daughter Christmas gifts, and hopes to move to California to find better
times. "Okie from Muskogee" offered Haggard's Vietnam War–era com-

mentary consistent with President Nixon's silent majority. Haggard sang of his disapproval of draft card burning and disrespect for authority while stating his belief in old-fashioned love. "Grandma Harp" relates Haggard's own grandmother's difficult life, and "Amber Waves of Grain" tells of the contemporary threat to the American farmer.

A wide variety of country music artists provide references consistent with traditional values and the humble origins of the country music audience and performers. John Conlee's "Common Man" tells of his desire to eat at McDonald's rather than at an expensive restaurant, his preference for a Chevrolet over a Mercedes, and a thirst for Budweiser beer instead of a glass of wine. The Nitty Gritty Dirt Band sings of humble southern origins in "Long Hard Road," subtitled "The Sharecropper's Dream." Alabama pays homage to a wide variety of pink- and blue-collar Americans in "Forty Hour Week," ranging from the Kansas wheat farmer and the Detroit autoworker to truckers, coal miners, waitresses, mail carriers, and police. Alabama claims that such ordinary Americans are the workers who truly hold America together and states that such Americans are worth much more than their pay.

Some country songs combine southern roots with bold proclamations of low socioeconomic status. The low status associated with the term *redneck* made its way into country music as a form celebrating humble origins. Johnny Russell's "Rednecks, White Socks, and Blue Ribbon Beer" positively proclaims redneck status while dealing with drinking, women, and violence. In a similar vein, Conway Twitty described the attraction of a wealthy woman to a "good ole boy" in "Tight Fittin' Jeans." Travis Tritt's "Country Club" dealt with the attraction of a working-class male to a high-status female. Tritt proclaimed that he too was a member of a country club because he loved country music.

The relationship between country music and modest socioeconomic status may be seen in a surprising manner. The Grand Ole Opry radio program helped market life insurance by providing listeners with country music. Nashville, Tennessee, radio station WSM began featuring country music in 1925. Over time, the Grand Ole Opry took form, with Friday and Saturday night performances that continue to the present time. The call letters WSM stand for "We Shield Millions." Owned by the National Life and Accident Company, the Grand Ole Opry became a marketing tool for insurance agents who sold policies for amounts rarely over $1,000 to people of modest means. The same agents collected small premiums on a weekly basis on street corners or in the home of the policyholders. Such a system required close personal relationships between the agents and the policyholders. Agents even introduced themselves as representing the Grand Ole Opry Insurance Company, provided clients with photographs of Opry cast members, and in 1933 distributed a picture book, *Fiddles and Life Insurance*.

The humble circumstances of country music performers may be seen in the life of Lewis Crook, who has been a regular performer on the Grand Ole Opry since 1929. Born in 1909 to sharecropper parents, Lewis Crook grew up in rural Trousdale County, Tennessee, some thirty miles northeast of Nashville. In 1910, the county consisted of 5,974 persons, split between 70 percent white and 30 percent African American. Only 0.4 percent of the Trousdale County population was classified as foreign born. Approximately 32 percent of the African-American population and 13 percent of the white population were illiterate. Sharecroppers operated 32 percent of Trousdale County farms, which featured tobacco, corn, poultry, and eggs as dominant farm products. In this setting young Crook learned to play his father's banjo and taught himself the two-finger (thumb and index finger) picking style he uses today. Afterward, Crook began saving money and purchased his own guitar for $9.95 through the Sears Roebuck catalog. Music played an important part in the life of the Crook family as friends and relatives would gather for socializing in homes or on picnics in which fiddles, banjos, and guitars contributed to the occasions.

Lewis Crook quit school by age fourteen to satisfy his father's desire for more labor. In the summer of 1926, Lewis boarded a bus and moved to Nashville, where he roomed at Aunt Willie Dixon's house and worked as a laborer for the Nashville Park Commission. After being laid off, he returned to Trousdale County to help his parents. In 1929, he moved with his family to Nashville and began performing on the Grand Ole Opry as a member of the Crook Brothers. Only Lewis remained in Nashville on a permanent basis; urban life provided his father and mother with no easier living conditions than did sharecropping. The remainder of Crook's working life has featured a variety of blue-collar or low-paying white-collar jobs, ranging from working in a chicken processing plant to selling life insurance to working in the Acme Boot factory. As Lewis Crook candidly states, "I was born poor and I still am."

Country music provided Lewis Crook with an important creative and social outlet at the same time it provided desperately needed income. Weekly Grand Ole Opry performances during the depression provided five dollars additional income. Lewis also organized a string band that played for dances and booked country music performances for himself in small-town schools and courthouses in rural middle Tennessee. In addition, he performed in various Grand Ole Opry package shows in the South. Only during World War II did Crook miss performing on the Grand Ole Opry. From February 1943 to November 1945 he served with the 43d Infantry Division throughout the Pacific campaign. He performed country music for others while in his tent close to the front lines, in landing ship transports waiting to storm ashore in island assaults, and for United Service Organization shows as filler prior to appearances by personalities such as Bob Hope. His performances helped spread the country music audience to people and locations that previously had known little or nothing about country music.

After World War II Lewis Crook returned to Nashville, to his weekly performance on the Grand Ole Opry as a member of the Crook Brothers, and to his modest life-style. In retirement, Crook lives in the same Trousdale County home where he grew up on country music and hard work walking behind a team of mules. Each Saturday evening he drives to the sprawling Opryland complex, which houses the modern Grand Ole Opry house. There he performs one or two numbers with the Opry Square Dance Band. With the death of group founder Herman Crook, the Crook Brothers ceased to exist. Lewis took his place to play for the square dance and clogging groups that provide a rural, down-home touch to Grand Ole Opry performances. From childhood to old age, country music and Lewis Crook have reflected a simple, humble existence that has brought together city and country, farmers and workers of modest circumstances, and major events of the twentieth century.

Major contemporary country music artists also tend to rise from humble circumstances similar to that of Lewis Crook. The Forester Sisters learned their tightly knit harmonies singing in a rural church in north Georgia. Clint Black labored as an ironworker. Dolly Parton grew up in near poverty in the east Tennessee hills. Randy Travis worked in the kitchen of a Nashville nightclub while attempting to obtain a recording contract. Ricky Van Shelton worked as a pipefitter. Although exceptions may be found, country music performers came from, and continue to come from, modest socioeconomic circumstances. Country music thus provides a potentially lucrative alternative occupation for persons brought up in modest economic and cultural circumstances. Such circumstances provide the context and content for the country music that the same artists use to reach their audience. These artists can communicate with their audience because they have "been there."

A variety of forces have operated in consort to bring country music to an international audience and generate impressive revenues for a wide range of goods and services. Beneath the commercial success, country music remains in its heart and soul a music with southern roots. Performed predominantly by southerners of modest class origins, country music will continue to reflect its roots as it offers its images of life to an audience that identifies with the rigors of daily life in the real world.

BIBLIOGRAPHY

Flippo, Chet. *Your Cheatin' Heart.* Garden City, N.Y.: Doubleday, 1985.

Horstman, Dorothy. *Sing Your Heart Out, Country Boy.* Rev. ed. Nashville: Country Music Foundation, 1986.

Malone, Bill C. *Country Music U.S.A.* Rev. ed. Austin: University of Texas Press, 1985.

Peterson, Richard A. *Single-Industry Firm to Conglomerate Synergistics: Alternative*

Strategies for Selling Insurance and Country Music. John Edwards Memorial Foundation, Inc. Reprint no. 34. Los Angeles: University of California, 1976.

Peterson, Richard A., and Russell Davis, Jr. "The Fertile Crescent of Country Music." *Journal of Country Music* 6 (Spring 1975): 19–27.

Porterfield, Nolan. *Jimmie Rodgers: The Life and Times of America's Blue Yodeler.* Urbana: University of Illinois Press, 1979.

Wolfe, Charles K. *Tennessee Strings.* Knoxville: University of Tennessee Press, 1977.

6

The Music of the Dispossessed: The Rise of the Blues

WILLIAM BARLOW

The blues have a century-long history in the development of American popular music. They emerged as a unique musical style among black agricultural workers in the rural South during the 1890s. Over the next three decades, this new music and its makers spread to urban centers in the South and the North with the rising tide of African-American migrants. Once in the cities, the rural blues were transformed, stylistically and in content, to express better the grim realities of urban living. By the 1920s, blues were the music of choice among the growing black work force migrating to the cities in search of jobs and a better life. The popularity of the blues finally attracted the attention of the music industry, particularly the record companies, which began manufacturing blues recordings for sale, primarily to black consumers. The blues continued to be the favorite music of the African-American working class throughout the Great Depression and World War II. During this period, their popularity reached its zenith in urban black communities. But by the onset of the 1950s, urban blues were being eclipsed by a more diverse mixture of black musical styles, which came to be known as rhythm and blues. This was especially the case among the younger generation of African Americans growing up in the cities. The blues were still alive in certain black musical enclaves around the country, and they continued to influence other styles of American popular music; however, they were no longer as culturally and commercially dominant as they had been in the pre–World War II era.

Ironically, the demise of urban blues as a popular black musical style coincided with their sudden popularity among young white middle-class listeners, who began discovering the blues, and then learning to play them, in the 1950s. During the 1960s, these white blues enthusiasts spearheaded the so-called blues revival, which "rediscovered" a number of the older blues veterans while broadening their appeal to a white audience. Within the music industry, however, the blues have been segregated from the pop mainstream and relegated to the bottom of the economic pecking order since the 1920s. Blues records and albums have historically been under-promoted by the industry; hence, they seldom get airplay on commercial radio or make it to the pop charts. Even the most popular blues musicians do not fill large concert halls, much less football stadiums; for the most part, they are treated like minor league properties. In a nutshell, the blues get little respect or support from the music industry, despite their many contributions to its prosperity over the years. Nevertheless, the blues have shown a remarkable resiliency; they have managed to survive as both a musical style and a subculture. Accordingly, they continue to inspire and influence current trends in popular music, if only beneath the surface as an insurgent roots music. Moreover, since the end of World War II, the blues have been discovered and acclaimed by people from various cultures all over the world. Today they are universally perceived as a music capable of articulating the sorrows, grievances, hopes, and aspirations of downtrodden people everywhere.

From the beginning, the blues have been characterized by a twelve-bar, three-line (AAB) stanza structure within which the second line is almost a repetition of the first line, and the third line is a response to the first two. Complementing the vocal line of the stanza is at least one instrumental accompaniment, usually a guitar, which establishes the groundbeat and the chord progressions, while also responding to the vocal lines in a call and response pattern. Although the twelve-bar blues became standard fare, the length of the blues stanza could, and often did, vary, especially in the early years.

The musical roots of the blues can be found in African-American field hollers, work songs, and ballads, all popular in the rural South during the post-Reconstruction era. The field hollers, also known as "arhoolies," can best be described as African yodels—a kind of tonal language used by slaves working on plantations in the South. As such, they were used not only as audio calling cards but also as a means of disguising messages between the captives. Arhoolies always employed "blue notes" in their descending vocal lines. Blue notes are "bent" or "flattened" notes sung in between certain major and minor keys of the European diatonic scale but more musically attuned to the African pendantic scale. They were the major musical break-throughs, along with the use of cross rhythms, in early blues music.

The collective voice and labor-intensive work songs were also sung during slavery and then remained in circulation on prison farms in the South with large black convict populations. They were call-and-response vocal chants sung by a lead singer and chorus, to the rhythms of forced penal labor. The subject matter of the work songs often drew on local prison folklore; it was ready-made for early blues repertoires. The black ballads were first sung by African-American songsters in the post-bellum era. These songsters were in many ways the precursors of the early blues musicians, their ballads based on traditional Anglo-American ballads from the rural South. They were, however, much more rhythmic compositions, and they featured African-American folk heroes, including renegade outlaws, in their storylines. The fusion of these three musical entities led to the formation of blues styles and repertoires in the rural South before the turn of the century. These rural-based musical formations took place in at least three discernible regions, thus generating three separate blues traditions: the Mississippi Delta, East Texas, and the Piedmont.

The Mississippi Delta is located in the heart of the soil-rich farmlands spreading out on both sides of the Mississippi River, between Natchez, Mississippi, and Memphis, Tennessee. The farmlands in this area were initially wild, lush swamplands. After the indigenous Indians were driven from the area, the swamps were drained, the vegetation burned off, and the land prepared for cotton cultivation. With the help of a federally funded levee system to hold the river's seasonal floods at bay, large cotton plantations were eventually carved out of the Delta wilderness, using slave labor in the antebellum era, and then hired and convict labor, in the postbellum era. With the passing of slavery, the Delta plantation owners turned to sharecropping and tenant farming, which enabled white planters to reap huge profits from their cotton crops while keeping their black fieldhands in economic servitude. By the 1890s, the Delta had the most concentrated black population in the nation, with blacks outnumbering whites by close to a four-to-one ratio. The economic peonage inherent in the sharecropping and tenant farming system, the rigid jim crow legal system, and the lynch rope were all used to keep the region's large black work force segregated from the white populace, dependent on their white landlords, and resigned to their second-class status in the social order. This was the historical situation out of which the earliest Delta blues emerged; in many respects, they were a defiant response to the oppressive social conditions engulfing their inventors.

Blues in the Delta may have originated in the cotton fields, but they soon became the centerpiece of black plantation workers' recreational life. At house parties on weekends, they supplemented the traditional country dance music; guitars and harmonicas took the place of banjos and fiddles. In the barrelhouses and the juke joints, the blues replaced ragtime as the music of choice. Delta blues pioneers like Charley Patton, Tommy Johnson, Son House, and Skip James made their reputations playing for crowds at these places and occasions. They were followed by a second wave of Delta blues legends: Robert Johnson, Rice Miller, Muddy Waters, and Howlin' Wolf, who not only made a name for themselves among Delta blues fans but also played a major role in transforming the blues from a regional to a national phenomenon. The Delta blues were dominated by two contrasting vocal styles: the rough, guttural declamatory shouting of Charley Patton and Howlin' Wolf, and the tormented and introspective falsettos of Skip James and Robert Johnson. The most prominent guitar techniques associated with the Delta blues were the use of intense chord repetitions building toward a droning crescendo and the use of a slider, such as a bottleneck on a finger, to create a poignant voice like a crying effect. The latter was derived in part from the widespread use of homemade one-string guitars by the black youth in the Delta.

East Texas was also a cotton-producing region tied to the South's plantation economy. As slavery's last refuge in the waning days of the Confederacy, the Lone Star state took in a sizable black slave population in order to keep them in bondage as long as possible. After being released, most of the former slaves had no choice but to continue to work in the East Texas cotton fields as sharecroppers and tenant farmers. However, they were not as concentrated there as their Delta counterparts, due to the paucity of the soil and the availability of land to the west. The exception was along the Trinity and Brazos rivers, where the topsoil was rich and thick. These riverlands were not only the site of the state's most prosperous cotton plantations but also a chain of the South's most notorious prison farms. The work songs shared among the black prisoners on these penal farms proved to be a motherlode for the East Texas blues tradition. A number of these work songs, or portions of their verse, were integrated into the repertoires of the major East Texas blues pioneers: "Ragtime Texas" Henry Thomas, the father of the railroad blues; Blind Lemon Jefferson, the blind blues bard who went on to become the nation's most recorded rural bluesman; and Alger "Texas" Alexander and Huddie Leadbetter ("Leadbelly"), both of whom served time on the infamous Texas prison farms. Leadbelly later recorded his entire repertoire of Texas prison work songs for the Library of Congress. The next generation of East Texas blues innovators— guitarists Sam "Lightnin' " Hopkins, Clarence "Gatemouth" Brown, and Arron "T-Bone" Walker; pianists "Ivory" Joe Hunter, Joe Liggins, and Charles Brown; and saxophonists Buster Smith and Arnett Cobb—all helped to shape the region's blues into a taut, dance-oriented ensemble music highlighted by rolling piano accompaniments, riffing horns, and imaginative single-string-guitar solos. T-Bone Walker is credited with being the first blues musician to experiment with this style on an electric guitar, which changed the sound of the blues irrevocably. Along with peers like Hopkins, Liggins, Hunter, and Brown, Walker helped to position East Texas blues at the center of West Coast rhythm and blues during and after World War II.

The Piedmont is the largest of the three rural blues homelands, stretching from Richmond, Virginia, south to Atlanta, Georgia. It is bounded by the Atlantic coastal plain to the east and the Appalachian Mountains to the west. The area from Richmond down to Durham, North Carolina, and then west to the mountains has historically been tobacco country; farther south, cotton was king. Black workers in the cotton and tobacco fields were the source and inspiration of the Piedmont blues, which seem to have emerged almost a decade after their initial appearance in the Mississippi Delta and East Texas. The first documented folk blues in the region were reported in rural southeast Georgia in 1908. In the 1910s, Greenville and Spartenburg, South Carolina, were the centers of gravity for a loose network of blind blues oracles, including Simmie Dooley, Willie Walker, and Gary Davis. In the 1920s, Atlanta was the hub for Piedmont blues giants like Blind Willie McTell, Peg Leg Howell, Eddie Anthony, and the Hicks Brothers, Charlie and "Barbecue" Bob. By the depression era, Durham was the region's blues hotspot, with musicians like Blind Boy Fuller, the Reverend Gary Davis, Sonny Terry, and Bull City Red based there. The Piedmont blues sound was sweet, light, and flowing—a dramatic departure from the deeper and darker Delta blues and the more jazz- and dance-oriented ensemble sound that came to the forefront in East Texas blues. Piedmont blues pioneers favored lilting melodies for their solo blues numbers, which they sang in high, plaintive voices. They drew their material from the folk songs, ballads, and show tunes performed by songsters working in black minstrelsy, which had a large following in the region from its origins in the Reconstruction era to its demise in the wake of World War I. In addition, the early Piedmont blues innovators, like Blind Arthur Blake, incorporated ragtime playing techniques into their guitar styles; they did so by "ragging" their blues melodies in order to create the desired cross-rhythms between voice and guitar, which gave the songs their tension and drive. Blake's ragtime-influenced blues guitar style stressed finger-picking dexterity; his fast-paced runs with a deft touch on the strings became the dominant blues guitar style in the Piedmont. Another musical trait of the region was the guitar and harmonica duos, which flourished in the northern Piedmont in the pre–World War II era. They featured intricate call-and-response patterns that were interchangeable and often overlapped. Unlike the Delta and East Texas traditions, however, the Piedmont blues were unable to adapt to an urban environment. They never found an equivalent urban sound and hence never caught on in eastern seaboard cities with large black migrant populations, like Washington, D.C., Baltimore, Philadelphia, and New York. The popularity of the Piedmont blues peaked in the region in the 1930s and were a musical relic of the past by the late 1940s.

When the blues reached the cities in the South and then the North, they came under the influence of two disparate cultural forces; the music industry and the ghetto tenderloins, also known as red-light districts. Both of these urban phenomena had contradictory effects on the blues—effects that dramatically transformed their soundscape and their lyrical content. The music industry introduced blues recordings to a nationwide black audience, as well as to a more select white audience; in the process, it documented some of this new folk music for posterity. However, the music industry also attempted to standardize the blues form, trivialize their contents, and financially exploit blues artists. The red-light districts also had a paradoxical influence on the music. The underworld economies at the heart of these tenderloins provided blues musicians with jobs playing their own music, which in turn gave them the social and physical space to experiment with their art form among peers. In addition, the red-light districts infused the blues with the restless and rebellious ethos of the resident black underclass. But the decadence, violence, crime, vice, alcohol and drug addiction, disease, and poverty endemic to the ghetto tenderloins eventually took their toll on blues musicians, like everyone else living there. As a consequence, many of the most talented urban blues artists of the twentieth century never got a chance to record their own music or to reach their full potential due to their premature deterioration or death. Ultimately all of these contradictory factors came into play in the sudden rise, and then the slow decline, of urban blues in the twentieth century.

Show business proved to be the high road for the blues migrations into the cities. In the wake of the Civil War, black entertainers began to replace their white counterparts in the blackface minstrel shows, popular since the 1830s. By the end of the century, black minstrelsy was well established as a favorite leisure-time activity among African Americans living in the South, especially in the Piedmont region. The traveling tent shows featured a wide variety of entertainers: dancers, comics, songsters, and an all-purpose band. In the postbellum era, male comedians like Billy Kersands became black minstrelsy's major attractions, but by World War I, the up-and-coming new blues divas began to rival the male comics for top billing. Foremost among these women were Gertrude "Ma" Rainey and Ida Cox, both of whom ran their own tent shows during this period. Concurrently the launching in 1909 of an urban vaudeville circuit for African Americans, the Theatre Owners Booking Agency (TOBA), gave black minstrelsy a new lease on life. Staging the shows at theaters in the cities was more lucrative, and they soon attracted the attention of the urban-based music industry. By the 1920s, blues divas like Bessie Smith, Ethel Waters, and Mamie Smith were the major stars of the TOBA; moreover, they were the first African Americans to record the blues. By that time, the music industry's Tin Pan Alley tunesmiths, following the lead of W. C. Handy, had already popularized their own watered-down versions of the blues. The bulk of these early 1910s recordings, however, were made for a white middle-class audience and featured white singers like Sophie Tucker. Only inadvertently, the music industry discovered that there was a more profitable blues market among African Americans, especially if the music was recorded by black artists. At first, only the smaller record labels ventured into the black blues market; this enabled some of the new record companies, like W. C. Handy and Harry Pace's Black Swan label, to gain a foothold in the industry. But eventually the larger companies, like RCA Victor and Columbia, bought out the smaller labels and took over the race record market, as it came to be known. Black women, later referred to as the "classic blues singers," first recorded the blues in the early 1920s. Later in the decade, the major race record operations sponsored field trips to the South to make recordings of rural and urban bluesmen. They were not especially interested in giving these indigenous blues artists national exposure or in documenting their folk blues; they were seeking new songs to use for financial gain. This was done by copyrighting the blues compositions they recorded under the auspices of their own music publishing firms, which then collected all the royalty monies generated by the songs; the original composers were left out of the financial equation, save for the few dollars they were paid to record their blues composition. This exploitation of black musicians by the record companies and their agents was business as usual in the music industry, especially where the blues were concerned.

The ghetto tenderloins proved to be the low road for blues migrations into the cities. The emergence of these red-light districts coincided with the accelerated growth of industrialism in the nation's burgeoning urban centers in the late 1800s and early 1900s. The rapid influx of immigrant and migrant laborers seeking work in the new industries changed the landscape of the cities. Overcrowded ethnic ghettos gave birth to local ward political organizations; they delivered the ethnic vote to city hall in exchange for patronage. These organizations became the backbone of a number of urban political machines, which gained control over the political and economic life of key industrial cities with large working-class populations. The machines not only doled out patronage to their ethnic constituencies (Irish, Polish, Italians, African Americans, and others); they also sanctioned the underworld vice operations—gambling, prostitution, illegal drugs and alcohol—that flourished in the ghetto tenderloins; this was done for a share of the profits from these operations.

New Orleans has a long history as the nation's foremost city of pleasure, dating back to the pre-Revolutionary War era. The legendary French Quarter is world renowned as both a red-light district and an incubator of innovative black music. Although recognized as the birthplace of jazz, New Orleans also played an important role in the origins of urban blues. In fact, it was the inclusion of blues in the repertoires of local black musicians, like cornet legend Buddy Bolden, that led to the birth of jazz in New Orleans around the turn of the century. The pioneering blues pianist, Ferdinand "Jellyroll" Morton, recalled first hearing the blues in New Orleans in 1902. The performer who introduced him to this new music was Mamie Desdoumes, one of the many local pianists who made a living playing in French Quarter bordellos. In addition to being adopted by tenderloin pianists, the blues were being featured in the music of local black bands. Bolden's jazz band was the most famous example; "Funky Butt Blues" was its signature piece. But a number of local bands played the blues during this period; the Johnson Family string band, for example, performed in the streets of the French Quarter.

The youngest member of this band was Lonnie Johnson, who blossomed into the 1920s premiere urban blues guitarist. Unfortunately, Johnson, like many other talented black musicians from New Orleans, had to move on to make his mark in music. The French Quarter went into a decline with the advent of World War I and was even shut down for awhile at the behest of the U.S. Navy. As a result, many black musicians left New Orleans to seek work in the red-light districts that continued to flourish in urban centers throughout the war years and well into the 1920s.

A number of cities in the South featured their own unique brand of early urban blues, the most prominent being Atlanta, Birmingham, Dallas, and Houston. The southern city that had perhaps the most profound influence on the development of urban blues in their formative years was Memphis, Tennessee. Like New Orleans, it was a bustling riverport trade, transportation, and manufacturing center, with a tenderloin haven for pleasure seekers and for talented black musicians. The city's political machine was lorded over by "Boss" Crump, a wily segregationist politician who garnered the local black vote in exchange for patronage and the sanctioning of a wide-open tenderloin nightlife on Beale Street. Cocaine use was rampant in this red-light district, as was murder. Due to the skyrocketing homicide rate, Memphis was christened the "murder capital" of the nation in 1923 by the local press. As for music, Beale Street became a magnet for Delta blues performers, as well as for rural blues musicians from the surrounding Tennessee and Arkansas countryside. In the 1920s, the city was base for a number of influential jugbands that played a rudimentary but lively brand of urban blues. These bands used guitars, banjos, harmonicas, kazoos, and whiskey jugs. The most prominent were Gus Cannon's Jug Stompers, which featured the legendary Noah Lewis on harmonica, and the Memphis Jug Band, featuring Will Shade on harmonica and "Laughing" Charley Burse on guitar and vocals. Burse's suggestive hip-shaking routine and his use of his guitar as a phallic symbol would be imitated much later in his career by an impressionable young white guitarist and singer named Elvis Presley. These borrowed stage antics helped to launch Presley's career as a rock and roll star. Other important Memphis-based blues musicians active in its pre–World War II heyday were guitarists Furry Lewis, Frank Stokes, and Memphis Minnie Douglas; pianists Jab Jones and Memphis Slim; harp players Hamie Nixon and John Lee "Sonny Boy" Williamson; and Sleepy John Estes, the groups' most talented blues composer. In the postwar era, Memphis continued to be a hub of blues activity, although Boss Crump's political machine was finally dismantled and Beale Street fell into disrepair. Urban blues artists like Howlin' Wolf, B. B. King, Bobby Blue Bland, Junior Parker, and James Cotton all cut their teeth on the postwar Memphis blues scene before moving on. In the case of B. B. King, this involved becoming the nation's premiere electric blues guitarist and ultimately an international symbol of the music.

Chicago proved to be the mecca of urban blues in America. The city was not only the site of a large ghetto tenderloin, overflowing with black migrants, mostly from the Mississippi Delta; it was also the site of a large race record operation, which was second only to New York's size and influence. The massive influx of rural African Americans began in earnest during World War II, when the *Chicago Defender* launched its "Great Northern Drive" to bring southern black migrants to the city. By the 1920s, Chicago's Southside ghetto had more African Americans living there than anywhere else in the country, with the exception of Harlem in New York City. The major blues musicians active in the city during this early period included guitarists Big Bill Broonzy, Tampa Red, Lonnie Johnson, and Kokomo Arnold; pianists Cow Cow Davenport, Cripple Clarence Lofton, Hersial Thomas, Clarence "Pinetop" Smith, Thomas Dorsey, and Jimmy Yancy; and vocalists Washboard Sam, Sippie Wallace, and Alberta Hunter. During the depression years, boogie-woogie pianists like Albert Ammons and Mead Lux Lewis came to the forefront of the Southside blues scene. In addition, the early urban blues bands, like those organized by Sonny Boy Williamson and Memphis Slim, began to transform the traditional Delta blues into the forceful ensemble dance music that would characterize Chicago blues. Sonny Boy's band featured his harmonica playing, an electric guitar, a rhythm guitar, then a bass, and eventually drums and piano. It was a prototype of what would follow in the postwar era, which proved to be the golden age of Chicago blues. The bands of Muddy Waters and Howlin' Wolf, along with their recordings on Chess Records, not only pioneered the soundscape of postwar Chicago blues but influenced the future course of popular music in America for years to come.

There were other urban blues hotbeds in the Midwest, in particular, Louisville, Indianapolis, Cincinnati, and Kansas City. Yet none was as bountiful as Chicago's during its heyday. After the ascendancy of urban blues in the 1920s and their impressive resiliency over the next three decades, they were finally overtaken in the late 1940s and early 1950s by fresher black musical styles favored by African-American youth. This decline in popularity coincided with a diffusion of the blues into the more current musical trends, both black and white—a process that accelerated in the 1950s. Hence, blues diffusions can be traced to African-American rhythm and blues, soul, and even rap musical styles. Moreover, they can be traced to the flowering of rock and roll, and then rock music, among white youth. As for country music, it has been diffused with the blues since its commercial origins in the 1920s.

In addition to the diffusion of the blues into much of American popular music, they have played a vital role in African-American cultural resistance to white domination. The blues texts were black working-class discourses on American society, as seen and experienced from the bottom up. The blues sounds were "off key" and "dirty" by Eurocentric musical standards, while being true to their African musical roots. Blues performances were collective healing rituals involving audience and artist in a self-affirming catharsis that purges the despair and pain of the past. And blues artists historically have been cultural rebels; their music and their life-styles were implicit critiques of their second-class status in the white-controlled social order. These four aspects of the blues tradition have helped to infuse African-American culture, from the bottom up, with a resilient outlook that has resisted domination, from both outside and top down. For example, the rural blues were a grass-roots cultural response to the domination of older styles of fiddle and banjo music in the South. In a similar fashion, urban blues were a grass-roots cultural response, this time to the domination of Tin Pan Alley musical styles. Even today, after having changed the landscape of American popular music, the blues remain a working-class-roots music constantly at odds with the commercially dominated pop mainstream.

BIBLIOGRAPHY

Albertson, Chris. *Bessie*. New York: Stein & Day, 1974.
Bastin, Bruce. *Red River Blues: The Blues Tradition in the Southeast*; Baton Rouge: Louisiana State University Press, 1986.
Bruyuoghe, Yannick. *Big Bill Blues*. New York: Oak Publications, 1969.
Charters, Samuel. *Sweet as Showers of Rain*. New York: Oak Publications, 1977.
Dance, Helen Oakley. *Stormy Monday: The T-Bone Walker Story*. Baton Rouge: Louisiana State University Press, 1987.
Handy, W. C. *The Father of the Blues: An Autobiography*. New York: Macmillan, 1942.
Harrison, Daphine Duval. *Black Pearls: Blues Queens of the 1920s*. New Brunswick, N.J.: Rutgers University Press, 1988.
Levine, Lawrence. *Black Culture and Black Consciousness: Afro-American Folk Thought from Slavery to Freedom*. New York: Oxford University Press, 1977.
Lieb, Sandra. *Mother of the Blues: A Study of Ma Rainey*. Amherst: University of Massachusetts Press, 1981.
Oakley, Giles. *The Devil's Music: A History of the Blues*. New York: Harcourt Brace, Jovanovich, 1976.
Oliver, Paul. *The Story of the Blues*. New York: Chilton Books, 1966.
Palmer, Robert. *Deep Blues*. New York: Viking, 1981.
Rowe, Mike. *Chicago Breakdown*. London: Eddison Press, 1973.
Sawyer, Charles. *The Arrival of B. B. King*. Garden City, N.Y.: Doubleday, 1980.
Shaw, Arnold. *Honkers and Shouters: The Golden Age of Rhythm and Blues*. New York: Macmillan, 1978.

7

Emerging from America's Underside: The Black Musician from Ragtime to Jazz

Burton W. Peretti

The music called ragtime, like the word itself, derived from obscure origins in late nineteenth-century America. Ragtime is primarily a piano music noted for the jagged syncopation (or "off-beat" rhythm) that the pianist plays with the right hand in the melody, creating exciting rhythmic tension with the sturdy on-beat line (usually in march tempo) in the lower, left-hand line. The name and the music derived from the language and music of free Afro Americans, probably those living in the Mississippi River valley, in the decades following the end of slavery in the 1860s. (The name *ragtime* probably came about to denote the ragged syncopated rhythm but has also been attributed to the slang of black vagrants and prostitutes.)

Ragtime gained national attention in 1893 when a number of the best black pianists from Illinois, Missouri, Arkansas, and other river states congregated at Chicago's Midway. They came in search of lucrative work; the low-rent Midway district was teeming in 1893 because the great Columbian Exposition, or world's fair, was taking place nearby, attracting millions of visitors. The fair was a stately, serious extravaganza with great artistic pretensions, but the pianists—along with the medicine salesmen, freak exhibitors, "exotic" dancers, prostitutes, and others who established businesses on the Midway—realized that many visitors might eventually flee the fair's august White City for more visceral entertainment. To the embarrassment of the fair organizers, the boisterous Midway received as much attention from the press and foreigners as the fair itself. The new piano music, not yet commonly called ragtime, gained special notoriety. Five years later, with the publication of piano "rags" by Missouri's Scott Joplin and others, ragtime became the most popular and publicized music in the United States.

The ragtime explosion of the 1890s was one of a number of events in American music history, stretching from 1800 to the present, that fit into a rough pattern. Like minstrelsy before it and jazz afterward, ragtime emerged from obscure folk origins, far away from schoolhouses and conservatories, arising almost unnoticed among poor Americans who did not keep detailed records of their cultural accomplishments (and who were generally ignored or oppressed by more powerful segments of society). Also as with minstrelsy and jazz, the poor Americans who made ragtime possible were largely black. We know this because the earliest known figures in minstrel, ragtime, and jazz history were African American and because these musics possess rhythmic and melodic qualities that clearly derive from black African musical traditions. Also, ragtime (like other styles) became famous when itinerant musicians, usually black and from rural areas, came to the city and attracted the attention of large crowds and the press (in the case of ragtime, in 1893 in Chicago). Finally, ragtime was a typically American popular music in that it spread rapidly with the help of America's aggressively capitalistic music industry, which marketed popular music nationwide with unprecedented speed and reaped handsome profits for its promoters.

This pattern of change in American music history saw one folk or popular music after another emerge from what might be called the vibrant underside of American society—the poor and disdained, often African-American groups in the fields and the ghettoes—and come into the glare of mass marketing, publicity, and popularity among the white majority. The 1990s popularity of rap music among millions of Americans who have never seen a ghetto and the new-found wealth of previously poor rap performers is perhaps the most recent incarnation of this phenomenon. This chapter focuses on pivotal parts in this story, the ragtime and jazz eras of 1900 to 1930, when popular music and poor musicians (largely black) most dramatically fled the American underside for national and global fame.

Before ragtime became the rage, the white majority in the United States had already taken black music and turned it into a widely popular style. The blackface minstrel show, originating in the 1820s, was in its final form a white creation; the outrageous slang and gestures and the gently syncopated music were white caricatures of black culture, and blacks had no role in minstrelsy at first beyond initially inspiring its white creators. After the Civil War, in an interesting turn of events, white stage performers turned away from blackface, but the minstrel show continued—now with black performers. They too wore burned cork on their already dark faces, probably in order to give white audiences a sense of continuity with the earlier era. Black minstrels were thus humiliated in many ways by this postwar change, but they were also newly prominent, well advertised, and famous. Some performers in the late 1800s, such as songwriter James Bland and comedian Bert Williams, were able to become well known and prosperous without appearing in blackface, and in the 1890s such black composers as Will Marion Cook began writing stage revues for black audiences. When ragtime arrived on the scene, therefore, some features of twentieth-century popular music—sheet music publishing, touring circuits, and music with black or pseudo-black themes—were already in place.

Ragtime syncopation was almost solely the invention of black musical culture, primarily along the lower Mississippi River and in points west, in Arkansas and Texas. Still, in conformity with the American pattern, it was white musicians who first popularized ragtime with the largely white public. William Krell published the first labeled "rag," the "Mississippi Rag," in 1895, and Ben R. Harney billed himself the next year as "Originator of the Only Absolute Novelty in this Season's Vaudevilles, Piano Playing in cynocopated or 'rag time,' singing his own 'Coon' melodies and doing his original dancing." Harney's reference to "coon melodies," the name for minstrel-style songs popular among whites for a decade, indicates that ragtime was sold to whites as an outgrowth of an existing popular genre. This sense of continuity also enabled New York's song publishing industry, Tin Pan Alley, to embrace ragtime after 1898, publishing tens of thousands of titles that allegedly "ragged" the beat. The popularity of white rag writers, some of whom had an affinity for the black style (such as Joseph Lamb and May Aufderheide) but most of whom did not (including the best-selling composers Harry Von Tilzer and Irving Berlin), made ragtime a major American music. This was to be expected, since the white majority was not yet willing to acknowledge black primacy in any major cultural endeavor.

Despite this dominance, ragtime created some significant advancement for black practitioners, seen most clearly in the rise to prominence of Scott Joplin, who moved eastward from Texas to Sedalia, Missouri, to St. Louis and New York City as his career prospered. Joplin possessed a unique genius for transmitting black ragtime's vitality to written form in a manner that won over white listeners; in 1899 he was fortunate to gain the assistance of John Stark, a white publisher in St. Louis who vowed to make Joplin (and Stark's own company) successful. By 1903 Joplin's rags had sold more than 100,000 copies, the composer moved his family into a large house in St. Louis, and soon white publicists and journalists were echoing Stark, who named Joplin the King of Ragtime. Other black composers from the river states, such as Tom Turpin, James Scott, Louis Chauvin, and Scott Hayden, also prospered in the early 1900s.

Their public image (especially Joplin's) was unprecedentedly dignified for African-American composers. Although these musicians had no apparent involvement in social movements, their dignified portraiture, respectful publicity, and (in the case of Joplin, Hayden, and others) refusal to write music for racially offensive popular genres mirrored black America's first movement for equal rights, launched at the same time as ragtime. The major black activist W.E.B. Du Bois praised music as the great cultural achievement of blacks and lamented the social and political oppression that otherwise had virtually destroyed black morale and accomplishment. His fight to halt lynching and to provide blacks with legal and political rights and decent education and employment coincided with Scott Joplin's rise to fame. Similarly, Joplin sought to make the most of his talent; not content with writing popular rags, he wrote operas about black folk and their ambition and tried to gain the exalted recognition that white classical composers received. His work, like Du Bois's, was dedicated to bringing African Americans to a level of equality with whites.

The ambitions of both men were deeply significant, but their inability to achieve their goals was also representative of the era. Joplin's opera *Treemonisha* was performed only once in 1916 in a rundown New York theater, since he received almost no backing or assistance from white promoters. This neglect was a shocking contrast to his success as a rag writer. Du Bois's failure to move legislatures against lynching and jim crow segregation was total, a symptom of the general American belief that blacks ought to rise in their own separate communities—and at a pace slower than that of whites.

In keeping with this continued oppression, black ragtime performers, the true masters of the style, largely were forced to operate on the fringes of American commercial music. As on Chicago's Midway in 1893, ragtime pianists were confined to performing jobs in the poorest neighborhoods, frequently on the dangerous waterfronts of riverports or in illicit gambling and prostitution districts. (More respectable employers of musicians usually avoided hiring blacks, and to them ragtime retained a disreputable aura even when it was performed by whites.) While musicians welcomed even this employment, the work environments were often dangerous and detrimental to their careers.

The most musically active city in the ragtime era may have been New Orleans. Its heavy port trade created a large waterfront, the city allowed prostitution in one downtown region, the black population swelled in recent years, and the city's musical traditions had long been rich and diverse, with black, Anglo, French-Creole, and Latin elements blending and thriving. Musicians there in the 1900s and 1910s—who called themselves "ragtime musicianers," although their music would later be termed jazz—worked in a low-pay, violent environment. Small bands (especially prevalent in this city) would often play for picnics, as pianist Fess Manetta recalled; late at night these would often break up as gangs from other neighborhoods raided the parties, usually forcing the bands to return home without pay. Bands would often play on wagons that advertised goods and merchants through city streets; these too might be attacked if they ventured into the wrong territory. Nightclub and brothel owners were always seeking to drive competitors out of business, and bands often suffered in the course of nighttime raids, club closings, and hostile takeovers of various workplaces.

For black musicians, though, a more subtle violence was the most pervasive: the general poverty of their class in New Orleans, where 40 percent of nonwhites could not read or write, health and education services were scarce and underfunded, and high unemployment was chronic. None of the great young players of that era could support himself with music: Louis Armstrong hauled coal, drummer Zutty Singleton was a drayman, bassist Pops Foster worked on the docks, and cornetist Natty Dominique rolled cigars. And there was always racial discrimination with whites to contend. New Orleans was especially dangerous; it had played host in 1901 to the most destructive antiblack rioting ever seen in the South.

By the late 1910s, it had become characteristic for black musicians in New Orleans and other river cities to escape this grinding environment. Bassist Bill Johnson and trombonist Kid Ory took bands to California; others, drafted during World War I, went to Europe for a time. The main destination, however, was Chicago. When a rival clubowner set off a bomb in the New Orleans club in which Joe "King" Oliver led a band, Oliver finally fled to Chicago, where Armstrong, Dominique, and many others from the city and other southern places soon joined him. The musicians' exodus was not isolated; like the ragtime composers' quest for dignity, the move north was part of a general attempt by blacks to improve their lives. As war industry jobs became available by the thousands in the industrial North, it became clear to southern blacks that leaving the South might be the best hope for improving their status and lives. A Great Migration of nearly 1 million African Americans swept into Chicago, Detroit, Pittsburgh, New York, and other cities in the 1910s and 1920s, creating the first large black communities there. In Chicago's livestock industry alone, 12,000 blacks were earning a family wage by 1920.

The migration north was a mixed blessing for southern blacks. To the surprise of many of them, northern whites were also racist; blacks were excluded from many neighborhoods, jobs, and labor unions and were refused service at stores and other establishments. Some whites met the migrants with violence, sparking a series of summer race riots that culminated in the Chicago tragedy of 1919, in which more than forty people were killed. Black migrants acquiesced to this ominous violence and segregation by remaining in sizable "ghettoes"—Chicago's South Side, New York's Harlem, South Boston—where their jobs and opportunities were inferior and limited.

Throughout the 1920s, however, the high expectations of newcomers, and their relief at having escaped the South, gave the northern black ghettoes an ever-renewed sense of progress and optimism. In Harlem, Marcus Garvey's popular parades and rallies promoted ideas of black separatism and self-sufficiency, and a stable of writers and artists envisioned a culture for the "New Negro," expressing special black values and paying homage to the African heritage. Black musicians shared in this optimism. Lee Collins, like King Oliver, was a New Orleans cornetist who fled that city's dangerous nightclub scene. "My going to Chicago changed everything," he later recalled; once there, "I didn't know my own power." Milt Hinton, a young bassist, felt that Chicago "in the early 20s . . . was paradise . . . everybody's kids are doing fine, everybody's working, all these great jazz musicians are playing in all these places."[1] Hinton had witnessed a lynching of a black man in Vicksburg, Mississippi, a few years earlier, and thus he, like others, realized that despite its problems, the North was a great improvement over the South.

As Hinton notes, by the 1920s the music that energized and exemplified the northern ghettoes was no longer ragtime but jazz. The origins of jazz— both the word and the music—are only a bit clearer to us than are ragtime's. Jazz is usually described as differing from ragtime in a number of ways. Jazz is primarily a band music, not rooted in the technique and repertoire of the solo pianist. Like ragtime, jazz features syncopation, but jazz (as musicians put it) also swings—in other words, the fundamental beat, played by the bass instruments in a band or by the pianist's left hand, is not steady but is subtly syncopated or "displaced" itself. Many observers attribute both the seductive, sensual element in jazz and its special excitement in fast tempi to this swinging of the beat. Jazz was also often played without reference to sheet music; a jazz number might be made up of a string of eight- or sixteen-bar solo improvisations by various members of the band. Finally, jazz (unlike ragtime) almost always made use of blues harmony, the special use of minor key notes and scales (as the European tradition would call them) to construct melodies and group singing (derived from African roots) that southern blacks developed in the 1800s.

All of these modifying features, which transformed ragtime so effectively as almost to exterminate it, were developed most obviously in New Orleans in the 1900s and 1910s. The city's rich band heritage, its multiracial and multicultural musical life (which contributed to loosening and swinging the march beat), and its musically illiterate black population (who brought the blues with them from the plantations) undoubtedly caused these variations. As was typical in America, this new style of ragtime was first made nationally famous by whites—in this case, by the white New Orleanians in the Original Dixieland Jazz Band (ODJB), who first recorded in 1917. These men had grown up among white New Orleans's band culture, which was also substantial and influenced by some of the Latin and African tendencies that shaped black band music. The ODJB's playing today sounds like a comic caricature of the classic early jazz to come, but it served to introduce the elements of the new style in a crude way. White America also took a special liking to the odd-sounding name *jazz*; theories regarding the origin of the word, too numerous to mention here, were propounded by journalists. In the late 1910s it seemed that jazz might develop in a manner similar to minstrelsy in the 1800s: in other words, a largely black music would be simplified and caricatured by whites, and the seminal black contribution to jazz would be ignored or ridiculed. Indeed, the ODJB's leader, Nick La Rocca, insisted late in his life that jazz "melodies are white man[']s music and not African in origin" and that if black jazz had "existed in New Orleans

I'm certain these [white] people here would have heard about it [but had not]."[2]

Blacks did assert their primacy in jazz in the 1920s. Black musicians were confined by their union to jobs in the ghettoes, and even there the elite clubs did not allow black customers, but still the ghettoes played host to a thriving nightclub and ballroom culture. Locales such as 35th Street and Calumet in Chicago and 135th Street and Lenox in Harlem held scores of large and small clubs, where blacks and whites could spend their newfound entertainment money and leisure hours, in search of bootleg whiskey (it was the prohibition era), in relaxed or exciting environments. Promoters, some connected with organized crime, strove to meet the need by opening new clubs and hiring bands.

King Oliver's band, playing at Chicago's Lincoln Gardens beginning in 1922, set a standard for swinging the beat and group improvisation to which other black bands aspired. In 1926, Oliver's second trumpet, Louis Armstrong, left the band to lead his own groups, and his extraordinarily expressive and rhythmic solos showed others that jazz had great potential as a creative musical medium. Soon other horn players, as well as pianists, clarinetists, and even vocalists, were emulating the soaring and swinging sound of Louis Armstrong. In Harlem, as in New York City in general, jazz was slower to displace ragtime, and when it did in the mid–1920s, black bands brought the New York tradition of elegant pretensions (the society tradition, strong for a century) to the new music. Both Fletcher Henderson and Edward "Duke" Ellington developed large jazz orchestras, which gave their image and often their music (not so often in Ellington's case) a smoother, more urbane quality than was found in Chicago. Ellington, with his dignified bearing and noble nickname, would succeed in the 1930s where Scott Joplin (composing his operas) had failed: he would gain recognition as a master of a rich musical style and as one of America's leading artists.

Black jazz succeeded in part due to aid on two fronts. First, communications technology evolved rapidly in the decades before 1920. The white ODJB's phonograph recordings spread the news of jazz worldwide in a matter of months; when black bands started recording in 1923, their special skill at jazz became known to Russians, Japanese, and Egyptians as soon as distributors were able to ship the records. That same year, regular radio programming began on some American stations, which led to an explosion of musical broadcasts by 1928 (although jazz did not dominate the airwaves until the swing craze of 1935). Besides spreading their music everywhere, records and radio gave black musicians fine new employment opportunities, especially since their skin color was hidden in these media. As Milt Hinton put it, jazz was an "auditory art. A guy hears you, he don't see you. It's one of the greatest arts in the world for a black man."[3] As a result of this exposure, jazz bands began touring the world; by the mid–1930s Sam Wooding's band had been to the Soviet Union, Buck Clayton led a group in Shanghai, and Teddy Weatherford fronted a band in Calcutta. Modern technology made black American musicians popular world citizens within a few years.

The other assistance came from white American admirers of black jazz. Beginning in the 1920s, many prominent white commentators and composers argued that jazz was the nation's most distinguished native music, rich in potential for future development. (A few people had said the same of ragtime, but their opinions were not nearly as influential.) Not all of them gave African Americans their due as creators of jazz, but they did give jazz in particular, and popular music in general, a new prestige and image as the "sound" of the American scene. Even more significant was the fact that many young whites were inspired by black jazz to become musicians. In particular, young sons of immigrants in Chicago and other cities—such men as Benny Goodman, Artie Shaw, Gene Krupa, and Mezz Mezzrow— as well as other working-class young men were lured by the excitement of the black clubs and were deeply moved by the expressive music they heard. Guitarist Eddie Condon recalled that he was "immobilized" when he first heard Louis Armstrong, and Mezzrow was persuaded after hearing King Oliver that he "was going to be a musician, a Negro musician, hipping the world about the blues the way only Negroes can."[4] For the first time in almost any American context, whites adopted blacks as artistic mentors, considering them the masters of a worthwhile art and studying at their feet. Due to the prevailing racial hierarchy, however, these white "pupils," while less skilled, usually received better-paying and longer-lasting jobs than their mentors. Only rarely in the 1920s would a black musician be able to sit in with a white band for a recording, radio, or club job. In the 1930s, however, as the legions of white admirers of black jazz grew, various kinds of jazz groups began to integrate. Benny Goodman, Woody Herman, and Charlie Barnet were among the first leaders to hire black musicians for their bands. The pervasive racism in America continued to slow and disrupt these efforts, but by the 1930s it was clear that jazz music was a major area of biracial cooperation and equality in America.

It is easy to exaggerate the success of jazz as a cultural institution in the 1920s and 1930s. Although some bands made lucrative incomes, most black and white players were in constant danger of unemployment and poverty. The new technology, while it spread music far and wide, also eliminated the need for live bands, thus deeply constraining the market for musicians; the onset of the Great Depression dealt further blows to jazz musicians. And when they had jobs, musicians often fell prey to exploitative employers, in and out of the underworld.

Despite these continuing difficulties, the transition from ragtime to jazz is a revealing story of the growth of black American aspirations and accomplishment and of how whites gradually came to respect this growth. In 1900 there had been little evidence that black America was fighting to rid itself of the legacy of slavery; ragtime, the most successful black music at that time, was only an initial break from the oppressive minstrel tradition of white America. Black ragtime musicians were confined to underworld jobs, and geniuses like Joplin could not expand their artistic goals. By 1930, however, dozens of black jazz performers were making substantial incomes, treated by many whites as equals, praised nationally, and given some respectful exposure on radio, records, and film. Much remained to be done before musicians and their art received the respect they should have earned, but in the first decades of jazz, the black musician and his culture had at least escaped permanently from the underside of American life.

NOTES

The author thanks the Smithsonian Jazz Oral History Project, the Institute of Jazz Studies (Dan Morgenstern, Director), and the Music Division of the Library of Congress (Wayne Shirley, Director) for their permission to use sources in this essay.

1. Lee Collins, *Oh, Didn't He Ramble: The Life Story of Lee Collins* (Urbana: University of Illinois Press, 1974), p. 43; Milt Hinton, Smithsonian Jazz Oral History Project (JOHP) transcript, April 1976, 5:16.
2. Nick LaRocca to Brian Rust, November 15, 1957, Music Division, Library of Congress; Nick LaRocca, Tulane Jazz Oral History transcript, 15.
3. Hinton, JOHP transcript, November 1976, 1:49.
4. Mezz Mezzrow and Bernard Wolfe, *Really the Blues* (New York: Random House, 1946), pp. 10–11.

BIBLIOGRAPHY

Blesh, Rudi, and Harriet Janis. *They All Played Ragtime: The True Story of an American Music.* New York: Knopf, 1950.
Collier, James Lincoln. *Louis Armstrong.* London: Pan, 1984.
Haskins, James, and Kathleen Benson. *Scott Joplin.* Garden City, N.Y.: Doubleday, 1975.
Hasse, John Edward, ed. *Ragtime: Its History, Composers, and Music.* New York: Schirmer, 1985.
Henri, Florette. *Black Migration: Movement North, 1900–1920.* Garden City, N.Y.: Doubleday, 1975.
Ogren, Kathy J. *The Jazz Revolution: Twenties America and the Meaning of Jazz.* New York: Oxford University Press, 1989.
Schuller, Gunther. *Early Jazz: Its Roots and Musical Development.* New York: Oxford University Press, 1968.
Shapiro, Nat, and Nat Hentoff, eds. *Hear Me Talkin' to Ya: The Story of Jazz Told by the Men Who Made It.* New York: Dover, 1955.
Toll, Robert. *Blacking Up: The Minstrel Show in Nineteenth-Century America.* New York: Oxford University Press, 1974.

— 8 —

Race, Class, and Ethnicity among Swing Musicians

KENNETH J. BINDAS

From the spring to fall of 1935, a popular music labeled swing went from relative obscurity to popular mania. The credit for this change goes to the son of a Russian Jewish immigrant, Benny Goodman, who used the arrangements of an African American, Fletcher Henderson, and who led a band made up of Italians, Germans, poor white southerners, sons of railroad workers, orphans, and, shortly after, African Americans. One reason that swing was able to achieve popular status concerned its ability to unite musicians of different races and ethnicities in the production of this American music.

To define swing as simply popular dance music misses its jazz lineage. As Gunther Schuller's *The Swing Era* effectively outlines, swing is the evolutionary extension of jazz performed by talented musicians. Yet swing is not limited to jazz. Almost any composition played by certain musicians under a particular set of circumstances can swing. When asked to define the music he helped popularize, Count Basie said swing "is a matter of some good things put together that you can really pat your foot by."[1]

The ambiguous definition of swing, it can be argued, derives from the fact that it comes from so many sources. Obviously not just jazz, dance music, or commercialized pap, it is a combination of the three because the musicians who created and performed swing came from backgrounds where they were exposed to all three. White musicians not only played black-inspired jazz but played with black musicians. Ethnic music that emphasized dance and rhythm, both black and white, joined with jazz to make dance swing. Musicians of different races and ethnicities borrowed from one another and unified on ground similar to them both: music. Their class connection helped them to understand the value of making money by playing the music the people wanted to dance to and hear. Swing, neither too black nor too ethnic, was a truly American music that offered escape, joy, and a sense of identification for both musicians and audience.

Central to the development of swing was the unity among musicians fostered by economic hardship. Many from both racial groups involved in the popularization of swing came from the American working class. This helped instill in them a desire to work for upward mobility, which, in turn, stimulated creative career choices. For some, this meant crime. Artie Shaw believed that he could have become a criminal as easily as a musician. Benny Goodman tells in his *Kingdom of Swing* that given the "neighborhood where I lived, if it hadn't been for the clarinet I might just as easily have been a gangster."[2]

Education was not considered a viable means to achieve status and wealth. In fact, in many cases, school actually got in the way. Barney Bigard went to work in his uncle Ulysses's cigar factory as a tobacco sifter, earning fifty cents a week, at age twelve. Soon he was promoted to roller, at a rate of eight dollars per one thousand rolled, and worked there until he was seventeen. Hoagy Carmichael found high school a waste of his time and quit to enter the work force on a cement mixer and then in a slaughterhouse. He performed these tasks out of necessity, not joy: "I sweated and I worked and I was cheerless."[3] For young Cab Calloway, school was a place to go between hustles. He would wake in the morning and ride the streetcars peddling the *Baltimore Sun* until ten in the morning and then go to school, leaving again around noontime to get the afternoon *Sun* and the *Star* to hawk. After this, he would ride the streetcars to Pimlico race track to sell racing forms and watch the races. Around 6:30, when the races ended, he would shine shoes at Pimlico until eight or nine and then go home. He did this from the time he was eleven until he was fifteen. In spite of his mother's stress on the value of an education, he would soon be back on the streets making money. For others, school attendance prevented the development of a musical career. Eddie Miller, born and raised in New Orleans, had established himself as a fine clarinetist and alto saxophonist by age fifteen. He traveled with bands throughout the South and by age seventeen was married and the father of a baby boy. The same held true for Jack Teagarden, who after his father's death and his family's move to Oklahoma City set out on his own as a professional musician. He was barely fifteen at the time.

The classic example of how school got in the way of a music career is Benny Goodman. Raised in a poor Russian Jewish family where the father worked in a variety of factory labor jobs, young Benny learned at an early age the value of a well-paying career. When the young Goodman entered school, his teenaged sisters were working as bookkeepers and stenographers, a profession well above unskilled labor. The father encouraged his children to work to get ahead, including taking his boys to the local synagogue and later to Hull House for musical training. By the time Benny was thirteen in

1923, he was working regularly around Chicago, and by fourteen he quit in order to play music full time.

Many swing musicians grew up watching their parents participate in the daily struggles of the laboring class. Although certainly levels of mobility differed between the races, generally both groups faced the problem of transitory and limited employment. Dizzy Gillespie, growing up in Cheraw, South Carolina, was forced to help his mother make ends meet; she earned only $1.50 a week washing clothes for a white family. Gillespie felt he had to help out: "I tried everything I knew to help Mama. The trouble was I just didn't know very much."[4] Count Basie watched his father's job as coachman for a local judge become obsolete in the face of the automobile. Without his prime source of income, the elder Basie turned to caretaking, tending to people's estates during the off-season and preparing them for the owner's arrival. The pay enabled him to own his house, but the mother still had to take in laundry to supplement the family income. Jess Stacy's father worked on the railroad in Missouri, and Jess was born during a train layover. His early years were spent near the family home, an abandoned boxcar. By the time Stacy reached his teens, his father's eyesight began to fail, and the railroad job ended. The family then lived off the income of his seamstress mother and Jess's job as a messenger for Western Union. Benny Goodman remembered that because of his father's low wages as a factory worker and other jobs, the family constantly moved, and there were times when there was little to eat.

Many other swing musicians grew up on the move, following their parents in search of steady work. Some, like Benny Carter, did not have to move far; his father's frequent job changes—from low-paying janitor, to night watchman, to postal clerk—allowed the family to stay in the San Juan Hill area of New York City. But Carter watched as his father's frustration led him to search for answers in alcohol. Stan Kenton's father wandered with his family throughout the Midwest and Far West in search of work. During this quest, the elder Kenton sold tombstones, worked as a mechanic, roofer, and carpenter, and attempted to own a garage, grocery store, car dealership, and butchershop; all resulted in failure. Finally the family settled in the Los Angeles area, where he found steady work. But the father was committed to ensuring his son would not follow in his footsteps, frowning on his musical skills and hoping the boy would find a steady job with a pension fund.

The tendency for the children to inherit their elders' jobs was high. Given the precarious nature of employment, parents encouraged their children to follow in their paths. Willie "the Lion" Smith's mother asked her husband to add him on as his helper on weekends at the local pork slaughterhouse to provide him job training. Young Harry James sought to follow his father's employment footsteps. Born into the Mighty Haag Circus, where his mother performed as a trapeze artist and his father led the band, he began working in the troupe at an early age, first as part of a contortionist's act. By the time he was seven, his father promoted him to the band where he pounded on the bass drum, and by age ten he became a full-fledged member of the band as a trumpet player. He eventually became the soloist in the band.

The great Billie Holiday was torn between two parents to follow: a mother as a domestic and a father as a musician. When in her teens, Holiday went to New York City to live with her mother, who got her a job working as a domestic for a woman who apparently spent all her time at the beach. When she returned, she would scold Holiday for not cleaning the house. Holiday quit believing that "there had to be something better than this."[5] After a stint as a prostitute, she would follow her father's musicians footsteps.

There were others, of course, who were not groomed to follow their parents' path but who nonetheless worked throughout childhood. Out of familial need, these children supplemented a usually limited income, becoming valuable wage earners at an early age. This experience would be important, for the hard work and little pay as youngsters made the lives and pay of musicians seem attractive. By age nine, Clark Terry earned his own room and board by charging pennies to haul away people's ashes. Quentin Hall's job at age twelve was to light and clean seventy-five gas lamps in his home town of Springfield, Illinois. His paycheck usually went directly to his mother. "Sir" Charles Thompson shined shoes, washed cars, bellhopped, operated elevators, and caddied golfers; he also served with Roosevelt's Civilian Conservation Corps. Willie Smith remembers that during his childhood in Charleston, South Carolina, he woke up every day at 4 A.M. to deliver papers on two routes. He later quit for a better job of working with his father hammering down boards. For Elmer Snowden, his early skill on the guitar caused friction in the home. By the time he was nine years old, he was regularly earning more per day than his father made during the entire week. The father destroyed the guitar as it threatened his role in the household, but the mother replaced it because it brought money into the home. Soon after, Snowden got a job earning ten dollars a week as a theater (movie) musician. His father quit his job because his son earned more than enough to support the family.

For working children from laboring parentage, music became a means to make easy money. Stan Kenton remembers: "I guess all young musicians are the same. I used to dream about the possibility of maybe making a little money at playing the piano because I could not believe that anyone could make money for something they loved to do so much."[6] In many cases these musicians were making more money than their parents by their teenaged years. Most times the experiences of their childhood, coupled with their parent's hard lives, made music their career.

I have purposely avoided racial identification to detail how, without labels, the circumstances of swing musicians' childhood are similar. This distinction is important; it provides a basis for understanding how swing, and especially its musicians, was able to surmount ethnic and racial differences to achieve widespread popularity. The class association and identification, combined with the hard times of the Great Depression, enabled swing's audience and its musicians sometimes to forgo generational racism and prejudice to enjoy the music as an escape and to derive a living from performing it.

Not that economics forced the merging of ethnicity and race. Although playing a key role in the ability of swing to promote musical integration, the merging usually took place when the musicians, and their audiences, were growing up. Assimilation by immigrants, first and second generation, by blacks moving to the North, and by rural people moving to urban settings forced association. These three groups made up the nation's underclass in the early twentieth century and inhabited similar neighborhoods, worked next to or near to one another, and were exposed to each other's culture regularly. While swing received its impetus for popularity from the economic hardship of the 1930s, the merging of race and ethnicity by the laboring classes who would write, play, and star in the swing revolution started during their childhoods.

In the period that shaped the swing musician and his audience (1900–1935), America experienced a tremendous movement of people. This migratory process occurred not only in terms of immigration but also internal movement. By 1940 almost one of every four Americans was a first- or second-generation immigrant. The largest percentage of these new Americans came from Italy, Russia (and its territories), Germany, and Poland.

One-quarter of the population is significant, but when one considers where these people migrated to, the importance is magnified. Most of these immigrants became unskilled or semiskilled laborers in the U.S. urban, capitalist, industrial landscape. Cleveland, Ohio, contained two-thirds ethnic population, New York City three-fourths, three-fifths in Newark, New Jersey, and Chicago, Toledo, Detroit, Pittsburgh, and Boston also had large immigrant populations. In these cities, the ethnic groups lived together in close proximity to one another and generally worked in similar occupations.

The other dominant migrant to the nation's cities was the African American. With the outbreak of World War I, immigration dried up, and with it, its cheap labor. To offset this, the industrial and commercial leaders turned to the South, where millions of unskilled and semiliterate blacks toiled as sharecroppers in conditions bordering on feudalism. These people would work cheap and cause divisions within the laboring classes.

From 1910 through the 1930s, the need for cheap labor and the lack of opportunities on southern farms pulled and pushed some 1.5 million African Americans to the North. They, like their ethnic counterparts, moved to the industrial urban North and lived and worked together. Their neighborhoods bordered Jewish, Italian, Polish, or any number of other ghettos of semiskilled and unskilled urban workers. Also, like their ethnic neighbors, they toiled for low wages, typically well below their white counterparts and usually in the most menial of occupations. They were last hired and first fired and suffered job discrimination in almost every field.

Both groups—African Americans and ethnics—comprised the working class. These were the bulk of the laborers who provided the skilled, unskilled, and semiskilled labor in the factories, as well as lower-level white-collar clerks. What the ethnics and races had in common was class. During this time, class membership determined nearly everything in a child's life: school subjects, career choice, church membership, marriage, debt, housing, crime, and so forth. Upward class mobility, the foundation of the American dream, in reality rarely occurred.

This class identification would be significant to the development and popularity of swing. It enabled groups of people from different cultures to exchange their ideas and use what was traded to make a living. Whether it was a Jewish delicatessen in a newly black Harlem of the 1920s where Fats Waller grew up, or in a Chicago ghetto where the Goodmans lived, the idea of making a living playing music was not necessarily done out of skill, training, or practice but out of the desire to earn a good living doing something enjoyable—a luxury few in their class were afforded.

The streets of the city exposed different races and ethnicities to one another, but music forged connections. Nappy Lamare, growing up white in New Orleans during the height of the jazz explosion, safely within his class pattern as a printer's assistant (a job he relished), turned his back on the job of his father and grandfather to take up the guitar and jazz, all because one day he happened to see a musical parade in New Orleans and was struck by the beauty of the music. The leader of the band Lamare saw was Louis Armstrong, and his band was made up of all blacks. Wingy Manone, also raised in New Orleans, recalls taking his traditional, white music teacher up the river to a place called Tobacco Road. Here, in houses built on quicksand, local blacks gathered to play the rudiments of what would become jazz. Manone told his teacher he wanted to play in that style. She called the blacks "fakers" for using skills not in the book. While she admitted they had talent, she told Manone that if he wanted to play in that style, she would not teach him. From that point forward, every chance Manone got, he "went over there and listened to 'em. They didn't want no white folks around, but they let me come, as long as I stayed on the boundary line."[7]

In the Southwest, similar transference took place. Charlie Christian, the great and mysterious guitarist, adopted a country-western swing style of playing while growing up and playing in his father's band in Oklahoma City. The band performed in the white sections of town, and the black musicians adopted the style that best pleased their paying audience. The black church and gospel singing played a major role in Jack Teagarden's musical training. Growing up in Texas during the height of jim crow segregation in the late 1910s, Teagarden was attracted to the musical sounds coming from local black churches and the occasional camp revival meeting. It was in listening to the hymns and shouts of the disaffected African Americans that Teagarden was awakened to the importance of the beat. His biographers wrote, "It came to young Teagarden in the rhythmic hand claps, the laments and hosannas of half a hundred Negro voices. It came from a tawdry tent, grey and shapeless under the Texas stars. Long after he had gone to bed its swing pulse kept him throbbing all night."[8] Andy Kirk, raised in Denver, Colorado, grew up listening to the popular Tin Pan Alley songs of the 1910s, and while citing Jelly Roll Morton as a musical influence, he admits that he rarely heard or saw any bands made up of blacks during his youth. In fact, in the early 1920s, when his band was playing in Oklahoma City on a shared bill with Jack Teagarden, the Kirk band played music "more white than Jack's," and Kirk remembers learning a few things about playing jazz that night.[9]

The exposure and acceptance of these cultures had important future ramifications. First, when these children grew up, the connection to multiethnicity remained part of their life-style. They did not fear the practices and cultures of other ethnic groups and races, as the more traditional white middle class did, but absorbed, understood, and, in the case of music, utilized them. The cultural exchange begun in their youth as a result of their class connections continued as they grew older. Swing musicians, like their audiences, broke down the racial and ethnic barriers that separated them—not overnight and not everywhere but slowly and then in bursts, until finally, no one even noticed that musical integration had taken place.

Benny Goodman's use of black performers serves as an excellent case in point. In 1935 Goodman hired Teddy Wilson and Lionel Hampton to play with his band, but he was forced to feature them with him as an intermission trio. Goodman's band, with Wilson and Hampton, toured the country with few genuine difficulties. Goodman argued that "for a lot of people that came to hear us, the [trio] was a special kick—and when we played, nobody cared much what colors or races were represented just as long as we played good music. That's the way it should be."[10] Good musicians meant good music, which might mean a popular and profitable swing band. While individual musicians and their audiences might have harbored prejudice, they submerged it in the joy of the music. Up on stage were musicians, and the music they created made one want to dance, move, escape in musical abandon. The audiences and musicians temporarily lost their sense of racial and ethnic identification and simply enjoyed the sound.

This is not to suggest that either the musician or the audience was not aware of the differences. For many swing musicians, it was precisely because they were different that made them unified. In his autobiography *Really the Blues*, Mezz Mezzrow recounts that regardless of his middle-class Jewish upbringing, he felt out of touch with mainstream America. Only after his flirtations with petty crime landed him in a reformatory in Pontiac, Michigan, did he discover his peer group: the other outsiders in jail, the African Americans. Others did not view their outsider status with Mezzrow's enthusiasm. For most, the lack of acceptance based on race or ethnicity led to shame or embarrassment. Arthur Arshawsky (Artie Shaw) recounts that being born on the Lower East Side of New York City into a Russian Jewish dressmaking family made him like the other ethnic immigrant children in his neighborhood: "Any kid growing up on the Lower East Side of New York City is apt to find himself playing with lots of kids with long, foreign-sounding names. There were all kinds of kids and all sorts of names. Romanoff, Liebowitz, Anzelowitz, Fiorito, O'Clanahan, Borazybski."[11] When his parents decided to move to New Haven, Connecticut, when he was eight years old, Shaw felt out of place—a fish out of water. In New Haven, a traditional White Anglo-Saxon Protestant, community, Shaw discovered that being ethnic meant being different, and when his classmates first heard his name called out, they laughed.

This alienation would force many musicians to accept situations that were out of the norm. For example, many black musicians and arrangers accepted their less than equal status with their white counterparts because it held more promise and security than many other nonmusicians in their community. While paid less and denied the lion's share of the exposure, both economically and culturally, they nonetheless acquiesced because their status was much better than that of most of their contemporaries. Some white performers, like Shaw, Goodman, and Krupa, deemphasized their ethnicity and became "American." James Collier recounts in his biography of Benny Goodman how the King of Swing's marriage into the Hammond family was important for just this reason—acceptance and assimilation. Goodman's marriage into an accepted family in the community of Westchester, New York, became so complete that he soon began to talk as his new family did.

Why would Goodman want to deny his ethnicity; or why would Fletcher Henderson allow Goodman to take credit for his arrangements? Or a better example, what made Arthur Arshawsky change his name to Artie Shaw? Was it simply the desire to succeed? Or were there other motivations? The idea of success, so vital in the modernist era of the 1930s, played an important role in the assimilation. Among many ethnic and racial groups, the alienation of being different could be breached by success, by fitting into the social machine. If one was a great boxer like Joe Louis, a gifted baseball player like Joe DiMaggio, an exciting actor like James Cagney, or a talented musician like Duke Ellington or Benny Goodman, the racial and ethnic barriers would certainly lower. As Goodman argued, all that counted was whether someone was a good musician, and during the performance, no prejudice existed.

The alienation of being an outsider, whether racial or ethnic, proved a great motivator. For many, the alienation led to isolation and introversion, and combined with the class restrictions and economic situation of many of the swing musicians, creative outlets like music became their only comfort, their only expression of their situation. For example, Sidney Bechet grew up working and had no toys as a youth. Years later, he wrote a song about a child who had no one or nothing to play with except a song. The boy sang and practiced this song "about being lonely, and as soon as he had the song, he wasn't lonely anymore. He was lucky. He was real well off; he had this thing he could trust, and so he could trust himself."[12]

The popular swing bands broke the musical color and ethnic barrier. Benny Goodman, the King of Swing, used his power to help break down the racial barriers because he understood the black contribution to his success. He used Lionel Hampton and Teddy Wilson as part of his show, and although he received letters of protest and lost some possible supporters, Goodman remained committed to their employment. His support was not lost to Lionel Hampton, who connected Goodman's musical integration to the post–World War II desegregation of baseball and other professions. Teddy Wilson's observations are more to the point. To him the inclusion of the black musician filled out the picture of the swing band: "Southerners ... Jews and Christians and Lionel and I represented the Negroes in the band. . . . We were like brothers, the whole outfit."[13]

NOTES

1. Count Basie, in *The World of Swing*, ed. Stanley Dance (New York: Da Capo, 1979), p. 1.

2. Benny Goodman and Irving Kolodin, *The Kingdom of Swing* (New York: Frederick Unger, 1939), p. 31.

3. Hoagy Carmichael, *The Stardust Road* (New York: Rinehart, 1946), p. 17.

4. Dizzy Gillespie, *To Be or Not ... to BOP* (Garden City, N.Y.: Doubleday, 1979), p. 16.

5. Billie Holiday with William Dufty, *Lady Sings the Blues* (New York: Avon Books, 1956), p. 20.

6. Stan Kenton, in William L. Lee, *Stan Kenton: Artistry in Rhythm*, ed. Audree Coke (Los Angeles: Creative Press, 1980), p. 5.

7. Wingy Manone and Paul Vandervordt, *Trumpet on a Wing* (Garden City, N.Y.: Doubleday, 1948), p. 13.

8. Jay D. Smith and Len Guttridge, *Jack Teagarden: The Story of a Jazz Maverick* (New York: Da Capo, 1976), p. 22.

9. Benny Goodman, in *Hear Me Talkin' to Ya*, ed. Nat Shapiro and Nat Hentoff (New York: Dover Books, 1955), p. 319.

10. Artie Shaw, *The Trouble with Cinderella* (New York: Farrar & Straus & Young, 1952), p. 27.

11. Sidney Bechet, *Treat It Gentle: An Autobiography* (New York: Da Capo, 1978), p. 5.

12. Teddy Wilson, quoted in James Lincoln Collier, *Benny Goodman and the Swing Era* (New York: Oxford University Press, 1989), p. 175.
13. Ibid.

BIBLIOGRAPHY

Collier, James Lincoln. *Benny Goodman and the Swing Era*. New York: Oxford University Press, 1989.
Dance, Stanley. *The World of Swing*. New York: Da Capo, 1979.
McCarthy, Albert. *Big Band Jazz*. New York: Putnam, 1975.
Schuller, Gunther. *The Swing Era: The Development of Jazz, 1930–1945*. New York: Oxford University Press, 1989.
Shapiro, Nat, and Nat Hentoff. *Hear Me Talkin' to Ya: The Story of Jazz as Told by the Men Who Made It*. New York: Dover, 1955.
Simon, George T. *Simon Says: The Sights and Sounds of the Swing Era*. New Rochelle, N.Y.: Arlington House, 1955.
Walker, Leo. *The Wonderful Era of the Great Dance Bands*. Garden City, N.Y.: Doubleday, 1972.

9

Rock and Roll and the Working Class

JAMES R. MCDONALD

- The folksinger Woody Guthrie, composer of "This Land Is Your Land" and "If I Had a Hammer" and a major influence on Bob Dylan, began his career in the late 1930s by performing as a "hillbilly" on KFVD radio in California for twenty dollars per week. A few years later, he sold his song "So Long It's Been Good to Know You" to the manufacturers of Lucky Strike cigarettes for well over two hundred times that earlier weekly salary.

- Elvis Presley's first contract with RCA Records in 1955 paid him a total of $3,000 and a Cadillac convertible. In 1984, ZZ Top sold the song "Legs" to the manufacturers of Legg's pantyhose in a multimillion-dollar arrangement for twenty television commercials.

- John Lennon of the Beatles was born dirt poor in Liverpool, England, a dirty manufacturing city on England's west coast. At the time of his death in 1980, Lennon lived in New York City and had an estimated worth of over $200 million.

- Mick Jagger of the Rolling Stones, who was raised in a middle-class London environment and studied at the London School of Economics, has presented himself as a former poor boy who could do nothing else but play in a rock 'n' roll band ("Street Fighting Man"). Jagger is also a multimillionaire and has long been a member of the international jet set.

These examples raise several divergent questions about the relationship between the working class and rock 'n' roll. For instance, can one be a rich rock star and still represent the values of the working class *to* the working class, as Bruce Springsteen attempts to do? Does rock 'n' roll offer any insights into what it means to be working class: into its values, life-styles, and economic and political priorities? Does rock 'n' roll represent a positive image of the working class? Is its resultant portrayal realistic or merely an illusion? Do the economic advantages of being a rock star preclude one from maintaining an artistic interest in the working class? Does having "paid one's dues" justify rock stars' singing about the working class when they live in million-dollar homes? And, most important, what does rock's position regarding the working class say about America and its culture?

There can be no doubt that rock 'n' roll often represents a road to riches. The success of the rapper M. C. Hammer is the most recent example of a poor boy making good. Whether Hammer maintains a relationship with his roots—in his case, the inner city of Oakland, California—remains to be seen.

Unlike Hammer, many stars have not only changed their class status but their country status as well. Rod Stewart and Joe Cocker, natives of England, now reside in California, largely due to the lower income tax regulations in America. Other stars, perhaps, have done more to maintain their pasts.

Both Presley and Lennon lived rich but were able, because of those riches, to isolate themselves from the world around them. Yet neither forgot his roots. Presley surrounded himself with family members in his "Memphis Mafia" and routinely gave elaborate gifts to people with little money. In addition, he often recorded religious and gospel songs similar to those that influenced him musically, and perhaps spiritually, in his early years.

Lennon, in spite of his relative isolation during the last five years of his life, maintained an intense interest in the working class. In addition to songs during his Beatle period, such as "Eight Days a Week," Lennon protested the plight of the working class in songs such as "Working Class Hero," released in 1970. The latter song presented the working-class hero as a person controlled by a political system uncaring about its citizens. And in "Watching the Wheels," released on his last album, *Double Fantasy*, in 1980, Lennon explains why he dropped out of the fast-paced music world to devote time to his family—just like a (very rich) working man.

That rock 'n' roll should have a close relationship with the idea of the working class should not be surprising given the musical areas from which it evolved. American blues, long suggested as an early form of rock 'n' roll, if not one of its greatest influences, has the working class as one of its major themes. Issues of physical labor, work, family, marriage, relationships, money, and alcohol pervade blues songs from the work of Robert Johnson, one of the main influences on Eric Clapton, Robert Cray, and other contemporary blues artists, right up to the latest release by John Mayall, a British artist who has recorded blues albums since the early 1960s.

Blues songs have always been sung by musicians with working-class backgrounds for people with working-class values. Since their music was normally performed on what was referred to as the "chitlin' circuit"—small bars and clubs throughout the country—it has been rare for a blues artist to make substantial sums of money. Even at their peak, B. B. King and Muddy Waters, two of the biggest stars in blues, never achieved the financial success of their rock counterparts.

Nevertheless, the blues artistry—its style, its tone, its honest emotion— led directly to its adoption, or perhaps adaptation, into a rock 'n' roll artistry. One can see that adaptation in groups ranging from the early work of the Rolling Stones and Cream, to newer groups like the Black Crowes, or even in recent releases by long-established groups like Aerosmith and Badfinger.

Similarly, a second musical influence on rock 'n' roll with a working-class background was certainly American folk music. Like the blues, folk developed from work songs, spirituals, and religious hymns, in addition to ethnic and European influences, and had been in the American musical tradition long before it became prominent in the early 1960s. Early folk artists, most notably Woody Guthrie, set the tone for those to follow, including Bob Dylan, Phil Ochs, Joan Baez, and Judy Collins.

Rock has the working-class values of blues and folk music as historical tradition; does that necessarily mean that rock continues to demonstrate an interest in those same values? After all, during rock's early days, it was music for the young: Chuck Berry singing about the problems of teenagers and Elvis and Buddy Holly singing about teenaged love. Could rock stars realistically expect teenagers even to care about the working class?

The teenagers of the 1950s, one must remember, enjoyed a postwar economy that placed more disposable income—and the time to enjoy it—in their pockets than had been done with any previous generation. Teenagers in the 1950s became the first yuppies, buying rock 'n' roll records in increasingly large numbers, thereby making their heroes richer and richer. It is no wonder that "sex, drugs and rock 'n' roll" became the rallying cry for the hard rock music that followed the tamer, perhaps more sentimental, work of 1950s' rockers, since the economic affluence of the 1950s carried over to the 1960s. All one had to do was party, or so it seemed.

Music in the 1960s, however, began to develop a social conscience. Songwriters led by Dylan and followed quickly by Lennon and McCartney and a host of others dealt with issues that engaged real people in real situations. While love remained a predominant theme in music, songs also addressed the Vietnam War, civil rights, feminism, the economy, education, and other issues. Suddenly rock 'n' roll was a stage from which messages could be sent. And listeners began to realize that music had meaning and influenced many facets of their lives. Suddenly, rock 'n' roll was not just the music of teenaged rebellion and issues of adolescent interests but was a music of the masses, the middle class, the working class.

Some rock 'n' roll commentators, however, suggest that rock 'n' roll has always been a classless music, performed by those bent on escaping a class system and listened to by those bent on doing the same thing. They suggest, for instance, that rock 'n' roll is a way out of the working class, a rebellion against the values of that class, and therefore a move toward bohemianism— freedom to engage in music without class values. They argue further that once groups reach stardom and attain significant wealth, their concern for their roots, their middle-class backgrounds, is no longer of concern.

Certainly the economics of rock music suggest that this is a strong possibility. Much is made of the fact that rock stars routinely make the Top 100 income lists. But that is really nothing new, even as far back as Frank Sinatra's early status as a teen idol. In 1974, for example, it is estimated that at least 100 British rock stars were earning an annual income in excess of $500,000. Although popular music has always had potential for lucrative earnings, there are numerous accounts of the money evaporating. Mick Fleetwood, for instance, a member of the group Fleetwood Mac, filed bankruptcy in 1988 in spite of having made millions over the years.

Moreover, enormous wealth, in and of itself, does not always change the life-styles of rock artists or the values of those artists. Paul McCartney, certainly one of the wealthiest rock stars, to this day continues to live in Scotland, claiming that family ties and traditional values are more important to him than residing in a warmer climate and enjoying better tax rates. John Mellencamp, one of the most successful recording artists in the 1980s, continues to reside in rural Indiana, his home state. Bob Dylan, in spite of his economic status, continues to engage in musical statements as critical of social issues today as they were in the mid–1960s.

The issue of rock 'n' roll economics, however, as important as it is, cannot help define the position of rock stars with regard to the working class or rock 'n' roll's position regarding the working class. The bohemianism referred to earlier is most likely a positive goal for rock artists to strive for. In attaining it, or at least striving toward it, artists create for themselves the freedom real or imaginary, to criticize both the working class and the system it supports. This is one of the motivating factors behind the emergence of punk rock in the mid–1970s, and, one might speculate, behind the continuation of the so-called alternative music of the mid- to late 1980s.

The punk rock scene developed in Britain and America almost simultaneously, although the British influence was more pronounced and the paths taken somewhat divergent. Invariably, British punk rockers were art students, those traditionally identified with a bohemian attitude. This is quite common in British rock history, where several musicians were former art students, including John Lennon.

But the British punk rockers, by comparison to their 1960s' counterparts, were anti–working class, preferring to be among the unemployed, the dispossessed, the economic bottom. Johnny Rotten of the Sex Pistols said, "I know it's tough on the dole but it's not that bad. When I was on it, I was getting paid for doing nothing. I thought it was fucking great. Fuck up the system the best way."[1] Instead of creating music inspired by a generation gap—teenagers against their parents—punk rock was more inspired by class conflict: the musicians against everybody involved within the system. The emphasis was on total freedom. Economics, the recording industry itself, even musicianship—all were despised.

Eventually the punk rock scene dispersed, most likely due to those things the initial punk performers were against. The second and third wave of punk groups signed recording contracts, formed recording labels, and made more money; in short, they, too, became part of the working class.

But punk succeeded in doing what rock 'n' roll has ostensibly always wanted to have as its goal. It allowed disaffected middle-class youth the opportunity, if even temporary, to express extreme dissatisfaction with contemporary society, particularly economic pressures brought on by an increasingly hostile world economy, and parental expectations to conform to those pressures.

While expressing dissatisfaction with society is a main theme of punk music, it has been done from an anti–working class perspective. However, several songwriters have engaged in social criticism from a perspective more sympathetic to the working class: Bruce Springsteen, John Mellencamp, Bob Seger, and Bob Dylan. Each has contributed heavily to what some commentators have labeled the blue-collar protest rock.

Springsteen has recently had the most to say about the plight of the working class. On his tour for the 1984 album *Born in the USA*, he often sang an acoustic version of Guthrie's "This Land Is Your Land," introducing it by saying, "I'm not sure this song is true any more. I hope it is, but I'm not sure. It's about a promise that's eroding every day for a lot of people."[2] It is ironic that Springsteen's song "Born in the USA" was adopted by Ronald Reagan during his reelection campaign, particularly considering the anti-Republican stance Springsteen has projected over the years on his albums.

From Springsteen's anthem song, "Born to Run," with its description of the necessity of flight, of escape, of an American dream gone wrong, through "Darkness at the Edge of Town," "The River," "Nebraska," and on into the 1980s, Springsteen has sung of the plight of the American worker, his lost dreams and fading hopes. Springsteen's goals seem to involve infusing the idea of hope into situations involving insoluble circumstances. One must also not ignore his efforts on behalf of unions nationwide, not to mention charity organizations, local food banks, and various Vietnam veterans' organizations.

Similarly, Mellencamp, Seger, and Dylan, all artists born in the Midwest (Indiana, Michigan, and Minnesota, respectively), have written about the plight of the urban poor and, perhaps as a gesture of support for the working class, about midwestern values and life-styles. Mellencamp, in the songs "Pink Houses" and "Blood on the Scarecrow," addresses the problems of the rural poor—American farmers. Seger, in songs like "The Ring" and "Makin' Thunderbirds," deals with the problems of the factory worker. And Dylan, who has addressed more issues regarding the working class than can begin to be discussed within this chapter, focuses on the working class in songs like "Union Sundown" and "Clean Cut Kid."

While Springsteen, Mellencamp, Seger, and Dylan have all demonstrated social concern in their work for many years, one must also remember that the 1980s was a decade in which rock 'n' roll itself paid a great deal of attention to issues of social concern, particularly to those involving the working classes and the economically disadvantaged worldwide. Further, artists involved in social causes include Sting, Don Henley, Bruce Cockburn, U2, Billy Joel, and all the other groups involved in various benefit concerts.

With the advent of Live Aid in 1985, over $200 million has been raised by rock groups of all kinds for various causes: USA for Africa ("We Are the World"), Band Aid ("Do They Know It's Christmas"), and the Live Aid concert, the Farm Aid concerts, and Amnesty International's Human Rights Now! world tour in the fall of 1988. In the 1980s, it has been said, rock 'n' roll again developed a social conscience. Ironically, that conscience, if developed as described, was done during a time when rock music was also under attack by various groups for being overtly violent, sexist, and pornographic. That attack, now directed toward rap groups, continues into the 1990s.

One of the assumptions of the attacking groups is that rock 'n' roll yields an unusually negative power on its listeners, even going so far as encouraging some teenagers to commit suicide. Nevertheless, there have been studies for years that demonstrate that the lyrics of songs are largely ignored by the audience, that the beat and, since the age of the video, the imagery are what captures an audience's attention.

In spite of the disagreement about the values rock 'n' roll espouses, what merits further examination in the area of rock 'n' roll and the working class is the issue of power, of influence, which is given to rock stars. In 1984, for instance, conservative columnist George Will wrote about attending a Springsteen concert and the impact Springsteen seemed to be having on American youth. A few days later, in September 1984, President Reagan, campaigning in New Jersey, said, "America's future rests in a thousand dreams inside your hearts. It rests in the message of hope in songs of a man so many young Americans admire: "New Jersey's Bruce Springsteen."[3]

When the president of the United States attempts to make an ally out of a rock star to enhance his own image—particularly when that star's political feelings run opposite to the president's—one must question the influence rock stars have on their audience, both economically and socially. Without the Live Aid benefit, for instance, how many people would have donated money to a cause designed to alleviate starvation in Africa? Without the Farm Aid concerts, how many would have donated to a cause supporting the plight of the American farmer? Jackson Browne, involved in political activism since the early 1970s, has often complained that he has no special expertise in issues on which he is often asked to comment. If a group of politicians had attempted to organize the various Aid fund-raising drives, rather than an assemblage of rock stars, it is doubtful whether the same effects would have occurred.

To answer why this phenomenon occurs is difficult, but the answer most likely is that the rock 'n' roll audience has an insatiable desire for product demand, whether it is the music itself, those who create the music, or the merchandise associated with the music (T-shirts, posters, and so forth). Because of this demand, marketing strategies are cleverly formulated not only to help satisfy the demand but to create more demand in the process. The situation becomes a never-ending cycle: consumers demand; consumers are supplied but asked to demand more; consumers demand. The irony is that consumers *are* members of the working class.

The issue of rock 'n' roll and the working class is clearly one that presents many potential areas of investigation. There can be little doubt that the working class is, at the least, a springboard for many rock artists, and, at the most, a central area of concern. While it is certainly possible to label many rock artists' concerns with the working class as transitory at best, so too is it possible to label the working-class obsession with rock artists as a futile hope that they too might aspire to capture their own portion of the American dream.

But it is that obsession of the working class that also affords it power. By focusing on rock 'n' roll, in whatever form it may take, the working class also forces those involved in rock 'n' roll from a production standpoint to deal with it. Therefore, whether rock 'n' roll represents an eventual escape from the working class or not is pretty much a moot point because rock 'n' roll will be nothing else than a music for the working class because the working class, as consumers, will not permit it to be otherwise.

NOTES

1. Johnny Rotten quoted in Simon Frith, *Sound Effects: Youth, Leisure, and the Politics of Rock 'n' Roll* (New York: Pantheon, 1981), p. 266.
2. Bruce Springsteen as quoted in Ray Pratt, "Is a Dream a Lie If It Don't Come True, or Is It Something Worse? A Commentary on Political Implications of the Springsteen Phenomenon," *Popular Music and Society* 11 (Spring 1987): 51.
3. Ronald Reagan, as quoted in Mikal Gilmore, "Bruce Springsteen," *Rolling Stone*, November 15, 1990, pp. 87–88.

BIBLIOGRAPHY

Coon, Carolyn. *The New Wave Punk Rock Explosion*. London: Orbach & Chambers, 1977.
Denisoff, R. S. *Sing a Song of Social Significance*. Bowling Green, Ohio: Bowling Green University Press, 1983.
Eliot, Marc. *Rockonomics: The Money behind the Music*. New York: Franklin Watts, 1989.
Frith, Simon. *Sound Effects: Youth, Leisure, and the Politics of Rock 'n' Roll*. New York: Pantheon, 1981.
Fryer, Paul. "Punk and the New Wave of British Rock: Working Class Heroes and Art School Attitudes." *Popular Music and Society* 10 (4) (1984): 1–15.

Grossberg, Lawrence. "Another Boring Day in Paradise: Rock and Roll and the Empowerment of Everyday Life." *Popular Music* 4 (1984): 225–28.

———. "Is There Rock after Punk?" *Critical Studies in Mass Communication* 3 (March 1986): 50–74.

Lewis, George H. "Cultural Socialization and the Development of Taste Cultures and Culture Classes." *Popular Music and Society* 4 (4) (1975): 226–41.

Lipistz, George. *Time Passages: Collective Memory and American Popular Culture.* Minneapolis: University of Minnesota Press, 1990.

London, Herbert I. *Closing the Circle: A Cultural History of the Rock Revolution.* Chicago: Nelson-Hall, 1984.

McDonald, James R. "Censoring Rock Lyrics: A Historical Analysis of the Debate." *Youth and Society* 19 (3) (March 1988): 294–313.

———. "Politics Revisited: Metatectual Implications of Rock and Roll Criticism." *Youth and Society* 19 (4) (June 1988): 485–504.

Pratt, Ray. "Is a Dream a Lie If It Don't Come True, or Is It Something Worse?": A Commentary on Political Implications of the Springsteen Phenomenon." *Popular Music and Society* 11 (1) (Spring 1987): 51–74.

Rodnitzky, Jerome L. *Minstrels of the Dawn: The Folk-Protest Singer as a Cultural Hero.* Chicago: Nelson-Hall, 1976.

Tillman, R. H. "Punk Rock and the Construction of Pseudo-Political Movements." *Popular Music and Society* 7 (1980): 165–75.

10

Rock Is Youth/Youth Is Rock

Deena Weinstein

Rock music and youth are inseparable. Adolescents walk around with boom boxes blaring rock, hang out at record stores, and sit glued to MTV. But there is far more to the connection between rock and youth than what everyone can see and hear around them. Although there have always been young people, only after World War II did there arise a social category called youth with distinctive features that separated it from other social groups. From the beginning, the most significant emblem of the youth group has been its music, known first as rock and roll, then as rock, and more recently as a bewildering array of kinds of rock music.

The relation of youth to rock music is reciprocal; each one defines the other. But they are not identical. Rock grows out of musical traditions that did not cater especially to youth, and it is produced by an industry controlled by adults. Youth, on the other hand, has more complexity than is allowed by rock, which stresses only certain themes that are relevant to the condition of young people. But the points of connection between youth and rock music are far greater than their aspects of indifference or antipathy. Rock and youth entwine with each other.

Rock, narrowly defined, refers to the music that was initiated and made famous by British bands in the mid- to late 1960s, such as the Who, the Rolling Stones, the Kinks, and the Beatles. The terms *rock* and *rock music* will be used here in the broad sense to refer to the rock and roll of the 1950s, the rock of the 1960s, and the many descendants of 1960s rock that appeared in the 1970s and 1980s.

Rock music arose, in its early form of rock and roll, in the mid–1950s in the United States. Rock and roll emerged from a coupling of black and white musical traditions that were not specifically youth oriented. From the black tradition, rock inherited race music, the popular music made by and for urban blacks in the years immediately following World War II. Much of this music was blues and, especially its urban offshoot, rhythm and blues From the southern white tradition, rock got country music, particularly in its more raw and earthy forms. Rock and roll's early luminaries, such as Little Richard, Jerry Lee Lewis, Chuck Berry, Elvis Presley, and Bill Haley, had roots in at least one of these musical traditions. They transplanted these roots into pop music, rejecting pop's smooth vocal tradition for a more ragged and emotionally charged vocal sound. They appropriated pop's mass commercial apparatus.

Rock and roll's emergence cannot be understood merely as an independent cultural development. It was fundamentally tied to changes in the condition of adolescents and also related to technological changes and economic transformations.

Television came into the American home in the first part of the 1950s, decimating radio. It stole radio's stars, its audience, and its commercial sponsors. Particularly during the after-dinner to bedtime period, television replaced radio as the prime-time family attraction. The television set sat in the position of honor, dominating the living room or, in the burgeoning suburban split-levels, the "family" room. The family gathered around it for the evening ritual. Had the television sets been smaller and far less expensive, there might have been several of them in the household, but they were expensive, and few households could afford more than one.

Although they were not opposed to television, adolescents removed themselves from the nightly family ritual. Generally they went to their bedrooms, furnished with the older medium, radio. In their rooms or cruising in cars, they played the radio. As they flipped the dial, they ran into race music and the wilder forms of country music. Some were attracted by the adventure and excitement of the experience and became converts. Meanwhile, as the radio industry began to realize that the composition of its prime-time audience was heavily weighted toward teenagers, it began to direct its programming toward the tastes of this demographic group.

The marriage of music and marketing was made by disc jockeys. In cities such as Cleveland and New York, deejays at first selected those pop records that appealed to their young audience and omitted songs that it disliked. When they recognized that a small but significant portion of white teenagers were tuning in to black radio stations and listening to race music, disc jockeys like Alan Freed began to play black music on their white-oriented programs. The record companies caught on and began to seek songs and performers to appeal to the teenaged audience.

Radio sold records. The members of the increasingly affluent teenaged audience were disposed to spend their allowances on items of leisure consumption such as records. A significant economic factor was born: the teenaged market. At first small, independent record labels, such as Chess Records in Chicago, supplied this new market. Once the market proved to be lucrative, the risk-phobic major record companies entered and quickly took it over. The music sold to teenagers in the 1950s is what became known as rock and roll, a term coined by Alan Freed, who borrowed it from rhythm and blues songs in which it served as a code word for sexual intercourse. Rock and roll was a musical style fashioned for and directed at the specific audience of teenagers. The music industry—radio, record companies, and musicians—served and created the market for the first exclusively youth-oriented music in history.

Rock and roll had special qualities that made it connect with its audience. It was youth music in both a biological and a social sense. Later it came to define youth as a distinctive culture and state of being.

Biologically, youth is a transitional period between immaturity (childhood) and full maturity (adulthood). As Chuck Berry put it, youth is when one is "Almost Grown." Energy and strength peak, and the skeleto-muscular system becomes fully developed. The strong beat of rock music, whether it encourages dancing or headbanging, reflects and appeals to youthful strength. Loudness, a prominent feature of much rock, especially in forms such as punk and heavy metal, reflects the physical prowess of youth. Children and older people want a softer beat and are physically distressed by loud sounds. Males, in comparison to females, develop greater strength and a higher capacity for powerful bursts of energy. The faster and louder style of rock music appeals especially to males. The vitality of rock music connects with the young body, which is at a peak of energy. Youthful vitality has remained a constant factor in rock music from its beginnings.

Biological youth is also a period of sexual maturation. In addition to reproductive abilities, secondary sex characteristics emerge. These transformations are due to hormonal changes, which can be influenced by diet. Over the past century in America, due to a diet rich in proteins and fats, the age of sexual maturation has markedly declined. The onset of menstruation in girls had been at about the age of sixteen, but it now occurs at about age twelve. Partly because the equipment is new and partly because of high rates of hormonal production, sexual interest is particularly intense among adolescents.

Many aspects of rock music appeal to, enhance, and reflect the sexual dimension. Sexual themes in rock lyrics abound, from the Rolling Stones's "Let's Spend the Night Together" to W.A.S.P.'s "Animal (F**k like a Beast)." Rock and roll continued the sexual euphemisms of rhythm and blues. The 1950s were a rather repressive era, and much of the language now common in rock songs would have been banned at that time. The term *dance* often stood for sex both lyrically and practically. The terms *rock* and *rock and roll* were used as code words for sex, as names for a style of music, and more generally as ways of naming a gratifying emotional expressivity.

Sexuality in rock is not confined to words but is reflected in the rhythms of the music. Much of 1950s' rock and roll was made up of slow doo-wop songs, encouraging movement in the pelvic area more than in the legs. The erotic resonances of this music are captured by the name of a dance done to it, the "bump and grind." The emphatic beat of rock music in all eras, usually produced by the combined attack of drums and bass guitar, produces a sonic sensuality. The music moves the body, not merely the eardrums.

Socially, youth is an invention of the twentieth century. At the start of the century, most people were engaged in full-time, adult work activity prior to becoming sexually mature. A combination of several factors, many of them economic, changed this time-honored pattern. Affluence became increasingly prevalent in the United States after World War II. Many families no longer relied on the earnings of their adolescents, freeing young people from the need to enter the labor market. Also, labor groups attempted to restrict the labor market in order to support a higher level of wages. They pushed for labor laws setting higher age limits for entry into the labor force. Finally, the number of years of required schooling and the number of years of schooling required to "get a good job" increased, as jobs changed from manufacturing to white-collar positions. Add to these economic changes the biological factor of a decrease in the age of sexual maturation and the result, fully in place by the middle of the century, was a prolonged period in which one is neither child nor adult.

Youth became an increasingly long period, a limbo in which the individual is caught between childhood dependency and adult responsibility. From the viewpoint of parents and other adult authorities and adult-controlled institutions, youth is supposed to be a transitional period. It should be when one learns to take on adult responsibilities and is trained to be an effective participant in the economy. Many young people, however, have a different perspective. They seize the opportunity to live hedonistically for the moment and to rebel against assertions of adult authority and impositions of adult plans for them. They attempt to escape from transition and hold on to their vital and rebellious freedom.

Much of rock music can be understood in terms of the dualistic consciousness of constraint versus hedonism and rebellion. Rock is a reflection of and a response to youth's desires for freedom and the immediate goods that the independent and irresponsible life offers. Rock regards this freedom as both absolutely desirable and extremely precarious and damns the ever-present threat to it presented by any coercive routine. For example, a commonplace source of domination for adolescents is school. Rock is replete with anthemic responses to the educational system. Listen to Chuck Berry's "School Days," Alice Cooper's "School's Out for Summer," and Pink Floyd's "We Don't Need No Education." But anyone even mildly acquainted with rock music from any era will be able to name a host of songs focusing on the theme of constraint versus freedom.

Alteration in the position of adolescents has gone along with rapid social and cultural changes that have made much parental wisdom obsolete. For the first time in human history, the young can no longer rely on the parental generation to provide them with the skills, knowledge, and attitudes required to enable them to become successful adults. Breaking away from parents, rather than following their views, has become a necessity for "making it." At first this was truer for males than females, since women saw their success in terms of being wives and mothers, roles that are somewhat less affected by changing sociocultural conditions than are occupational careers. But more recently, due to changes in the labor market and the women's movement, young females have also had to confront a changing world without the guidance of parental wisdom. This growing need of all young people to break away from the family became known as rebellion.

Youth in the 1950s were termed teenagers, a word that connoted not merely age but a rebellious attitude. Rock and roll was perceived by parents and teenagers alike as a rebellious music. Racial segregation and sexual repression were a fact of the 1950s. Rock and roll, emerging from black music and featuring black performers such as Little Richard and Chuck Berry, scandalized many whites. The scandal was that white adolescents were adopting black cultural styles and black heroes. This was miscegenation, racial mixing, and was seen as a rebellious act against the dominant group. Of course, the music itself also came in for criticism. It was viewed as sexually arousing and thus grossly improper. Teenaged refusal to be proper, to go along with sexual repression, was also seen as rebelliousness.

Teenaged rebellion in the 1950s was expressed in other popular media. In movies such as *Blackboard Jungle*, with its theme song "Rock around the Clock" rock music was symbolically tied to juvenile delinquency. This outlaw view of adolescents was epitomized in the movie *The Wild One* by Marlon Brando's sneering remark to a query about what he was rebelling against: "Waddya got?" Defiance has been a constant of rock music, although its contents keep changing with developments in the wider society.

In the late 1960s, espousing the use of mind-altering drugs and opposing the government's military policies were rebellious stances. Several years later the punks, instigated by groups such as the Ramones in the United States and the Sex Pistols in England, articulated an uncompromising rebellious attitude, as in the Sex Pistols's "Anarchy in the U.K." Heavy metal came into being around 1970 and took a thoroughly rebellious stance against the dominant culture. Judas Priest, a quintessential heavy metal group, created an array of songs in this vein, including "Breaking the Law," "Beyond the Realms of Death," "You've Got Another Thing Coming," and "Screaming for Vengeance." Metal's vaunted "satanic" themes are nothing but the appropriation of the central western symbol of rebellion: Satan. Rap music's graphic pornography and mannered ghetto braggadocio also serve as expressions of rebellion.

One need only review the constant spate of denunciations of rock to confirm that these lyrical features are correctly understood as defiance. They have come from those who actually or symbolically uphold the values and/ or interests of the dominant society and culture. Parents, as individuals or through organizations that act in their name, such as the Parents Music Resource Center, speak out against rock music. Religious and government leaders have denounced and taken action against rock. The parental interest group phrases its opposition to rock in terms of its negative impact on youth. Its complaints can be read as attempts to uphold parental values and the positions of adult authority in society.

As rock and roll was replaced by rock (in the narrow sense) in the 1960s, the designation and meaning of the group of young people also changed. Teenagers were transformed into "youth." Among the reasons for this change were the arrival of the Beatles, the assassination of President Kennedy, and the growing civil rights movement. An increasingly large percentage of the postwar, baby boom generation was attending college. The upper age limit of youth increased from the teens to the early twenties. A college-based free speech movement turned into the youth-based anti–Vietnam War movement.

The change from teenagers to "youth" was not merely a matter of words. As "teenagers," young people were basically a category defined by others, though they were gaining an awareness of their distinctiveness as a group. In the 1960s youth became conscious of itself as an actor on the world stage, aware of its power. The commercial awareness and creation of a lucrative youth market helped raise the status and importance of youth in the society. Rock music was only one of the products directed at this group, which had gained a great deal of disposable income. The civil rights and antiwar movements drew the commitment of many young people, some of whom began to compose and perform their own rock music, giving vent to their special concerns. Bob Dylan's "Blowin' in the Wind," Barry McGuire's "Eve of Destruction," and Country Joe and the Fish's "Fixing to Die Rag" gave voice to youth's objections to their sociopolitical circumstances.

The transformation of consciousness was another item on youth's agenda in the 1960s. Mind-altering experiences induced by drugs began to overshadow sociopolitical concerns as youth's political ambitions were forcefully repressed by the authorities. The police riot in Chicago at the 1968 Democratic presidential nominating convention and the later killing of protesting students by the Ohio National Guard at Kent State University put a damper on political activity and led to an emphasis on more private pursuits. Rock songs lyrically exhorted their listeners to take a "journey to the center of your mind" and get "eight miles high." More significant than lyrics was the sound of psychedelic rock, represented by Jimi Hendrix, the Grateful Dead, and early Pink Floyd, among many others. Psychedelic rock is intended to simulate and enhance drug trips and is often played by and for those using illegal drugs.

The rock of the 1960s was also youth music in the special sense that it celebrated youth as such. The Who's "My Generation" expressed the self-conscious affirmation of the youth group by its members. The Woodstock Festival in 1969 was a ritual celebration of the youth community. Rock music of many different types was appreciated by a single audience. The live, mud-soaked audience at Woodstock became the symbol of youth everywhere. Rock concerts ever since Woodstock have been ritual reminders of the lost ideal of a community of youth with shared values, vitality, and social prestige and influence.

The fabled sixties receded into history sometime in the mid-seventies. With recession, Watergate, and the end of the draft, the view of youth as a single, distinctive entity lost its dominance. Its last rock gasp was John Lennon's "Imagine." Here there are no calls to action, just wistful dreaming. Adolescents split into mutually antagonistic groups, their different musical tastes becoming emblems of their separation. The keepers of rock's flame, heavy-metal headbangers and punk rockers, were not generally acknowledged to represent all youth.

In the mid–1970s *youth* began evolving into a term that signified more than a biological or a social grouping. *Youth* (especially in the sense of youthfulness) could now apply to someone of any age who upheld the values of "youth": vitality, rebellion, sexuality, and freedom to live for the moment and to reject constraint.

The easiest entry into youth in its cultural sense is to listen to current rock music or to rock from the age when youth ruled the roost, the fabled sixties. The mass media celebrate the baby boom generation's nostalgic obsession with attempting to (re)live its youth by continually playing the rock music of the 1960s. Radio calls this the classic rock format. That music and its continuation by decades-older sixties' stars is not only popular with aging baby boomers but also with the biologically young. The Live Aid Concert in 1985 can be understood as a celebration of youth in the cultural, not the biological or social, sense.

Rock music is youth music. Those who wish to define themselves as youth, whatever their age, can do so through this music. In part this identification is simply nostalgia for a golden age that never was. The music recalls the hopes that were dashed when the period of utopian assertion came to a close. But in another sense youth has been a cultural category at least since rock began. Indeed, youth in great part is created by rock music. Rock not only expresses and reflects youth but defines it. Through the music, adolescents learn how they should behave, what values they should espouse, and what complaints and desires are appropriate to them. The value of analyzing rock music is not simply to assess a controversial, economically significant, and pervasive cultural expression. Analyzing rock music also tells us about or what is meant by youth. Rock expresses youth as much as youth expresses rock. That is, rock is youth music, and youth, to a large extent, is an expression of rock.

BIBLIOGRAPHY

Betz, Carl. *The Story of Rock.* New York: Oxford University Press, 1969.

Brake, Michael. *Comparative Youth Culture: The Sociology of Youth Cultures and Youth Subcultures in America, Britain and Canada.* London: Routledge & Kegan Paul, 1985.

Frith, Simon. *Sound Effects: Youth, Leisure, and the Politics of Rock 'n' Roll.* New York: Pantheon Books, 1981.

Hall, Stuart, and Tony Jefferson, eds. *Resistance through Rituals: Youth Subcultures in Post-war Britain.* London: Unwin Hyman, 1975.

Hebdige, Dick. *Subculture: The Meaning of Style.* London: Methuen, 1979.

Lull, James, ed. *Popular Music and Communication.* Newbury Park, Calif.: Sage, 1987.

McDonald, James R. "Censoring Rock Lyrics: A Historical Analysis of the Debate." *Youth and Society* 19 (3) (March 1988): 294–313.

Martin, Linda, and Kerry Segrave. *Anti-Rock: The Opposition to Rock 'n' Roll.* Hamden, Conn.: Archon Books, 1988.

Weinsteen, Deena. "Rock: Youth and Its Music." *Popular Music and Society* 9 (3) (1985): 2–15.

———. *Heavy Metal.* Boston: Lexington Press, 1991.

Part III

Economics

11

Music as Commodity: Effect and Influence

Scott John Hammond

Popular music at its best is a form of artistic expression that enables extensive communal participation in both performance and appreciation. At its worst, it is a product of the value-neutral, leveling effects of market forces—forces that quite often impair artistic integrity and imagination and replace these diminished properties with conformity to standards set by the market rather than the musician. In the following commentary, we will consider the forces within this process, as well as their effects, and consider the relationship between commerce and music as commodity.

Human creative activity, which generates production and its discrete objects and processes, is affected by the dynamics of the general social and economic relations that human beings have shaped for themselves within the community. It can be said that both the act of production and the products of that production reflect and encapsulate the social and economic totality of a given society. A product is the result of human needs, tendencies, and desires. If the creation of the product is concentrated on the realization of genuine needs and authentic desires, or natural tendencies, the product will enable the producer to fulfill its immediate goals. Should a product be manufactured or created as a result of artificial needs, contrived tendencies, and inexplicable desires, the product may not address authentic necessity and thus may not enable the producer to fulfill its immediate goals. The distinction between products that fulfill genuine needs and those that do not can be discerned with fair ease when examining use products, for they are simply the products that allow the producer to secure the sustenance required for essential living and reproduction. Aesthetic products are more difficult to define and comprehend, for they are the work of inspiration, the result of the passion for elevation. Whether the aesthetic expression is for the sake of beauty, conscience, or rebellion, the common purpose is toward the exertion of a free, creative will that is not simply bound to the production of instrumental things for the acquisition of the means of life. The uses of art are uses of the autonomous human agent, and in its uses it aims at the ultimate abolition of living under the narrow constraints of basic necessity. There will always be a connection between the material and the aesthetic, the production for use and the production of art, and when that mode of production that is directed toward use is corrupted by inauthentic needs, tendencies, and desires, the mode of production that is directed toward the aesthetic will also be corrupted, for art cannot be treated as an autonomous realm of human creation. Music is a vital part of life, with roots in the material conditions of human beings; should the latter be dominated by a certain form of production, distribution, and consumption of goods and services, the former will also be influenced in kind by those dominant forces. In societies based on the structure and processes of capitalism, popular music that is commercially prepared for the market will also be shaped by that very structure and those very processes.

Capitalism is characterized by, among other things, a sophisticated network of exchange based on an economy that operates through sharp divisions in labor and the development of consumer dependencies. The primary unit of commercial exchange in capitalism is the commodity form, and the balance of all products that are supplied by this type of economy are commodified, receiving their principal valuation in the market. Owing to this system of valuation based on the concept of the commodity as unit of exchange, products are invested with a measure of value that is not necessarily connected to their use in sustenance and reproduction. The commodity does not address our material needs in the same way as simple products manufactured and distributed for use. Eventually, as the market becomes an increasingly important element in measuring the value of things, the essential use of products becomes ancillary, as a measure of worth, to that which a thing will command at market. This is what Marx called "exchange-value," the direct indicator of a commodity's value in commercial circulation. Genuine value and authentic need become obscured by the factor of exchange-value layered over use-value, and new needs, tendencies, and desires are present in the consumers who purchase and use the products sold as commodities. Essential human needs may not be addressed in the distribution of commodities as opposed to products; indeed, because of the creation of new needs, desires, and tendencies, the consumer becomes increasingly dependent on the objects and services intended to fulfill those contrived needs and wants. As a consumer, the individual fulfills both natural and contrived needs, but it is the contrived needs that create unnecessary, and perhaps unnatural, dependencies, dependencies that are alien and self-perpetuating because they are formed around an economic system, capitalism, that demands a high volume of consumption in order to stimulate growth through a steady increase in demand. The primary end of production is dependent on exchange, which amplifies consumption and adds a layer of superficial value that often conceals the substantive use-value of the product behind the commodity. Not how a thing can be used for human satisfaction or fulfillment but rather what the thing will command in the market: this is the shift in emphasis that separates and differentiates exchange-oriented commodities from simpler economies based on more essential human need.

Art is not immune from the relations and processes that occur within capitalism. When art and music become entrapped within the relations of commodity circulation and exchange, the functions and delights that allow us to define art in itself and independent of additional factors such as commerce become subject to possible subordination to price. Art becomes commodity, and the measure of its use becomes linked to its capacity for exchange—the price that is attached to it in the market. Hence, art for its own sake, or for the sake of conveying any sort of meaning, is altered by the presence of exchange-value. By becoming a part of the flow of commodities and receiving its primary value from the dynamics of exchange, the measurement of art may be reduced to what that art, or music, will cost the consumer. The content of the art or music may or may not suffer, yet clearly the purpose of the art is partially, if not fully, controlled by the forces of mass production and commodity exchange. Music, both within the categories of "formal," "serious," or "classical" (as defined in the broad connotation of "classical") and "popular," is included within these processes. The clearest example of the manner in which music is subject to the effects of capitalism is discerned in the production and consumption of the popular form and its various idioms. In its marketing, performance, and ultimately its credibility as an art form, popular music is deeply affected by the relations of commodity exchange.

Mass production is dependent on steady increases in demand and geared toward the expansion of profit through economic growth. Hence, production is oriented toward high consumption rather than pure use. In order to sustain the steady growth of production for profit, the degree of consumption must be accelerated, leading to conditions wherein a large portion of general demand for goods must be invented in order to ensure that consumers will maintain interest in buying and consuming commodities. As a commodity, music receives its immediate economic value from the amount of currency that it can command in the process of exchange. Music still contains its intrinsic value as art (Beethoven's "Fur Elise," Scott Joplin's "The Entertainer," John Lennon's "Imagine," and Tracy Chapman's "Fast Cars" will always maintain a substantive value as art and great music regardless of their level of popularity); yet as music becomes further entangled within the motion and meaning of business and marketing, the property of music as commodity becomes central in its creation and consumption. Popular music is largely shaped by these various forces that accelerate consumption, and in order for music to command the highest price in combination with the greatest possible volume of sales (thus leading to a bounty of profit), it must be manipulated not only as a commodity included in the market through the selling of the artist and the artist's work, but it also must surrender, explicitly or tacitly, control over its content.

Music in its popular form, by definition, is shaped by and directed to the sentiments and preferences of the people. Many composers and performers of popular music are concerned about the art, but they do not detach that concern from the need to address the general attitudes and tastes of the popular audience. Popular musicians such as Scott Joplin, Cole Porter, Thelonius Monk, and Paul Simon have been able to affirm their art with ability, integrity, and skill while at the same time reaching extensive audiences. By addressing common, popular themes, avoiding the complexities of "serious" music, and keeping their overall compositions and performances instinctively accessible, the popular artist who cares about the work can produce good music that can be easily appreciated by a broad base of listeners. Most popular musicians, if they are to succeed and endure as popular entertainers and artists, must realize the guiding perimeters that surround and define popular production. In order to maintain wide appeal, popular music must contain certain elements. For example, in rock music, there is generally a hard, steady beat played by a powerful rhythm section that is mixed forward in the performance or recording, enabling the listener to "feel" the music in the body without concentration or reflection. Instrumental mix, compositional length, vocal technique, and lyrical themes are generally defined by the structure of the form, although since the Beatles, Bob Dylan, Paul Simon, and Jimi Hendrix, some of these components have become somewhat more flexible but still remaining within the recognizable characteristics and usages of rock music. The same applies to other forms such as country or blues; both possess certain instantly identifiable features that allow the listener recognition as well as providing performers clear compositional rules. There are even subtle variations of form that communicate to the listener the use of a particularly specialized style, especially in dance music where a scarcely detectable shift in tempo and rhythmic patterns can indicate a change from one type of dance music to another, a difference that may be important enough to cause a collective exchange of dancers on the nightclub floor. Even the improvisational style of popular jazz is structured and follows a basic understanding of the elements of style needed to define the form. Above all, popular music must play to the audience and must acknowledge the rules established by the taste and judgment of the people. All categories of popular music and their various crossover combinations are in some degree dependent on the audience in ways that the "classical" or "serious" forms are not. The "serious" forms are intended to be shared, but they are shaped by standards of composition and performance far more formal, indifferent to the influences of popular opinion and tolerance and the quest for the general approval of a wide audience. This is contrasted to the popular modes, for they must eventually bow to the standards of composition and performance that will best entertain broader audiences. "Stormy Weather," "My Back Pages," "In the Mood," "Eleanor Rigby," "Stardust," and "Take the 'A' Train," for all their virtues as great music, are still basically written for the popular audience and are largely shaped by the tastes and tolerance of the popular listener.

Within the matrix of economic relations driven by the factors of commodity production and consumption, popular sentiments, preferences, tastes, and tolerance are influenced, if not largely determined, by the forces of the market. Popular music is that form of music most influenced by and connected to the attitudes and tastes of the general public, and this factor is further affected by those market forces that determine the production and circulation of commodities as such. As popular music becomes an entertainment industry for the generation of profit, this form of music has increasingly been treated as a commodity for consumption in such way that the artistic content of the art is attenuated, and in some cases vitiated. Markets depend on the circulation of commodities, and expansive markets must encourage and ensure the conditions for accelerating the rate of that circulation. Therefore, what is needed in order to sustain the growth in consumption is the creation of a product that will not only appeal to a wide market base but will move with rapidity through those markets. Popular music must satisfy as many people as possible within a specific market. One must recognize that popular forms are not always general but will be ardently embraced by a particular following in some instances. These more particular forms have such a loyal and devoted aggregate of believers that they will prove as profitable as those forms that have a more general and less intense following—a following that is not inclined toward the fanatic end of devotion. Forms such as heavy metal and gospel incongruously spring to mind, for neither commands the type of general following that we find associated with mainstream artists within other styles, such as Motown or soft country. Their disparate audiences are true believers and follow their music with a fixity and zeal rarely duplicated in less specialized styles of popular modes. Thus, the level of consumption is guaranteed and perhaps even intensified, for the true believer usually commits unbridled devotion to the article of faith or musical form of choice.

Popular music in general must, however, achieve a common denominator that will guarantee the market success of the artists if it is to continue to provide an amenable and attractive product for consumption. As a certain style appeals to "the common," it is able to generate high levels of demand for that style, a demand that is related to and dependent on an increase in volume of consumption. Volume sales require volume demand, and that style of music that expands volume will, logically, expand sales; hence, as commodity directed, the industry tailors its product to fit as many tastes as possible. The popular mainstream is created, and popular music is increasingly geared toward success in terms that are dictated by indexes such as the Billboard chart, an index based purely on sales, and is an indication of the market potential and power possessed by particular commodities. A song with a strong chart position is seen as a popular hit, a successful song—but a success that is defined by its purchase and consumption and not by its intrinsic aesthetic properties and is, therefore, treated by the industry as a commodity item that is profitable and good. Of course, it must be conceded that good music is not excluded from these commodity charts; songs such as "Hey Jude," "Bridge over Troubled Water," and "(You Make Me Feel) Like a Natural Woman" were enormously popular and artistically acclaimed; yet songs such as "Sugar Shack," "Having My Baby," and "Teen Angel" are less edifying in comparison to the former group, while still enjoying considerable popular success. The measure that is most important to the industry in these examples is the factor of sales. Naturally, the key is the need to discover and then exploit the style that will sell the most records to a wide audience over a sustained period, and this requires the creation of that common denominator of tastes that will appeal to the largest possible audience.

Differentiation that is substantive is not compatible with the fluidity of exchange requisite for a consumptive market. Mass consumption almost invariably defeats variation in production, for mass production and mass consumption tend toward the reduction of choice due to the principles of efficient, routine, uniform, and interchangeable methods of creativity and manufacture. As music becomes increasingly transformed into commodity and subject to the dynamics of mass production and consumption, the greater are the demands for a homogeneity of style upon the product itself. All music is imitation to an extent, and popular music is imitation par excellence, an imitation that is largely the result of the way that it is produced. Therefore, as commodity, music that is radically innovative is likely to fail in meeting the conditions set by the market unless the artist is a rare exception of innovation and appeal. Even when certain seemingly innovative artists extend the boundaries of popular culture, they must do so only within the fundamental principles that are developed in the style. Artists such as the Beatles serve as good examples of innovation within the popular medium. Their music deserves critical acclaim, but it still remains primarily within the perimeters of composition and performance needed to capture the general public. Songs such as "Help!" "Not a Second Time," "Norwegian Wood," "Yesterday," and "All My Loving" are fresh and stimulating because they add new musical concepts to the field while remaining firmly with the comfortable limits of the familiar and thus appealing to the public tastes. Later creations from the quartet did in fact stretch the imagination beyond the accepted norms of popular culture—songs such as the landmark "Strawberry Fields Forever," the extraordinary "Tomorrow Never Knows" (which was never a hit), and the experiments on the remarkable *Sergeant Pepper's Lonely Hearts Club Band* album (especially songs such as "A Day in the Life" and "Lucy in the Sky with Diamonds") were artistically valuable but perhaps only commercially successful as popular recordings due to the sheer force of the Beatles persona, which by that time had reached mythic proportions and afforded them the luxury of such experimentation without the risk of losing their stature in the industry. In contrast, the Thirteenth Floor Elevator, led by the innovative master of psychedelia, Roky Erickson, was unable to achieve the same degree of popular acceptance and volume of sales even though a few critics deemed their work artistically equal to the experiments of the Beatles during the same period. Even so, in spite of their popularity, the Beatles were careful, for the most part, not to alienate their listeners with dissonant modes, and in the rare occurrence when they did make such attempts, (for example, the underrated "Revolution #9"), the reception among even their most ardent following was not enthusiastic. The Beatles enjoyed a latitude of innovation because they had achieved a position in popular music that was without precedent; they could be both imitative and true to the basic components of their style but also develop new styles that served as real departures from previous forms. ("I Saw Her Standing There" is much closer to "In the Mood" or "What'd I Say" than it is to "Within You, Without You" or "Strawberry Fields Forever" or even "Norwegian Wood" for that matter.) Other artists, such as Roky Erickson or Lou Reed, could not combine innovation with the same kind of popular success. Less comfortable, more innovative, and even honest forms of popular expression are not encouraged by the industry save in the extreme case, such as the Beatles. Unless the artist can draw upon previous success, support, and sustained loyalty, respond directly to developing fads or include enough familiar popular elements of style within even the more daring music, innovation will be ignored or rejected.

The maxim of the "greatest happiness for the greatest number" combined with a uniform standard for that happiness based on simple and immediate gratification emerges predominant within the production and consumption of popular music. Music that can measure its success on the index of sales is the most successful and lucrative commodity, and its exchange value becomes the only justification for its creation. A "sure hit" or "bullet" will usually be a record that stays well within the compass of familiarity, adhering to the patterns imposed by the industry and able to gratify the public's tastes in the most general way. Some forms will be accepted by as many consumers as possible and must fit into the formulas accepted by the greatest number of consumers possible.

By pressing the envelope of its style, experimental music of any kind exposes itself to risks of rejection for aesthetic and emotional reasons; therefore, the neglect within the market is only partially based on profit concerns. Politically radical rock and militant folk music share the fate of neglect rather than blatant or intentional rejection. Protest music will always command the allegiance of the disaffected, socially conscious, and naturally rebellious. However, it will experience general acceptance only when the themes articulated are in response to growing public disturbance, concern, or outrage about a specific issue or issues or during times of intensified social flux. Abolitionist protest songs such as that which was performed by the Hutchinson quartet during the antebellum controversy, the critical folk music commentary of Woody Guthrie during and after the Great Depression, and the antiestablishment songs sung by both militant folksingers and rock bands from the mid–1960s to the early 1970s, received a level of acceptance during times of great social stress but were still unable to dominate their markets in spite of the general need for cultural articulation of social anger. Even when protest music increased in demand, only a few giants in the industry could gain and secure the volume of audience needed to generate enough sales to be considered commercially successful. Guthrie, Seeger, and Dylan became famous voices for the people against the banker, the bosses, the masters of war, and those who rob with a pen, but their success was also linked to other factors. Guthrie's music was uncompromising; he sang with a direct and trenchant voice of criticism and compassion against the injustices and hypocrisies of his day. Nonetheless, his music was well within the musical form and traditions of folk and not incompatible with the political values of American populism. Furthermore, Guthrie, for all his popularity, never achieved the mainstream status of his more popular contemporaries, and while becoming the folk music legend in American music, he remains today a somewhat diluted, even neglected figure within the mainstream of American culture. Dylan's example is more supportive of the proposition that an artist can drift toward the mainstream formula upon the ascent into popular markets. The famous "electrification" of Bob Dylan can be seen as a conscious need to gain a wider audience by employing a fashionable style, a move that risked a large percentage of the true followers among his folk and politically progressive audience, one that would result in the eventual expansion of his following and the further enlargement of his legend. Dylan, like the Beatles, is more exception than rule. For the most part, innovative or bold changes in style remain neglected by the balance of the popular music industry and its consumers, and only those who are able to draw upon other elements to expand and sustain their audiences are able to succeed and still attempt some innovation. Furthermore, one could argue that the most successful protest music tends toward abstraction rather than specifically attacking single issues. The abstract protests against "the Man" and the havoc wrought by the "establishment" fit the rebellious qualifications of successful rock and roll quite well, in much the same way that rock and roll always complained about the repressive, destructive, and "uptight" authority and morality of the older generation (the sentiments expressed in "Summertime Blues" are not that different from the supposedly radical antiwar songs that were produced in the period from 1968 to 1972). A specific commitment by an artist of stature was infrequent, and even then, rarely successful or sustained.

Neglected forms such as experimental jazz, militant folk, and radical rock at times enter the mainstream but for the most part join other forms at the margins of popular culture. Those artists who remain devoted to performing the music and preserving the tradition of the form rather than selling records at the expense of the integrity of the music remain largely at the margins of the popular market. Muddy Waters and Bob Marley have entered the lexicon of American popular culture due to their influence on mainstream musicians, as well as due to their own immense talent and performing tenacity; however, they still remain, like Guthrie and Lou Reed, pushed to the side—acknowledged as creative sources of incalculable influence but not receiving the enormous following of less artistically committed performers who may have benefited from the initial innovation and work of others. Reggae, blues, and bluegrass have enjoyed extended recognition at different times, but their loyal audiences remain confined within a small portion of the popular market. Their influence is felt in the general market in the same way experimental jazz has affected the more popular styles, and on occasion legends such as Marley will enjoy temporary moments of popular acclaim before receding back into the margins of popular culture. In terms of real popularity measured upon the paramount criterion of sales, these styles have never captured the massive audiences of less flavored or distinctive forms.

As commodity, the genuine countercultural form remains largely outside the industry and can become a part of the industry only through outside compromise and co-optation or the selective use of those elements of the countermovement that can augment the familiar and make it appear more fashionable or hip without risking the discomfort of the audience. Forms such as punk, psychedelia, and rap began at the margins of popular culture, possessing a certain integrity within the music that resisted the tendency to sell out to the popularizers with the bankroll and the glitter. If these forms do become widely popular, it is because they are absorbed into the musical industry and refashioned into a more broadly palatable product, a product that is more benign and even quaint in comparison to the uncompromising substance of the initial form. The initial integrity of the music is over-whelmed by the sheer power of the market, and the artist becomes as much a part of the pop middle as Frank Sinatra or Elvis Presley. The radical performer may try to preserve the purity of the art, but as long as the market pressures are a factor in the performance, the substance will eventually be rendered secondary to the potential market value of the music. Radical politics becomes radical chic, punk becomes contained anarchy (reminiscent of the taming of early rock and roll), experimental jazz and psychedelia become hip and fashionable, and protest song is heard through the conveyance of state-of-the-art fidelity systems within the sterile cocoons of the affluent consumer. Tracy Chapman, a composer and performer who speaks within the more radical tradition of protest music, inadvertently becomes a voice not for the disaffected, as she intended, but rather for the affected. Facing co-optation, Chapman becomes the rising star and new hero of an industry driven by the accumulation of the kind of material wealth based on the injustices that she laments in her songs. Her message, taken in small doses by the consumer, is fitted into the current fad of providing the affluent with easy and palatable methods of sympathy for the socially misfit and even vicarious atonement for the sins of luxury within the circle of the advantaged. The music is just enough consciousness raising to calm temporarily the inner tensions of the self-absorbed but not dangerous enough to force the popular audience to risk thoughts and emotions outside the familiar and comfortable.

When all economic and artistic factors are considered, popular music is, above all else, consumer music. The imposition of commodity and consumptive relations threatens to discourage free expression and cultural differentiation, and not only is there a reduction of originality and honest individuality, there is also a loss of control of the popular sound by the artist and audience as a result of the forces of the exchange market. Fashions and common tastes are paramount components of any product that is widely distributed and rapidly consumed, and by definition fashion requires a considerable amount of conformity among consumers. Fashions are established in the market based on what product will be most easily produced, circulated, and sold, and this requires the manipulation of public tastes in order to control trends to the advantage and profit of the industry. Popular music naturally contains certain limitations that provide it with clear definitions, but as the tendency toward the common denominator and the bland commodity gains strength, formulas for the music restrict popular expression within the standards controlled by the leaders of fashion—the producers in the mass industry. Popular music becomes a popular commodity, but it loses its base in the popular will and passions and is no longer popular in the true sense of the word, connoting that which is of the people. Rather than being a song of the vox populi and the natural expression of a free culture, pop music becomes another object of consumption provided to the mass in response to a need not necessarily in accord with the aesthetic aspirations and yearnings of the people. Contained within the limits of formula that are diluted by the presence of a bland common denominator that is appealing to the mass culture, the product music is sold as a business and not as an art, treated as an industry, and consumed by the purchaser as a quick means to achieve the immediate gratification of a deeper and more serious and less easily satisfied need, a need that cannot be filled through the ephemeral charms of the products offered at the top of the charts. Popular music is not truly popular, for it is no longer controlled by the populace and the artist but rather by the market forces and industry producers that determine what the listener will consume based upon the calculus of sales and profit refracted through the bending medium of fashion. Market command thereby determines how the popular culture is shaped, rather than the aesthetic needs and inclinations of the people themselves. A loss of personality ensues, and the commodity becomes a means to immerse the self through conformity to the current trend—usually a trend that may provide temporary amusement but the kind of amusement that inhibits the growth of personal experience and self-discovery in favor of mass consumption, a level of amusement that is wholly unreflective and in some ways counterreflective. This is a hollow form of entertainment, one that is used to fill the empty spaces of time and empty pocketbooks without filling or providing substance for the mind and spirit. Popular music can fill our lives when it is free to express itself authentically and in full voice, but when it becomes transformed into commodity and primarily subject to market dynamics, it loses its liberating potential and becomes just another thing that must be bought by a consumer-oriented collective. The "free" market is anything but free, for the choice is offered with variations that remain beyond the agency of the audience, and the chains of consumption command the manner and value of what is produced and sold. Market forces, rather than stimulating the development of music, actually inhibit, even repress the musical imagination, imposing acceptable standards that will enhance the music's stock in trade as an entertainment commodity. The belief that "free" markets are open and challenging to the creative producer is a myth. Some popular artists are indeed brilliant and bold enough to create quality music in spite of the market, but these cases are infrequent, and the general trend is toward the music of the banal rather than the development of human inspiration.

In *The Birth of Tragedy out of the Spirit of Music*, Friedrich Nietzsche used Apollo and Dionysus as metaphors for the animating power behind the creation of music and the Greek tragedy that concurrently emerged. In examining the spirit of music today, we must include Hermes, the god of commerce, as an additional source for metaphor. Commerce is now the force that animates the spirit of music, and it is the business of music to provide quick and accessible entertainment without necessarily stimulating the conscience or consciousness of the mind. There is little place for the serene, meditative Apollo or even the intensely passionate Dionysus in the creation of commercial music, but there is considerable room for the god of thieves. Music is industry, and the music industry as it exists today is not unlike what Paddy Chayefsky called the "boredom killing business" in the scathing and astute critique of television, mass entertainment, and commercial culture contained within his powerful and prophetic screenplay for the film *Network*. Entertainment that does not encourage the growth of art and the discovery of the human self is primarily directed to the instant amusement of bored consumers, who listen to the music without really listening, who need the easily ingested and digested music in order to fill the empty time with a noise that does not require thought, but is still temporarily capable of gratifying a very human need for some sense of rhythm and love for song. Not that all music needs to echo the highest hopes of the aesthetic consciousness, for that is a demand that can be filled by only a few great artists. The products of genius stand as clues to human meaning and the possibilities of our own transcendence and are not easily produced or readily detected. Music as commodity tends toward the direction away from such work, toward the production of a rhythm and occasionally melodic noise that, like fast food and "instant karma," offers instant satisfaction of an immediate urge without supplying substance, a consumer product that is plain, homogenous, familiar, reliable, fashionable, popular, and, when all things are considered, of little intrinsic value save for its property of killing time and filling space. "Boredom killing" is big business, indeed, in a culture that actually encourages banality, and as tastes and preferences are increasingly homogenized, the control over the production and distribution of the commodities that amuse all boredom becomes more efficient and, ultimately, more profitable. All profit is based on some investment and cost; in this case, the investment is in mediocrity, and the cost is the freely creative imagination.

BIBLIOGRAPHY

Adorno, Theodore. *Philosophy of Modern Music*. Translated by Anne G. Mitchell and Wesley W. Bloomster. New York: Seabury Press, 1973.
———. *Aesthetics and Politics*. Edited by Frederic Jameson. London: New Left Books, 1978.
Berlin, Edward. *Ragtime*. Berkeley: University of California Press, 1980.
Bindas, Kenneth, and Craig Houston. " 'Taking Care of Business': Rock Music, Vietnam, and the Protest Myth." *Historian* 52 (1) (November 1989).
Frankfurt Institute for Social Research. *Aspects of Sociology*. Preface by T. Adorno and M. Horkheimer. Translated by J. Viertel. Boston: Beacon Press, 1973.
Frith, Simon. *Sound Effects: Youth, Leisure, and the Politics of Rock 'n' Roll*. New York: Pantheon Books, 1981.
Hamm, Charles. *Yesterdays: Popular Songs in America*. New York: W. W. Norton, 1979.
Hampton, W. *Guerilla Minstrels*. Knoxville: University of Tennessee, 1986.
Harker, David. *One for the Money*. London: Hutchinson and Company, 1980.
Marcuse, Herbert. *Essay on Liberation*. Boston: Beacon Press, 1968.
———. *The Aesthetic Dimension*. Boston: Beacon Press, 1977.
Marx, Karl. *Capital*. New York: International Publishers, 1979.
Pattison, Robert. *The Triumph of Vulgarity*. Oxford: Oxford University Press, 1987.
Smith, Adam. *An Inquiry into the Nature and Causes of the Wealth of Nations*. Oxford: Clarendon Press, 1976.

12

The Development of Tin Pan Alley

CRAIG H. ROELL

"That piano sounds like a tin pan." So said journalist and composer Monroe Rosenfeld about the old, untuned upright piano being played by Harry Von Tilzer, one of many composer-publishers banging out tunes on such instruments along publishers' row on West Twenty-eighth Street in New York City. "Matter of fact," Rosenfeld continued, "this whole street sounds like a tin pan alley."[1] So was coined, according to popular legend, one of the most famous phrases in American culture. Writing for the *New York Herald* about 1903, Rosenfeld described a new era in American music publishing, a business closely linked with the piano industry. From about 1890 to 1930, during the revolutions of ragtime, the player piano, and new business structures and marketing techniques, the modern American music industry came to power, becoming dominated by New York sheet music publishers and piano manufacturers. In those years Tin Pan Alley came to define not only this business but also the style of popular music being produced and even the historical time period itself. Having such complex and significant context allows Tin Pan Alley to serve as a barometer of change in American musical and business life as the nation shifted to its modern age.

The rise of Tin Pan Alley both reflected and was influenced by the historical time in which it developed. Several trends emerged in the last decades of the nineteenth century that propelled American industry, including the music trades, into big business, trends that were primarily a response to expanding urban markets. These currents, which continued into the twentieth century, changed forever American ways of business, as well as American culture. The development of Tin Pan Alley must be seen in this context.

Cities were growing rapidly as rural populations migrated to urban areas and as immigration from abroad continued. Transportation improved considerably with the motorcar, railroads, and city streetcars. Technological innovations allowed mass production, and an increasing railroad network aided the mass distribution of consumer goods to a growing national market. To control this process more efficiently, American business adopted the corporation structure and vastly increased capital, efficiency, and production. To limit disastrous competition and stabilize production and marketing, business consolidated; industry combined, integrated, and diversified. One result was huge companies and almost monopolistic control.

Accompanying this move toward monopoly capitalism were the trends toward a wider dispersal of ownership among many small stockholders, the increasing separation of ownership and management, and the rise of a class of professional managers and salaried experts who governed the operation of a company by order of an executive committee. Alfred D. Chandler, Jr., the distinguished historian of business, has called this development "the managerial revolution in American business."[2] As part of this development, innovative advertising and marketing techniques created a new world of material options for consumers, and new products significantly eased the lives of Americans. Although not as common in the music publishing and instrument manufacturing trades as in some industries, these structural innovations were adopted in the music industry and helped transform and modernize it. This contributed to the near monopolies of piano manufacturing by a few New York firms and of popular songwriting by New York tunesmiths, arrangers, and publishers. (Certain large piano manufacturing corporations in Chicago and Cincinnati shared in this market control.)

Ultimately, industrialization and urbanization transformed American culture from a Victorian ethic that dignified hard work, creative skills, frugality, and traditional roles for women to a consumer ethic that emphasized leisure, convenience, machine production, and mass consumption and redefined the roles of both women and the home. The entire music industry, from sheet music publishing and piano manufacturing to teaching, competed with not only new commodities but a new ideology, shifting recreation away from the home and redefining social distinction, leisure time, and personal identity in terms of consumption.

Leading manufacturers in the piano trade and music publishing business developed and adopted merchandising techniques that became characteristic of this emerging culture of consumption. They sought to create desire for a product, educate and survey consumer consciousness, and present persistent and consistent sales messages to stimulate public interest in music as one of life's greatest sources of enjoyment and inspiration. But the piano and its sheet music, symbol of the toil and perseverance required in playing it, center of the Victorian home and family life, inevitably declined as this transformation occurred. Radio and the phonograph became more accessible and cheaper sources of musical entertainment. Alternative amusements, such as movies, spectator sports, and the automobile, increasingly shifted the focus of recreation outside the home. Unprecedented numbers of new material goods in seemingly endless variety competed for the consumer's attention. In other words, the piano and piano playing in the home did not decline simply because alternative amusements became popular but because the Victorian ethic in which they were so valued was being replaced by a new set of beliefs dominated by consumerism. It is against this backdrop of modernization that the rise and maturation of Tin Pan Alley took place.

In an age witnessing the consolidation of business enterprise, New York became the focus of the popular music industry by the 1890s, in both publishing and instrument manufacture, especially pianos. Thomas B. Harms, who established his firm in 1881, is considered the first Tin Pan Alley publisher, though other businesses soon followed, particularly those of Willis Woodward and Isidore Witmark (M. Witmark & Sons). Their success drew many more companies, which tended to collect in New York's theater district on East Fourteenth Street in Union Square. Prior to this development, successful publishers were located in various American cities and published a variety of music, ranging from classical and instructional to popular and religious. But these New York firms concentrated on popular music alone and employed in-house songwriters and song pluggers to manufacture, distribute, and market their products. In this respect, the music trades paralleled business developments in other American industries that allowed command of raw materials, production, distribution, and even the market itself. By 1900 most of these New York firms had moved to West Twenty-eighth Street ("Tin Pan Alley") and gained control of the popular music publishing industry in the United States.

It is no coincidence that the rise of Tin Pan Alley songwriting coexisted with the American heyday of the piano, when young people were most likely to gather around it and sing. Before the advent of radio and the high-fidelity phonograph, the piano spread music appreciation and added prestige to the home. Appropriately, as American culture modernized, as technology and urbanization made life faster paced, a new type of music developed, the first music of modern America. It propelled Tin Pan Alley to unprecedented success. It was called ragtime. Composer Irving Berlin, whose hit, "Alexander's Ragtime Band" (1911), became the most commercially successful ragtime song, asserted that the "speed and snap" of American ragtime was directly influenced by the automobile. "All the old rhythm was gone," he said, "and in its place was heard the hum of an engine, the whirr of wheels, the explosion of an exhaust. The leisurely songs that men hummed to the clatter of horses' hoofs did not fit into this new rhythm—the new age demanded new music for new action.... The country speeded up."[3]

The popularity of ragtime involved the big businesses of piano manufacturing, Tin Pan Alley songwriting and sheet music publication, and the emerging culture of consumerism. Unlike classical music, sentimental Victorian songs, or hymns, ragtime was not meant to build character or convey morality but to be consumed and enjoyed solely as entertainment. Ragtime, predominantly a piano idiom, enjoyed unparalleled success and spread across the United States and to other countries from the 1890s to the 1920s through dance bands, pianists, sheet music, and song pluggers. Several trends contributed to ragtime's novel popularity. Department stores, a decidedly modern concept in retail selling, had special areas displaying scores of sheet music and employing a performer to play the hits to customers. Tin Pan Alley publishers hired pluggers to perform new songs to the public in vaudeville houses and theaters, centers of entertainment enjoying immense and increasing attendance. These distribution and marketing innovations were momentous. Nevertheless, this was still much the way music had always been popularized—played by hand from musician to audience.

But the ragtime phenomenon was significantly aided by mechanical sound reproduction, especially the player piano (the early phonograph, though popular, was limited by poor sound fidelity and brief recording time). Chiefly written for piano, ragtime music was successfully transcribed to perforated rolls and played mechanically on the player piano and, to a lesser degree, the phonograph. It is revealing that pianos and published piano rags reached their sales peaks at approximately the same time. Ragtime and the piano were interdependent, the popularity of one spurring sales of the other. Indeed, ragtime songs became known primarily through sheet music and piano rolls but also because they were well promoted and easily consumed— artifacts characteristic of the emerging consumer ethic.

Many could not afford the luxury of mechanical piano music; others wanted to enjoy it outside the home. To solve this problem, piano manufacturers led by the Rudolph Wurlitzer Co. introduced coin-operated player instruments in the 1890s. This "nickle-in-the-slot" trade, forerunner of the modern jukebox, became a big business popularizing the tunes of Tin Pan Alley writers. Wurlitzer and the J. P. Seeburg Piano Co. remained the two largest manufacturers of these pneumatic, roll-activated, automatic music machines, placing them in bowling alleys, excursion boats, cafés, clubs, cigar stores, department stores, grocery stores, hotels, railroad depots, restaurants, ocean liners, skating rinks, ice cream parlors, theaters, bars— virtually every public gathering place. Although the coin-operated phonograph paralleled this development and was also popular, the superior technology and fidelity of automatic pianos and the entrenched industrial and cultural strength of the piano manufacturers allowed them to dominate the music recording industry until after World War I. (Significantly, the modern phonograph jukebox industry, which developed after the decline of the player piano in the mid–1920s, was virtually monopolized by the Wurlitzer and Seeburg firms.) Popularizing the songs of the Tin Pan Alley tunesmiths, the coin-piano industry grew into a big business while significantly contributing to the growth of the New York music writing and publishing industry.

Another factor in the popularization of Tin Pan Alley melodies was the invention and development in the 1890s of the motion picture. Music was vital to silent films. According to the Theater Exhibitors' Chamber of Commerce in 1921, music influenced 40 percent of attendance for good films and 95 percent for bad ones. Supplying this crucial element became big business for both the songwriting and instrument manufacturing trades. Although large metropolitan theaters used pipe organs or even orchestras, most motion picture establishments used an automatic piano designed especially for the movies. Called "photoplayers," these instruments were manufactured by nearly every coin-piano maker (Wurlitzer and Seeburg again dominating) and could supply music and special effects through perforated rolls, levers, and pedals. In addition to the tunes accompanying the silent film—producers increasingly commissioned special theme music among Tin Pan Alley writers—movie audiences heard new hits performed during intermissions by Alley song pluggers who encouraged them to sing along. If the audience liked them, sheet music and perforated roll sales soon reflected popular fancy with these new tunes.

Through these revolutionary developments, for the first time in history unprecedented numbers of people were exposed to music, and songs enjoyed unprecedented success. Yet Americans increasingly consumed music passively by listening rather than actively performing it. This trend continued into the 1920s and 1930s with the rise of the high-fidelity phonograph, radio, and sound films. Indeed, by the 1930s when motion pictures had become the most popular form of public entertainment, film companies recruited hundreds of Tin Pan Alley songwriters and arrangers. The speed with which popular tunes circulated across the nation (and indeed around the entire world) increased greatly, as did the numbers of people exposed to these songs.

Ironically, this increased speed and exposure eventually hurt the music publishing and piano manufacturing trades while helping to propel the music recording industry. Formerly (when played only by hand), a sheet music hit would sell for months as fascination with it slowly swept across the country. The new technology, especially the high-fidelity phonograph and radio, both of which displaced the player piano in the 1920s, familiarized the public with a hit song in only a few weeks and encouraged passive listening rather than actively learning to play a song. Sales of phonograph discs eventually displaced sheet music. As Tin Pan Alley matured, the industry became concerned chiefly with music recording and broadcasting rather than with publication. Indeed, E. C. Mills, chairman of the board of the Music Publishers' Protective Association, lamented that the radio and phonograph caused sheet music sales to fall by more than 33 percent in 1924 alone, and piano manufacturers witnessed declining sales so severe after 1923 that their entire industry was almost ruined. "It's that Gal in Kalamazoo don't buy sheet music," explained one Tin Pan Alley insider about this decline in amateur performing in the wake of automatic music. " 'Try this over on your piano,' " once the byword of Alley tunesmiths to familiarize the public with new songs, "is a dead slogan."[4]

This growing public preference for recorded music and the rise of the music recording industry had far-reaching legal ramifications. By law, composers received royalty payments from the publisher for sales of their copyrighted sheet music. After the advent of recorded sound, manufacturers of piano rolls and phonograph discs freely recorded songs, frequently at the request of music publishers, who were quite aware that the new media would greatly aid both the popularity and the sales of sheet music. These manufacturers and publishers, and even many composers, viewed mechanical reproduction of copyrighted music as an aid to sales, a form of advertising. This emerging music recording industry, which itself benefited from innovative corporate, managerial, and marketing innovations, became monopolized by New York player piano and phonograph manufacturers and sheet music publishers—to the virtual exclusion of composers.

By 1906, under the leadership of John Philip Sousa and Victor Herbert, the Authors' and Composers' Copyright League of America pressed Congress for a new law recognizing that composers should be paid royalties for the sale of recorded songs on piano roll or phonograph disc. After a long battle in Congress and the Supreme Court, the Copyright Act of 1909 became the first copyright law to deal with recorded sound technology. Composers thereby gained some control over the mechanical reproduction of their works and were granted a small royalty upon the sale of either piano roll or disc. The American Society of Composers, Authors, and Publishers (ASCAP) organized in 1914 and continued the fight to protect songwriters from the unauthorized performance of their music. ASCAP became a giant and practically monopolistic force working for the financial interests of publishers and songwriters, but much like a guild, its membership was restricted. The organization continued to challenge and change copyright laws as recording and broadcasting technology became more sophisticated in the 1920s and 1930s with the phenomenal popularity of radio.

With the decline in popularity of piano playing in the wake of radio and high-fidelity phonographs, the developmental years of Tin Pan Alley were complete. A major shift would then occur as the American popular music industry became more a recording and broadcasting business than one chiefly concerned with piano manufacture, sheet music publishing, and amateur performing. Although the term "Tin Pan Alley" continued to be applied to the American popular music industry into the 1950s, the phrase lost any real meaning as Hollywood, Nashville, New Orleans, and other musical centers grew in importance and as sheet music declined as the chief disseminator of musical culture.

As a musical genre, Tin Pan Alley has been widely written about; many sources offer a full discussion of this musical style so characteristic of America's early modern age. Nevertheless, several important composers and trends can be noted here. Turn-of-the-century popular songs depicted changes in American life, at least as seen by Tin Pan Alley writers. "Do not offer them anything which in subject matter or melody does not appeal to their ears," advised Charles K. Harris about the untrained musical public.[5] One of the era's most successful composer-publishers, Harris understood the formula for accessibility and simplicity in songwriting that so characterized Tin Pan Alley (as well as the new culture of consumerism). His "After the Ball" (1892) sold millions of copies of sheet music in only a few years and is representative of the first generation of Tin Pan Alley writers. Harry Von Tilzer (Monroe Rosenfeld's legendary inspiration), who claimed to have written eight thousand songs, enjoyed immense success through such hits as "A Bird in a Gilded Cage" (1900) and "Wait 'Til the Sun Shines, Nellie" (1905). Significantly, Harris and Von Tilzer became powerful in the emerging popular music business not simply because they were talented composers but because they also became innovative publishers and distributors. In an age of big business, they were also talented businessmen.

As ragtime became the rage, Tin Pan Alley writers secured even greater success, eclipsing the controversial sources of the genre. (The music originated in American black culture and was made famous by Scott Joplin's phenomenal "Maple Leaf Rag," published in 1899.) Through Tin Pan Alley—especially the Jerome H. Remick company, which issued over five hundred rags, about one-sixth of the entire published output—ragtime was mass produced and marketed much like the products of other American industries in the emerging age of consumerism. Irving Berlin, whose "Alexander's Ragtime Band" has already been noted, is among the most familiar and successful names of the ragtime era, though Berlin's long and productive career spanned virtually the entire Tin Pan Alley period of American popular song and is associated not only with sheet music publishing but also stage musicals, electronic recording, radio, and film well into the 1950s.

Following the decline of ragtime's popularity, these developmental years of Tin Pan Alley saw America through World War I, the jazz age of the 1920s, the Great Depression of the 1930s, and World War II. Many alley songwriters of this period have become cherished names in American and even international culture: Berlin, George Gershwin, Jerome Kern, Johnny Mercer, Cole Porter, George M. Cohan, Richard Rodgers, Oscar Hammerstein II, and Frank Loesser. Their music collectively represents the urbanization of American song, reflecting the cultural climate of New York, and appealing generally to middle-class, white, urban, literate Americans. In time, country music, jazz, blues, gospel, and big band music became part of the immense Tin Pan Alley repertoire in the 1920s, 1930s, and 1940s. But these styles, while appealing to a wider American audience, ended the dominance of the New York publishing district that gave the musical era its name. This diversification also marks Tin Pan Alley's modern period, characterized by recording and broadcasting concerns rather than sheet music publication.

Tin Pan Alley developed at a revolutionary time in American business and cultural history, a reflection of the culture of modernization and urbanization. New methods of business organization and marketing techniques concentrated Tin Pan Alley's power in New York and resulted in unprecedented sales of pianos and sheet music. Popular music, which may appropriately be called the product of Tin Pan Alley industry, characteristically reflects the new consumer ethic out of which it developed. Like all other products of the consumer age, they are easily accessible, short-lived, and sold in a market of intense promotion and competition in a society distinguished by an emphasis on consumers' passive use of machine-made products and immediate gratification without effort. "The Old Home Ain't What It Used to Be," expressed C. A. White in a song published early in the development of these changes. Indeed, Mr. White, indeed.

NOTES

1. Ronald L. Davis, *A History of Music in American Life*, vol. 2, *The Gilded Years, 1865–1920* (Malabar, Fla.: Krieger, 1980), p. 181.

2. Alfred D. Chandler, Jr., *The Visible Hand: The Managerial Revolution in American Business* (Cambridge, Mass.: Belknap Press, 1977).

3. *New York Times*, August 17, 1924, sec. 8, p. 10.

4. "The Ragtime Queen Has Abdicated," *New York Times Magazine*, May 24, 1925, p. 21.

5. Charles K. Harris, *After The Ball: Forty Years of Melody* (New York: Da Capo, 1987), pp. 60–61.

BIBLIOGRAPHY

Blackford, Mansel G., and K. Austin Kerr. *Business Enterprise in American History.* 2d ed. Boston: Houghton Mifflin, 1990. Excellent, readable historical overview, essential to understanding the general business culture in which Tin Pan Alley developed. Bibliography.

Davis, Ronald L. *A History of Music in American Life.* Vol. 2, *The Gilded Years, 1865–1920*, Vol. 3, *The Modern Era, 1920–Present.* Malabar, Fla.: Krieger, 1980–1981. Scholarly and informative chapters on Tin Pan Alley and much more. Instructive bibliographical essay.

Ewen, David. *The Life and Death of Tin Pan Alley: The Golden Age of American Popular Music.* New York: Funk and Wagnalls, 1964. Long the standard treatment. Though now somewhat dated, it is still rewarding reading. Appendixes of song hits; bibliography.

Hamm, Charles. *Yesterdays: Popular Song in America.* New York: W. W. Norton, 1979. A readable and excellent treatment of popular music in all periods of American history, with two full chapters devoted to Tin Pan Alley. Nicely illustrated. Several appendixes list hit songs. Excellent bibliography.

Hasse, John Edward, ed. *Ragtime: Its History, Composers, and Music*. New York: Schirmer Books, 1985. An enjoyable and scholarly collection of the many facets of the ragtime phenomenon by leading ragtime experts. Well documented, up to date, and informative.

Kinkle, Roger D., and R. McCaffrey. *The Complete Encyclopedia of Popular Music and Jazz, 1900–1950*. 4 vols. New Rochelle, N.Y.: Arlington House Publishers, 1974. Noteworthy and instructive treatment of a variety of topics relating to Tin Pan Alley.

Meyer, Hazel. *The Gold in Tin Pan Alley*. Philadelphia: Lippincott, 1958. Revealing treatment of the commercial aspect of the American popular music business.

The New Grove Dictionary of American Music. 1986 ed. S.v. "Popular Music," pt. III, "The Tin Pan Alley Era," by Charles Hamm. *The New Grove* is the best starting place for further reading on all American music-related topics. Hamm's essay is essential reading for any understanding of Tin Pan Alley. An excellent overview, well written, and broadly conceived. Superb bibliography.

Roell, Craig H. *The Piano in America, 1890–1940*. Chapel Hill: University of North Carolina Press, 1989. Traces the history of the American piano and musical culture by focusing on the interaction of the piano industry, musical education, and the instrument itself with the broader American society. Appendixes and bibliography.

13

Small Business and the Recording Industry

Martin Laforse

Autograph, Arista, Okeh, Sun, Chess, Blue Note, Commodore, Brunswick, Vocalion, Rich-R-Tone, and King are just a few of the innumerable independent record labels that circulated American popular music throughout the country and much of the rest of the world. These names are the merest beginnings; hundreds, perhaps thousands, of others graced various aspects of the music business in the twentieth century. They made significant contributions to the popularization of key styles and performing artists.

In many ways, this situation evokes Adam Smithian economic models. Many independent record companies began as the outgrowth of a music store or a furniture shop. These enterprises tended to add record sales departments most readily. Often they were located in small towns, many times in the South where black talent lay hidden from the public ear. This process often characterized the earliest days of recording in jazz, blues, and country. Later, sophisticated business operatives with considerable knowhow in the music business would record regional talent, and sometimes this output would transcend local markets.

In time, the centrifugal forces of the American economy worked to the advantage of the major companies, which would either take over the independent or lure away its major talent. A number of independents perished along the way from these and other causes. In a number of instances, particularly creative and aggressive independents pursued talent in several fields. The Okeh label, an offshoot of the General Phonograph Company, issued important discs in jazz, blues, and country. Okeh's superb talent scout, Ralph Peer, pursued artists energetically and recorded jazz and country performers in their own habitat. During field trips to several southern cities, Peer brought the work of many important artists to the public's attention.

Without the recording of African-American talent, the independents probably would not have been able to survive as long as many of them did. A few companies were black owned and operated but did not have the opportunity that afforded them a lasting place in recording history. Two all-black record companies flourished for a brief period in the early 1920s. Black Swan began activities in 1921, led by W. C. Handy and Harry Pace, and proudly asserting that all of its personnel, stockholders, and talents were black. The director of music was Fletcher Henderson, who later would lead one of the greatest of the big bands and write arrangements for Benny Goodman and others. Black Swan recorded blues artists Trixie Smith, Ethel Waters, and others and sought a wider audience by recording current pop and opera. The company floundered in 1924, and Paramount bought its assets. Black Patti, led by black talent scout and record producer J. Mayo Williams, followed Black Swan in being an all-black company. Both companies failed not through lack of imagination but because of troubles in distribution.

Okeh's heyday came in the 1920s and 1930s, and many of the recordings issued on this label helped shape the development of jazz and made a major contribution to the preservation of America's unique art form. Louis Armstrong's history-making discs with his Hot Five and Hot Seven on Okeh changed music history. His performance on such Okeh outings as "Potato Head Blues," "Wild Man Blues," and "West End Blues" remain collectors' items. These performances established for the first time the soloist as the key figure in jazz improvisation. Even before Armstrong's historic recordings of the mid- and late 1920s on Okeh, other independents had made important contributions to jazz recording. King Oliver's Creole Jazz Band is often regarded as the most significant of the bands; after leaving New Orleans, it spread the sound of jazz throughout the country. This band, led by the legendary pioneer cornetist King Oliver, toured the Keith-Orpheum vaudeville circuit from coast to coast and recorded on several independent labels, including Gennett, Paramount, and Vocalion.

In the 1920s and early 1930s, the key independent companies, in addition to Okeh, were Gennett, Paramount, Vocalion, Brunswick, Harmony, Cameo, Romeo, Perfect, Oriole, Commodore, Keystone, and Blue Note. These companies recorded an extensive catalog of jazz, swing, vocal, and instrumental blues. Fletcher Henderson, whose big band in the 1920s and early 1930s showcased a who's who of great black soloists, including Rex Stewart, Roy Eldridge, and Coleman Hawkins, recorded for Brunswick, Vocalion, and Harmony under his own name and various pseudonyms. The same can be said of Duke Ellington, who in addition to his Victor outings appeared on more independent labels than perhaps any other jazz artist. Gennett, founded in Richmond, Indiana, by the Starr Piano Company, sought out a variety of jazz and blues performers. The Wolverines, a young white group of the mid–1920s, which played widely in the Midwest and included Bix Beiderbecke, Jimmy McPartland, and Tommy Dorsey at various times, journeyed to the Gennett acoustic studios in Richmond to record. It is said that the studio lay near a railroad track, and horsemen were sent up the tracks in either direction with orders to fire a pistol if a train were approaching so that recordings would not be interrupted.

Jelly Roll Morton played an important role in race recording for Victor Records with his studio band and Red Hot Peppers. Like others, he also recorded for independents, among them Paramount, Autograph, Rialto, and Gennett. Morton also recorded piano solos of several of his greatest versions of his immortal compositions. "Wolverine Blues," "The Pearls," "Kansas City Stomps," and "King Porter Stomp" found a place in the Gennett catalog. In 1924, he recorded duets with King Oliver for Autograph, in 1926, piano solos for Vocalion, and the next year, trios with Dodds Brothers for Vocalion and Gennett.

Any perusal of a reasonably scholarly discography reveals the extent of the contribution of independents to jazz. In addition to the artists already mentioned, one finds Louis Armstrong on Vocalion and Brunswick, Sidney Bechet on Blue Note, Jimmy Blythe on Champion, Gennett, Paramount, and Vocalion, Cab Calloway on Banner, Cameo, Conqueror, Jewel, Oriole, Melotone, and Perfect, and Benny Carter on Crown and Vocalion. The historic recordings of the Chicago Rhythm Kings, which signaled the entry of whites into jazz, took place on Brunswick and Vocalion.

The first Blue Note Record Company session took place in New York in January 1939. The great boogie-woogie pianists Albert Ammons and Pete Johnson played piano duets in their irrepressible style. For almost a decade, Blue Note records featured premier jazz talents James P. Johnson, Vic Dickenson, Sidney DeParis, Sidney Bechet, Edmond Hall, and Sid Catlett. Beginning in the late 1940s, Blue Note recorded important transitional figures, players who were beginning to break out of the swing mode, like Charlie Christian, Red Norvo, Teddy Wilson, and Ben Webster.

The 78 rpm period was especially rich for Blue Note groups, which did not exist outside the studio. Sidney Bechet recorded his famous version of Gershwin's "Summertime," and as early as the third Blue Note session a group called the Port of Harlem Jazzmen recorded an extensive collection of 78 blues discs. This studio band included Frankie Newton on trumpet, J. C. Higginbotham on trombone, Sid Catlett on drums, and boogie-woogie artist Albert Ammons on piano. These constituted a major force in the jazz record market, and Bechet's "Summertime" was the first big hit the label presented. While exploring some of the as yet inchoate new thought in jazz, Blue Note continued to record established artists and turned out several 78 rpm album sets that featured the explosive cornetist Wild Bill Davidson in concert with the equally volatile Sidney Bechet in some of the hottest traditional collective jazz ever recorded. Blues pianist Art Hodes, who earlier had established a place in the blues piano tradition, waxed several sides for

Blue Note and appeared on some of the Davidson-Bechet recordings as well. His approach to the piano affected such players as Ray Charles and Professor Longhair. In the 1950s Blue Note issued sides by the soulful tenor saxist Ike Quebec, and at the end of that decade the label began issuing singles in the 45 rpm format featuring Quebec, Milt Hinton on bass, Sir Charles Thompson on organ, and J. C. Heard on drums. Quebec also acted as artists and repertoire (A&R) man for Blue Note and in that capacity brought to the label the advanced modern jazz ideas of Thelonious Monk and Bud Powell. Herbie Nichols waxed his elegant modern complexities on several Blue Note LPs in 1955 and 1956, clearly demonstrating the willingness of independents to seek out artists shunned by the more cautious majors. Nichols was an original force in jazz, off the mainstream. His Blue Note output included five LPs in sessions that included Art Blakey and Max Roach on drums. One could hardly mention two more original and important percussionists in modern jazz.

In both the 78 and LP eras, independents brought out experimental modern jazz issues that would assume a key place in the history of the music. Dial Records first recorded modern jazz featuring Charlie Parker, who also recorded on Savoy, Musicraft, Comet, and Jazztone. Miles Davis's trumpet contributed to some of these sessions. The iconoclastic pianist Cecil Taylor recorded on New World and Unit Core, Sara Vaughan on Pablo, and Ornette Coleman on Horizon. Typical of the immortal quality of many of these recordings were the Savoy, Verve, and Dial recordings of Parker, Gillespie, and Davis, which produced, among others, "Ornithology," "Night in Tunisia," and "Yardbird Suit."

Milt Gabler's vision and energy fueled the fire that produced Commodore Records. He worked in his father's electrical store, which eventually added radio and then a record department after World War I. Young Milt listened to jazz bands in his neighborhood and on the radio and became knowledgeable about the history of jazz recordings by the early 1930s. The store changed its name to the Commodore Music Shop and was located on Forty-second Street in New York. Jazz musicians became frequent visitors to the Commodore Music Shop in search of reissues of out-of-print 78 records. Encouraged by the academic scholar and jazz historian Marshall Stearns, he became involved in recruiting for Forty-second Street; many of the greatest players in several schools of jazz recorded for Commodore from the 1930s until its demise several decades later. The recordings and the jam sessions were perhaps the most intensely integrated jazz performances up to that time. In one, Jimmy Ryan's outing, the bandstand held the white players Eddie Condon, Brad Gowans, Marty Marsala, and Max Kaminsky and the black players J. C. Higginbotham, Charlie Shavers, Pete Brown, Billy Kyle, and John Simmons.

The period from January 1938 to December 1943 was an especially rich one for Commodore. Eddie Condon led off with a Chicago jazz session, and afterward a host of jazz stars recorded on the label, among them Bud Freeman, Teddy Wilson, Jess Stacy, and Lester Young (with a Kansas City group that included Basie Buck Clayton, Freddie Green, Walter Page, Eddie Durham, and Joe Jones). Piano duets between Willie "The Lion" Smith and Joe Bushkin and a Jelly Roll Morton session followed. Billie Holiday waxed a series of vocals that included the famous "Strange Fruit." Jack Teagarden, Art Hodes, Joe Marsala, and Coleman Hawkins all recorded. Lee Wiley sang for Commodore, and Joe Sullivan displayed his Chicago-style piano. Chu Berry led a Kansas City group that featured the trumpet of Hot Lips Page.

In the period from 1944 to 1945, Commodore continued to record and issue discs by most of the same artists, while adding Eddie Heywood's group, the DeParis Brothers' Band, Miff Mole, and an Edmond Hall–Teddy Wilson group to the list. This company, like Blue Note, became a part of jazz history with its historic sessions by seminal players. Also like Blue Note (although perhaps not as extensively), Commodore would record the modern jazz in the post–World War II period.

Parallel to and intersecting with jazz recordings was the recording of blues performances. Many of the same companies pioneered the genre, among them Okeh, Pathe, Cameo, Gennett, Black Swan, Banner, and Paramount. The first blues recording occurred on Okeh in August 1920 and featured Mamie Smith in the "Crazy Blues." Black women would dominate the form in this era, led by Bessie Smith, who recorded her entire output on Columbia, which paid her a flat, nonroyalty fee for each session.

The independents produced a host of great blues records. A month after Mamie Smith's Okeh session, a much bluesier singer, Lucille Hegamin, recorded "Jazz Me Blues" for Arto Universal Records. This company issued six of Hegamin's discs in the following year. In these early days Emerson, Pathe, Perfect, and Gennett also put out female blues singers' discs. It would be an unusual company that did not have an outstanding black woman blues singer under contract. Black Swan recorded Alberta Hunter's plaintive "How Long Sweet Daddy, How Long?" which helped pull the company out of the red.

Paramount challenged Okeh's dominance with issues featuring Alberta Hunter, Lucille Hegamin, and the signing of Ma Rainey, who, after Bessie Smith, was perhaps the most important blues singer. The 1924 Paramount catalog named her Mother of the Blues, and indeed she had tutored the young Bessie Smith. Over the next seven years, her records would prove to be perhaps the most popular of their time. Other Paramount blues stars were Sippie Wallace and Victoria Spivey. Although most blues singers continued to be women, men began to edge into the field, and Paramount enjoyed success with Papa Charlie Jackson and the reknowned Blind Lemon Jefferson. Paramount also turned up Blind Blake, Son House, and the legendary Charlie Patton. Although it remained the one blues company that refrained from field trip recording, preferring its Chicago studios, Paramount developed several subsidiary labels, which put out cheaper discs and tried a number of merchandising ploys, including a mail order service and putting Blind Lemon Jefferson's likeness on his records. Paramount continued to keep abreast of the times when in the late 1920s the more urban style of blues emerged. Yet when the depression hit, the company failed.

Vocalion tried to broaden its market by advertising "cleaner race records," an effort to back away from the historic double meanings that had marked some blues lyrics. Talent scout Mayo Williams brought two famed artists to Vocalion—Georgia Tom Dorsey and Tampa Red. It was Dorsey who wrote and recorded "Its Tight Like That." Georgia Tom also recorded for Gennett's cheaper Champion and Superior labels. These artists appeared on the Perfect race label in the mid–1920s after a merger that produced the various labels put out by the American Record company. In addition to Tampa Red and Georgia Tom, ARC garnered Big Bill Broonzy. The agglomerate of labels also put out country and jazz.

In the early 1930s, blues- and jazz-oriented independents began to fall at an alarming rate. American Record Company restricted blues to one label, Perfect, and devoted the others to pop and hillbilly. Warner Brothers, busy buying up music publishers for its forthcoming musicals, also acquired record companies, among them Brunswick.

In 1923 over a dozen independents contended in the blues market, but in the ensuing eleven years, failures, mergers, and takeovers narrowed the field. By 1931 the blues market was down some 20 percent, and by 1932 that figure was halved again. In the weeding-out process, Cameo, Crown, Gennett, Harmony, Pathe, and Paramount went under. Gennett failed at the end of 1934, and by the next year, only three companies remained. Decca bought up several independents, and by 1938 CBS had purchased companies put together in previous mergers. Urban blues styles were prominent by the mid–1930s, and sales rose, but by then majors and their subsidiaries dominated the field. The 78 era came to an end with an oligarchy of companies controlling the market.

The post–World War II period saw more black movement to the urban areas outside the South. Out of this experience came a harder, stronger, and more insistent sound that reflected anger, hope, and assertiveness— rhythm and blues (R&B). The Atlantic label signaled the way in its R&B recordings by the irrepressible Louis Jordan and his Tympany Five and the big hit, "Is You Is or Is You Ain't My Baby?" Guided by Ahmet Ertegun, Atlantic would have a long career in various forms of popular recording.

The catalysts for the new music were the transplanted black southerners. In this environment, the recordings of B. B. King, James Brown, Little Richard, Ivory Joe Hunter, Willie May Thornton, Esther Phillips, Cleanhead Vinson, and T-Bone Walker, all of whom first recorded for independents, sold handsomely. After 1950 Los Angeles emerged as a major center of rhythm and blues recording. Among the independents flourishing in the city were Modern, RPM, Specialty, Swingtime, Hollywood, Imperial, Art-Tone, and Big Town. Chicago was home to over fifty companies, some which issued discs on several labels. Muddy Waters left Mississippi and brought to his new home and updated version of Delta blues, which was a concoction of many influences. His colleague, the stand-up bassist Willie Dixon, contributed to the Chicago recording tradition as composer, A&R man, band leader and record producer. Most of his work would come out under the independent Chess Label, and both Muddy Waters and Howlin' Wolf recorded a number of Dixon's blues songs on Chicago-based Chess. Houston and Detroit rivaled Chicago and Los Angeles as blues playing and recording centers. The great Lightin' Hopkins was a Houston man and recorded some of his greatest numbers on Arhoolie, Imperial, Modern, and Aladdin. John Lee Hooker, who had traveled north from Mississippi in search of war work, lived in Detroit and performed there. He was a major figure in urbanizing the country blues, which he had ingested from Charlie Patton and Blind Lemmon Jefferson. He helped bring the hard, amplified sound to the blues, and he recorded on a number of labels under a variety of pseudonyms. Among the independents that marketed his records in this way were Fortune, Chance, DeLuxe, Modern, King, and Savoy.

The R&B experience seemed to help certain independent companies when they turned to rock. The independents' low overhead would prove to be an advantage over the majors in the mid–1950s rock era. Many small companies fell by the wayside in the transitional period, and the survivors fled in the direction of rock. Independents aggressively sought out new artists and, aided by less sales pressure, took chances with untried talent.

While Chicago retained its pivotal role in independent activity, new cities came to the fore. Nashville, Cincinnati, and Memphis played key roles in the rock revolution. Several rock historians contend that the majors played a relatively small part in recording rock and that most of the important recordings came from independents. Precursors like Otis Blackwell, Ray Charles, and Bobby Bland, originators of soul sounds that enriched rock, plied their music on labels like Duke and Davis. Blackwell, in particular, had a significant influence on Elvis Presley; several of Presley's early discs reveal an almost note-for-note aping of Blackwell's stylings.

As in the other genres, certain enterprising individuals made all the difference in shaping and popularizing the new music—pop, R&B, or rock. Berry Gordy, Jr., Colonel Tom Parker, and Brian Epstein come immediately to mind. Gordy's family moved to Detroit from Georgia, and there the young man made his impact as a songwriter. Most important, he founded the Motown agglomerate of labels and in the process became one of America's most accomplished black businessman. A clever organizer, Gordy launched both publishing and recording enterprises and a talent agency as well. His Motown enterprise put out a series of labels and pioneered the new rock and roll sound outside the South. Gordy recorded the Miracles and Mary Wells on Tamal and Motown. Gordy was fortunate; Detroit offered a harvest of recordable singers and musicians. It was Motown that made a successful soloist of Marvin Gaye, whose vocalizing included a distillate of successful past styles. Again the housing projects, which yielded up the Supremes, gave forth with the Temptations.

The Motown recordings thrived not only on generous Detroit talents but also as a result of Gordy's insistence on recording material designed to appeal to the teenaged market. Thus, a kind of musical blending took place in Detroit. Gordy's taste and business acumen allowed him to outlast many of his independent contemporaries. Eventually Motown surfaced a series of labels, which included Tamal, Gordy, Motown, Soul, and V.I.P. The product came to be called the "Detroit sound," and the youth of the nation literally danced to it. In the early 1960s, the combined Motown labels produced an incredible number of Top 20 hits.

It was a Supremes solo assignment on Motown that made a star of Diana Ross. Among the stars who also first recorded for Gordy's enterprises were the Four Tops, Martha and the Vandellas, Ivory Joe Hunter, the Andantes, and the Marvelettes. This innovating company with its limited studio technology nonetheless produced the work of Junior Walker, Kim Weston, and perhaps above all, Marvin Gaye, Stevie Wonder, and Gladys Knight and the Pips, a truly astonishing catalog.

Of all the era's independents, Motown was probably the most well administered. Moreover, unlike other labels, it continued to sponsor the careers of their youngest singers as they matured. This enabled Stevie Wonder to make the transition to adult-oriented artist. Motown remained resolutely independent in the face of increased pressure from the majors who were taking over other labels. If, for example, Atlantic fell under the direction of Warner, Motown continued its waxing of increasingly popular black artists, who now achieved popularity with the wide American audience— white as well as black. Eventually a series of troubles beset Motown; key producers left, some artists began to waiver, and legal suits ensued. Still, the company persevered by finding talent and sensing the new directions of popular taste.

In 1970, Gordy moved his company to Los Angeles, and from that base Diana Ross, Marvin Gaye, and Stevie Wonder continued to grow in critical and popular success. During this period, Stevie Wonder recorded his famous one-man band recording in which he played all of the instruments, and the Jackson 5 first appeared on the label.

What Motown was for Detroit, Chess was for Chicago and King for Cincinnati. Chess and King were the most important Midwest labels. Chess was the 1947 brainchild of the Chess brothers, Leonard and Phil, and was known as Aristocrat until 1949. Their roster was like Motown's—a who's who of recording artists in several pop fields. Willie Dixon became in-house musical adviser and wrote rhythm and blues songs for Howlin' Wolf and Muddy Waters. At Chess, doo-op surfaced, and a heartfelt soul feeling emerged. Electrification also set a mode for an increasingly strident urban blues sound. Chuck Berry, whom many critics think set rock on a new road, recorded "Maybellene" in 1955. Other premier music acts recorded on this label and its subsidiary Checker were Sonny Boy Williamson, John Lee Hooker, Bo Diddly, Gene Ammons, and the groups Flamingoes, Moonglows, and Monotones.

King, one of the most successful independents of the 1950s, came out of Cincinnati. Founded in 1944, King produced major rhythm and blues artists like Tiny Bradshaw, Lucky Millinder, and Earl Bostic. Vocalists Bullmoose Jackson, Eddie Cleanhead Vision, as well as the country singers Moon Mullican, Cowboy Copas, Grandpa Jones, and the Delmore Brothers recorded on King. The Platters, a 1950s music group, Otis Williams, Johnny Guitar Watson, Hank Ballard, and the Rockets also cut wide-selling discs for founder Syd Nathan.

Of all the independents that launched careers, none outdid the success of Sun Records, which promoted the music of the most important figure of his time, Elvis Presley. Rock and Roll success continued to elude most majors in the mid- to late 1950s, but the Presley sound broke open the southern white market. Presley's fusion would be called rockabilly and country rock in some quarters, a term denoting the blending of southern country with black blues. No other white artist effected so telling a meld as did Presley. Like other independents, Memphis-based Sun was the creature of an entrepreneur, Sam Phillips, who worked the rhythm and blues and rock genres. Beginning in 1953, Sun issued recordings by Junior Parker, Little Milton, and, on its Phillips International subsidiary, Charlie Rich. Memphis soon became a center for ambitious new talents. Carl Perkins's recording of "Blue Suede Shoes," which would also be a Presley hit, made the Top 10 charts in 1953. Johnny Cash waxed his smash hits "I Walk the Line" and "Folsom Prison Blues." More than most other independents, Sun featured a house full of stars and potential stars, but, as was often the case, it lost key people. Johnny Cash and Carl Perkins, for example, moved to Columbia. Still among the riches were Jerry Lee Lewis, who outdistanced other Sun artists. But in 1960, when he departed for Mercury, Sun began to fade.

While Sun seems to have been the prime source of country rock, it was not alone. Chess, King, Specialty, and a number of southern regional independents issued country rock and other forms of contemporary pop. Excello Records in Nashville began as a subsidiary of a gospel label and was among the first to issue blues in that music city. Country's Eddy Arnold recorded for Excello, as well as the country rock group the Crescendos, who were Top 10 hit makers. Imperial Records recorded Fats Domino in New Orleans, and in Houston Duke-Peacock featured rhythm and blues and gospel with "Gatemouth" Brown and Willie Mae Thornton. Duke subsidiaries in Memphis put out Bobby Bland and Junior Parker discs. Ace Records of Jackson, Mississippi, experienced some success in rhythm and blues and rock and roll in the local region. A paradigm example of this was a Clovis, New Mexico, lounge owner who in 1956 financed his own recording studio in that town near the Texas border. Both Roy Orbison and Buddy Holly were born there, and the latter would make his first test pressings for the entrepreneur Norman Petty. Eventually Dot and Roulette issued hit discs on license from this small enterprise.

In the 1960s, more recording output came to be centered in cities. Philadelphia became an important music city, with Phil Spector's Phillies label, recording what was coming to be called soul, Ike and Tina Turner, and the Righteous Brothers. Chubby Checker, a late 1950s rage, surfaced on another Philadelphia label, Cameo. Disc jockey idol Dick Clark, also quartered in Philadelphia, plunged into the record business with part ownership of several labels, among them Hunt and Jamie, which produced rhythm and blues and rock. Roy Orbison, after failing to sell well on Petty and Phillips, turned to Nashville's Monument Records in the early 1960s and sold well. Monument executive Fred Foster engineered a new packaging for Orbison's vocal properties, and success was immediate. Nashville, long the home of the Grand Ole Opry, was about to emerge as the premier music city, and it was fast becoming a major location for singers, musicians, arrangers, and agents.

Los Angeles became the site of flourishing independent record labels after 1945. The list was a formidable one. Alladin, Challenge, Imperial, Exclusive, Excelsior, Specialty, Modern, Liberty, Dot, Era, Dore, Keen, and Demon surfaced there in the postwar era. Even firms that established themselves elsewhere tended to open California operations, as Motown did.

Country and western as popular music emerged with post–World War I recording and radio. Neither factor can be overestimated. The Grand Ole Opry and National Barn Dance were merely the best known of the evening radio programs, which increased the listening audience for country and western or, as it was originally known, hillbilly. Brunswick, Paramount, American Record Company, Vocalion, and Gennett were particularly active in pioneering country music recording in the 1920s. In 1928 Brunswick recorded the East Texas Serenaders, whose style grew out of an itinerate fiddling tradition. Their typical all-string band featured banjo, guitar, and fiddle. As conditions changed, country instrumentation would shift, as jazz did. Late in 1929 Paramount entered the country market with a song recorded under the name of the Martin Brothers, which depicted the massacre of striking workers in North Carolina. Much of the so-called hillbilly material would tell a story, in the grand folk-minstrel tradition. Gennett debuted with Bradley Kincaid's "The Fatal Wedding." His career also followed one of the main paradigms of country careers. Born in the Kentucky mountains in an environment saturated with old-time songs, he moved to Chicago in the 1920s to work in a YMCA. Proximity soon led him to broadcast on the National Barn Dance over station WLS, which led to a recording contract.

From the 1930s on, independents recorded some of the greatest figures in the idiom as they had in jazz and blues. Gene Autry in 1931 recorded "Silver-Haired Daddy of Mine" for Vocalion and, in 1933, his famous "The Last Round-Up" for Conquerer. These were his first big hits and helped launch his fabled career in Hollywood and on radio. Like many others, Autry came from the Oklahoma-Texas region and had worked on the railroads, although he would be billed as "The Singing Cowboy."

Both the American Record Company and Crown issued important country records in the early 1930s. Karl Davis and Hartfort C. Taylor, National Barn Dance radio stars, recorded an early prison song for American Record Company, which was subsequently issued simultaneously on its various labels. This same company also issued the Carter Family's first outstanding hits, "Can the Circle Be Unbroken?" and "Gospel Ship." Crown issued a disc by the Georgia Wildcats, an important early string band that exemplified the southeastern style.

But no independent was more active than Vocalion in the mid–1930s. In 1934 the company issued discs by the Callahan Brothers, a leading southeastern style duo and, in 1935, Patsy Montana's well-known "I Wanna Be a Cowboy's Sweetheart." Her Vocalion efforts marked the first major hit for a solo woman country yodeler and opened the door for others. Vocalion recorded western swing in the mid–1930s, first with W. Lee O'Daniel and his Light Crust Doughboys and later with the leader in the field, Bob Wills and his Texas Playboys. The latter's "Steel Guitar Rag" set a style and made the Wills's approach, which included the introduction of soloists, characteristic shouts, and moans of "Aha," familiar to country fans everywhere. Wills's band exemplified a real feeling for jazz and included creditable jazz solos by trumpet and sax and recorded genuine blues and jazz materials, including Bessie Smith songs on Brunswick as early as 1929.

The interfacing of jazz and country was a particularly southwestern phenomenon. Wills's group also featured improvisation and under the influence of Charlie Christian and T-Bone Walker introduced electrified guitars. Wills's groups were the most famous of all southwestern swing musicians. They loved the blues, and in 1941 Okeh, by then directly under the control of Columbia, issued their greatest hit, "San Antonio Rose." So acceptable had country become to the wider audience by then that Bing Crosby also recorded a hit version of the tune.

The American Record Company stayed with more traditional performers and in 1936 recorded Roy Acuff and his Crazy Tennesseans' huge hit, "Great Speckled Bird." Acuff's background was paradigmatic and included Baptist church going, listening to country records, and singing in medicine shows and on radio. Eventually, like other outstanding country artists, he appeared on the Grand Ole Opry.

As was the case with blues, hordes of southerners moved north and west during World War II to work in war industries. They carried with them a nostalgia for home and for their music. Cincinnati's King Records capitalized on the situation and in the 1940s recorded Grandpa Jones, "Eight More Miles to Louisville," a traditional Kentucky song. Cowboy Copas, Moon Mullican, Clyde Moody and the Delmore Brothers, Tennessee Ernie Ford, Merle Travis, and Red Foley also made discs at King during this period.

Independent companies did not slacken their efforts in the postwar period. In fact, those that featured country proliferated. Among them were Gold Star, Marcy-Abbott, Four Star, Dot, Folkways, Imperial, Pep, Sun, Monument, Zero, Tally, Event, Vanguard, Old Homestead, Rick-R-Tone, Rebel, Starday, and Sonora. The list of country artists who in the 1940s and 1950s first recorded for independents is a long and honorable one. Texas farmboy Jim Reeves first surfaced on Macy-Abbott; quite typically he would later gain fame with the Grand Ole Opry and sign with RCA Records. The Maddox family's incipient rockabilly appeared on Four Star, as did Patsy Cline and Jimmy Dean. Cline's recordings set the pace for updated women country singers, and she too went from Grand Ole Opry to a contract with Decca Records.

Okeh's Ralph Peer, who had played an important role in jazz and blues, also pioneered country recordings. He was the first to make field recordings of newly discovered talent; in June 1923 in Atlanta, he recorded Fiddlin' John Carson's "Little Old Log Cabin in the Lane." Peer discovered and recorded Jimmie Rodgers and the Carter Family. Accompanied by recording technicians, his field trips in search of talent took him to Ashville, Dallas, Bristol, and St. Louis, where he would consult local scouts and advertise for music makers in local newspapers. Peer's efforts constituted nothing less than the beginnings of commercial country music, and he was soon joined by other scouts representing both majors and independents.

A number of the earliest country recordings graced independent discs. Okeh recorded Ernest Stoneman, and Vocalion waxed Uncle Dave Macon. Women country singers followed. Loretta Lynn recorded her first disc, "Honky Tonk Girl," for Zero and Dolly Parton, the poor mountain woman from a churchgoing family of thirteen, recorded for Monument and Goldband. Buck Owens first recorded for an independent, Pep, before moving to Capital. Bluegrass singer Mac Wiseman recorded on Dot in Nashville in 1951, and Merle Haggard followed in the same city in the early 1960s for Tally with the chart-making hit, "Sing a Sad Song."

Two subcategories of country music deserve special mention for the important role the independents played in their popularization. Honky-tonk and bluegrass signaled new directions in country and reflected underlying social and geographic shifts. Honky-tonk became widely popular in the 1950s and dominated the jukebox trade. As a musical form, it borrowed heavily from western swing, the blues, jazz, and even Hawaiian music. Honky-tonk bands avoided drums but made extensive use of fiddle, string bass, piano, and the all-important electrified pedal steel guitar. The lyrics reflected the frustration and anger of the displaced in a bewildering new urban locale. At a time when country music was beginning to appeal to the wide American public, honky-tonk remained closest to the feelings of the dislocated southern working class. The lyrical scene was usually the tavern, and the songs highlighted an environment of dancing and brawling. Pastoral images were absent. The new themes expressed the anguish of the rural-to-urban migration. The uncertainties of love, marriage, and work contrasted with the escapist joys of drink-oriented good times. If much of the feeling was escapist, guilt and morose self-pity also dominated lyrics. As in the case of the not-unrelated rock music then emerging strongly, honky-tonk also included strikingly louder volume, perhaps necessitated by the noise level of bars. Technological adaptation in the form of electrification facilitated this upturn in volume. Web Pierce, Tammy Wynette, and George Jones, in particular, caught the spirit of the times.

In contrast with honky-tonk, bluegrass constituted an attempt to move back to the roots of the country music tradition. Unexpectedly, it seemed to catch something of the sixties zeitgeist, since one of its chief appeals was to the hip college students of that time. In fact, this audience also produced some of its important performers. In line with sixties traditions were the numerous bluegrass festivals that sprang up in many parts of the country. Leading figures in the movement included Bill Monroe, Flatt and Scruggs, and the Osborne Brothers. At first the major record companies showed little interest in signing with these artists and their cohorts, opening the way for independents to fill the vacuum. In came a host of labels: Country, Rebel, Rural Rhythm, Rounder, Sugar Hill, Rich-R-Tone, and Old Homestead, to name a few that recorded significant material. Companies like King and Dot also entered the field. As in other genres, some companies endured; some did not. Starday Records proved to be the most active producer in this field. Originally a Texas company, it moved to Nashville in the 1960s. The Stanley Brothers, who used a mandolin-guitar lead style similar to Monroe's, recorded for King and Rich-R-Tone in the late 1940s before moving to Mercury. Scruggs-like bluegrass musician Jesse McReynolds recorded for Kentucky Records in the early 1950s and then signed with Capital. In the ensuing decades, the pattern persisted. Outstanding bluegrass artists recorded first for independents and then signed with majors.

The story of independents is a fascinating one from the point of view of business, art, popular culture, and social import. In rock, blues, jazz, and country, the independents invariably brought new talent and new styles to the fore when the majors held back. In any collection of historically important recordings in any of these fields, independent recorded work occupies an important and even central place.

BIBLIOGRAPHY

Balliett, Whitney. *American Musicians: Fifty-Six Portraits in Jazz.* New York: Oxford University Press, 1986.

Collier, James Lincoln. *Louis Armstrong: An American Genius.* New York: Oxford University Press, 1983.

Curtis, Jim. *Rock Eras: Interpretations of Music and Society.* Bowling Green, Ohio: Bowling Green Popular Press, 1987.

Dixon, R.M.W., and John Godrich. *Recording the Blues.* New York: Oxford University Press, 1988.

Gelatt, Roland. *The Fabulous Phonograph: From Edison to Stereo.* New York: Macmillan, 1965.

George, Nelson. *The Death of Rhythm and Blues.* New York: Pantheon, 1988.

Gillett, Charlie. *The Sound of the City: The Rise of Rock and Roll.* New York: Pantheon, 1983.

Malone, Bill C. *Country Music U.S.A.* Rev. ed. Austin: University of Texas Press, 1985.

Oakley, Giles. *The Devil's Music: A History of the Blues.* London: Taplinger, 1976.

Schuller, Gunther. *Early Jazz: Its Roots and Musical Development.* New York: Oxford University Press, 1968.

Whitcomb, Ian. *After the Ball: Pop Music from Rag to Rock.* New York: Limelight, 1986.

Williams, Martin. *The Art of Jazz: Ragtime to Be-Bop.* New York: Oxford University Press, 1981.

—— *14* ——

The Business of Popular Music: A Short History

Patrick R. Parsons

Among the most successful rock groups of 1990 was a marketing phenomenon known as New Kids on the Block, a creation of record promoter Maurice Starr (aka, Larry Johnson). Starr assembled the New Kids in 1984 hoping they would be *the* new teen idols, and with a combination of hard sell and savvy promotion, the group was soon generating more than $400 million annually. Most of the money, as much as 80 percent, came not from record sales or concert tours but from merchandise licensed by the group: clothes, toys, key chains, lunch boxes, bed sheets and pillow cases—almost anything with space for a picture or a logo. The group's recording company, MCA records, was one of the corporate giants that dominated popular music, and its marketing division, Winterland, designed the New Kids products with a particular audience in mind, girls aged nine to fourteen. The typical preteen fan could spend her money on up to three hundred different New Kids items, according to one Winterland executive, who added, "and she wants one of everything."[1]

The New Kids represented an extreme example of what constitutes success in the music industry: sales. Most groups are not "manufactured" in the same manner as New Kids or the Monkees and do not start out intending to become simply commodities, but unless they eventually perform like successful commodities, no group will last in the *business*. The word is emphasized because popular music industry is, and always has been, first and foremost, a business enterprise.

In 1989 it was a nearly $6.5 billion business, and close to $20 billion internationally. Like many other large industries, the recording business is controlled by a handful of companies. The six majors are CBS, Warner, Polygram, RCA Arista, Capitol/EMI, and MCA, each part of a larger media conglomerate. CBS is owned by Sony Corporation; Polygram is part of the Dutch electronics giant, Philips; RCA/Arista is owned by the European conglomerate Bertelsmann; Capitol is a division of the British corporation, Thorn/EMI; MCA records is a division of the larger MCA Corporation; and Warner Records is part of the largest media company in the world, Time-Warner, Inc. Finally, many of the smaller labels most people see on their albums and tapes are only corporate subdivisions of these firms. Columbia, Epic, Atlantic, A&M, Geffin, Mercury, and the legendary Motown are but a few examples.

To understand popular music, then, it is necessary to understand the popular music business. The keys to this understanding include an appreciation of the economic structure of the industry, the organizational process by which records are selected and promoted, and the philosophies and motives of the businessmen (there are few women executives) who make the decisions.

Depending on what one includes under the rubric rock 'n' roll, the category accounts for anywhere from 35 to 50 percent of all record sales. The closest competitor is country and western, with about 13 to 15 percent; classical provides only about 5 percent of total sales. The industry, in other words, is largely driven by rock. While one might suspect that the birth of rock 'n' roll in the mid–1950s is a reasonable starting point for the discussion of music as a business, one should actually look back much further.

It was just before the turn of the century that a number of New York City music publishers began doing something that had not been done on any significant scale before—writing music for money, creating music as one would create toothpaste or snow tires, on demand and for a profit. Most of the music enjoyed by the American public until then was classical, folk, or popular tunes that had been in circulation for many years or written as a side business by people in other areas of the music industry.

The increase in leisure time and prosperity that accompanied the industrial revolution meant greater demand for music, musical instruments, broadway shows, vaudeville, and so forth. Bright entrepreneurs realized they could make money by writing and publishing sheet music for this expanding market. The music was not necessarily a means of giving voice to any personal experience or an attempt to communicate something of cultural or social importance. It was designed to sell, and so it was designed to appeal to a mass audience.

The business that engaged in producing and buying the rights to the new music concentrated in an area of New York that soon came to be known as Tin Pan Alley, for the cacophony of sound emanating from the music offices. In 1912, these publishers formed the American Society of Composers, Authors, and Publishers, or ASCAP, to serve as a collection and distribution service for the growing music royalties, something that would later become critical in the record business. The Tin Pan Alley "product" was sheet music, however, not records.

Invented in the late 1800s, records started to become serious business around the turn of the century. The first record companies were Columbia Phonograph Record Company and Victor Talking Machine Company. Columbia sold Thomas Edison's round cylinders, and Victor sold the competing flat disk technology. Patent agreements between the companies and the inventors helped establish the early dominance of the two firms, and their subsequent organizational size helped them maintain it; business acumen soon eclipsed technical prowess in the race for market share. Through the 1910s and 1920s, the industry prospered.

Hard times came to the business in the late 1920s and 1930s, however. The introduction of radio meant people could receive music for free, rather than having to buy records, and the depression meant that people had little money for records or record players. The sales of both collapsed. In 1921 some 100 million records were sold in the United States; by 1932 the figure was 6 million.

The entire industry came close to folding; only jukeboxes helped maintain a trickle of sales. The two major companies weathered the storm only through their absorption by the radio networks; in 1928, RCA bought Victor, and in 1938, CBS bought Columbia. Small record companies, the minor labels, which had begun to succeed in areas of specialty music such as hillbilly and race genres in the 1920s, were wiped out or purchased by the majors. Only one company, U.S. Decca, rose to success in the 1930s, and it only by cutting the price of its records below that of its competitors. But the musical diversity that accompanied the rise of the minors in the 1920s disappeared. Product lines contracted. The folk, ethnic, and country or hillbilly musical forms were eliminated or radically restricted. Only the lucrative mass appeal material, the show tunes and big band material, remained.

The specialty genres did start to make a comeback near the end of the 1930s, but World War II brought another contraction as shellac, the principal component in making the 78 rpm disks, became a rationed material. Popular music remained relatively narrow in scope through the depression and World War II. Only with the end of the war did the business begin to expand, although in ways no one would have predicted.

The birth of rock 'n' roll and the formation of the modern billion-dollar record industry were the products of a confluence of technical, social, and economic forces that surged together in the late 1940s and early 1950s. Television, which had been put on hold during the war, was unleashed on an innocent and unsuspecting public. Hesitantly at first and then in stampeding packs, radio shows—the dramas, comedies, mysteries, and soap operas—abandoned radio for television. Radio relied more and more on records for cheap programming. Large amounts of playtime on the radio eventually came to be critically important to the success of a record and therefore was lusted after by the record companies. But music publishers, the ASCAP group, were much less enthusiastic about radio. The ASCAP members historically had made their money from the sale of sheet music. For the publishing industry, music played on the radio meant music not played at home. When people stopped playing the piano and started playing the radio, sheet music sales dropped. ASCAP's long-standing remedy was to charge the radio stations for the use of the music, but as royalty fees went up, so did the friction between ASCAP and the radio industry. It came to a head in the late 1930s when the radio stations decided to boycott ASCAP music and set up their own licensing organization, Broadcast Music Incorporated (BMI). Since ASCAP had a virtual monopoly on most of the popular music of the time, BMI was forced to go to the musical fringes for material. BMI "rediscovered" country and western (hillbilly music), various forms of folk music, and rhythm and blues.

The economic prosperity that followed World War II and the discovery in Germany of audiotape provided the capital and technology for small record companies to record this type of nonmainstream music. And BMI itself supplied funding for some of the new labels. Unknown talent and use of just a few musical instruments meant no need to pay large sums of money for big band musicians and well-known performers.

Furthermore, as the radio stations began playing these records, a newly affluent generation of teenagers, with radios in their cars, began listening. In the early 1950s, the new rhythm and blues, country, jazz, and popular genres began to fuse and grow in popularity among the young. In part because of the nature of doing business in the record and radio industries, rock 'n' roll, the product of this fusion, was born.

In the early 1950s, six majors controlled the record industry: RCA/Victor, Columbia, Decca, Capitol, MGM, and Mercury. Research has shown that the four largest majors (Columbia, RCA, Decca, and Capitol) accounted for more than 70 percent of all hit records between 1948 and 1955, and the top eight firms controlled more than 90 percent.

But the majors were hesitant to get into rock 'n' roll. In each company, an artists-and-repertoire department (A&R) determined which artists would be developed and released, and at the head of each department was a single, powerful executive. The few A&R men who controlled the music selection at these companies were personally resistant and sometimes even hostile to the new sounds, and professionally they felt it lacked the mass appeal of their staple product, the show tunes and popular music of artists such as Perry Como, Mitch Miller, Dinah Shore, and Rosemary Clooney. Rock was considered an unfortunate cultural fad and an economic risk. While the major companies signed the early rock 'n' roll stars, the proved money makers, it was left to the smaller labels to generate new talent. Elvis Presley, for example, began with Sun Records. Sun's owner, Sam Phillips, sold the contract to RCA for $40,000 and used the money to develop new acts, such as Jerry Lee Lewis.

As a result, the number and diversity of record labels and companies expanded radically through the early 1960s, breaking down the dominance the majors had held over the industry after World War II. By 1963, the top four firms accounted for only 26 percent of the year's Top 10 hits, and the total number of record labels making the Top 10 had increased from ten in 1951 to fifty two.

The rock 'n' roll boom of the late 1950s hit a slump in the early 1960s. Many of the stars fell from the sky: Elvis joined the army, Little Richard went into the ministry, Buddy Holly was killed in a plane crash, Chuck Berry was convicted on a morals charge, and Jerry Lee Lewis was disgraced when he married his teenaged cousin. The replacements—artists such as Fabian, Bobby Darin, and Chubby Checker—failed to capture the earthiness of their predecessors and the excitement of the fans.

The possibility that the majors had been correct about the rock 'n' roll fad was not to be borne out, however. The mid- and late 1960s saw a resurgence of rock, led in large part by the British invasion. The Beatles, the Rolling Stones, and a host of other British groups joined U.S. acts such as the Beach Boys in southern California and the acid rock groups of the Bay Area to demonstrate the purchasing power of a new generation. Sales soared, and rock finally caught the profit-oriented eye of the major record companies. The idea that a single artist could regularly sell 2 million records or more, as did these groups, was something new in the business. In 1967, for the first time, records sales surpassed $1 billion. Recognizing the growing youth culture and the money it was willing to spend on music, the majors began entering the field. Rock historian Serge Denisoff marked the "summer of love," 1967, and the Monterey Jazz festival of that year as the start of a kind of feeding frenzy among some of the majors to acquire new talent. The infusion of interest and capital quickly began paying off.

While the majors' share of the market in the early 1970s remained significantly below that of twenty years earlier, they were beginning to reassert their monetary muscle. By 1973, the top eight firms again controlled more than 80 percent of the Top 10 hits of the year, and they were spending significant sums to maintain their edge. In 1971 Neil Diamond was given a Columbia contract guaranteeing $400,000 per album, and in 1972 Elton John signed an $8 million deal with MCA. These deals acted, the companies hoped, as insurance against the risks being taken with the unknown groups that also were being signed, groups that only promised to achieve star status. In fact, the reliance on a few acts to bring in most of the profit for a record company was, and is, a hallmark of the industry.

According to most accounts, only about 15 percent of all the records released actually turn a profit. The small percentage that do make money must support the company and the losers. The problem, of course, is that no one ever knows which 15 percent will become hits. This business reality has been the source of a variety of industry practices designed to cover the bet. Companies may try to steal established acts from competitors. Denisoff, for example, noted that James Taylor, Bob Dylan, the Rolling Stones, and the Beach Boys were all lured away from Warner by CBS.

Getting an act is only the first step, however. In the late 1960s and 1970s, many companies spent lavishly on promotion and advertising. Since the days of Tin Pan Alley, it has been axiomatic that the road to success in the record business is paved by promotion—the process of getting people who count to listen and endorse the music. Getting airtime has been crucial; radio station programmers (disc jockeys and program directors) must be convinced first to listen and then to play the record. As of 1981, getting the video on television has been of equal or greater importance. Without airplay, radio, and television, the chances that a record will make it are slim. Getting the record industry and popular press to take notice is also essential. Press kits, press parties, and press conferences are part of the process.

While it is the job of the A&R departments to find and develop the musician, group, or singer, it is the job of the promotion, publicity, and marketing arms of the corporation to get it sold. They are charged with everything from arranging newspaper advertisements and television interviews to assembling the T-shirts, the buttons, the fliers, billboards, coffee mugs, and skywriting—anything that can serve to get out the word about the act. And all of this costs money.

Lavish catered press parties running to tens of thousands of dollars were not unheard of in the 1970s. According to critics, the spending went beyond necessary promotion and into extravagant indulgence of the acts and the industry executives themselves: multimillion dollar contracts, chartered jets, and postconcert limousines stocked with freshly chilled champagne and various exotic imported refreshments. There was, in short, a great deal of free spending in the 1970s. But in 1979, the bubble burst; the party was over and the hangover had arrived.

The industry suffered a small slump in the mid–1970s but rebounded quickly. Sales went from 533 million units (singles, albums, and tapes) in 1975 to a peak of more than 726 million in 1978. In 1979, however, the bottom dropped out of the market; sales went into a tailspin for the next four years, falling to a low of 550 million in 1982. There were a variety of explanations for the "crash of '79."

Part of the problem was a general economic recession; people had less money to spend on records. The industry also placed a great deal of the blame on record piracy—illegal home or factory duplication of tapes. Why buy an album when you can make a tape copy of a friend's disc, or tape it off the air when a radio station played a new release in its entirety (a practice that had record industry executives screaming and pounding on tables)? The industry estimated losses from illegal taping at more than $1 billion in 1983. There were other problems as well.

With a few significant exceptions, such as Michael Jackson and Bruce

Springsteen, the superstars who drove the industry and accounted for the 15 to 20 percent profit rate failed to materialize. Instead of a large stable of hit makers, the industry was living off disco, considered to be faceless, manufactured dance music. Very few new hit groups were associated with it; the Bee Gees and Village People were among the few exceptions. And like the musical *Grease*, disco turned out to be a short-lived—and somewhat controversial—fad. Some critics went so far as to hold disco responsible for "killing" popular music in the late 1970s. Some said good rock 'n' roll simply was not being made, and teenagers were taking their money to the new videogame parlors instead. There was probably some merit in all of these arguments.

Thoughtful observers saw an additional, deeper problem, however. Denisoff pointed out that demographic changes constituted a fundamental business dilemma for the industry. Simply put, the rock audience was getting older and losing interest. The baby boomers, that national demographic bulge that constituted the rock audience of the 1960s and 1970s, were aging. Many of the acts that did sell well were ten and fifteen years old, such as Fleetwood Mac and Paul Simon. It was difficult for new groups and new music to get national exposure. The traditional outlet for such work, the album-oriented (AOR) or progressive radio stations, refused to play it. The stations were forced to cater to the demographics of the older, and more affluent, audience, the target of radio advertisers.

The results for the industry were dramatic and unpleasant. Some majors were financially hard pressed by multimillion-dollar star contracts made years earlier. There were massive cutbacks and layoffs. CBS fired more than three-hundred people and closed nine branch offices; among the casualties were nine vice-presidents. Many of the independent labels folded. The days of champagne press parties, chartered jets, and wear-once-then-toss promotional T-shirts were gone.

Some companies exacerbated the problem by cutting back on the development of new talent, maintaining only the older, more established (and more expensive) stars. A general malaise came over the industry as it struggled with problems of talent, demographics, and money through the early 1980s.

In the summer of 1988, *Business Week* did a cover story on the popular music industry entitled "Now Playing: The Sound of Money." The industry had recovered, and explosively. Sales were up on the order of 10 and 20 percent over the previous year, and companies such as RCA and MCA were having the best year in their history. What happened?

The answer lay in a combination of technological and marketing changes. One of the most critical was the recapturing of the younger audience, which was made possible by the blossoming of cable television and the success of the music video, or, to put it simply, MTV. The suggestion by some observers that MTV literally saved the music industry probably overstates the case, but there is no question that the Music Television Channel had a profound impact on the industry, as well as the culture.

MTV began in 1981 as a joint venture of Warner Amex Corp. and American Express. The stated intent was to capture the twelve to twenty-four-year-old market segment, which had been raised on television. Because they were more readily available, many of the early videos used by MTV were European. Television was a more common vehicle for record promotion there, especially in Britain, due to the lack of privately owned radio outlets.

The result was the exposure of a previously neglected audience to a previously underpromoted music. Videos were credited with introducing new groups such as Men at Work, Stray Cats, and Human League. MTV was bringing into the industry both new music and new music consumers. As more homes connected to cable and to MTV, the power of music videos to sell records became increasingly clear. The initial MTV audiences were relatively small, but the viewers proved to be energetic record buyers. Even companies that initially refused to supply videos to MTV, such as Polygram and MCA, quickly saw the wisdom of getting their groups on the music channel. By the mid–1980s, music videos were an essential part of the music industry and MTV a dominant force in the business.

While MTV helped prime the money pump by generating fresh talent and fresh customers, the industry did not rely on the new teenaged audience alone. The lessons of the magazine industry, the cable television industry, and a wide variety of consumer products industries in general were too clear: The conception of the consumer audience could no longer be restricted to the notion of a national, uniform, mass market. The potential market for popular music, as for most other consumer goods, was broadening in a global dimension and fragmenting in taste and demographic dimensions.

The multinational character of the majors already positioned them to take advantage of the expanding international market. Bertelsmann's purchase of RCA in 1986 provided expanded U.S. markets for the German firm's existing international coverage. Sony's $2 billion acquisition of CBS Records signaled the seriousness of the Japanese company's global intentions. In 1990, in fact, CBS opened offices in Eastern Europe to take advantage of the markets opening up in those emerging capital economies.

At the same time, the majors began refocusing their product lines to deal with the increasing diversity in consumer taste that was especially prominent in the postrock generation. Record companies began buying into market niches that previously would have been considered too specialized, such as new age music, college or alternative rock, and various forms of international music, including artists from the Caribbean, South America, and Africa.

As part of this process, the majors began acquiring the smaller, more specialized labels. Polygram bought Island Records, known for its reggae library, for some $280 million, and for $500 million it also purchased one of the largest and most successful independents, A&M Records. In one of the more dramatic buyouts, Motown records was purchased for $61 million by MCA.

The majors also entered into deals with independent music distribution companies. In 1990, CBS purchased 50 percent of Important Records Distributors and its specialty labels. Such distributors and labels traditionally focused on smaller groups (and smaller sales). CBS saw it as a way of tapping into the specialty market and providing a kind of farm club for the development of new talent. Some of the industry giants began buying music publishing companies to solidify their hold on the product and squeeze more profit from each song.

The trends, in short, included accelerating concentration of ownership contrasted with accelerating diversification in product. Market diversification meant more than just greater heterogeneity in the music; it also meant parlaying successful acts through an array of merchandising schemes made possible by the conglomerate nature of the companies. The New Kids example is only one of the most extreme illustrations of cross-merchandising. Younger teenagers and preteenagers have growing disposable income, several billion dollars worth, and the corporations that own the major records companies are well situated to take advantage of those resources. *Batman* was one of the best examples of conglomerate marketing that included a record division. In its comic book form, Batman was owned by DC comics, a subsidiary of Time-Warner, Inc. The heavily promoted film was released by Warner Bros. film company, and the music by Prince was released on Warner Records. *Batman* artifacts—the lunchboxes, T-shirts, toys, and games—were licensed through Warner. All told, *Batman* generated more than $500 million for Time-Warner, Inc.

Technology also is playing a significant role in the business. Consumers increasingly find, sometimes to their surprise, that the one thing they cannot buy during a visit to the local record store is a record. The familiar black plastic disc is being phased out, replaced by compact discs (CD). The industry shipped about 341 million records in 1978; by 1989 that figure had dropped to 34 million. CDs offer superior sound and durability. But with about 80 million turntables in the United States and fewer than 15 million CD players, many consumers view the displacement of records as a bit hasty. Some record store owners sympathize but point out that record companies are discouraging the sale of plastic. The majors no longer accept returns on unsold albums, as they had historically, and new releases are being made available only on CD or tape. According to the industry, it is market demand that has prompted the accelerating phase-out, but some critics suggest additional motives. The higher quality of CDs is bringing older customers back into the market, and industry research shows that people who buy a new CD player subsequently purchase an average of thirty

CDs within the year. In addition, consumers are no longer satisfied with the quality of their old albums and have begun replacing their entire libraries with CDs. All of this has meant a frenzy of new buying for the industry. Sales of CDs more than doubled between 1987 and 1989, from 102 million to 207 million units, and they accounted for nearly one-third of all recording sales in 1989. The sales of albums, meanwhile, dropped from 107 million to 34.6 million in the same period.

In addition, whereas the record companies made about a dollar on every record album sold, the increased price of CDs means the companies make about two dollars per disc. Given these figures, it is not surprising that the old 45s and 33s are quickly becoming collectors' items.

The 1989 sales year saw a slight slowing in the growth of the industry, but the trend was still steadily upward. Total unit sales increased from about 762 million to 800 million and dollar value sales went from about $6.2 billion to $6.5 billion domestically. New talent, new products, new marketing strategies, new technologies: the business of popular music looks promising once more, and for the industry, as always, that is the bottom line.

NOTES

1. Sherryl Connely, "Manufacturers Know When to Target Kids for Products," *Centre Daily Times* (State College, Penn.), September 30, 1990, p. 6E.

BIBLIOGRAPHY

Chapple, Steve, and Reebee Garofalo. *Rock 'n' Roll Is Here to Pay*. Chicago: Nelson-Hall, 1977.
Denisoff, R. Serge. *Solid Gold: The Popular Music Industry*. New Brunswick, N.J.: Transaction Books, 1975.
———. *Tarnished Gold: The Record Industry Revisited*. New Brunswick, N.J.: Transaction Books, 1986.
Frith, Simon. *Sound Effects: Youth, Leisure, and the Politics of Rock 'n' Roll*. New York: Pantheon Books, 1981.
Frith, Simon, and Andrew Goodwin, eds. *On Record*. New York: Pantheon Books, 1990.
Gillett, Charlie. *The Sound of the City: The Rise of Rock and Roll*. New York: Pantheon Books, 1983.
Hirsch, Paul. "Sociological Approaches to the Pop Music Phenomenon." *American Behavioral Scientist* 14 (1971):371–88.
Jansen, David. *Tin Pan Alley*. New York: Donald I. Fine, 1988.
Lull, James. "Popular Music: Resistance to New Wave." *Journal of Communication* 32(Winter 1982): 121–31.
Pavletich, Aida. *Rock-a-Bye, Baby*. Garden City, N.Y.: Doubleday, 1980.
Peterson, Richard A., and David Berger. "Cycles in Symbol Production." In *On*

Record. Edited by Simon Frith and Andrew Goodwin. New York: Pantheon Books, 1990.

Rothenbuhler, Eric, and John Dimmick. "Popular Music: Concentration and Diversity in the Industry, 1974–1980." *Journal of Communication* (Winter 1982): 143–49.

Stokes, Geoffrey. *Star-Making Machinery.* Indianapolis: Bobbs-Merrill, 1976.

—— *15* ——

Taking Care of Business: The Commercialization of Rock Music

GEORGE M. PLASKETES

Elvis Presley wore a ring with a lightning bolt and the letters "TCB" imprinted on it. It meant "Taking Care of Business." Perhaps more than any other popular culture figure, Elvis and his image—whether in solid gold, velvet, rhinestone, black or blue suede—became the embodiment of commercialization. To a younger generation who did not grow up listening to Elvis or experiencing his liberating impact on American culture, he represents nothing more than a registered trademark, and Graceland stands as a ripoff.

Yet the jewelry that fit Elvis has also been worn by the music industry. The TCB logo not only became a symbol for Elvis's career but foreshadowed the direction rock music would take. Over four decades, rock has evolved into a billion-dollar industry and the most recognizable U.S. export. By 1990, TCB was no longer limited to a record's unit sales, hit singles, and radio airplay. Rock's commercial sprawl includes highly organized world tours, videos, merchandising, multimedia marketing campaigns, and corporate sponsorship. The dollar signs pointing to the magnitude of rock's economic growth are widespread. Consider that in 1969, the highest paid performer at Woodstock—the Jimi Hendrix Experience—received $18,500, a sum that is mere pocket change when compared to the Rolling Stones's earnings for their Steel Wheels Tour thirty years later, estimated at $85 million. During the 1980s, rock stars dominated *Forbes Magazine*'s Top 40, an annual list of entertainment's top earners. Michael Jackson, *Forbes*'s financial first, appeared ready to give Elvis a run for the money with an empire built around the biggest selling record of all time, *Thriller* (35 million units), an unprecedented million-dollar advertising deal with Pepsi, and his $47.5 million purchase of the rights to the Beatles song catalog.

And Elvis? He is still selling, with the commercialization reaching immense proportions. As one critic put it, "Elvis has made more personal appearances than any dead person since the Virgin Mary."[1] It even became possible to charge a plastic Elvis on the Elvis Mastercard—"Live like a King . . . in Elvis We Trust."

Since its inception, rock music has been one of American culture's most exploitable artifacts. The commercialization of rock has been an inevitable process—a creeping, clinging, controlling, consuming, controversial, constant companion to the music through its stages of formulation, maturity, stylization, and more stylization. The evolution of rock into a big business illustrates the basic economic principle of supply and demand. As rock developed as a form and its audience grew, the music industry grew to accommodate it.

Through much of rock's initial period from the mid–1950s through the 1960s, the emphasis was on the music, its artists, and the youth culture, with its own vision, vitality, voice, and values. By the 1980s, rock's audience expanded with constant additions of new teenagers, as well as older fans from the previous two decades who were now adults into their thirties and twenties. As it evolved into a mass, the rock culture lost much of its shape and became increasingly fragmented and absorbed into mainstream culture. Whereas the 1960s was a rebellious period, the 1970s, widely characterized as the "Me Decade," brought normalization and a collective turning inward. Woodstockian ideals and gestures of defiance were parceled into individuality and adult success stories. Consciousness shifted from backpacks, bands, and protest banners to briefcases, button-downs, and bank accounts.

Rock music accompanied youth in its redirected focus from community and counterculture to career and commodity. Although hints of rock's commercial potential lie in earlier festivals such as Monterey Pop, it was not until the early 1970s that entrepreneurs recognized the opportunity to reach an unprecedented number of people with music and to make money, maybe even get rich, while doing it. Music became a product—a commercially viable item to be packaged, promoted, merchandised, and marketed. Rock musicians, unable to sustain their 1960s' role of missionary in the commercial world, became "professionals." Middle-class youth enjoyed new levels of affluence, a reflection of rising parental income, and rock's audience channeled much of its discretionary income into music.

Signs of the increasingly sophisticated business surrounding rock quickly emerged. The music industry began to approach its product as a series of alternatives, or choices, to offer its consumers. Record companies stereotyped artists and categorized their music for marketing purposes—folk, country, rock, disco, reggae, punk. This demographic strategy was also employed by radio stations; the primary programming practice became formating—targeting a specific audience with a certain type of music. Other economic indicators could be seen in record sales. During the previous decades, a record was a hit if it went gold (500,000 units sold), whereas in the 1970s there were multiplatinum (million) sales expectations attached to big hits. And the spontaneous gatherings, festival scenes, and events such as Woodstock and Altamont evolved into efficiently organized concert tours, with major acts performing in stadiums and arenas rather than muddy farm pastures and dusty speedways.

Rock's widespread commercial conversion had begun. During the early 1970s, the music industry grew at a steady rate of 25 percent annually. By mid-decade, music had established itself as the most popular form of entertainment in America, surpassing sporting events and movies. Rock critic Dave Marsh suggests that the music industry itself may have been the biggest star the 1970s created, as the business of music had become more potent than any of its parts. During his 1979 Rust Never Sleeps Tour, Neil Young could be seen dwarfed by oversized amplifiers, instruments, and stage props—a visual expression of Young's belief that the music business was bigger than its performers.

The industry's star, however, soon faded. Increased costs, declining sales (widely attributed to home taping), and an undeclared war with radio over programming and promotion plagued the music business by the early 1980s. A revenue decrease from $4.31 billion in 1978 to $3.52 billion in 1982 had a devastating impact on the artist-business relationship. As production costs increased, record companies, almost totally dependent on proved superstars, were less inclined to invest in marginally commercial acts; nor would they push hard to break new ones because of cutbacks in promotion. "Most radio these days sounds like AM radio in the late 1950s and 1960s," said Peter Wolf. "You're basically getting the Top 20, and that's it. Unless you have a hit single, the visibility and airplay is not there, which makes it harder for new groups and groups trying not to be commercial. It doesn't change, because radio stations are corporately owned and into highly competitive ratings. They all adhere to formulas that are safe rather than taking certain chances and dropping behind."[2] Standards also changed, and there were soon distortions other than those on Neil Young's Rust stage. "Suddenly records were judged not on their artistry—or even whether they're hits— but on their chances of putting the machinery back into gear," wrote Marsh in his State of the Music Industry address in January 1980. By the 1980s, rock had become a marketplace dominated by entrepreneurs who were united by their financial focus on product units sold. "Almost nowhere, and from no one, does anyone presently feel a sense of reaching," observed Marsh. Critics lamented the loss of community and a commitment to unconventional values, which were replaced by competitiveness in the industry. Many felt that spontaneity and creativity were lost to stylization, structure, formula, and routine. "In the process it has become easier for businessmen and behind-the-scenes manipulators to structure their approach to merchandizing music," argued producer Jon Landau.[3]

MTV's arrival in 1981, coupled with the superstar successes Prince, Michael Jackson, Bruce Springsteen, and Madonna a few years later, led to the record industry's economic recovery. Despite the widespread optimism, some ills lingered, and others were masked by the industry's revitalization. Music video may have forged a valuable new aesthetic, but it hardly represented a music renaissance. There was still little experimentation on any front as artists and record companies, now committed to video potential and imaging, were reluctant to explore new musical directions. The primary focus remained on the safest formula and easy marketing. Any departure from the norm was likely to be deemed risky business, taken as an affront rather than a challenge, and discouraged because it was not sellable. "There is an environment in which music can live and breathe, and right now the environment is suffocating," said U2's Bono Hewson.[4]

Critic Jon Pareles labeled the process taking place in music "Rock Reaganomics," as the richest part of the record business pulls rapidly away from the smaller companies: "Don't look for independent labels in the Top 200 without a magnifying glass. Apparently record companies aren't willing to take many chances on unexposed music. Just as in the supply-side economy, nothing trickles down from the top.[5]

A friend from Nashville recently called and said he had spotted Steve Forbert with his twin sons, Sam and Dave, in a pizza parlor parking lot. He said Forbert looked quite haggard and world weary. The description was not surprising, considering what Forbert had been through as a musician during the 1980s. Forbert is one of those critically acclaimed, medium-level acts who became a victim of Rock Reaganomics. Pronounced *Alive on Arrival* (his first record) in 1978, Forbert's debut brought claims of his being "the next Bob Dylan," a seemingly annual industry designation for some folkie with a harmonica. Forbert's next three records could not establish a suitable aesthetic direction for him or, more important, generate enough sales to keep his label happy. In 1984, Columbia refused to release his fifth record. For the next six years, Forbert lived a musician's nightmare, touring the small club circuit while tangled in the music industry's web of producers, managers, lawyers, and record companies. "It was terrible; a no-win thing," said Forbert. "Record companies can put you in something called 'suspension,' which means time is going by, but not by their clock. Your hands are virtually tied. You learn that it's all a big working engine and you've got to have a record to fit in that engine. It's the way things are handled in this rat race/snake pit they call the music business."[6]

The cut-out bins steadily expanded with the deleted catalogs of labelers' artists who, like Forbert, found themselves in record company limbo, shopping demonstration tapes with hopes of signing a new deal. The casualties of commerce were not limited to new acts or critical and cult favorites such as Forbert, Warren Zevon, T-Bone Burnett, and the Roches. Even established artists, several whose careers spanned twenty years, became economic exiles. In July 1984, one of the industry's largest companies, Warner Brothers, dropped thirty artists from its roster, an unprecedented housecleaning that included stars Van Morrison and Bonnie Raitt.

The released were based on the company's financial return for its investment in an artist. Morrison, always one to sing his own song, commented, "I'm not a rock star. I'm not playing their game. If I can't be myself, retain my own dignity, then whether I have a wider audience doesn't matter. The record companies don't accept me because I haven't laid down and said 'I give up, manipulate me.' "[7]

For most of the artists, there was life after label limbo. Forbert returned from his six-year suspension on Geffen Records with *Streets of This Town* (1988). Morrison quickly signed with Mercury/Polygram; Zevon, after a five-year absence, joined Virgin; and Burnett, though he continued to record (on Columbia), also produced records by Marshall Crenshaw, Los Lobos, Peter Case, the BoDeans, Elvis Costello, Jerry Lee Lewis, and Roy Orbison.

The most ironic chain of events involved Bonnie Raitt. She signed with Capitol, and her *Nick of Time* (1989) not only won four Grammys but reached number 1 on the charts. As a classic example of taking care of business in a flash, the opportunistic Warner quickly got around to cashing in on its ex-artist's success by releasing a twenty-song collection from Raitt's nine-album, fifteen-year association with the label.

The artist-business relations became a legal issue involving Geffen Records and Neil Young. In June 1984, Geffen filed a $3 million suit against Young, claiming he produced two "noncommercial" records for the label—the techno (synthetic computer sound) *Trans* (1982) and the retro-rockabilly *Everybody's Rockin'* (1983). Geffen alleged that the two records were "uncharacteristic" of Young's earlier work; the company wanted "Neil Young records." Young appeared surprised and somewhat amused by his record company's legal action. "That was confusing to me because I thought I was Neil Young. But it turns out that when I do certain things, I'm not Neil Young. Well, to get sued for being non-commercial after twenty years of making records, I thought was better than a Grammy," said Young.[8]

Geffen would be hard pressed to find tangible evidence to build a case for the prosecution against Young. As an artist, Young has been difficult to classify, having been more committed to musical exploration than to any one style. It was difficult to determine what was a "characteristic Neil Young record." Young's catalog of works, dating back to the Buffalo Springfield in the 1960s, is a collection of fragments that wanders the spectrum between folk/country strumming and power chording. Young's 1980s records might best be characterized as a series of stylistic extremities that moved from heavy guitar work to synthesizers and computers, to rockabilly, to country, to rock, to brassy blues. The stylistic progression understandably frustrated Geffen and alienated many of Young's followers.

Considering David Geffen's reputation for providing a supportive environment for his artists and his friendship with Young's manager, Ellit Roberts, a lawsuit seemed as extreme as Young's musical directions. The company's stance appeared to be motivated by fear as well as confusion. If the record-buying audience did not accept or allow Young creative license to experiment, a sharp decline in sales was inevitable. By Geffen's standards, the "characteristic Neil Young records" were works comparable to Young's most commercially successful and widely accessible records: *Harvest* (1972), *Comes a Time* (1978), and *Rust Never Sleeps* (1979).

Young, who, like Morrison has been uncomfortable with commercial and mainstream acceptance, viewed his musical exploration as part of a natural, inevitable progression as an artist. "Sure, I can do this over and over for a while and that would be the easy way out," said Young. "Financially, I'd have everything I wanted because the idea business-wise, is to go with a winner. But even more than the money and everything, I hate being labeled. I just don't want to be anything for very long."[9]

Geffen eventually changed its mind about putting Young on trial; both sides reached a tentative compromise. Following further contractual conflicts and artistic differences, the strained relationship ended in a presumably mutual separation, and Young returned to his original label, Reprise. "They didn't look at me as an artist, they looked at me as a product, and this product didn't fit their marketing scheme," said Young.[10] On his final record for Geffen, *Life* (1987), Young gets in a few parting shots at the label and "record company clowns" with the garage anthem, "Prisoners of Rock and Roll." And it may have been vengeance more than irony that Young's recent Reprise records, *Freedom* (1989) and *Ragged Glory* (1990), are his most commercially accessible and critically acclaimed records in years and more like the "Neil Young records" Geffen had been hoping for through the 1980s.

By the 1980s, the Age of Aquarius had become the Age of Acquiringness; the Woodstock Nation was the Pepsi Generation. Yippies, who decades earlier were rebellious youth trying to make sense of the world, became yuppies—adults focused on making cents in the business world. Money became the long hair of the 1980s, and music was a means of making money. "Making it in music is lucrative on such a humongous scale compared to ten, fifteen, or twenty years ago," said promoter Bill Graham. "The video is sold, there are sponsorship deals, tours, and merchandising income. The peripheral income is enormous."[11] The Steel Wheels Tour is an obvious example of the multidimensional commercial complex Graham speaks of. It is estimated that ticket sales brought in over $100 million, with merchandising, averaging $10 a person, adding $32 million. Another $8 million came from miscellaneous revenue, including sponsorship deals with Anheuser Busch, a Showtime pay-per-view special, and merchandise sold in stores like J. C. Penney and Macy's. At the pretour press conference, the Stones scoffed at the suggestion that they were doing it for the money.

Music's machinery had expanded into an elaborate exposure network. Music, video, and film embraced one another and increasingly explored the potential for cross-promotion of their products as records, movies, and videos all were marketed to sell one another. This multimedia marketing concept, labeled synergy or symbiosis, came to signify an increase in each medium's effectiveness. The symbiotic relationship between music and film, which dates back to the 1940s, was particularly noticeable in Robert Stigwood's *Saturday Night Fever* in 1977. The Stigwood strategy was to release segments of the soundtrack to promote the film. The Bee Gees–dominated soundtrack sold over 22 million units, 850,000 of those prior to the film's release in December 1977. This marketing strategy was widely used in 1980s film and music as hit singles were released weeks, and sometimes months, prior to the accompanying film's premiere. Video joined this marketing marriage to form a lucrative triangle when MTV arrived as a new avenue of exposure that embraced both film and music. By mid-decade, the money-making combination of movies, soundtrack, and video was firmly in place. The chart action and box office receipts for *Flashdance*, *Top Gun*, and *Purple Rain* were shining examples of the synergy formula operationalized.

The commercialization of rock was so immense that by 1987 it appeared that money was beginning to overshadow the music. Several top bands, concert promoters, and merchandisers made more money than ever. Merchandisers alone sold $250 million worth of T-shirts and rock paraphernalia, a total that is nearly two-fifths of the $650 million spent on concert tickets. At many shows, merchandise exceeded ticket sales. In October 1987, a record $17 per fan was spent on merchandise at a Bon Jovi concert in Worcester, Massachusetts. During the tour, the band changed T-shirt designs three times because repeat business was so strong. "In the mid–1970s, the magic number was one dollar a head," said Dell Furano, president of Winterland Productions, the biggest American music merchandising company. "Today, it's eight or nine dollars a head."[12] For many bands, that means sales of $100,000 a night, with superstar acts easily in the millions.

The number of people who get a piece of the pie contributes to the inflated costs of merchandise. The $18 a concert goer typically pays for a T-shirt is divided between the artist (32 percent, or $5.76), the merchandising company (12 percent, or $2.16), and the venue (38 percent, or $6.84). The shirt itself costs $3.24, which accounts for the remaining 18 percent. Most acts earn from 25 to 37 percent of the gross, or between $5.50 and $6.66 for each shirt sold. Superstars like Springsteen and Madonna, who routinely receive multimillion-dollar merchandising advances, can command from 40 to 45 percent, or $7.20 to $8.10 per shirt. The American concerts on Springsteen's Born in the USA Tour earned him nearly $7 million from merchandising alone.

Rock merchandising is not a 1980s phenomenon. Not surprisingly, that too, began with Elvis in the mid–1950s as his manager, Colonel Tom Parker, sold programs, song books, and glossy pictures of Elvis. In the 1960s there was Beatlemania, complete with bubble gum cards, lunch pails, and wigs, although the group lost millions because so many unlicensed products were sold. Through much of the 1970s, merchandising was considered crass and commercial. By the 1980s, that stigma faded, and most artists were allowing their likenesses to be placed on T-shirts. Many get creatively involved with the design and view it as part of their artistic vision, no different from an album cover. They no doubt also recognize that a T-shirt can be both an artifact and a marketing tool. By the late 1980s, rock merchandising represented a source of income that ranked with record sales and touring. The three top merchandising companies—Winterland, Brockum, and Great Southern—grossed an estimated $125 million, $80 million, and $25 million, respectively.

Merchandising income became more important to rock acts as the price of going on the road increased. Artists commonly financed start-up costs for their tours—stage building, lighting, sound, freight expenses—with merchandising advances. With tour costs in the 1980s escalating, both record companies and promoters were reluctant to support anyone other than superstar acts because the financial risk was too great. The emphasis was on larger shows, and consumers paid the price. Tickets for most major shows started at $20, with surcharges often added by outlets. Add to that parking, merchandise, and drinks, and a date could cost around $100. In perhaps the perfect expression of Rock Reaganomics, seats for the Jackson 1984 Victory Tour were initially available only by purchasing a four-ticket, $120-block minimum. In response to the price gouging, WKKD in Akron, Ohio, featured a radio promotion, "I Can't Afford the Jacksons' Concert." The spots asked, "So what will it be this month? Rent? Car payment? Or the Michael Jackson concert?" and "Need a co-signer to buy Jackson tickets?" Charges of greed as a contributing factor to rising tour and ticket costs were widespread beyond the Victory Tour. Promoters and venues jumped on the merchandising bandwagon and demanded bigger cuts from the souvenir stands. As a result, when rental costs were equal between two sites, artists often based their choice on merchandising deals rather than box office splits.

Some of the high costs were unavoidable. The biggest expense, and threat to promoter's business, was insurance. Every member of a concert audience has to be insured. By the late 1980s, those costs had risen from four cents per person in 1984 to anywhere from forty to sixty cents per person. Rates are expected to jump higher due to the increase in the number of violent outbreaks at shows. Twenty years earlier, the Stones hired Hells Angels for $500 worth of beer to "keep order" at their free concert at Altamont. The bikers did not earn their keep; eighteen-year-old Meredith Hunter was fatally stabbed. By the 1980s, fear of rioting, violence, and gang warfare prompted extensive and expensive security measures, including airport-style metal detectors at some shows, armies of security patrols, and mounted police officers. It is estimated that New York taxpayers paid $678,000 for police protection at the Jacksons' Madison Square Garden concerts.

A popular insurance policy against mounting tour costs and the road to financial ruin for artists is corporate sponsorship. Until the 1980s, companies were reluctant to associate their names with rock and roll or recruit rock stars as spokespersons for their products. Advertisers viewed involvement in music's unpredictable scene and its "sex, drugs, and violence" atmosphere as a risk, both financially and image-wise. Jay Coleman, who founded the entertainment marketing firm Rockbill in 1976, says companies rejected rock ties with reservations like, "What if he rapes someone on the tour bus or gets busted with drugs?"[13]

Those attitudes changed as more people who grew up with rock and roll advanced to the management establishment of corporate America. Sponsors realized that rock's sound and image were ideal marketing tools for targeting audiences they most needed to reach, for brand identification, and to justify their billion-dollar expenditures. In 1982, advertisers spent $66 billion, a figure that doubled by the end of the decade. That same year, the Rolling Stones accepted over $1 million from Jovan/Musk Oil for their American tour, and the practice of receiving money from companies for associating music with products became "acceptable."

By the mid–1980s, a seemingly endless string of rock performers tied their tours or sold the rights to the songs to advertisers. Although there was a handful of resisters, many in the industry predicted that by 1990 every tour would go on the road with a sponsor. Musicians and business people viewed their alliance as necessary because of costs.

The ties to sponsors extended beyond tours. Advertisers scanned the oldies in the rock and roll catalog for songs that might have nostalgic appeal and connect with consumers, in particular, the baby boomers. "This music was once the most important thing in the lives of the people we're trying to sell cars to now," commented a Young and Rubicam vice-president. "This music creates a good feeling. People start remembering some of the best times in their lives, when they were carefree."[14]

The baby boomers were not the only demographic group targeted with music. Pepsi's scope was international, with the world tours of Jackson, Tina Turner, and David Bowie, as well as ethnic, as it financed the Hispanic group Gloria Estefan and Miami Sound Machine. While Anheuser Busch appealed to twenty-four to thirty-four-year-olds with stars like Phil Collins and Steve Winwood in its Michelob ads, Miller's commercials aimed at college students with club bands like Del Fuegos and Long Riders. Adidas allied itself with rappers Run D.M.C., whose fans include many inner-city blacks. And Coke reached down to teenagers with the New Kids on the Block.

The approaches were as subtle as Reebok's underwriting of the Human Rights Now! Tour or as elaborate as the long-form musical commercials featuring Pepsi pitchers Jackson, Bowie, and Lionel Richie. Either way, both the artist and the advertiser benefited from the exposure. For example, the

California Raisins Advisory Board paid $120,000 for the rights to Marvin Gaye's "I Hear It through the Grapevine." Projected raisin sales for 1988 were $200 million, with merchandise featuring the dancing raisins bringing in another $250 million.

The artist's degree of involvement in commercials varied. Many simply sold the rights to the songs for a specified period of time, while others covered their earlier hits for advertisers. Jackson rewrote "Billie Jean" into a Pepsi jingle, and Winwood tailored "Don't You Know What the Night Can Do?" for Michelob. Many artists appear in the commercials, whether performing their songs, or just doing a hip cameo like Lou Reed and Grace Jones for Honda.

With much of the oldie territory mined, advertisers began looking to use current hits. As they did, the commercial conversion of a song accelerated. *Billboard* began to feature a weekly index for marketers listing names, addresses, and telephone numbers of those holding the rights to the week's top songs. And *Rolling Stone*'s publishers printed a monthly newsletter, *Marketing Through Music*.

Advertisers also devised methods of dealing with the high price of music licensing. Golden oldies became "stolen" oldies at stock music houses that specialized in producing "counterfeit" songs almost identical to the original but different enough to be legally acceptable. If an advertiser could afford the song but not the singer, sophisticated electronic equipment in recording studios allowed companies to come close to duplicating a popular singer's voice. The legalities of sound-alikes are more complicated, as B. F. Goodrich can attest to following a suit filed by Tom Petty for its unauthorized use of "Mary's New Car." And if artists refused to license their music, determined advertisers borrowed the sound, style, persona, or image and reworked them into commercials. After Springsteen turned down Lee Iacocca's $12 million offer to sing for Chrysler, the company nonetheless proceeded to reshape "Born in the USA" into "The Pride Is Back, Born in America." The Springsteen/Mellencamp T-shirt and blue jeans, small town, home town, heartland images were routinely reduced to a formula for many 1980s' commercials.

Whether originals, remakes, or ripoffs, songs were used to sell everything from colas, candy, cars, and computers to desserts, detergents, beer, jeans, and fast foods. While many appreciated the "memories of carefree days gone by" that advertisers hoped the music would trigger, the commercial conversion also resulted in some, "Look what they've done to my song" sighs and criticism that the music had been stripped of its meaning.

Then came the Nike Revolution. In 1986, the black and white documentary style ad featuring the Beatles "Revolution" struck a responsive chord. Much of music's meaning derives from human experience, both of the creator and the audience. While some songs evoke feelings of nostalgia, others were deemed more sacred. Using the Lennon/McCartney political song from 1968 to promote a $75 pair of athletic shoes was not the same as using the Fifth Dimension's "Up, Up and Away" for an airline commercial or the Lovin' Spoonful's "Do You Believe in Magic?" to sell laundry soap. In the eyes of many, the Nike commercial had crossed the line and was nothing less than sacrilege. The song's meaning went beyond being a Beatles fan. For many, the song marked experiences that included rioting and getting teargassed in the streets in 1968.

The ad may have been "brought to you by" Nike, but it was "made possible by" Michael Jackson. Through a complex series of legal and financial transactions dating back to the 1960s when Lennon and McCartney gave up ownership of their songs, Jackson—wearing his Sergeant Pepper outfit at the London negotiations in 1985—secured the copyrights to much of the Beatles catalog from ATV Music for $47.5 million. After agreeing to license "Revolution" to Nike for $250,000 for one year, Jackson persuaded Capitol Records, owner of the rights to the Beatles recordings, to license the original record. The $7 million ad campaign and controversy followed.

Nike eventually suspended the ads because of a suit brought by Apple Records, controlled by George Harrison, Ringo Starr, McCartney, and Yoko Ono. Ono appeared to object the least to the commercials, and she even saw value in them. "This ad is a way to communicate John's songs to kids today, to make it part of their lives instead of a relic of the distant past," she said.[15] Jackson reportedly has plans to make forty other Beatles songs available for commercial exploitation.

The Nike Revolution magnified rock's commercialization. Although both companies and artists benefited from the sponsorships, rock marketing also carried a sellout stigma. Questions of ethics, integrity, and greed often surfaced, and "selling one's soul" became more than a reference to the Motown sound.

The "sellouts" easily outnumbered the "holdouts." The corporate payroll even included some surprises, like Lou Reed, a rock hero known for his rejection of everything soft and safe in the pop world, who nonetheless licensed his signature song, "Walk on the Wild Side," for Honda scooters. "When you hold up a lot of money there are few people today who stand on principle," observed a J. Walter Thompson ad executive.[16]

The exceptions were few. In 1985, Dave Clark refused to let Union Carbide have his group's 1960s hit, "Glad All Over," to sell Glad Bags. Linda Ronstadt would not redo "Get Closer" for the Thompson firm's Close Up toothpaste campaign. Chubby Checker refused to do "The Twist" for Skil's power screwdriver, but only because they would not pay him enough. Bob Dylan's comment from years earlier—"Money doesn't talk; it swears"—seemed more appropriate than ever in the 1980s music.

Critics characterized the corporate state of music as "McPop" and "Wing Tip Rock." Many artists also expressed their frustrations with the commercialization and the "money changes everything" movement in rock.

"When we look back at this decade, we'll have to say that in the Eighties, rock and roll went to work for corporations and got up at 6:00 A.M. to go jogging," said U2's Bono Hewson. "And it wasn't just to keep fit. It was to get ahead, to improve the prospects of the corporation."[17] For others, they were the ones "who held out and we lost. We're antiquated. We're a 1956 Cadillac running down the road getting passed and we're stupid," said John Cougar Mellencamp. "My daddy and my friends tell me I was stupid when I wouldn't take five million from a beer company [for "Small Town"]. And I look around me and I think, goddamn, maybe I was stupid. There's no honor here anymore."[18]

In some cases, the point about greed may be well taken. McCartney and Jackson are easily among the wealthiest individuals in music, if not the world. Where does one draw the line in distinguishing between what is greed and what is shrewd business sense? Was it greedy or shrewd of Jackson to outbid McCartney and Yoko Ono for the Beatles songs—and then to demand the $15 million from Pepsi up front, not only to help with tax breaks on the $47.5 million he spent on the Beatles but because, as reported, getting the money up front "would make Michael happy"? Certainly $15 million could make anyone happy. And while McCartney may have been upset over the use of "Revolution," he is less protective of other works. The owner of many songs, McCartney sold Buddy Holly's "Oh Boy" to Buick in 1987. Again the question arises: shrewd business or greed?

While marketers are aware that artists and critics have made sponsorship an issue, they doubt that consumers are affected and believe they are for the most part indifferent to the commercial conversion of songs and rock's corporate ties. It is not important, not to mention likely, that audiences believe that Michael Jackson drinks Pepsi or that if the Beatles were touring today they would be wearing Nike Airs rather than black pointed boots, or that Keith Richards "meant a Bud Light" in a pub and not a match to light his ever-dangling cigarette. Exposure and product identification are the advertiser's goals. Executives also point out that art through the ages has depended on commerce. Market researcher Mike Shallet, creator of Sound Data survey of music buyers, compares Michelob to the Medicis, calling it modern patronage.

Yet the commercialization of rock appears to be more glaring than the other popular art and entertainment forms. Perhaps it is because rock was founded on antiestablishment values and has always been an expression of rebellion, the unconventional, and antisocial. A rock artist or a song's being associated with a corporation or product is mainstream and counter to those values. Whether accurate or not, there is a perception that the artist has more soul to sell than a movie star or professional athlete. And songs are passion statements containing meaning and human experience. They are the soundtracks of our lives. The late rock critic Lester Bangs believed that the primary reason people listen to music is to hear passion expressed. When that passion is parceled into promoting a product, is something lost—perhaps the soul or the meaning—in the process?

Success and security now play such a central role in our cultural consciousness that even rock artists have learned to strive along a scale of career values and commercial strategies and incentives. In the gradual shift of the cultural value scale, commercialism, professionalism, and bureaucracy have steadily displaced independence and the romantic ideals of creative community. Suzi Gablik, in *Has Modernism Failed?* writes that culturally we are witnessing the rise of a new psychological type of artist, "the bureaucratic or organizational personality who lives in submission to a cultural and economic power system." Also emerging is a new value system emphasizing the importance of the modern organization. "The goal is security: to be part of the powerful machine, to be protected by it and feel strong in the symbiotic connection to it," writes Gablik.[19]

Is it possible for artists living in a capitalistic culture centered on production, consumption, and success to create without compromising personal and artistic integrity? Must all conform to organizational structures and commercial imperatives? Will even the most determined, independent artist be restricted and destined to be reduced to being a cog in the music machinery, punching the clock and working on the assembly line at the hit factory?

Undoubtedly, much of the choice, or responsibility, lies with the artists themselves and how each defines personal values, needs, motivations for creating, and aspirations. The decision is not easy. As Bluesman Mose Allison said, "If you wanna sing your own song, you're gonna have to lose a few." Resisting can result in frustrating ordeals, alienation, suspension, lawsuits, or self-doubts and wondering if "you're stupid." It is a "they give you this but you pay for that" proposition.

The questions of quality and the issue of art versus commerce become somewhat relative in the popular arts. Even the term *artist* becomes a misnomer within the organizational and commercial framework. The artists themselves are well aware that they are employed by a company and are expected to produce a product—music—to be bought and sold in a marketplace. "Artistic merit" is not a column in a record company's accounting ledger. "It's not about quality, it's about money," said Mellencamp. "People are always gonna talk charts and money to me. I'm in the business." "As far as I'm concerned, 'Art' is just short for 'Arthur,' " adds Keith Richards.[20]

Although there are conditions that allow for creative freedom and the pursuit of individual artistic and musical goals within the commercial complex of the popular arts, the individual artist and his or her work seldom emerge above the organization and commerce. Rock is no exception. It is business as usual; the record industry remains as the stream of individual artists comes and goes. Elvis was right on the money: Taking Care of Business is the essence of America.

NOTES

1. Jim Greer, "Ten Best," *Spin* (April 1990): 46.
2. Quoted in Jeffrey Ressner, "Touring: The Road to Ruin," *Rolling Stone* (December 1987): 82.
3. Dave Marsh, "Rock and Roll 1980: Hold On Hold Out," *Rolling Stone*, January 8, 1981, p. 2; Jon Landau, *It's Too Late to Stop Now* (San Francisco: Straight Arrow Press, 1972).
4. Quoted in David Breskin, "Interview," *Rolling Stone Twentieth Anniversary*, November 5, 1987, p. 284.
5. Jon Parles, "Work Hard, Play Hard," *Rolling Stone*, December 20, 1984, p. 137.
6. Quoted in Bill Flanagan, "Steve Forbert Escapes from Hell," *Musician* (October 1988): 72.
7. Quoted in Fred Schuers, "Van Morrison Won't Play Industry's Games," *Rolling Stone*, November 22, 1984, pp. 61–62.
8. Quoted in Bill Flanagan, "The Real Neil Young Stands Up," *Musician* (November 1985): 34.
9. Ibid., p. 36.
10. James Henke, "Interview with Neil Young," *Rolling Stone*, June 2, 1988, p. 46.
11. Ressner, "Touring," p. 82.
12. Michael Goldberg, "Rock's New Gift of Garb," *Rolling Stone*, November 3, 1988, p. 15.
13. John Schwartz, "Wing Tip Rock and Roll," *Newsweek*, September 26, 1988, p. 49.
14. Mark Crispin Miller, "Gonna Hawk around the Clock," *Mother Jones* (November 1988): 40.
15. Jon Weiner, "You Say You Want a Revolution: A Case Study of Rock and Roll as a Commodity," *Utne Reader* (May–June 1988): 108.
16. Miller, "Gonna Hawk," p. 41.
17. Breskin, "Interview," p. 284.
18. Bon Guccione, Jr., "Mellencamp Melancholy," *Spin* (June 1989): 79.
19. Suzi Gablik, *Has Modernism Failed?* (New York: Thames and Hudson, 1984), p. 301.
20. Steve Perry, "John Mellencamp's Brutal Honesty," *Musician* (August 1989): 40; Bill Flanagan, *Written in My Soul* (New York: Contemporary Books, 1988), p. 207.

BIBLIOGRAPHY

Chapple, Steve, and Reebee Garofalo. *Rock 'n' Roll Is Here to Pay*. Chicago: Nelson-Hall, 1977.
Denisoff, R. Serge. *Solid Gold: The Popular Music Industry*. New Brunswick, N.J.: Transaction, 1975.
———. *Tarnished Gold: The Record Industry Revisited*. New Brunswick, N.J.: Transaction, 1986.

———. *Inside MTV*. New Brunswick, N.J.: Transaction, 1988.

Frith, Simon. *Sound Effects: Youth, Leisure, and the Politics of Rock*. New York: Pantheon, 1981.

———, ed. *Facing the Music*. New York: Pantheon, 1988.

Hendler, Herb. *Year by Year in the Rock Era*. New York: Praeger, 1987.

Marsh, Dave. *The First Rock and Roll Confidential Report*. New York: Pantheon, 1985.

Podell, Janet, ed. *Rock Music in America*. New York: H. W. Wilson, 1987.

Stokes, Geoffrey. *Star-Making Machinery*. Indianapolis: Bobbs-Merrill, 1976.

Ward, Ed, Geoffrey Stokes, and Ken Tucker. *Rock of Ages: The Rolling Stone History of Rock and Roll*. New York: Rolling Stone/Summit, 1986.

Part IV

Race

16

The African-American Contribution to Jazz

WILLIAM HOWLAND KENNEY III

Black Americans established each of the definitive stylistic departures that guided the course of jazz history. From ragtime composers Scott Joplin and James Scott to jazz composer Ferdinand Jelly Roll Morton, from Louis Armstrong to Count Basie and Duke Ellington, Charlie Parker to Thelonius Monk and Miles Davis, and John Coltrane and Ornette Coleman to the Marsalis brothers, African Americans transformed jazz into the most developed and respected idiom in American popular music. Two closely related questions arise, however, about the definitive position of black musicians in jazz: what their respective contributions have been and why African Americans rather than Americans of other ethnic backgrounds made them.

Two interesting lines of development have characterized African-American contributions to jazz: the twin arts of solo improvisation and of jazz composition and arrangement. The first of these, solo improvisation, began with Louis Armstrong's invention of grandly sweeping, dramatically structured, and urgently swinging cornet and trumpet improvisations. The records Armstrong made in Chicago during the 1920s—"West End Blues," "Muggles," and "Tight Like This," among many others—are usually cited as some of the most influential in jazz history. Armstrong and the fiery reedman Sidney Bechet first demonstrated the impressive range of individual expressiveness made possible in the freedom of jazz improvisation.

Armstrong influenced most of the jazz solo instrumentalists who followed him, particularly trumpeter Roy Eldridge, and tenor saxophonist Coleman Hawkins was no exception. But Hawkins, in ideal jazz fashion, added to his early influences his own remarkably sophisticated harmonic knowledge, which blossomed during a most creative period from 1939 to 1944. He contoured long lines of precisely selected chordal tones into lush, powerfully phrased improvisations on records like "Body and Soul" (1939) and "The Man I Love" (1943), and he deeply influenced a long succession of tenor saxophone stylists from Herschel Evans to Buddy Tate, Illinois Jacquet, Yusef Lateef, Don Byas, and Ben Webster. Hawkins's style contrasted sharply with the more dancing, lightly articulated melodic and rhythmic playing of Lester Young, whom writer Martin Williams has called "the most gifted and original improviser between Louis Armstrong and [alto saxophonist] Charlie Parker."[1] Young, who made many remarkable solos on records with the Count Basie band—"Taxi War Dance" and "Lester Leaps In" (both in 1939)—and with vocalist Billie Holiday—"He's Funny That Way" (1937) and "All of Me" (1941)—opened the way to later bebop concepts, but important tenor soloists like Dexter Gordon managed to synthesize qualities from both Lester Young and Coleman Hawkins.

Each influential African-American solo breakthrough in jazz has interacted with a parallel concern for the overall form and structure that may be given to any performance. Where, for example, Armstrong focused attention on the individual's instrumental creativity, Ferdinand Jelly Roll Morton, drawing on the compositional heritage of Scott Joplin, invented jazz compositions and arrangements like "Black Bottom Stomp" and "Dead Man Blues," which provided several techniques for balancing the solo statement with varied ensemble voicings so that jazz performances became much more than just a statement of the melody followed by a string of solos. His "King Porter Stomp" later became a staple of the big band repertory during the swing era of the 1930s.

The tradition of jazz composition and arranging championed by Morton received its most creative boost from pianist and bandleader Duke Ellington, whose orchestral work reached its height from 1938 to 1942. Ellington composed over a thousand tunes, notably such subsequent jazz standards as "Satin Doll," "Take the A Train," "Mood Indigo," and "Don't Get Around Much Anymore," and arranged many more. On such recordings as "Harlem Air Shaft," "Ko-Ko," and "Concerto for Cootie," Ellington perfected a musically unsophisticated orchestral balance featuring the highly individual sonorities of his instrumentalists, unusually voiced harmonies, and his own and Billy Strayhorn's original and memorable compositions. His influence permeated the music and career of bassist, composer, and bandleader Charles Mingus and pianist and orchestra leader Sun Ra, both of whom retained many of Ellington's principal ideas while exploring the outer limits of free jazz.

At the end of World War II, just after the Ellington band's peak years, Charles Parker, trumpeter Dizzy Gillespie, and pianist Bud Powell created a major renewal of the solo language labeled bebop. The boppers played complex eighth-note patterns in varied, unexpected rhythmic accents, which stimulated the label applied to the new music. At the same time, they combined the new subtlety and complexity with a searing emotional power. Recordings of "Shaw Nuff" (1945) by Dizzy Gillespie's All-Star Quintet and the exciting Massey Hall concert of 1953 in Toronto, Canada, provide two peaks in bebop creativity. Parker's influence can be heard in the playing of pianist Bud Powell, drummer Max Roach, and many saxophonists, most notably Cannonball Adderley, Sonny Stitt, Phil Woods, and Richie Cole.

Ellington and the boppers drew attention to jazz as a music for serious listening rather than social dancing or accompaniment for stage and night-club acts. During the 1950s and 1960s, individual African-American musicians and black groups continued to set the pace of jazz experimentation with improvisation and structural arrangement. Pianist Thelonius Monk, for example, invented a form of highly structured melodic improvisation, which replaced the flurries of eighth notes of Charlie Parker with a spare compositional style. In his compositions "Straight," and "Misterioso," Monk married sophisticated, often dissonant, harmonies with compacted, silence-filled melodic lines that demonstrated his concern for form in improvisation. Similarly, tenor saxophonist Sonny Rollins, who carried solo innovation into the 1970s, discovered order and logic in his improvised lines, which presented a sense of symmetrical balance in a whole greater than its parts. So, too, many of the performances of John Lewis and the Modern Jazz Quartet evolved a balance of solo, accompaniment, and ensemble that was as delicate as it could become raucously emotional under the direction of Charles Mingus.

Among African-American jazz innovators, few have surpassed trumpeter Miles Davis's ability to set new stylistic trends as both a bandleader and composer. Beginning in the bebop era, Davis swiftly moved in new stylistic directions that departed widely from the bebop emphasis on rapid harmonic rhythm, breakneck tempi, and agitated, note-filled solos from the wind instruments. In 1949, Davis recorded *Birth of the Cool*, an album that influenced the light, soft, gentle style of "cool jazz" or "West Coast" jazz. Ten years later Davis's *King of Blue* set the trend for modal jazz, with minimal harmonic movement. In 1969, his long-playing records *In a Silent Way* and *Bitches Brew* strongly influenced the fusion of jazz with rock and roll, a concept subsequently developed by Joe Zawinul's and Wayne Shorter's Weather Report, Herbie Hancock's Headhunters, and Chick Corea's Return to Forever. Like Jelly Roll Morton, Duke Ellington, and Thelonius Monk before him, Miles Davis was both a composer and solo instrumental improvisor, absorbed by the interwoven concerns of improvisation and planning.

In 1960, alto saxophonist Ornette Coleman's long-playing record album *Free Jazz* nearly matched the artistic influence of the Miles Davis records; Coleman encouraged a more frequent use of collective improvisation without preset harmonic patterns. That is not to claim that his music lacked any rules (for horn solos with rhythm section accompaniment, constant tempo, and even some chordally based instrumental improvisations enriched his recordings), but Coleman certainly did stretch the conventional relationships of harmony, melody, and rhythm. He pushed his turbulent, churning, high-energy jazz toward greater improvisational freedom and away from preconceived, memorized, and written structures, at least as they had customarily been understood. Coleman's ideas were developed and transformed by, among others, orchestra leader Sun Ra, pianist Cecil Taylor, trumpeter Don Cherry, and tenor saxophonists Abert Ayler and John Coltrane.

The freeing of jazz from the major melodic, harmonic, and rhythmic conventions developed from the 1930s through the 1950s has preoccupied most African-American musicians who worked in the idiom from 1960 to 1980. Following the lead of Ornette Coleman and Cecil Taylor, the Association for the Advancement of Creative Musicians and the Art Ensemble of Chicago attracted critical attention with their free-form rhythms and solos based largely on particular moods rather than chord sequences. The most influential of these musicians, composer Anthony Braxton, mixed various jazz styles with avant-garde concern music. The adventuresome spirit that propelled the leading jazz pioneers of the 1960s through the 1980s to expand greatly or defy happily the accepted musical definitions of jazz also informed the concepts and performances of the World Saxophone Quartet. Oliver Lake, Julius Hemphill, Hamiet Bluiett, and David Murray mixed arrangements with improvisations while experimenting with new and unusual saxophone sounds.

Tenor and soprano saxophonist John Coltrane experimented with new performance styles, creating a searingly intense voice that climaxed in chordlike shrieks and screeches in which several different subtones could be heard. Coltrane, whose influence (while he lived) rivaled that of Miles Davis, pioneered in his album *Giant Steps* quadruple-time improvisations over exceedingly complex, difficult chord changes of his own creation, progressions between very rapidly changing and distantly related chords. He turned to more modally oriented improvisations in later recordings, such as *My Favorite Things*.

A brief appreciation of the greatest of the African-American jazz improvisors and composers raises some important questions: Why have African Americans, and not another ethnic group, whites in general, or musicians of various ethnic backgrounds created the major stylistic breakthroughs of jazz history? The traditional answer, forcefully articulated by Martin T. Williams and echoed implicitly in the musicology of Gunther Schuller, has been that American blacks have a natural rhythmic sense drawn from their African background. While quick to point out that this "natural rhythm" is not possessed by all blacks and that nonblacks may acquire it, Williams still insists that "Negroes as a race have a rhythmic genius that is not like that of other races."[2]

This may or may not be true; certainly there is no way of proving the proposition, which may well be a form of self-fulfilling prophecy. It is much more certain that the notion of innate racial characteristics has had a long history in North America. In the colonial South, slaves were encouraged by their white masters to sing rhythmic work songs in the fields in order better to apply a concentrated group effort to the task at hand. During precious leisure hours, plantation masters encouraged slave music making as a sign of docile contentment under enslavement. Particularly gifted slave instrumentalists were ordered to the plantation house to play for the innumerable balls that made southern plantation life such a gay affair.

During the nineteenth century, the persistently popular minstrel shows, in which whites made themselves up to look like caricatures of black people, spread the idea of an innate racial predisposition for lighthearted music and dance. After the Civil War, some blacks formed minstrel companies and performed "under cork," too, so that whites and blacks carried the minstrel tradition over into variety, the forerunner of vaudeville, the popular turn-of-the-century theater entertainment.

While the reality of innate racial predispositions to much of anything, much less to "natural rhythm," appears painfully problematic, powerful racial and cultural attitudes in the dominant white American society have without any doubt shaped the range of contributions that blacks have been allowed to make to popular music in this century as well. These pressures, moreover, came to bear heavily on vaudeville, nightclubs, and phonograph record industry, each of which played a central role in the creation of jazz. Racial segregation in each of these popular music media resulted in a strong and nearly exclusive association of African Americans with vernacular music performance. Racial segregation also encouraged the separate development of black and white styles in musical entertainment.

Vaudeville, the nineteenth-century form of popular stage entertainment, included most forms of popular music on programs, which ran the gamut from trained animal acts to comedians. Vaudeville encouraged the dissemination of new popular music styles across the country during the late 1910s when jazz was born. Under racial segregation, black ragtime musicians normally could expect to work only in vaudeville theaters located in ghetto neighborhoods and tour the country on the segregated chain of black theaters called the Theatre Owners Booking Association. As they got their careers underway, black jazz musicians and vocalists like King Oliver, Duke Ellington, Louis Armstrong, Bessie Smith, and Ethel Waters rarely broke into more lucrative and well-publicized white theater chains.

Since their career ambitions in vaudeville were limited, black musical entertainers also focused their efforts on nightclubs, actually small, action-oriented, intimate theaters, performing in what were called at the turn of the century black-and-tan cabarets. There were clubs located in black ghetto neighborhoods of the country's major cities but patronized overwhelmingly by "slumming" whites interested in black musical entertainment. Before World War I, African Americans owned a few of these clubs and catered to an interracial clientele, working a fine line between the entertainment market in the local black neighborhood and a natural economic drive to reach the larger and more lucrative interracial market. Black-and-tan owners in Chicago—for example, Robert Motts, Teenan Jones, William Bottoms, and Virgil Williams—were largely pushed out of the black-and-tan business by whites who ran the bootleg liquor operations (often gangsters) or by white urban reformers, who retained influence over black activities, if not over those of the mobsters. As in vaudeville, therefore, Duke Ellington, King Oliver, and Fletcher Henderson were limited to roles as performers in the cabarets and barred from the commercial management of lucrative black-and-tans like New York's famous Cotton Club and Chicago's Plantation Cafe. The former was so racially segregated that blacks were not even allowed in as customers.

The national popularization of phonograph records after World War I further identified blacks as performers of blues and jazz. Beginning in 1920, white-owned phonograph companies, which had overwhelmingly produced popular dance records by white combos and dance bands, introduced a separate product category known as race records, usually produced by subsidiaries and aimed at the African-American market. Blacks were hired by Okeh, Paramount, Vocalion, and other race record companies to produce and perform identifiably ethnic music for black record buyers. Race records enjoyed a privileged but strictly limited position in the popular record business. The major record companies of the 1920s, Victor and Brunswick, reserved the recording of new Tin Pan Alley hit tunes for white dance bands such as those led by Leo Reisman, Ben Bernie, Isham Jones, and Art Hickman in the major hotel ballrooms in New York, Chicago, and San Francisco. Black combos were accorded market share for novelty, blues, and jazz records on the special, cheaper labels. The industry and trade papers like *Variety* and *Billboard* agreed that only a black band could do justice to "indigo" material.

The history of Harry H. Pace demonstrates that blacks would have sought careers in other forms of music had segregation not prevented them. Pace, a black, became owner and director of the Black Swan Record Company and in this position recorded a broad range of music enjoyed within the black community. He was swiftly isolated and forced out of business by the more heavily capitalized white race record companies. Had ambitious, musically inclined African Americans wanted to become something other than performers of jazz and blues, their chances of success in the record business were limited.

These cultural pressures on the commercialization of African-American musical enterprise in the 1920s, when so many new technologies revolutionized the experience of popular music in America, indelibly marked the subsequent history of jazz in the twentieth century. First, blacks interested in careers in popular music recognized that their energies would have to be focused on innovations in musical performance. They might not be allowed to become owners of major theaters, dance halls, clubs, record companies, and radio and television stations, but they were expected and encouraged to create new forms of musical performance. Blacks usually have exercised control only over the actual playing of the notes; they have had every reason to become extremely good at it, creating thereby islands of independence in the troubled seas of the music business.

The time has come to take note of the concrete historical circumstances that channeled African Americans into blues and jazz performance. No one would argue that these musical forms were created for or imposed upon blacks. Both were deeply rooted in the African and the African-American cultural experience. But to ignore history may too readily encourage the sort of reverse racism that credits blacks with a racially inherited musical superiority. Recording their primacy in the musical history of jazz is merely giving credit where it is due. Perhaps even more than the rest of us, the great black jazz musicians in this century have clearly understood both the limits and the possibilities before them, both taking control of and beautifying the space allotted to them.

NOTES

1. Martin Williams, *The Jazz Tradition* (New York: Oxford University Press, 1976), p. 115.
2. Ibid., p. 8.

BIBLIOGRAPHY

Gridley, Mark C. *Jazz Styles: History and Analysis.* 3d ed. Englewood Cliffs, N.J.: Prentice-Hall, 1988.
Jones, LeRoi (Amiri Baraka). *Blues People.* New York: Morrow, 1963.
Kernfeld, Barry, ed. *New Grove Dictionary of Jazz.* New York: Macmillan, 1988.
Levine, Lawrence W. *Black Culture and Black Consciousness: Afro-American Folk Thought from Slavery to Freedom.* New York: Oxford University Press, 1977.
Ogren, Kathy J. *The Jazz Revolution: Twenties America and the Meaning of Jazz.* New York: Oxford University Press, 1989.
Schuller, Gunther. *Early Jazz: Its Roots and Musical Development.* New York: Oxford University Press, 1968.
Williams, Martin. *The Jazz Tradition.* New York: Oxford University Press, 1976.

17

The Day Hank Williams Died: Cultural Collisions in Country Music

Nolan Porterfield

January 1, 1953, was a cold, blustery Thursday on the plains of West Texas. A blue norther howled down out of the Panhandle, and the sky was thick with gusting sand. New Year's Day, coming in the middle of the week, was just another slow workday in my dad's crossroads grocery store and gas station, ten miles from nowhere and about twice that far from the junky little town where I went to high school. In the early hours of that sandstorm morning, while I slept my zombie adolescent sleep and dreamed (if I dreamed at all) of misty English countrysides, flashy cars, and Nanabeth Cox, Hank Williams died in the back seat of his '52 Cadillac, somewhere in the wilds of eastern Tennessee.

I do not remember how I learned of Hank Williams's death, a realization that I now find strange and rather puzzling. But I was a strange and puzzled kid, square as a bear, and I missed a lot of what was going on. I was equally unaware of another great passing that very week—that of Fletcher Henderson, the musical genius who was largely responsible for the swing revolution that Benny Goodman got most of the credit for. But I had no reason to know about Henderson; after all, he was black and several cultural removes from the West Texas world of a decidedly unhip, muddle-headed white boy. Hank Williams, on the other hand, was one of us, as close to blood as blood gets, and I probably would not remember anything about his death if it were not for what happened four days later, when I went back to school, on a still sand-blown Monday morning, after the Christmas holidays.

It took a while to figure out what was taking place. Country kids in my day tended to be cold-eyed realists, too simple to be sentimental, and we desperately avoided public displays of emotion. But something was going around, quietly, awkwardly, out of a need too great to contain, in the first whispered communications that morning, eerily everywhere: "Hey. You

hear Hank Williams died?" Even more unsettling was the invariable response: a solemn nod of the head, a troubled sigh, even now and then (but
only from girls, of course) a tear or two. All that morning, kids gathered
in small clumps in out-of-the-way corners and vacant classrooms, talking
in hushed tones, sharing the news.

It was at once comforting and disturbing; I had never seen my schoolmates
behave this way, and before that morning it had never occurred to me that
anyone else paid much attention to Hank Williams, not the way I had. I
am sure I did not realize then the full implications of what was happening—
that I would remember it and someday recall it in such detail, in such awe
and extravagance—but I knew that it was a turning point. It was like being
a lone member of the Resistance, afraid your identity will be betrayed to
the barbarian Nazis all around, then suddenly discovering, through the
exchange of a secret sign, that you are safe among fellow conspirators.

For me the crucial point came just after lunch, when I went up to the
second-floor nook, just off the tiny auditorium balcony, where Peggy McKee
and I worked on the yearbook. Peggy was the solidest rock I knew, a senior,
two years older than me, bright, long of limb, funny as hell—a girl with
lots of sand, as Huck said of Mary Jane. Because she was older and naturally
protective, I chose to think of her as the big sister I never had. My fraternal
attitude may also have been influenced by the fact that she was already
dating a tall, hardrock cowboy whose daddy owned half the county.

I had never seen her without a smile and a ready toss of the head. But
when I got to the yearbook room that day, she stood up from her desk,
without a word, chin quivering, and came up to me and put her arms around
me and began to cry. I confess to having had occasional fantasies about
hugging Peggy McKee but not this way, in this circumstance. I was much
embarrassed, worried that someone would see us. Hugging, even in grief,
between opposite sexes on school property was not considered acceptable
behavior in 1953. But I stifled my worser, nerdier self and comforted her
as best I could.

What I could not do in front of her was cry too. When she seemed better,
I went downstairs behind the stage and let go—for Hank, for Peggy, for
me, for that whole sad, sand-blown, inexplicable West Texas day.

In later times, in other places, and among other people, there would be
quite a lot of this going on—fashionably, in the wake of Janis and Jimi,
Elvis and John Lennon. But in 1953, for the young, innocent, straight-arrow
fans of just one more redneck troubadour (and one whose career was, after
all, in serious decline), it was bizarre and rather baffling behavior. To understand even vaguely the impact and meaning of that day, it is necessary
to understand something about the character back then of country music
and its audience.

I am annoyed as much as puzzled that I do not remember the moment I
learned of Hank William's death. But I think that the very fact that I do

not remember is an essential part of the story. More than likely, I heard about it from the cheap little Wards Airline radio that played incessantly in my father's store, a static hodgepodge of swing bandstand, western roundup, time-news-temperature, Patty Page singing "How Much Is That Doggie in the Window," Les Paul's "Lady of Spain." It is possible that I read about Williams's death in the back pages of the next day's edition of the *Lubbock Morning Avalanche*—"Hill-Billy Song King Found Dead in Automobile by Chauffeur"—along with late bulletins from the Korean War, warnings that our schools and colleges were filled with communists, and, on a note of social progress, the news that, for the first time in decades, no one had been lynched in the United States during the previous year. Eisenhower was about to take office, Stalin still reigned, our schools were segregated, Elvis was a wimpy senior at Humes High, the whole world was dark and windy.

In 1953 nobody paid much attention to country music, at least not publicly. If you had any pretensions at all to culture and sophistication—if you just wanted to be "normal" and have nice people like you—you ignored country music wherever possible. If you could not ignore it, you made fun of it. Historians of country music like to think of the 1940s and 1950s as "The Golden Age," but in those days everybody called it "hillbilly music," and practically no one took it seriously.

What we mostly did was take it for granted. After all, country music was everywhere around us, as common and inevitable as the dust in the air we breathed. The twenty-four-hour all-country radio station had not yet been invented (that happened a year or so later, right in our very midst, when Dave Stone put KDAV on the air from a cotton field just south of Lubbock), but every 250-watter for miles around programmed three or four hours of pickin' and singin' daily—usually an early morning wakeup show beamed at the farmers ("Sunrise Frolics"), an hour or so of mid-morning jamboree for the housewives, and an all-afternoon "western request roundup" that kept the cards and letters coming in. I spent a lot of time listening, more or less mindlessly, to High Pockets' "Country Tune Corral" from KSEL in Lubbock while I stocked shelves and pumped gas. When anyone else was around, I made a point of tuning to "The 950 Club" (950 kilocycles, not "hertz," on the dial), where a Peter Jennings sound-alike named Wayne Allen played Artie Shaw, Benny Goodman, and Stan Kenton.

There were no bars in Baptist-dry West Texas in those days, but every café and gathering place had a jukebox. There was even one in my dad's country grocery, a decrepit old Wurlitzer that held only ten records. For several months one fall, nine of the ten slots held Hank Williams's "Lovesick Blues," because the distributor got tired of changing worn-out records. (The tenth record, I clearly remember, was Theresa Brewer's "Music, Music, Music," obligatory for every jukebox in those days: "Put another nickel in, in the nickelodeon . . . "). After Nanabeth Cox broke my heart in the eighth grade, my pal Bobby Kitchen and I spent a lot of time hanging out at Jackson's Drive-In, consoling ourselves with hamburger steaks and hillbilly music from the jukebox. Bobby, who looked like James Dean and had a mildly tough reputation, broke the hearts of more girls than I ever said hello to, but he always seemed to be between romances and as much in need of a cheatin' song as I was. Hank's "Cold, Cold Heart" and "I'm So Lonesome I Could Cry" seemed to fill the bill—equal parts of she-done-me-wrong, Lord-how-it-hurts, and somehow-I'll-live.

Because we were not allowed to dance at school and there were no other places to do it, often on Saturday nights several couples would drive miles out of town to some point where two deserted dirt roads crossed, park their cars facing the intersection with headlights on, tune all the radios to the same station, and dance in the center, waltzing and two-stepping and hug-dancing in the dusty light to string-band strains from "The Big D Jamboree" or "Louisiana Hayride." We claimed to hanker for the uptown rhythms of city orchestras, but ballroom dancing, even if we had known how, seemed out of place.

These rustic orgies left no permanent marks. We scarcely ever stooped so low as "The Grand Ole Opry" (too corny and hayseed, even when Hank was on it). Afterward we went right back to Patti Page and Frankie Laine and Joni James and Eddie Fisher (rock 'n' roll was yet unknown, still little more than a gleam in Chuck Berry's eye). We spoke intensely of "classical music,"—our notions of classical tending in the direction of Mantovani or something by Sigmund Romberg—"Stouthearted Men," perhaps. I yearned for what I thought of as normalcy, "good taste," "respectability." In matters of popular culture, my idol had always been Jack Armstrong—"The All-American Boy," for those too young to remember—and I wanted nothing so much as to root-hog out of my country roots, get as far as I could from all the "howdys" and "you-alls," and sandstorms and hard-scrabble hickness that seemed to plague me everywhere I turned.

I never quite made it and lived to be grateful I had not. But I went on suffering from the symptoms of hypertoxic cultural dysfunction for some time. In the early 1960s, eight or nine years after Hank Williams died, when country music was still in the slump brought on by rock 'n' roll, and Hank was pretty much a fading memory, even in West Texas, one of my friends went to California to visit at UCLA one summer. He came back telling a wondrous tale of having lunched at the student center, where on grand terraces beneath huge spreading trees in which hung a network of loudspeakers, crowds of upscale, sophisticated children of the sun sat munching their avocados and alfalfa sprouts and listening reverently to the music of— you got it—Hank Williams, one record after another. I realized later that they were proto-hippies, although the term was not yet current. In my mind's eye, they were simply California preppies—clean-cut, rich, and respectable. After I got over my initial disbelief, there was a moment or two while I rejoiced that Hank and I were vindicated, his genius recognized in the real world beyond the arid intellectual climes of West Texas. Then I got mad. Where did they get off, liking Hank Williams at this late date? They were too young, and too affluent, and too citified; they had not earned the right, as I had—had not danced in dusty crossroads, scrounged for jukebox nickels, or suffered through the greasy meatloaf at Jackson's Drive-In. It was all quite irrational, but it illustrates the kinds of cultural mysteries inherent in country music.

The beat goes on, I'm afraid. Leap ahead to the mid–1970s, and it's country-music-with-a-capital-C. Country has gotten Cool. Hank Williams, duly canonized as a hero of the republic, supports a minor industry (record reissues, film biographies, general preservation of the legend), and these days everyone I know is sick to death of Hank, Jr., singing dumb songs about him.

There will, no doubt, be another installment on down the road. Country music makes for some strange cultural bedfellows, and they are never quite the same from one era to the next.

Vernon Dalhart, who recorded hillbilly music's first million-selling record, "Wreck of the Old 97," in 1924, was an ex-operatic tenor. Loretta Lynn and Luciano Pavarotti, warbling together from the stage of the Metropolitan Opera, were a hit on national television in the 1980s. Before that, Richard Nixon and Roy Acuff, played with yo-yos on the Grand Ole Opry. One of Bing Crosby's first national hits was "San Antonio Rose," which originated with Bob Wills and the Texas Playboys; another was "The One Rose," which Jimmie Rodgers, "America's Blue Yodeler," had recorded in 1930.

To witness some of the more extreme cultural collisions in country music, note simply that the Nashville Product is one of the most popular American exports around the world. A few years ago, traveling on the spectacularly bleak far northern edge of Scotland, my wife and I found that one of the jukebox favorites with the crowd in a small railroad pub was Kitty Wells's original 1952 version of "It Wasn't God Who Made Honky Tonk Angels," played over and over. Posters all around the British Isles regularly announce forthcoming tours by Johnny Cash, Tammy Wynette, Merle Haggard, and Riders in the Sky. American country music is equally popular in Australia, Japan, and Eastern Europe. It is a real experience to hear the Polish version of Waylon Jennings's "Good Hearted Woman" ("Bajecna Zenska").

While living in England in the 1960s, a young West German, Richard Weize, became so taken with old-time American pickers and singers that he started a company to reissue historic recordings. (Because Weize also likes bears, he named the company Bear Family.) Today, from its head-quarters in Bremen, Bear Family Records assembles, digitally remasters, and reissues in elegant boxed sets hundreds of recordings covering almost the gamut of American country music, from its beginnings in the 1920s down to contemporary artists such as Jerry Lee Lewis and James Talley. This

European organization has become one of the world's leading sources of supply for a distinctly American art form.

It is not difficult to understand country music's cultural affinities with English-speaking countries, but what explains its attraction in places like Czechoslovakia and Poland? Writes Miroslaw Desperak of Czestochowa, Poland: "I love so much blues, country, and those sad lyrics dealing with our everyday problems. They are immortal and they'll always be enjoyed, for we have the same problems all over—home, family, death, sorrow, loneliness, mother, bottle. Keep it country! I hate so much that modern junk, disco, etc. Keep it country, and don't forget your roots." He signs himself, "Your faithful and grateful Polish hillbilly."[1] Desperak is university educated and teaches German in one of the local schools. Some hillbilly.

It was only after reflecting on global encounters such as these—strange, awesome, and wonderful in their capacity to cut through national and ethnic barriers—that I realized a paradoxical but fundamental fact about country music here at home, in the good ole USA. In this supposed melting pot of many peoples and diverse cultures, in an era when social and racial barriers everywhere are falling, minority involvement in one of the nation's largest industries (and certainly its major native phenomenon) is essentially zero.

I have offered evidence that country music is a bundle of contradictions and that the mixture is always in flux. Here is an instance where the exception tends to prove the rule: If there is any sociocultural constant in country music, it surely lies in the almost total absence of racial plurality throughout its history.

Country music, we are told, is white man's blues. The well-intended, even humorous sense of that, of course, is that country music is what whites have instead of blues. And because a substitute is often inferior, there is the subtle implication, not unfounded, that country music does not reach the artistic and cultural level of the blues; it is not, at least, quite as classy. The statement suggests some sort of interplay or identity between the two forms, yet paradoxically it draws the old color line between them: blacks have the blues, whites have country music. Finally, since what the whites have is similar to, or borrowed from, what the blacks have, it is sufficient unto itself: no blacks need apply. That may be stretching an innocuous one-liner too far, but it is what reality attests to. You may have noted the lily-white cast of characters in my Hank Williams *fabliau*.

The almost total absence of blacks and other minorities from country music is not surprising, considering its origins among white southerners and its evolution through the years in the hands of performers, composers, agents, and promoters whose driving concern has always been commerce rather than social progress. What would attract paying black audiences to an art form that has traditionally reflected the values of staid, fundamentalist, xenophobic white society?

Historical accounts of hillbilly-country music typically cast a nod in the believe-it-or-not direction of racial and ethnic anomalies: blacks invented the banjo; Louis Armstrong recorded with Jimmie Rodgers; Deford Bailey, a black harmonica player, appeared on the Grand Ole Opry from 1925 to 1941; Freddy Fender is really Baldemar Huerta; Kinky Friedman's band is known as the Texas Jewboys; Ivory Joe Hunter's last album was entitled *I've Always Been Country*. In broader, even foggier fashion, a generic black influence is acknowledged; white pickers and singers "borrowed" songs, thematic elements, and instrumental styles from black country blues, work songs, church music—from countless unnamed, uncredited black entertainers. The biographies of a dozen major country stars dutifully record how the hero or heroine was taught to play or sing or perform by some kindly old black person. Indeed, a cherished element of the Hank Williams legend is the story of Tee-Tot, the black street singer who, according to doctrine, taught Hank to play the guitar.

And of course there is always Charley Pride. People who think "ET" means "extraterrestrial" and could not hum a bar of "Wildwood Flower" to save their lives know that Charley Pride is country music's first black superstar, the Jackie Robinson of the genre. Unaccountably attracted to broadcasts of the Grand Ole Opry as a boy, Pride wangled a cheap Sears, Roebuck guitar at the age of fourteen and taught himself to play. But he was also hooked on baseball, and it was only after several years of struggling to break into the major leagues that he gave up and eventually found his way to Nashville in the mid–1960s to pursue a career in country music. His demonstration tapes, submitted through an agent, invariably attracted interest—until he showed up in person. "He sings like us, but he looks like them," said puzzled white promoters. Anxious to capitalize on Pride's obvious talent but uncertain of how to do it, his white managers suggested that he bill himself as George Washington Carver III and dress in a minstrel costume. Pride, true to name, courageously refused to play the clown, and his initial records, performed as "Country Charley Pride" in a straightforward fashion, were eventually released—but without photographs or any hint of the singer's racial origin. In the face of growing popularity, his color could not be long concealed, and it is to the credit of his white audiences, as well as to the power of his talent, that he was readily accepted even when his "secret" became known. In 1971 he was named Performer of the Year by the Country Music Association, an act of major significance in country music history, and for a time it appeared that the racial barrier was broken. Unfortunately, Pride's vast appeal to members of his own race never matched that of his white audiences. As country music's eminent historian, Bill Malone, has noted, few other blacks have followed him across the color line. Today, with Pride aging successfully into his fifties and his own career having peaked, his influence on future generations of blacks seems negligible.

Given the provincial nature of hillbilly music historically and the racial attitudes of the white majority, North and South, over the years, it is remarkable to find that individual blacks such as Charley Pride (and, to a lesser degree, performers from other ethnic minorities) have from time to time played pivotal roles in country music almost from the beginning. To the extent that blues is truly a major element of country music, it is because Jimmie Rodgers, enshrined as the Father of Country Music, borrowed widely from the black blues he had heard as he was growing up in rural Mississippi and later popularized it for white audiences in the 1920s and 1930s with his thirteen famous "blue yodels" and another dozen related blues tunes.

Rodgers was perhaps the first major white recording star in any field to record with black accompaniment; even before he recorded with the young Louis Armstrong in 1930, he had cut one side (never issued) with a black jazz band in Dallas. He had also recorded earlier with Joe Kaipo, a Hawaiian, and with several Hispanics from San Antonio, Texas. It is sometimes pointed out that the cultural borrowing occasionally reversed direction; sporadic evidence of Rodgers's influence on black music turns up in records by the Mississippi Sheiks and in the work of various rhythm and blues groups later in the decade. But efforts to connect the black dots are ultimately futile. Between Jimmie Rodgers in the 1930s and Charley Pride in the 1960s, the involvement of blacks in mainstream country music was negligible. While their contributions remain isolated and fragmented, however, those contributions are no less artistically valuable, if only for what they tell us, in their very isolation and fragmentation, about the interchange between white and black cultures through the years. If country music is white man's blues, perhaps we can flip the coin and learn what it takes to make country music for blacks.

Appropriate to this tale of psychic and social oddities, a black man figures prominently in what is for me the ultimate revelation. For some years after Hank Williams died, country music was no more and no less to me than it had always been—an ordinary fact of a dull life I hoped to change. Then in the 1960s, about the time Nashville was rebounding into the national consciousness, increasingly fashionable if not yet respectable, I fell in with a rowdy crowd of Texas poets, anarchists, and musicians who treasured country music and knew a lot more about it, historically and philosophically, than I ever had. Through them I learned, with some mild shock, that educated folks with academic titles were writing high-powered, footnoted tracts and even entire books on the likes of the Carter Family, Fiddlin' John Carson, Bob Wills, and Johnny Cash. In time, I too wrote such a book, still absorbed by the cultural confusions that had begun to surface in my life the week Hank Williams died.

It took a long time for me to sort them out. I thought I had the job pretty much done, when along came McDonald Craig. The great-grandson of slaves, Craig lives near Linden, Tennessee, on land that his grandfather bought years ago with sweat and endurance and an integrity that most of us can only imagine. Like Charley Pride, he is one of those rare exceptions—a black man attracted from childhood to country music. He was born about the time Jimmie Rodgers died and was thus too young to have heard the original, yet he has a vast repertoire of Rodgers songs, learned from recordings and delivered in a remarkably faithful style. Craig is also a fan of other country artists, including Ernest Tubbs and Eddy Arnold. Speaking of his upbringing, he says, "It was country music that encouraged me to do right, as much as anything I was ever engaged in. If I belonged to all the religions, they couldn't have encouraged me to be any more respectful and honest with people than I have learned to be through the songs of men like Jimmie Rodgers, Ernest Tubbs, Hank Williams, and so forth."[2]

And so, just when I felt I had deciphered most of the holy mysteries of country music, I was privileged to hear what may well be the ultimate confirmation of faith in its efficacy, the simple truth of why we listen and what we hear.

NOTES

1. Miroslaw Desperak to the author, October 12, 1989.
2. Interview with James Akenson, Cookeville, Tennessee, March 1983.

BIBLIOGRAPHY

Kingsbury, Paul, and Alan Axelrod, eds. *Country: The Music and the Musicians.* New York: Abbeville Press, 1988.
Malone, Bill C. *Country Music, U.S.A.* Rev. ed. Austin: University of Texas Press, 1985.
Porterfield, Nolan. *Jimmie Rodgers: The Life and Times of America's Blue Yodeler.* Urbana: University of Illinois Press, 1979.
Williams, Roger M. *Sing a Sad Song: The Life of Hank Williams.* Urbana: University of Illinois Press, 1981.

─────── *18* ───────

Swing and Segregation

CHARLES A. NANRY

The great diversity of humanity can lead to consensus or constraint, tolerance or suppression, war or trade. The history of slavery and race relations in America provides an example of how a dominant group used everything from terror to subtle measures of institutional control to keep everyone "in place." With slavery formally abolished by a bloody civil war about halfway into our history as a nation, the doctrine of separate but equal segregation maintained many institutional arrangements supporting the hegemony of whites over blacks. As is so often the case, however, structural barriers were breached by popular culture.

American music often bridged the cultural gap between the races, even when those on the bridge were less than fully aware of their linking role. Jazz, including swing either as an element of all jazz or later as an accepted style of jazz, challenged rules about "proper" music. People were literally swept off their feet by the sounds and the feelings evoked by this infectious new music. Swing broke down cultural barriers; it also meant that conventional ideas of both popular music and those who played the music had to be redefined.

There are dozens of elements that can characterize music. One can argue endlessly about what the sound of music is, about when sound actually becomes music and why music to some ears is mere noise to others. Some musicologists make a career of doing just that. My purpose here is more modest. We need a simple definition permitting us to get started on our discussion of a kind of music that came to be known as swing.

Any characterization of the sound of music that also swings is elusive. Swing has to do with rhythm, with pulse and with beat, in a special harmonic

I acknowledge the useful and penetrating comments on an earlier draft from my colleagues at Rutgers University: Edward Berger, David Cayer, Robert McCaffrey, and Dan Morgenstern.

and melodic context. A Mahler symphony does not swing; neither does the music of John Cage; nor does a polka, most pop, rock, rap, or march music. In fact, the classical musics of Europe, which emphasize harmony and melodic line, and of Africa, with their focus on rhythm itself, do not swing either. Swing was, and continues to be, a product of African-American synergism—that is, the confluence of African rhythm and European conceptions of melody and harmony. Swing evolved as essential element of jazz, the unique music created by African Americans.

Most of Africa has had a rich set of musical traditions that emphasize complex, intertwined polyrhythms. With an astonishing number and variety of percussive (or struck) instruments unique to the African continent, African musicians and their listeners developed, over time, an ear for polyrhythms that accommodated long and complex alternations of sound and silence, accent or emphasis, meter or pattern, and tempo or rate of speed, in the forward propulsion of music. Africans, brought in chains to the New World from the seventeenth century onward, carried this sense of the importance of music as quintessentially rhythmic with them.

European social and cultural musical traditions were quite different than those from the African continent. In broad terms, we might argue that Europeans were just as focused on the up-and-down dimension of sound (harmony) as Africans were on the long and short of it (rhythm). Out of that concern grew a rich tradition of melody (which sounds followed which) and harmony (which sounds are grouped together) in both Europe and among European Americans. Spectacular inventions such as the organ, the piano—and its predecessors—as well as all sorts of plucked, bowed, and blown instruments, led to a great socio-musical need that became urgent in Europe at about the same time that Europeans came to the New World: the need to tune many instruments together so that their combined sound was pleasing.

The culmination of this search for a pleasing sound led as well to the search for a rational or scientific foundation for music as a part of the pan-European Age of Reason. Eventually the social convention of the well-tempered twelve-tone scale emerged, which, it turns out, is theoretically complex but not mathematically rational. "The great Western musical compromise" of the well-tempered approach is based on accepted convention and a willingness to overlook certain acoustical problems of nonscientific "irrationality" when certain tones occur together.

What any group calls music is socially defined; whether any group chooses to emphasize harmony, melody, rhythm, or anything else related to sound defined as music is arbitrary and often lost in the mists of cultural origin or sanctioned by the tyranny of social convention. The reverse is also true: some elements of music, critically important to one group, may be ignored by another.

Early jazz is often associated with New Orleans. One explanation for the rise of a new music there is that New Orleans, especially in the early part of this century, was the most cosmopolitan of American cities. It was also a port city where the Caribbean influence was great and where Spanish and French (Catholic) slaveholding permitted greater potential for preserving African and European traditions side by side than in the rest of the (Protestant-dominated) United States. While the argument behind this assertion is complex, it relates to the idea that Protestantism was focused on all aspects of worldly behavior more so than the Catholic tradition. It does not suggest that Catholic slaveholding was any less cruel—just less ethnocentric and more eclectic.

Prior to the Louisiana Purchase and lasting until after the Civil War, a complex and unique caste system of racial definition arose and declined in New Orleans. By the end of the nineteenth century, persons of mixed racial heritage, sometimes formally trained in the European musical tradition, had to find expression and/or work by playing with and accommodating to those with closer ties to the African way of musical thinking. Like race relations itself in America, jazz became a struggle to reconcile powerful traditions in conflict.

Part of the answer to this need to accommodate and to reconcile was the development of what later came to be recognized as swing. It was employed as a mechanism for each tradition, the European and the African, to provide the other a musical domain in which to manifest itself.

Someone is supposed to have asked the great New Orleans jazz innovator Louis Armstrong to characterize jazz. (His reply could just as well apply to swing as an essential element of jazz.) Jazz legend has it that he told her not to mess with it if she could not feel it. Swing itself is indeed a feeling and hard to describe in words; words fail to capture its total essence. Therefore, any "theory" of swing is best understood as but a starting point toward comprehension. One really must listen to swing in order to "dig" it.

In true jazz, with its emphasis on improvisation, creating new melodies out of old, and altering chordal structures, the whole becomes a great deal more than the sum of parts; the "feel" of swing is an essential element. Most listeners, however they understand the melodic and harmonic changes of jazz, at first feel the radical change in rhythmic structure. The exciting new musical conception called jazz, and felt as swing, gained an audience in the 1920s and the 1930s in America and abroad. It was novel and exciting and could not be denied; sweeping away convention in its path, it offered no quarter to racism, demanded recognition on its own terms, and attracted worldwide attention.

Propelled by the dissemination of the phonograph and the radio, nonprint and listened-to mass media, this new feeling in music spread like wildfire. Masters of both jazz and swing—as a form of jazz—took rules about such things as syncopation (accenting normally "weak" beats) as merely the starting point for establishing exceptions and new sets of rules to be broken in turn. Rule making and rule breaking, after all, is what improvisation is all about. And improvisation is the real key to understanding jazz in all of its forms. Our analytic need four score years from the very origin of jazz and three score years beyond the heyday of swing is to achieve perspective from the point of view of the audiences for what was a brand new world music. The paradox of mass audiences is that they both crave the familiar (and therefore distrust innovation) and at the very same time search restlessly for the new and the faddish. It is also important to understand that mass audiences tend to focus on particular aspects of complex art forms and that those aspects may be reduced to formulas. Certainly the swing formula was used by a lot of poor to average bands as merely a device during the heyday of the swing era.

It is one thing to assert a definition of swing; it is quite another to explain how swing became the popular music of the 1930s. It is necessary, in the first place, to understand that writers and commentators need labels to describe phenomena going on around them. We often see references to the 1920s as the jazz age. Does that mean that true jazz dominated popular culture? Not at all. The same thing can be said of the swing era. Most of what people listened to was not pure jazz-based swing but rather the music of large dance and concert bands playing written arrangements with occasional improvised solos and with enough syncopation to fit the category: familiar enough to be understood yet novel enough to be new and exciting.

The key to understanding the popularity of the big bands of the 1930s is to understand that they were tied to the passion of people to dance. It was "hip"; in the vocabulary of the day, the listeners and the dancers were "hep cats." In the same way that people dance to rock music today, their grandparents danced to swing music. Popular music in America, moreover, has always been the music of song and dance, and especially dance. Swing moved the masses.

African-American dance style has heavily influenced popular dancing in America. From the Charleston, the Lindy, and the Black Bottom of the 1920s and 1930s, through the Funky Chicken and the Mashed Potato popular in the 1960s, to the Moon Walking craze of the late 1980s, the leading edge of popular dance music has been based on styles that came out of the black community. Of course, other styles of dancing, both formal and folk, were widespread. Among youth, however, led by the new mass media, the radio and the phonograph, jazz-inspired swing won the day and captured the popular American imagination in the 1930s. Frequently the innovators were black; the imitators were white.

There were outstanding white jazz players and swing musicians. That they were "into" African-American music only a fool would deny. That they do not deserve credit for their contributions is unjust. The wonder of cultural traditions is that they are not based on genetics. Unlike bees, who have no choice about the dance they do, humans are free to cross over and dance (or hum or sing) to different drummers. Culture is the learned way of doing things; it is both created and learned in a social context. White musicians learned the African-American style and contributed to it. White musicians, excited by what they heard on records and in clubs, did all that they could to get close to the source. Competitions (cutting sessions) and opportunities to play across racial lines ("sitting in" and jam sessions) cropped up in major music centers throughout the United States, especially in Chicago, Kansas City, and New York.

In the preswing and early swing eras a number of "better" white musicians such as Bix Beiderbecke, Bunny Berigan, Artie Shaw, and Benny Goodman jammed frequently with black innovators such as Louis Armstrong, Earl Hines, Coleman Hawkins, Roy Eldridge, and Benny Carter. This undoubtedly influenced the adoption of a swing style by the big white bands of the 1930s and helped to integrate racially some of these bands toward the end of the swing era as the opportunity to do so arose.

Jazzman Benny Goodman found jazz cognates in klezmer music (the Middle Eastern–influenced music of the Eastern European Jewish shtetl), which also linked African and European music in a unique way. Goodman's approach to the clarinet certainly became a part of the jazz mix. It was Benny Goodman who most publicly broke the color line in the late 1930s by integrating his own band. One of the great technical players of all times, Goodman had the courage and honesty to acknowledge his roots in several musical cultures and used the muscle of his own popularity to force his sense of what was right on a duplicitous entertainment industry.

Once swing caught on, many musicians and bandleader-businessmen, such as Paul Whiteman, who achieved enormous popularity with the mass American audience in the 1920s, wanted to capture the essentials of what was turning people on. Segregation meant that blacks, who arguably were more authentic, were not acceptable. Therefore, whites who had learned the new style were brought in. Bix Beiderbecke, a white Iowan and a legend of early jazz, played in the Whiteman band. Bix was authentic. He was also constantly in trouble for his free spirit and often got into hot water for improvising jazz "too authentically." (This phenomenon was not limited to white players in white bands; Dizzy Gillespie, a living jazz legend, had similar problems a decade later playing bebop in Cab Calloway's black swing band.)

African Americans rarely were permitted to become stars in an entertainment system that grabbed themes and inspiration from any source but typically made sure that those who profited from it were from the establishment. American entertainers were caught in the system of segregation that was a legacy of America's very beginnings as a nation.

Segregation is an ugly word, and so are words like *discrimination, stereotype*, and *prejudice*, whenever they are applied to social relations. These terms, and others like them, imply that cultural forces such as music and art (as well as social, political, economic, and social institutions) can be held separate and apart from one another. It almost always means that those in control feel that some—those like themselves—are "by nature" superior to others.

The interaction of diverse groups and influence nonetheless are usually beyond mere political control, even coercive control. The infection of innovation and its spread often cannot be controlled. Folkways, moreover, almost always also tend to be a lot more resilient than their suppressors assume.

The paradox of America is that much of its impulse for nationhood came from its antiestablishment character. Black slavery never fit the American paradigm. Yet, and fitfully, our European forebears tried to square the circle by using formulas that defined slaves as equal to some proportion of full citizenship or, finally following a bloody civil war, that those who had origins in the slave category merited equal but separate facilities even though they were "full" citizens.

Not until 1954, well after the swing era, did the U.S. Supreme Court in its *Brown* v. *Board of Education* decision, finally and forcefully reject the separate but equal doctrine as unworkable and repugnant. At last, as a people, we said that one category of citizens, defined by ethnic origin, could not be dealt with as separate but equal because there was no practical way in which to ensure equal treatment. In other words, if a group is singled out for special treatment, it will fail to achieve positive treatment since the American political system is based on distributive representation and the need for basic protection of each citizen's rights, no matter what kind of minority that citizen may represent. As a people, Americans continue to grapple with this issue of race as a category of minority status.

To understand the swing era, it is necessary to place ourselves back in time before *Brown*. It was legal and acceptable to keep blacks and whites separate. Negroes (or blacks or colored people) were considered inferior by many in the majority; anything that white folks did for "them" was a matter of noblesse oblige.

The genius of African-American music, however, could not be contained within an unjust system of segregation. It kept breaking through cultural barriers. Within the American system of segregation, however, nonwhite innovators rarely received either their just desserts or acknowledgment of their contributions. A nearly all-white music industry controlled the cultural product and its markets. Even the mass black audience was serviced by white entrepreneurs who produced the race records of the 1920s and 1930s and controlled and profited from black entertainment in theaters and clubs and on phonograph records and the radio. The link between the growth in the 1920s and 1930s of a mass entertainment industry, youth, and the phonograph and radio can hardly be emphasized enough; a segregated strategy of containment could not hold the robust new forms. That so much unfairness and human suffering occurred is a part of the continuing tragedy of race relations in America.

By and large, musicians were segregated when they worked; audiences were segregated. But audience demand created some interesting anomalies. In major cities, special clubs arose where African-American entertainers played to white audiences. All-black shows, reviews, and plays were produced on Broadway. Black stars such as Noble Sissle, Eubie Blake, and Bill "Bojangles" Robinson broke through to national reputations. That they all suffered indignities that were not a part of the white performer/creators' lot is well known and well documented.

And, of course, whites bought phonograph records produced primarily for black buyers, and they heard black bands on the radio. In fact, since the performers on radio or on records cannot be seen, the music could be enjoyed on its own terms without a visual reminder of race.

Records were inexpensive and sold millions of copies. Radio was a sponsored medium, and advertisers were interested in reaching large audiences for their products. The selling of soda pop and cigarettes and soap provided a boisterous context in which swing emerged and thrived. In this period, dancers flocked to dance halls and nightclubs to swing and sway and to see and hear the bands and the singers heard on records and the radio.

A driving force was the emerging American system of consumer capitalism. Music was a business; it had become an industry. The mass music market demanded innovation and novelty; jazz and jazz simplified into big band swing met that market demand. Profit was the key, and the color of money turned out to be neither black nor white.

During the early swing era (the mid–1930s) the major black bands (Fletcher Henderson, Jimmie Lunceford, Count Basie, Duke Ellington, Earl Hines, Chick Webb, and Cab Calloway) managed to penetrate segregated America through the popularity of radio and phonograph outlets, which were accidentally color blind. Restricted in where they could play, the radio and phonograph helped them gain acceptance from better white popular musicians and "hip" swingers. Eventually some doors opened for them in previously segregated hotels and theaters. As the black swing bands became more commercially successful with white audiences and with the genuine musical admiration and imitation of white stars, a new pattern emerged.

A pattern of total segregation in America was never completely realized; there were always exceptions. Usually the blacks who did break through worked in the background. White bandleaders hired black arrangers. By the late 1930s, a few black players appeared in white bands. Within jazz there was also an after-hours tradition of jam sessions, with white players sitting in with black bands, and vice versa. Jazz and real swing was firmly supported in the black community. Trend-setting white hep cats and hipsters sought out the new music and pushed it toward the mainstream.

White band leaders of note such as Benny Goodman, Artie Shaw, Charlie Barnet, the Dorseys, Gene Krupa, Harry James, and Woody Herman emulated the African-American's style and hired blacks as arrangers and soloists. Black "stars" were employed to give authenticity to swing bands in large numbers by the early 1940s. The floodgate was open. It was, however, more than a decade and a half later that blacks were hired into regular studio jobs and permitted to earn a living from music in less than starring and highly public roles. Like major league baseball's integration nearly a decade later, jazz and swing did not end segregation; some senseless barriers, however, were lowered, if not removed.

During the entire swing era, America was on the move. Industrialization and urbanization and the search for employment sifted and sorted the population of the country and created networks of entertainment; radio networks, phonograph distribution systems, and the emergence of traveling troupes of entertainers, including dance bands, spread far and wide. Dance band circuits spawned territory bands that were loosely organized into a hierarchy, with the major population centers at their pinnacle. Los Angeles, Kansas City, Chicago, and New York were magnets for the best bands and individual stars from the territory bands. Live radio broadcasts from hotel ballrooms and the opportunity to make recordings solidified a national status hierarchy of bands and musicians. Smaller groups, often drawn from popular big bands, jammed and innovated, and some gained popularity.

In Chicago Louis Armstrong and King Oliver, both from New Orleans, dominated the musical scene. Later, Benny Goodman and others emerged. In New York, the bands of Chick Webb, Jimmie Lunceford, Fletcher Henderson (who also became a key arranger for Goodman), and Don Redman contributed to the swing style. Tommy and Jimmy Dorsey, Artie Shaw, and Harry James became household names. Glen Gray's Casa Loma Orchestra and the bands of Charlie Barnet and Ben Pollack became well known through radio broadcasts. Jean Goldkette fielded various bands that traveled the territory circuits throughout the Midwest. The new music called swing overwhelmed the popular music business, on the road and in the air.

The most famous band in Kansas City in the early 1930s was led by Benny Moten, who combined the blues tradition of the riff (or call-and-response pattern) with the hard-driving sound of a big band. The band was taken over in 1935 by a musician from Red Bank, New Jersey, named William "Count" Basie. Employing the blues-riff style (constant repetition of a theme), Basie transformed the big band into a platform for extraordinary soloists and a marvel of disciplined section playing.

John Hammond, the scion of a wealthy eastern family and an extraordinary talent scout for Columbia Records, sought out gifted singers and musicians without regard to race or ethnic origin. Hammond brought a wide diversity of talented people into the Columbia recording studios over many decades, including Bessie Smith, Billie Holiday and, much later, Bob Dylan. Hammond, who was scouting bands in the Chicago area, happened to tune his radio to an experimental radio station at the top of the AM dial. He heard a broadcast from the Reno Club in Kansas City by a local band led by Count Basie. Excited by the sound, Hammond flew to Kansas City. He talked a friend, Willard Alexander, an artist's agent, into going with him. They convinced Basie to bring his band to New York. The rest, as they say, is history. The Count Basie Orchestra became one of the most successful and long-lasting musical aggregations in America; alumni from the various Basie groups constitute a who's who of both swing and jazz.

The swing era came to close as a result of two factors. The dark days of World War II made travel difficult, and many musicians went into the armed services. Following a bitter labor dispute, the musicians' union imposed a recording ban in 1942 that kept the bands out of the radio and recording studios. Perhaps just as important, the music itself had become used up as a popular form. Better jazz players went on to experiment with a new style that became known as bebop, while the popular music audience waited for a new epiphany of African American–influenced music called rock 'n' roll.

In the current era with its debates about politically correct views and with the nation facing a massive shift in population characteristics, there is no better time than now to review our cultural origins. The swing era was a time of change. We are going through another. The oppression of a minority, African Americans, could not suppress their contribution to the American spirit. There is a lesson to be learned here about the contribution of women, Asian Americans, older citizens, and others who keep the national agenda open.

Things are far from all right with us. Now, more than ever before, tolerance and passion must be balanced. Respect for diversity—learning truly to value it—is not merely a nicety but a necessity. Conflict, accommodation, and change itself is the very core of the new world that has come into being. To see this new world as a rainbow, a mosaic, as a whole with many parts, is the challenge the global village offers us.

Only through serious and meticulous scholarship, investigation, and appreciation of the way things were—and will be—can we liberate ourselves from the temptation to impose false order and crushing control over the very medley of cultural diversity that makes life itself interesting. The lesson of swing is that in the longer run, closed systems cannot survive.

We owe a lot to the musicians of the swing era. From the fringes of an oppressive political and economic system, they blew a breath of fresh air that became a metaphor for what is best in all of us: freedom of expression, creativity, and the liberation of the spirit against all odds.

BIBLIOGRAPHY

Gridley, Mark C. *Jazz Styles*. 3d ed. Englewood Cliffs, N.J.: Prentice-Hall, 1988.
Sales, Grover. *Jazz: America's Classical Music*. Englewood Cliffs, N.J.: Prentice-Hall, 1984.

Schuller, Gunther. *The Swing Era: The Development of Jazz, 1930–1945.* New York: Oxford University Press, 1989.
Simon, George T. *The Big Bands.* New York: Macmillan, 1971.

RECORDINGS

Big Band Jazz. 6 LPs. RO30 DMM6–0610.
Singers and Soloists of the Swing Bands. 6 LPs. RO35 T6–19881.
Smithsonian Collection of Classic Jazz. 7 LPs (also available on CDs). RO33 P7–19477.

Recordings are available from the Smithsonian Collection of Recordings, Smithsonian Institution Press, Washington, D.C. 20560. 800–678–2677.

19

The Role and Image of African Americans in Rock and Roll

Charles R. Warner

Given the assumptions of musical influence implied by the title of this chapter, it seems an odd state of affairs that many readers of this book are undoubtedly able to conceive of the rock and roll phenomenon without any serious consideration of the importance of African-American artists and audiences to its development. Indeed, if one may assume that the bulk of the rock and roll audience is comprised of white youth, then it would seem an equally valid assumption that the musical and cultural landscape of these white youth would be populated by that type of performance imagery with which they could most accurately identify. It should come as no surprise that when one becomes lost in a reverie of rock and roll's past glories, the demographics appear to be the same on both sides of the limelight: Italian kids in a Newark bowling alley lounge dancing to Frankie Valli and the Four Seasons, a sea of blond hair and blue eyes ebbing and flowing to the wholesome harmonies of the Beach Boys, adolescent suburban girls screaming and fainting at the very sight of the Beatles.

Certainly part of the reason that rock and roll's history is vulnerable to this type of whitewashing is definitional in nature. Even the most rudimentary consideration of the music's genesis will reveal a separation of musical product on the basis of race at an institutional level. Music industry chart distinctions between popular music and race music were both a cause and a reinforcement of segregated radio airplay well into the 1950s, and humorous anecdotes of the industry's attempts to satisfy postwar youth demand for black music by offering sanitized cover versions by white artists have become part of the music's lore. (If the reader doubts the unintentional humor inherent in these attempts, I recommend a comparison of the Little Richard and Pat Boone versions of "Tutti-Frutti" as a classic example.) Even in today's comparatively enlightened pop music environment, less overt chart distinctions based on race still exist and continue to be both a cause and reinforcement of segregated radio formatting. Of course, the prospects for creating a crossover hit that can blur such chart distinctions are greater today than in times past, but it is not insignificant that many African-American artists feel that such a hit is necessary for their ascendance to true stardom.

This portrayal of a racially polarized history of rock and roll may—and should—cause a certain degree of consternation. Indeed, it is difficult to view the brief history of rock and roll without entertaining the notion that it may stand as a microcosm of our larger cultural dilemma concerning distinctions based on race. Still, it is precisely those enlightened readers who, more often than their less-enlightened social counterparts, take great pleasure in the consumption of rock and roll as a cultural product. But before we begin to lament this paradox and the psychological dissonance it portends, we must remind ourselves of an important fact relating to the precondition of rock and roll's development: it is no accident that the two national cultures within which rock and roll began and developed—the United States and the United Kingdom, respectively—are characterized by multiracial societies traditionally plagued by racial turmoil. In fact, one could say that therein lies the key to the genesis of rock and roll as a cultural form, for it is the distinctions that culturally define what it means to be black or white that serve as the catalyst, the fuel, and the justification for rock and roll as both a musical style and a life-style.

Today, almost forty years after its birth as a recognizable pop music form, it is common knowledge among its adherents that rock and roll is in some way a blending of Anglo-American and African-American musical cultures. Still, the significance of this blending is all too often limited to serving as a simple explanation as to why rock and roll sounds the way it does. Seldom is it employed as a tool for examining the greater issues of rock and roll's rise as a dominant pop music form or rock and roll's status as a microcosm of America's multiracial history. Actually, this blending of Anglo-American and African-American musics was not the unique invention of some visionary proto-rocker. In fact, the interface of black and white music and musicians predates not only rock and roll's birth in the 1950s but the birth of pop (recorded) music in the 1920s as well. In pop music's prehistory, Anglo-American and African-American musicians shared what Tony Russell terms "common stock materials," a collection of songs that stand as a testament to the intermingling of American musicians of African and European heritage dating back to the early days of slavery. These songs tended to be ballads in the Anglo-European tradition of oral storytelling, but their content centered on themes that reflected an expansionist, multiracial America. In addition, these odes to railroad heroes and traveling rogues featured many African musical "survivals" (standard song materials), not the least of which were emphases on harmony and rhythm. Eventually these common stock materials would become distilled into recognizable white and black musical forms: hillbilly music and the blues, respectively. It seems clear that these racially distinct musical expressions share not only a claim to rock and roll's parentage but a common ancestry as well. Still, in a national culture largely defined by its racial distinctions, only that music developed within the dominant white culture would be nurtured as pop music for the mass audience of twentieth-century America.

The genesis of pop music—that is, music published or transmitted to its audience in live performance or recording—can be traced back to the 1920s when the recording and broadcasting of regional southern music became commonplace. And while these regional musics encompassed both black and white musical idioms (e.g., gospel, blues, ragtime, hillbilly), it is important to note that their greatest impact was felt within the white-dominated music industry. Initially influencing the traditional folk music of the South, the resulting melange of recordings and broadcasts would eventually become institutionalized as country music in the 1930s, complete with such mass culture trappings as the Grand Ole Opry radio shows and a performer many consider to be the first pop star, Jimmie Rodgers. Remixing what had become the rather distinct blues and hillbilly (black and white) musical forms with their common boogie beat roots, Rodgers personified the process of musical hybridization that would fuel the development of pop music through the rock era. In other words, he became the first "white boy who stole the blues."

Throughout the 1940s, as communication technologies and the entertainment industry were becoming increasingly "massified," the exposure of America's dominant white culture to the products of African-American culture became more commonplace. Social boundaries based on race become somewhat unenforceable in the context of free radio transmissions, which are available to anyone, regardless of race. In addition, the armed forces during World War II provided an unprecedented opportunity for white American youth to encounter black American youth on a mass scale, at least in the sense that they shared a common national purpose. As postwar America continued to thrive with the paradox of legally sanctioned segregation and an increasingly persistent cultural interfacing of the races, the response of the pop music industry to this situation underwent some adjustment. Rather than encourage additional grafting of African-American musical technique to an essentially Anglo-American pop music form, the task became one of achieving the increasingly popular performance qualities of black music through the medium of a white performer with whom a predominantly white mass audience could fully identify. It was this task that became the obsession of Sam Phillips, a recording engineer from Memphis who claimed that if he could find a white man who had the "sound and feel of the Negro," he could make a fortune in the music business. Phillips found such a man in Elvis Presley, a performer whose career has become so legendary it need not be rehashed here. But what does merit emphasis is the distinction between the mere assimilation of a small list of African-American musical techniques by the country music industry of the 1930s and the quantum leap represented by the search for a white man who could somehow embody the sound and feel—the gestalt, if you will—of the African American. Once found, rock and roll was here to stay.

While separated by time and, to a lesser extent, style, the careers of Jimmie Rodgers and Elvis Presley exhibit one striking fact about pop music: regardless of a predominantly white audience's affinity for a music that features discernible Africanisms as part of its style, a precondition for that music's success on a mass level seems to be the discovery of a white performer as a vehicle for the music. This racial precondition for mass success is best exemplified through a comparison of Elvis Presley and his contemporary, Chuck Berry. If Presley can be said to represent a black musical consciousness in an acceptable white vehicle, Chuck Berry can be said to represent a black musical vehicle made palatable to a predominantly white mass audience. Originally Berry's musical inclinations were toward traditional blues, as indicated by his recording of "Wee Wee Hours" in 1955 and his efforts to have the song released on the blues-oriented Chess label. But it was the pop-oriented B-side, "Maybellene," that Leonard Chess chose to emphasize during that period of white teen affection for fast cars and young love and that propelled Berry into a position of prominence in the rock and roll pantheon. In his reappropriation of country guitar stylings, originally the province of African-American musicians, Berry went beyond his original conception of the blues and synthesized what would become the seminal rock and roll guitar style preferred by the youthful white mass market. Indeed, Berry's guitar playing was easily the greatest stylistic influence for white rock guitarists of the 1960s, clearly more influential than Presley's more countrified approach. But if this is the case, then why do we refer to Elvis Presley, rather than Chuck Berry, as the King of Rock and Roll?

The answer to this question lies in the cultural realities of twentieth-century America and the legacy of racial distinctions on which they are based. Certainly one of these cultural realities is the general control of the music industry by the dominant white culture, a situation that tends to hold true regardless of the racial composition of performers and audience. Perhaps a more significant reality of the twentieth century is the "massification" of cultural production, which virtually ensures a mass audience in which white Americans will be a majority. Such realities would seem to explain the necessity of a white performer as an initial vehicle for the popularization of any pop music form. But what they do not explain is the virtually simultaneous acceptance of Elvis Presley and Chuck Berry by the same mass audience. In order to explain this situation, one must come to the realization that Presley and Berry served different needs during the formative years of the rock and roll subculture. Berry's style of guitar playing has certainly been more influential than Presley's, and that stands as his personal legacy.

Chuck Berry is unrivaled as an instrumental technician; he is rock and roll's musical prototype. Elvis Presley fills a different, more crucial, role; he is rock and roll's attitudinal prototype. While the average (that is, white) rock and roll fan might not have had the talent to emulate Berry's guitar playing successfully, he certainly had the ability to emulate both the appearance and behavior of Presley. Both roles were necessary for the development of rock and roll because rock and roll is much more than a musical style; it is also a life-style.

To this point, I have provided a brief explanation as to how rock and roll developed as a hybrid of African-American and Anglo-American musical styles, combined with the enabling discovery of a white catalyst who provided both the "sound and feel" of the black performer and an object of identification for a predominantly white audience. But what remains a mystery is the reason this musical hybrid was, and continues to be, so appealing to its young mass audience. While any explanation would be subject to charges of oversimplification, it seems safe to say that the answer lies in the social realities that developed following World War II—the baby boom, in particular. Postwar America was characterized by an increasing degree of prosperity among the white middle and working classes, and the bulk of their unprecedented disposable income was directed toward the family and invested in children. This shift in family financial structure was accompanied by an equally unprecedented degree of uncertainty about the future in which these families would exist. Concerns as diverse as the increased mobility of the family and the prospect of nuclear destruction had the effect of calling many stable values and truths into question. And without such underlying meanings to provide cultural and social continuity, a postwar value structure loosely based on surface appearance and created imagery filled the vacuum created by their absence. In the context of this new value structure, the only things certain were change and uncertainty; the prewar conception of transcendent truths as a basis for community became a virtual impossibility. The vanguard of this new value structure was the postwar generation of financially empowered and increasingly autonomous children who knew little of that prewar stability. Of course, the parents of these children attempted to reassert their traditional values—a process that continues between parents and children to this day—but to no avail. The rift between generations continued to widen and eventually became institutionalized as the once-unified culture of white America grew a "tail" that would eventually "wag the dog": the subculture of youth.

Not only did this subculture of youth become institutionalized as a concrete, demographic grouping populated by individuals, but the very idea of youth became institutionalized as the central value of postwar consumerism. In other words, "youth" became a symbol of all things modern and progressive, not merely a state of physical development leading to maturity. This equation of youth and consumerism drastically affected the concept

of leisure in postwar America in that the new youth subculture represented
a class of people who were both financially potent and relatively unburdened
by the daily responsibilities of the adult world. This best-of-both-worlds
situation resulted in a plethora of consumer products designed to fill the
idle time of the young with diversion and entertainment. Perhaps a bit
envious of the privileged position they created for their children, adults soon
began to embrace the youth-consumerism ethic. No longer would the term
leisure simply refer to a brief respite from the obligatory workday. Leisure
would become a life-style in which everyone could purchase "fun" in the
form of consumer goods. This encroachment of the adult world on the
marketplace of the young dictated that the youth subculture would have to
locate a cultural product through which it could maintain an appearance
of autonomy. Rock and roll—sonically, visually, and socially inaccessible
to the adult world—was just such a product.

At the nexus of leisure, consumerism, and music, the rock and roll life-
style developed as the preferred, idealized mode of existence for the youth
subculture. But in a postwar world in which transcendent values were nonexistent, this newly constructed life-style would require the construction of
an appropriate guiding force—a hero figure—complete with all the attendant
imagery and created reality necessary for the task of giving the youth subculture its raison d'être. The hero figure was found through the mining of
the same ambivalent racial history that gave birth to rock and roll—what
Bane describes as a culturally constructed mythic image of the black man
as the locus of pleasure for American youth. Like all other mythic figures,
this imaginary black man functions as a sort of archetype—an image
not consciously referenced or subjected to verification but still serving as
the standard-bearer of the subculture's behavioral mode and aesthetic sense.
Clearly this mythic black stereotype accurately addresses the needs and
desires of the youth subculture as an embodiment of those qualities that
distinguish the postwar youth mind-set from that of their prewar parents:
an instinctual primitivism centered on the body as opposed to an intellec-
tually constrained rationality, an unambitious, anarchic nature rather than
an industrious Christian work ethic, and an emphasis on immediate rather
than deferred gratification. Perhaps these factors can best explain why Elvis
Presley, rather than Chuck Berry, became known as the King of Rock and
Roll. Presley embodied all the traits of this mythic black man in a white
vessel. Berry, on the other hand, was the genuine article, a black performer
whose physical appearance would constantly remind the audience of its
separate racial-cultural heritage, thereby destroying the power of the myth
through an infusion of reality. Appropriately, this mythic black man championed by the youth subculture is virtually identical to the negative stereotype that prewar white culture traditionally placed upon the African
American, a reversal that supports this postwar bifurcation of white America. Yet whether it is perceived as a positive or negative image, this racial

stereotype rests on the belief that the black man is free in ways the white man is not, and he is free in precisely those ways the white teenager wishes to be.

This mythic black man is not a device limited to the postwar youth subculture of the United States. Indeed, the minstrel shows of nineteenth-century America were comprised of song and dance created and performed by and for white culture yet based on a stereotyped, mythic black persona. Also, there is a great deal of evidence that postwar British youth were not only greatly influenced by this mythic conception of the American black man but that they strongly identified with the actual life-styles of black British immigrants as well. Interestingly, there is little evidence that these British youth identified in any way with the life-styles exhibited by Asian immigrants, who, like the white youths' parents, were perceived as conservative, traditional, and hard working. It should come as no surprise that these two national youth subcultures, which share similar mythic foundations, are also the two cultural entities routinely credited with the birth and development of rock and roll as a musical form and a life-style.

I feel somewhat compelled to emphasize the fact that this chapter is in no way intended to diminish the huge debt owed to both African-American music as a fundamental component of rock and roll and African-American musicians as essential contributors to its content. Indeed, there is much to recommend the contention of Living Color guitarist Vernon Reid that all rock and roll is fundamentally black music. Yet one must be sensitive to the mutations that occur when a musical form becomes recast as a mass culture product. In the context of the pop music industry, even the most authentic black music has been routinely reformulated with sale to a predominantly white mass audience in mind. Berry Gordy's Motown Records label virtually redefined formulaic pop music in the 1960s as something decidedly African American. Yet as this black musical idiom became a valuable mass culture product, it was touted as "the sound of young America," not *black* America. Similarly, rock guitar virtuoso Jimi Hendrix is best remembered not as a black performer playing for a black audience but as the star of Woodstock—a youth subculture event during which black faces were conspicuous by their absence. Even today, the Hendrix legacy is one of influence on subsequent generations of predominantly white rock guitarists. These points are raised not to diminish the importance of these contributions toward making African-American culture a significant feature of our cultural mainstream but as a reminder of the continuing white hegemony exerted over such mass cultural forms.

Perhaps the perfect metaphor for the uneasy racial dynamic that characterizes rock and roll lies in rap music. Clearly an African-American musical form, rap is replete with African musical survivals, such as the call-and-response vocal techniques, which inform much of the oral traditions of African tribal life. And the translation of these Africanisms to an American sociocultural context is often achieved with a high degree of elegance and, at times, irony. For example, the technique of sampling, in which snippets of previously released pop records are recombined through tape editing to form a distinctly new musical creation, seems to stand as a type of poetic justice as black rappers "steal back" the American musical heritage that was once taken from them through the contractual maneuverings of the music industry. Still, the acceptance of rap by a mass audience seemed to require the emergence of a white vehicle for the music. And while resoundingly "dissed" (put down) by the black rap community, the Beastie Boys proved to be that vehicle by making that all-important crossover into the white-dominated pop charts, thereby paving the way for more "authentic" rap acts. It is no accident that the most commercially successful (crossover) rap acts tend to be either white performers portraying a black sensibility (e.g., 3rd Bass, accepted by both black and white audiences largely because they were raised as middle-class whites and voluntarily chose to live a black life-style) or black performers whose personae are acceptable to a white audience (e.g., DJ Jazzy Jeff and the Fresh Prince, winners of the first rap Grammy Award, whose thematic concerns mirror Chuck Berry's mainstream youth obsessions of girls, cars, and skipping school).

Finally, a closing comment on rock and roll's tenuous racial balance concerns the rap group 2 Live Crew's battle with the State of Florida concerning obscenity in their lyrics. Regardless, one can only wonder if these powers of state would have been summoned to protect a culturally isolated, predominantly black audience from the supposed dangers inherent in their music. We will never know, since the album in question, *Nasty As They Wanna Be*, has gone platinum with sales in excess of 1 million units and has been resting comfortably on the pop charts for over forty weeks.

BIBLIOGRAPHY

Bane, Michael. *White Boy Singin' the Blues*. New York: Penguin Books, 1982.

Chambers, Iain. *Urban Rhythms: Pop Music and Popular Culture*. New York: St. Martin's Press, 1985.

Frith, Simon. *Sound Effects: Youth, Leisure, and the Politics of Rock 'n' Roll*. New York: Pantheon Books, 1981.

Hebdige, Dick. *Subculture: The Meaning of Style*. London: Methuen and Co., 1979.

Marcus, Greil. *Mystery Train: Images of America in Rock 'n' Roll Music*. 2d ed. New York: E. P. Dutton, 1982.

Part V

Gender

—— *20* ——

Equal Time: A Historical Overview of Women in Jazz

LINDA DAHL

When most people think of women in jazz, they think of Billie Holiday, Ella Fitzgerald, or Bessie Smith: singers of blues and ballads in smoke-filled nightclubs and concert halls or, at most, the occasional piano player. Yet there is a vast underground of women instrumentalists as well, not to mention bandleaders, composers, record producers, and artists' managers. This chapter looks at those talented women in jazz who have been mostly buried in the footnotes of the music and at the factors that have both held them back through the various eras and styles of jazz and all too often keep their accomplishments a secret. It is time to retrieve and celebrate the accomplishments of the jazzwomen.

Jazz is complicated to define because it has been an evolving, ever-experimental art form for more than a century, with many different styles to its credit. It is hard, therefore, to generalize about a musical body that includes ragtime, swing, bebop, and other offshoots. Generally, though, it is agreed that jazz involves individual improvisation, or "blowing," in a group context—improvisation that includes the creation of new melodic and/or rhythmic patterns on a given harmonic foundation. This is a highly sophisticated and technically demanding technique in which individual skill is crucial, as is the necessity to function musically within the group. Like other art forms where the group is important, jazz has always been a way of life, as well as a way of playing music. This must be kept in mind when examining women's participation; the jazz way of life has been, arguably, a masculine one.

Another feature of jazz is that it is African American in spirit and philosophy. That is, it derives from an uprooted African aesthetic in which (among other elements) celebration, incantation, and a spiritual-artistic merging were kept alive by slaves on American soil and gradually transmuted as European and other cultures influenced the music.

When black people were freed after the Civil War, what can be called prejazz music blossomed. Blacks with the talent and inclination were at last free to move around the country and could seek jobs in the emerging black entertainment venues of tent shows, carnivals, and nascent black vaudeville. In the latter 1800s the music included blues styles and spirituals, work songs, and cabaret-popular tunes—and ragtime. It was music heard at churches and picnics and at whorehouses and taverns. It was played by marching bands and by piano "professors," by orchestras and beggars. For women, the black church was (and is) a haven and a training ground for musicianship. But outside the church, most of the opportunities to learn and play music, to get jobs and recognition, were male oriented and male dominated. There were many reasons this was so. Among them was the stricture against "nice," respectable women working professionally—that is, for pay outside the home. At that time, there were hardly any women on stage in the popular traveling shows that catered to lower- and middle-class audiences. Minstrel shows and traveling troupes were segregated by race and by sex. Female impersonators stood in for women in many roles and were quite popular and respected. A woman musician who could get work risked losing her reputation.

Of course, there were always exceptions. Both white females and black men and women formed their own orchestras, bands, and troupes—a tradition that continues to this day in the case of women. In the 1880s, newspapers advertised the services of a number of all-women groups: the Ladies' Orchestra in Chelsea, Massachusetts; a Colored Female Brass Band in Michigan; a dance band at the Atlantic Gardens club in New York City; and the services of Madame Rentz's Female Minstrels. Minstrel shows were extremely popular across the country and gave women players the rare chance to work and be heard. Among the black troupes, black women were represented to some extent. Getting in on the ground floor of black musical entertainment gave these women exposure and opportunities, and black women would continue to be an important, if somewhat hidden, presence in black music in all areas into the next century. With both widespread poverty and a lack of employment opportunities more prevalent among black people than whites, to be a musical entertainer was seen more often as a way up and out of the ghetto than as a loss of respectability for women. Among the early women, Bessie Smith and Ma Rainey were the most famous to come out of the traveling shows, but a host of women played for tent shows and circuses—women like Mrs. Henry Hart with the Alabama Minstrels and Mrs. Theodore Finney with the Quadrille Band in Detroit.

One way up for women musicians was through family bands. As the name suggests, the whole family took part—and not only as players but as composers, arrangers, and directors. Such aggregations were especially important to women because they provided a rare opportunity for equal access to playing the instruments of one's choice. Famed saxophonist Lester Young recounted how his mother, sisters, and aunts played equal roles in the family band that was his training ground, as did the bassist Oscara Pettiford in remembering the skill of his mother and sisters. But these bands were not the norm; most were made up completely of men.

It was in New Orleans, that exceptional place that nurtured exceptional music, where we find that women did play early jazz. A few of these women are still alive and performing today, in their eighties and nineties. As a great cosmopolitan shipping port, New Orleans blended African American, French, Spanish, Caribbean, German, Irish, and other cultures into a gumbo unique in America. Its music has long reflected these various influences, and music has always been important in New Orleans, which had the first opera house in America and what might have been the first black orchestra. Storyville, New Orlean's famous and legal red-light district, nurtured early jazz in whorehouses, gambling houses, and taverns until the District, as it was called, was closed down by the federal government during World War I.

It was much more common for women to be on their backs than on their feet playing early jazz during the late 1800s and early 1900s. And yet among the male piano professors and the brass bands were a significant sprinkling of women players. Old-timers recall women who marched in the early brass bands. Women singers worked in the cabarets. One brothel keeper, Antonia Gonzalez, often played cornet for her clients. There was much music outside of Storyville, at picnics and resorts and beer gardens. Women like "Sweet Emma" Barrett, a piano player who was also called the "Bell Gal" because she tied bells to her wrists and ankles to jingle as she stomped and sang, had long-time careers; she played from the 1920s to the 1980s.

The best known of these early jazzwomen was not a New Orleanian although she played with New Orleans's most famous musician, Louis Armstrong. Lil Hardin Armstrong was trained, having studied at Fisk University, at a time when most jazz musicians (including Louis) could not read music. Louis Armstrong went with "King" Oliver to Chicago in the early 1920s, where jobs were plentiful, and Lil Hardin joined this hot band there, laying down a strong, sure beat and a valued addition for her arranging and reading skills. Records she cut with Armstrong—the Hot Five and Hot Seven sides— were sensations at the time and are collectors' items today. Lil continued to play and write music until her death in the 1970s.

Scores of other women were taking part in the early jazz of the 1920s, especially in the big cities of Chicago and New York. Many might have achieved national fame but were limited to local success by the need to stay at home and raise families. Some women married musicians or bandleaders and traveled with them, such as the trumpeter Leora Meoux, who married the famous early jazz orchestra leader Fletcher Henderson. It was the exceptional woman who managed to carve out a career on her own on the national, not to mention the international, level. One who did so was trumpet player Valaida Snow, a big star in the black community who went on to even greater success abroad. Snow, fellow musicians said, could hit those high Cs just as Louis Armstrong did. Like men in jazz, Valaida found that opportunities to work and the racial climate were better in Europe than in her native country. But she was confronted by a dilemma that has worked to the detriment of other attractive female musicians, which men did not have to face: should she give in to the pressure to play up her good looks and sex appeal as a crowd pleaser or concentrate on her musicianship? Few women were given the chance to succeed on either level that she was as she toured the world and recorded often. She always traveled in style, a sight to behold in her Mercedes-Benz, herself and chauffeur and pet monkey all dressed in her favorite color, orchid. After World War II began, Snow fled persecution in Europe and returned to the United States, but by all accounts she had become somewhat broken and bitter. Also, musical tastes had changed, and Snow's style of showmanship did not fulfill the promise of her early, spectacular trumpet playing.

One woman with giant talent and a lifelong career in jazz illustrates the possibilities for creativity that jazzwomen can achieve. Mary Lou Williams came of age during the 1930s, a vibrant time for the development of jazz, with swing bands playing across the country and offering plenty of jobs for players. There were hundreds of bands to feed the public appetite for dance music, some of them mediocre but many producing good music and a few of them superior. It was an era when women worked most often in the bands as singers; *canaries* and *chirpers* were two of the terms used to describe them. Although many of these singers were sex symbols who could barely carry a tune, dozens of fine talents got their start in bands and developed jazz as a vocal art tremendously as a result. They include Billie Holiday, Mildred Bailey, Lee Wiley, Ella Fitzgerald, and Helen Humes, followed a little later by Sarah Vaughan, Betty Carter, Carmen McRae, Anita O'Day, and others. As singers, these women were not competing directly for jobs as players; they did not invade male musical turf or upset rules and taboos about the proper roles and behavior for women, unlike the women instrumentalists. This was doubtless a major reason for the singers' success.

As a woman musician, Mary Lou Williams faced many of the obstacles in her career, which spanned five decades, that other women did. As a serious artist, she was mainly concerned with the music and the evolution of her own talent, but inevitably she hit some brick walls of resistance to her sex. Her superb talent usually won the day, however, for Mary Lou mastered most of the styles of jazz from preswing to swing, boogie-woogie to bop, and beyond.

Her story is instructive and inspiring. She was born into a poor black family in Atlanta, Georgia, in 1910 and moved when she was age four to Pittsburgh with her musically inclined mother (her father having left home about the time she was born and her mother later remarrying). Mary showed her talent very early, picking out tunes on the family piano. By the time she was six, this talent was known all over town, especially by black musicians who traveled through the black communities. They took her under their wing, exposing her to much good music early on. This and the musical instruction she got at her junior high school were crucial in giving her a foundation as a pianist.

Despite the attention and help of her early years, Mary (later to become Mary Lou) soon ran into trouble. Her family was poor, and she needed a job; by age fourteen she was out doing what she could do best: playing piano as accompanist at a local vaudeville show. There, in the polite phrase of the day, a boss tried to take advantage of her. Fortunately she was rescued by an older girl in the troupe who knew of the man's bad reputation. Such were the ever-present dangers for young girls on their own at a time when the victims of rape were routinely blamed. Poor young women working in the entertainment business had to fend for themselves as well as they could. Mary Lou fended, continuing to go out as accompanist with little traveling shows, a phase of her life that she later recalled simply as "a terrible life" until, at the age of seventeen she married a saxophone player named John Williams. Williams helped her by intervening and pleading her case when managers and performers were reluctant to hire her because she was a woman.

They moved to Oklahoma City in 1927, where they joined a new territory band, a musical group that concentrated on one region of the country, called Andy Kirk's Twelve Clouds of Joy. This group became one of the best of the preswing bands of the era, featuring jump rhythms, blues, and riff arrangements. Mary Lou Williams's contribution to the band was invaluable, but here too she had to overcome resistance to her sex. She began with the band as a kind of second player, filling in as a pianist and acting as chauffeur for the constantly traveling unit. She quickly demonstrated that not only was she a swinging, hard-rocking pianist; she could also write music. Her natural writing talent poured out of her, and she became the key writer-arranger for the band. As she described it, she could not write down her ideas, so she asked other musicians about chords and voicings and memorized what she wanted. By the latter 1930s, the greats in the business were all hiring her to write for their bands—Duke Ellington, Benny Goodman, and others. Traveling constantly with the Clouds, she would write by the aid of a flashlight in the back seat of a car to keep up. (Sadly, like so many other talented black songwriters, she did not know about copyrights and lost many of her potential royalties.) The Clouds were based in Kansas City, and there Mary Lou was at the heart of the hippest new jazz, the place where the new Count Basie Orchestra was cooking up a storm, and she often jammed with the greats. Yet when she played for pay, too often she felt constricted by the demand for her to be a "boogie-woogie mama," when that new style was hot.

By 1942, she was ready for a change and left the Clouds. She divorced

John Williams and started to explore new areas of music, working for a time as staff arranger for Duke Ellington and settling in New York. She was at the heart of the city where big changes were going on in jazz. Younger musicians were rejecting the stylizations of the swing era just past and working out advanced approaches—what would soon be called bebop or just bop. Mary Lou Williams became immersed in this scene. She formed close relationships with other great pianists like Thelonious Monk and Bud Powell. She was also writing, always writing. Her modern jazz symphonic work, *Zodiac Suite*, premiered in 1945 to critical acclaim.

Next she made the trek to Europe, where there was supposedly more respect for the music of jazz. But clubowners there wanted her to continue to be the "boogie-woogie mama" so popular in the 1930s. Mary Lou, though, wanted none of that, and for some time she stopped playing completely. Returning to New York, she devoted herself to aiding down-and-out musicians and street people. Eventually she was encouraged to play and write again. By the early 1960s, she had produced a fresh body of work, akin to the spiritual works of Duke Ellington. Now she became an honored presence on the playing scene, showing a breadth of ability that ranged from accompanying the swing era clarinetist Benny Goodman to playing piano duets with truly avant-garde musician Cecil Taylor. Her playing still swung hard but had deepened in meaning and intensity over the years. By the time of her death in 1981, Mary Lou Williams had become a living history of most of jazz music. About being a woman in jazz, Mary Lou Williams had this to say:

You've got to play, that's all. They don't think of you as a woman if you can really play. I think girls have an inferiority complex about it and this may hold them back. If they have talent, the men will be glad to help them along. [And] working with men, you get to think like a man when you play. You automatically become strong, although this doesn't mean you're not feminine.[1]

Many women in jazz performed and recorded in the 1940s and beyond but usually remained on the fringes of the mainstream. An exception was the proliferation of all-women groups in the late 1930s and again in the 1970s. By the 1940s, the big band era, a continuation of the swing era, led some promoters to try out all-women groups as a money-making gimmick. These bands provided experience, exposure, and a paycheck at a time when work for women was scarce in the main, male-dominated bands. (During World War II, with a shortage of men around, many more women found work with the bands.)

Some all-women big bands developed solid reputations and were commercially successful. Ina Ray Hutton and her Melodears was a fifteen-piece orchestra of white women players with, in those rigidly segregated years, the occasional black player passed off as "Oriental" or "Latin." From 1935 to 1939, the Melodears toured the nation and made recordings and film shorts and features. Another band was the International Sweethearts of Rhythm, begun as a fund-raising effort at a school for poor, minority orphans in the South. From the late 1930s to the late 1940s, the Sweethearts evolved into a band with an international following. They had the benefit of fine arrangements and attracted many of the best young black women players, playing top dance spots such as the Savoy and the Apollo in New York and making records and films. In the 1970s, there was a rebirth of the women's band—with the difference that the women's movement had caused many people to examine and discard sexual stereotypes as they had not done before. Also there was an abundant supply of well-trained women musicians, and women's jazz festivals featured talented females not from just the country but the rest of the world.

For every woman who joined with others to play music, there were, as always, more who preferred to go it alone or to try to work within the established system, competing for work with male peers. Their numbers have increased, but their difficulties, many would attest, are far from over. A veteran jazz drummer, Dottie Dodgion, musing over the problems she and her fellow jazzwomen have had getting work, said, "You don't know how many times I've sat with other ladies and listened to them let off steam— the rancor because guys were picked over them. But you see, the bottom line is you can't let it get to you. You can protest, make a little bit of noise ... but you can't let it get out of hand or else they'll *never* hire you.... You don't knuckle under, but you don't go out and try to club 'em over the head either."[2] The young black saxophonist Fostina Dixon observes: "There still is some active discouragement of you if you're a woman—not as much, but psychologically, there is still some. Guys can still try to belittle you, make it seem like you don't have it together. So being a minority, you have to be noticeably better or they're not to accredit you. If you're an okay player, then you're 'all right for a girl.' So you have to be an exceptional all-round player."[3]

Gone are the days when "nice" girls stayed home and kept their music to the parlor, but unseen, subjective barriers to women's equality in jazz seem still to exert an influence on their careers. Often these unconscious prejudices—these sex taboos in music—not only feed expectations about how well (or poorly) women can play; they are internalized by women themselves, lowering their own sights. And sex taboos go further, affecting what the sexes can play. When surveyed to rate instruments in terms of their appropriateness for males and females, many people rate the drums and the trumpet as strongly masculine. At least in part, these opinions are explained by history. The trumpet, for instance, was long used in war to call the troops to battle. What more aggressive role can an instrument have? The harp, on the other hand, is often viewed as feminine, with its angelic associations and its nonaggressive demeanor. Beyond the notions of what instruments are suitable for the sexes to play, there is the fact that playing jazz implies an aggressive attack. Slapping the bass, blowing out the cheeks like Dizzy Gillespie, honking on a saxophone, is behavior that traditionally has not been thought of as proper or suitable for women.

But taboos tend to lose their magical power the more they are broken. The more women are visible and audible as role models for others to follow, the less are they viewed as exceptions. To the extent that women—and men—choose the instruments and the technique of playing that they want, they overturn the old attitudes and show that talent, like justice, should be blind. As notions of femaleness and maleness have been generally questioned in our society, especially in recent years, the stereotypes wither, and the old prejudices begin to die. The future of jazz looks brighter for all because now women, too, can look around them and back in time at the accomplishments of others like them who say by their examples, "Yes, you too can play jazz."

NOTES

1. Mary Lou Williams quoted in *Down Beat*, October 17, 1957.
2. Linda Dahl, *Stormy Weather: The Music and Lives of a Century of Jazzwomen* (New York: Limelight Editions, 1989), p. 219.
3. Ibid., pp. 174–75.

BIBLIOGRAPHY

Albertson, Chris. *Bessie*. New York: Stein & Day, 1972.
Baxter, Derrick S. *Ma Rainey and the Classic Blues Singers*. Chelsea, Mich.: Scarborough House, 1970.
Chilton, John. *Billie's Blues: A Survey of Billie Holiday's Career, 1933–1959*. New York: Stein & Day, 1975.
Crowther, Bruce, and Mike Pinfold. *The Jazz Singers: From Ragtime to New Wave*. Javelin, England: Sterling, 1988.
Dahl, Linda. *Stormy Weather: The Music and Lives of a Century of Jazzwomen*. New York: Limelight Editions, 1989.
Handy, D. Antoinette. *Black Women in American Bands and Orchestras*. Methuen, N.J.: Scarecrow Press, 1981.
Jones, Hettie. *Big Star, Fallin' Mama: Five Women in Black Music*. New York: Viking Press, 1974.
Leder, Jan. *Women in Jazz: A Discography of Instrumental Music, 1913 to 1968*. Westport, Conn.: Greenwood Press, 1985.
Placksin, Sally. *American Women in Jazz: 1900 to the Present*. New York: Seaview Books, 1982.
Unterbrink, Mary. *Jazz Women at the Keyboard*. Jefferson, N.C.: McFarland & Co., 1983.

———— *21* ————

Women and Country Music

KAREN SAUCIER LUNDY

Country music is one of America's native musical art forms. As a musical genre, it has been called the folk music of white working-class America and tends to reflect traditional values. When one thinks of country music, images of good-hearted women, honky-tonk angels, lovable losers, and cheating boozers come to mind. Mass media have been acknowledged by social scientists to be one of the most powerful socializing forces. Country music, as a form of mass media, has perhaps received less attention as a shaper or reflecter of social behavior because of its image in the field of social research as an artistic and intellectual wasteland. The roles that women and men play have experienced great change in recent years, and research of all forms of media indicates that these changes have been reflected very slowly in the mass media. This chapter explores the images of women in country music in an effort to determine if those changes are being reflected in the most conservative and traditional of American music—country music.

All media sources are important influences on people's ideas about social reality. Popular music is considered to be a significant socializing mechanism that both transmits and reflects norms regarding all social behavior, including the way men and women should act. I make no attempt here to prove that listening to country music causes one to be a honky-tonk angel or a philandering cheating husband or that this music even reflects reality. Rather, I assume a relationship in terms of listener and song that is probably bidirectional. The maintenance of gender role stereotypes through the media helps people understand how and why ideas regarding male and female behavior continue to exist in a particular society. The symbolic realm of society, which includes the media, assists persons in a society in affirming and maintaining these gender role pictures even when the images do not reflect reality.

Country music lyrics are important because they are meant to be listened to (they are mainly ballads), they are straightforward and unambiguous, and they are an attempt by the writer-singer to convey reality—a complete story is told in what has been described as a three-minute soap opera.

In many ways country music represents reality that many people rarely like to think about and for that reason may choose not to listen. It represents a humanness that most can identify with and for that reason usually respond—either sympathetically or in anger but certainly with some emotion. Merle Haggard has summed up this relationship between listener and song: "No one could really know [country music] unless they've been there."[1]

According to many researchers, country music appeals primarily to urban and rural whites, ages twenty-five to forty-nine, who have only high school educations but work at relatively high-income, skilled jobs. Although associated with the rural South, in the last two decades country music has grown in popularity from the farm to the factory.

Traditionally country music has portrayed women as nurturing, submissive, loving, and forgiving of their cheating, wandering, and insensitive men. Previous research on lyrical theme analysis offers support that the symbolic world offered by country music represents a rather bleak, limited world for both men and women. The only aspect of their lives apparently under their control is the love relationship. As reflected in country music lyrics, a woman derives her status primarily through her ability to get and keep a man. Her family, children, and friends are seldom mentioned in the lyrics. The love relationship is the most intense and powerful aspect of their lives. When this relationship is threatened, the effects are crippling. However, recently there have been indications of changes in the way women view men and themselves in country music. Women performers and writers have begun questioning the authority of men and expressing dissatisfaction with their drinking, cheating, and outlaw behavior.

Until the 1930s love songs in country music existed as two distinct types: the parlor tradition love song dealing with fidelity, family, home, and God, such as "Oh, Susanna" by Stephen Foster, and the tavern tradition, which was much more sexually explicit, for example, Fiddlin' John Carson's "The Old Hen Cackled and the Rooster's Going to Crow." After World War II, these two traditions blended. Singer-songwriter Hank Williams in the 1950s sang about men who were lured by alcohol into illicit love affairs by loose women and left alone with the honky-tonk blues all the while knowing that they would have to make eventual confessions to wives and God. This dualistic blending of the two traditions continues in contemporary country music lyrics.

The majority of country music songs are still written and performed by men; little more than a quarter of songs today are sung by women. From 90 to 95 percent of most country music songs present a male-female theme, and the vast majority of the songs within this theme deal with the establishment and the disintegration of the love relationship. Other themes related to the male-female relationship deal with sexual prowess and a social commentary or advice theme. Other various themes include a desire for the good old days, the South, and nature.

Romantic involvement as the focus of country music has been consistent through the years. The anticipation of the love relationship is expressed differently by men and women in country music. Traditionally, the man is expected to play the dominant role by asking the woman out, which reflects acceptable behavior in the traditional male and female relationship. Such songs as Eddie Rabbitt's "Step by Step" illustrate this role as he advises a man to treat a woman as a lady first and foremost during the courtship. Male sexual prowess is symbolized in the songs "Older Women" and "Never Been So Loved" as male singers extol their virtues as lovers. Further examples of the male's tendency toward wanderlust and the need for a variety of sexual experiences are in the songs "The Wanderer" performed by Eddie Rabbitt and "My Baby Thinks He's a Train," sung by Roseanne Cash. Sexual boasting is generally unacceptable for the woman in country music. However, recent changes in country music lyrics, although exceptional, provide evidence that women are beginning to take the initiative in the sexual relationship and are even expressing an enjoyment of sex. The group Highway 101, with a female lead singer, pleads with her man to "Just Say Yes" to her sexual advances. Reba McEntire in the song "I Know How He Feels" laments the loss of a lover by describing his physical attributes and skills as a lover. As a departure from conventional gender roles, "One for the Money," sung by T. J. Sheppard, details the contentment of a woman who stays with her husband for material security but has a lover for her emotional and physical needs.

A major theme in country music lyrics has consistently been the establishment of the love relationship. By far the most common expression of this is in the celebration of the relationship by both women and men. These songs express affection, romance, and euphoria concerning the relationship. This celebration of romantic intensity reflects how important the male-female relationship is for the fulfillment of both men and women's lives. Alabama is well known for its love songs, which celebrate love and romance and has become one of country's most popular groups. In "Face to Face," the male singer details the sensual pleasures of a committed love relationship.

The only acceptable roles for "decent" women in country music are as lover, wife, or mother. The few times they are mentioned, women work as waitresses or barmaids; they are not viewed as co-workers or having careers. Men are depicted in jobs, not careers, that tend toward monotonous, blue-collar positions where the only reward is money. Neither men nor women in country music seem to gain much satisfaction from their work. In "Midnight Hauler" by Razzy Bailey, the man describes his work as the driver of an eighteen-wheel truck as just a means to getting home to, and providing for, his woman. Charlie Daniels, a popular country music performer, contends that rich men go to college, while poor men go to work. Eddy Raven sings in "Joe Sure Knows How to Live" about a co-worker from the assembly line who goes to Mexico with Betty, the waitress, for the weekend. Kathy Matea's "Eighteen Wheels and a Dozen Roses" is about the impending retirement of a truck driver.

The woman is often portrayed in country music as an emotional fixer—always there when her man needs her. When a woman's love, and consequently her emotional support, is pulled back from a man, the effect on him is usually devastating. Earl Thomas Conley sings in "Fire and Smoke" about the dark despair resulting from a failed love affair, and Johnny Lee's "One in a Million" tells about his reliance on his woman when things are tough. In this same song, he negates the influence that her friends have on her concerning him by reminding her of his value as a lover. When a man leaves a woman, the response is one of disappointment but without quite the intensity of the man. Anne Murray in "Blessed Are the Believers" describes the disappointment and eternal hope of everlasting love. Women tend to stay hopeful while men become more remorseful and depressed. When the woman is grief stricken over the loss of a lover, she is not completely shattered. She tends to need her man to stay with her temporarily until she can regain her footing. This theme is illustrated in Janie Fricke's "I'll Need Someone to Hold Me When I Cry" as the abandoned woman begs the departing lover to wait until the morning to leave. Crystal Gayle sings about her willingness to take her man back at any cost in "If You Ever Change Your Mind." The man does not need to be strong because the woman will be there to provide the emotional support in case the other woman does not.

Women tend to use sexuality as bargaining power more than men, as illustrated in Sylvia's song, "Drifter," about a woman's attempted use of affection to keep her man from wandering in and out of her life. Men express their inability to resist a woman's spell and her magic; the male in country music expresses fears of being dependent on and vulnerable to a woman's spell and being consumed by and weakened with desire. For example, in Razzy Bailey's "I Keep Coming Back," he expresses his inability to resist his woman's charms, although he knows she will eventually break his heart. Alabama sings in "Why Lady Why?" about a man's inability to resist a woman's charms. Rodney Crowell illustrates this same concern in "I couldn't Leave You If I Tried."

In country music, a man traditionally uses liquor as the only consolation to losing a lover. The liquor apparently works to anesthetize emotional despair, although he knows that he will feel guilt and eventually will pay for his excessive drinking. The man often blames himself for the failure of the relationship, which compounds the despair. Mickey Gilley sings about this dilemma in "A Headache Tomorrow or a Heartache Tonight." References to alcohol abound in country music in songs such as "What Made

Milwaukee Famous Has Made a Fool Out of Me," "Whiskey River," "I'm Gonna Hire a Wino to Decorate Our Home." "If Drinkin' Don't Kill Me, Her Memory Will," "Party Time," and "Think I'll Just Stay Here and Drink." Hank Williams, Jr., extols the virtues of alcohol and women in "I Like My Whiskey on Ice and My Women on Fire."

In recent years, references to alcohol have diminished, possibly due to public consciousness about alcohol abuse. In 1981, in three of the top four songs of the year, alcohol use was the main theme. In 1988, only one song in the Top 40 even mentioned alcohol use. This trend is noteworthy because of the traditional association of alcohol use by men in country music. Alcohol use, when mentioned, is most entirely limited to men as an appropriate way of dealing with grief. Drinking alcohol is associated with a machismo type of behavior and does not seem to be acceptable in any form for a woman in country music. This lack of reference to women's use of alcohol again supports the stereotypical roles of traditional males and females portrayed in country music. However, women do make their feelings known about their man's use of alcohol, such as in Loretta Lynn's "Don't Come Home a-Drinkin with Lovin' on Your Mind," and in "Your Squaw Is on the Warpath," she warns about her man's excessive drinking and his diminished manhood.

The male's role in country music does not clearly illustrate the strong, efficient man so often associated with a traditional gender role. Often the man portrayed in country music by both women and men display an ineptness, as in Johnny Lee's "One in a Million." The man sings about aimlessly stumbling through life with only his woman there to provide sense and comfort in his otherwise confused world. Rodney Crowell expresses a feeling of being lost and out of control, returning to his woman for stability and reassurance, in "It's Such a Small World."

There are indications that women singers in country music are beginning to express strong reactions toward their wandering, demanding, drinking mates. Kitty Wells in 1952 began this slow rebellion in defense of women with her song, "It Wasn't God Who Made Honky Tonk Angels." Loretta Lynn has long been one of country music's most outspoken singers who asserts the woman's needs in the relationship. Many radio stations refused to play her 1975 song, "The Pill," in which she proclaims that there are going to be changes made in the relationship now that she can control having children. Other similar songs include Dottie West's "(I'm Gonna) Put you Back on the Rack," which asserts her contention that she will not always take her man back when he messes up. Tammy Wynette became well known for "Stand by Your Man" in which she advises women to tolerate their men's failures and inept stumblings. By contrast, in the song "Another Chance," recorded in 1982, she asserts her independence and tells her man that he will not be bossing her around anymore. Although a revolution seems hardly at hand in country music, these feelings suggest that country music singers and writers are aware of the gender role changes in contemporary society.

Clearly the symbolic world offered by country music lyrics is rather limited for both men and women in regard to status and role. The only aspect of their lives under their control is the love relationship. The images reflected in country music lyrics serve to reinforce stereotypes, primarily those of traditional gender role expression. Women's roles are limited to lover, wife, and mother, and rarely as co-worker and professional career person. Men's roles are less clearly defined, appearing as those of lover and provider. For both, work is secondary and unsatisfactory, leaving primarily the love relationship as the most intense and most powerful aspect of their lives. When the love relationship is threatened or failing, the effects are crippling, particularly for the man.

The presentation of traditional gender roles in country music lyrics serves to reinforce the image of men as controlling and women as submissive and supportive even in the face of discontented suffering. Limited evidence suggests that women singers in country music are beginning to demonstrate a more assertive attitude toward sex and the love relationship. The study of country music can add to our understanding of the maintenance of gender roles in society because men and women learn how they should behave from what they tell each other.

NOTE

1. Ellis Nassour, "Hag's Songs Reflect Life," *Music City News* 13 (1975): 8.

BIBLIOGRAPHY

Bernard, Jesse. *The Sex Game.* Englewood Cliffs, N.J.: Prentice-Hall, 1968.
Buckley, John. "Country Music and American Values." *Popular Music and Society* 6 (1979): 293–306.
Chalfant, Paul, and Robert E. Beckley. "Beguiling and Betrayal: The Image of Alcohol Use in Country Music." *Journal of Studies on Alcohol* 38 (1977): 1428–33.
Freudiger, Patricia, and Elizabeth M. Almquist. "Male and Female Roles in the Lyrics and Three Genres of Contemporary Music." *Sex Roles* 41 (1978): 61–65.
Horton, Donald. "The Dialogue of Courtship in Popular Songs." *American Journal of Sociology* 62 (1957): 569–78.
Ivins, Molly. "Honk Tonking." *Ms.* (September 1988): 28–29.
Lewis, George. "Country Music Lyrics." *Journal of Communication* 26 (1976): 37–43.
Nassour, Ellis. "Hag's Songs Reflect Life." *Music City News* 13 (1975): 8.
Nietzeke, Ann. "Doin' Somebody Wrong." In *Mass Media and Society*, pp. 11–16. 3d ed. Edited by M. DeFleur, S. Ball-Rokeach, and A. Wells. Palo Alto, Calif.: Mayfield Publishing Company, 1979.

Saucier, Karen A. "Healers and Heartbreakers: Images of Women and Men in Country Music." *Journal of Popular Culture* 20 (1986): 147–66.

Tuchman, Gayle, A. Daniles, and J. Benet. *Hearth and Home: Images of Women in the Mass Media*. New York: Oxford University Press, 1978.

—————— *22* ——————

One Voice: The Legacy of Women Singers in Popular Music

THERESE L. LUECK

A survey of women's participation in popular music provides an essential view of the changing pattern of life in the United States. Although the types of popular music have been as diverse as the women themselves, common themes can be found as women grew with the musical culture and its technology and commercialism. Despite the diversity of their roles, they are mostly remembered as singers.

From the blues of Bessie Smith to the punk of Patti Smith, women have played an integral part in popular music throughout the decades. By the 1990s, women were prominent in every aspect of popular music. New names such as Sinead O'Connor and old ones such as Bonnie Raitt crested the popular tides of the century's last decade. Access to popular music in the 1990s is easy, whether one searches for new music, new renditions from bygone eras, or virtually flawless digital reproductions of original works. Surrounded by such diversity and easy access, it is easy to lose sight of historical perspective and the roles women have played in shaping America's popular music.

Women have always sung the blues. In fact, many women became famous singing those blues in the early part of the century. Although there have always been good female instrumentalists, many of them have eluded the pages of history. The singers are remembered. Their voices, as inspired instruments, rise through the gaps of history from the baby's bedside and the church choir to the stage. As the blues gave way to jazz and then to soul and rock 'n' roll, the nation enjoyed the voices of many women. Today women are heard in every aspect of popular music, from country to contemporary. In addition to capturing their voices, modern media have been able to focus on the singers as physical commodities; a new prominence has been bestowed on the sexy lead singer of a band otherwise male. Through the changing times, women are most often given attention as singers.

The 1989 return of Bonnie Raitt showed how her appeal has endured with the baby boom generation. Her compelling voice and sincere delivery combined to win her Grammy Best Album and Performer Awards. Suzanne Vega, with her straightforward manner of presentation and soft voice, helped carry folk music into the 1990s by invoking modern tales. She broke into the top ranks with "Luka," a story of abuse. A new line-up of country singers, such as Roseanne Cash and Canadian k. d. lang, has expanded the bounds of country music. Made-up almond eyes and a shaved head lend Sinead O'Connor an austere androgyny. In her video, she simpers into the camera lens as if to her estranged lover as she sings, "Nothing Compares 2 U." Janet Jackson, of the famous Jackson family, propelled the pop scene into the 1990s with *Rhythm Nation 1814*.

How could all these different women singing different songs achieve popularity in one country? From where do they trace their lineage?

At the beginning of the twentieth century, public performance by women was not considered to fit the role of wife and mother. Women were not allowed to speak at public meetings; they did not win the right to vote until 1920. It was fashionable for women to play music in the home, but their playing music in public was considered rather scandalous. Many musical instruments were considered improper for them to play. Women were told they were not strong enough or intelligent enough to play instruments such as tubas and drums. It was decided after much debate that if women had to play for a living, the violin could be considered ladylike, as was the piano. Women were often denied formal educations and the time and money needed to dedicate themselves to a career. They were told that these lacks would prevent them from playing serious material, so they should be satisfied with less serious music—thus, the prevalence of women in popular music.

Women found themselves caught in a circular argument: they could not earn as much as male professional musicians; they were denied access to an education and a living wage and then denied access to jobs because women's labor was thought to cheapen a respectable business, including the business of musical performance. Women were sometimes allowed to practice with an orchestra but not to sit in on the final performances. Since 1900, it has been fairly common for women to go to school for and even teach piano, but relatively few women have become famous pianists. In the public performance of music, as in other fields not directly associated with childbearing, women have had to struggle against general disapproval, which often manifests itself in restrictive cultural expectations and a lack of financial funding.

Orchestras rarely admitted women, and so they sometimes formed their own groups, often made up of string and keyboard players. Women's brass bands were also fairly common. All-female jazz ensembles performed throughout the 1930s and 1940s. Like blacks, women found that forming their own groups was often the only way they could appear in public.

Women's orchestras did not survive World War II. With major orchestras remaining predominantly male, women tended to gravitate toward the less formal restrictions of popular music.

Stemming from the oral tradition, folk music is perhaps the oldest form of popular music. It celebrates the heritage of its singers and the geographical regions of the country; it protests and laments the loss of land and heritage to the intensive industrialization and insensitive dehumanization in the United States in the twentieth century. Because each generation tends to learn folk songs by imitating the performance of an older generation, these songs generally differ from one performance to the other. Before recording equipment was available, folk songs had to be transcribed. Despite difficulties of transcription and differences of background, women have done important work in collecting and preserving many types of folk music, including hymns, spirituals, slave songs, Appalachian ballads, and American Indian music. This process is now a discipline known as ethnomusicology.

One woman nationally known for her work in preserving regional music is Anne Grimes, who was born in Ohio in 1912. In the process of preserving Ohio's musical heritage, she also dispelled myths, such as the notion that all traditional people live in log cabins and lack education. When she began traveling around Ohio in the 1940s singing folk songs, she started recording the songs she heard. She also began collecting data on dulcimer lore; her dulcimer collection is one of the largest in the United States. Eighty years old in 1992, she continues to work out of her home in Granville, Ohio, as an archivist of over fifteen hundred folk songs and as a folk performer. Many of the ballads she sings depict history as vividly as any textbook.

The South is another area rich in folk songs, with slave songs, gospel music, and the call and response of spirituals being the roots of blues, jazz, and soul. One way southern folk music reached other regions was through choral group recitals. The first and foremost of the choral groups was the Fisk Jubilee Singers from Fisk University in Nashville, Tennessee.

In addition to folk music's contributions to popular musical genres, it was incorporated into more formal musical forms. An early black woman of note, Florence Beatrice Smith Price, often used black religious music in her compositions. Her most famous arrangement of a spiritual is "My Soul's Been Anchored in de Lord," published in 1917. Price's pupil, Margaret Bonds, who is known for her arrangements of poems by Langston Hughes, was influenced by the blues and jazz of her native Chicago.

Women's performance continues in the folk tradition. Jean Ritchie is a traditional folksinger who sings and writes of her native Kentucky. From a musical family, Ritchie captures the bluegrass and hills as well as the black, acid water pouring from the mines into the rivers. Odetta is important for her own performances from the 1950s on, as well as her influence on musicians such as Bob Dylan and Janis Joplin.

Since folk music is an immortalization of the United States, women's participation is significant in that their perceptions are key to the folk portrayal of the nation: the diversity of its roots, from Europe to Africa; its regionalism, from streams to states; its expression, plain delivery and traditional instruments; its subject matter of love and lullabies; and its concern for the environment. The folk strains adapt to this new world, truly forming a melting pot. Emotional issues are often close to the heart of folk lyrics. The Civil War, which tore the nation apart, is relived in ballads. Similarly, a resurgence in the popularity of folk music coincided with the Vietnam conflict. The Weavers were one of the bands that revitalized folk music in the 1950s. One of their original members, Ronnie Gilbert, performing with Holly Near, helped bring folk music into the 1990s by singing invigorating women's music and folk songs of old and new origin. Another prominent singing family is the Carter Family, led by Mother Maybelle Carter, who has had tremendous impact on traditional folk and country music.

Many country music performances are traditional, incorporating biblical references and conventional sex roles. Country music also mirrors the changing lot for women, from Tammy Wynette's "D-I-V-O-R-C-E," brought out when divorce was becoming as prevalent as marriage, to Barbara Mandrell's "Midnight Oil," which dared to talk of women who cheat on their men. Another song of women's nontraditional roles is "Honky Tonk Angel," Kitty Wells's rite of passage from country girl singer to the Queen of Country Music. She still sings that song and other favorites such as her plaintive "Release Me." After over twenty number 1 hits, she stepped aside for women such as Loretta Lynn, a coal miner's daughter known for her singing and writing, and Dolly Parton, whose buxom and bewigged body playfully parody her sexuality. A writer as well as a show woman, she penned songs such as "I Will Always Love You" that echo through the emotions. Entering the 1990s, a new round of country women includes some who carry on family traditions while expanding musical boundaries, such as Crystal Gayle and Roseanne Cash. Newcomer lang adds her personal touch to country music yet often sings as if Patsy Cline had left her "in care of the blues."

In addition to carrying on traditions and broadening musical genres, women have adapted to the changing cultural tides and styles of music. One of the best examples of a woman who has employed adaptation as a survival strategy is Diana Ross. Initially recognized for her singing as one of the Supremes, originally known as the Primettes, the group had an incredible string of hits. Alongside the Beatles and other British invaders in mid–1964, the Supremes sold millions of records. For new songs, they often relied on the Motown writing team of Nick Ashford and Valerie Simpson. Their 1960s hit list was matched only by the Beatles, and the Supremes were by no means the only Motown women of note. Sharing the spotlight were the Marvelettes, Mary Wells, Martha and the Vandellas, and Gladys Knight and the Pips. On another record label, the Queen of Soul, Aretha Franklin, taught men that women demanded "R-E-S-P-E-C-T."

In 1970, Ross left the successful group. Diana Ross and the Supremes' last record together, "Someday We'll Be Together," ended an era. Using the Supremes as her foundation, Ross became a superstar. The year she left, she started a solo career that garnered her that year's NAACP Image Award for Female Entertainer of the Year.

In 1972, Ross ventured into other media, such as film, and other popular styles of music, such as disco. Her 1972 film, *Lady Sings the Blues*, was Ross's tribute to Billie Holiday, who combined blues, jazz, and popular styles in singing renditions such as "Ain't Nobody's Business." Holiday's best singing came in the 1930s with such classic songs as "Embraceable You." Holiday, in turn, was influenced by Bessie Smith, whose 1920s vaudeville blues came alive in much of Holiday's work. The soulful singing of Smith bridged the styles of blues and jazz. Smith's teacher was Ma Rainey, who brought the folk tradition to the blues in the early years of the century. Rainey is known as the Mother of the Blues because of her influence on the generation of singers who developed the classic style of the blues. In essence, then, Ross took her style from Holiday, who borrowed from Smith, who learned it from the mother—Ma Rainey.

Jazz brought out a truly indigenous American sound, embodied in powerful singers like Ella Fitzgerald and Sarah Vaughan who used their voices as finely tuned instruments and were influential jazz singers. Jazz artists today continue to perform traditional and modern jazz, and the influence of the many great women vocalists remains.

Rock 'n' roll might never have come about if not for blues, jazz, and rhythm and blues. Despite rock's infamous misogyny, women have been in the background as writers and instrumentalists and in the foreground as lead singers. It is not unusual, though, for rock to ignore its foremothers. When the Rock and Roll Hall of Fame chose its first inductees in 1986, no women were selected. The next two years saw Aretha Franklin and Diana Ross and the Supremes inducted.

Yet women have been in the forefront of rock's many changes. The psychedelic rock of the 1960s was a musical rendition of paisley and blue jeans, acid and marijuana, incense and the ethereal, with riffs played for a recreational high and words written for uncommitted lovemaking. Women such as Grace Slick of Jefferson Airplane helped define this era, contributing music to what is now considered classic rock. This was the music of the drug culture, which left more than one casualty entombed in its high, hard life. The dynamic Janis Joplin died of a heroin overdose in 1970. Rebellious and rowdy, she vaulted into the 1960s on music influenced by Bessie Smith and Odetta. Although brief, Joplin's was a significant contribution; her throaty blues rock left songs and images that symbolize an era, such as the cross-country hitchhiker of "Me and Bobby McGee." She was twenty-seven when she died.

Rock rolled from rebellion to establishment as its main performers grew older and became part of the society they had rebelled against. Newer forms of music filled the airwaves. By the mid–1970s, much of rock 'n' roll had ventured into electronic music or become an adjunct to disco music. Such alternating currents of sophistication and complacency frustrated not only listeners but new musicians trying to break into an established rock industry. Rock's reaching for the extremes of ultrasophisticated electronics and disco pandering created a strain in the fabric through which punk rock exploded with its basic chords and sociopolitical discontent. Punk had been welling up on the outskirts of the mainstream in people such as pre-punker Patti Smith and the sinful Marianne Faithful. Punk's commercialization, new wave music, was absorbed into the pop charts in the 1980s, led by Pat Benetar, Cyndi Lauper, and Madonna.

By 1990 many rockers were in their forties and fifties. Women such as Tina Turner contributed to a more vibrant version of middle age than cultural stereotyping had previously allowed. Yet these 1990s middle-aged rockers were mere teen-agers when actual pop music came about. In the mid–1950s *Billboard* magazine began to chart what was popular by following mass record sales, declaring top pop singles. A pop song often lasts two or three minutes. During its peak popularity, airwaves and record stores deluge consumers with it. Pop embodies a moment; it is a piece of personalized history that at the same time is shared with the culture. Pop does not always make much sense, playing instead on sensibilities. Anyone who has been out of the country will find gaps, voids in a popularized past that cannot be reclaimed. As an integral part of the culture, any particular pop song conveys a slice of what life was like during that song's peak.

Pop music is a business. Because of its exploitive nature and the fact that men rule the record industry, women have to please men in order to be successful. Their talent has to be recognized by the men in power for them to be given a chance at stardom.

A pop music portrait of the latter half of the 1950s is typified by sweet female voices singing sanitized versions of songs with much sexual innuendo. Women such as the McGuire Sisters and Debbie Reynolds were at the top, their singles often backed by a full orchestral sound. Sexual references became more overt in the 1960s with its songs of love and loss; then the decade plunged into the Age of Aquarius with the Fifth Dimension.

Sexuality in pop music was counterbalanced in the 1970s by the pop Christian sound of singers such as Debby Boone. Disco dancing was popular; singles flooded the charts, with throbbing tunes such as "Le Freak" by Chic. In the 1980s, women made an exceptionally good showing in pop music. It was literally a showing, given the prevalent video orientation. The top pop song of the decade was Australian Olivia Newton-John's "Physical," which fed off and spurred a fitness craze.

The 1990s might show that there is a lot of room for many types of music, especially with cable television channels open for music video material. Each technological advance in communication has altered the popular music industry. The advent of Music Television (MTV) in 1981 brought pop music into the video era. Once this manner of presentation was accepted, it became unthinkable for a pop song to be released unaccompanied by a video. Images gained increasing importance as did show(wo)manship. Women entered the video dimension of visual pleasure—heavy metal and soft pornography.

Women who closely conform to the cultural ideal have often been the ones to gain pop stardom, such as Madonna, modeled as the image of a latter-day Marilyn Monroe. One has to wonder if someone as talented as fat Mama Cass, of the Mamas and the Papas, would even have been given the chance to sing in this video age. Sex still sells—maybe more than ever. Three of the top ten singles artists of the 1980s—Newton-John, Kim Carnes, and Irene Cara—are on the album covers for those hit singles with their hands held suggestively on their lower bodies. A 1970s disco album poses sexy Donna Summer (a bad girl and proud of it) on the album cover to seduce buyers. Inside, she is shown fashionably strutting the streets. With an upbeat tempo, she sings about women gone bad and those used by men, a theme Tina Turner would return to in the next decade with *Private Dancer*. Promiscuity is by no means new to pop, though it had often been encoded earlier in order to appeal to the broader buying audience. As more liberal expression became socially accepted, popular music moved with the times. Less sanitizing was done on lyrics that had originated outside the main-stream. Over the decades, innuendo has become explicit, but mainstream acceptance remains more conservative than the radical nature of music on the margins.

Although women like Turner write pop tunes, more often it is men who put words into the mouths of women, having them say what men want to hear. Sex and sales go hand in hand. When sex idol Madonna sizzled in the 1980s with "Like a Virgin," the lyrics on her lips were words written by men. Men have women sing what they would want an idealized woman to say, even to the point of having her attribute her creation to men. They trap her in adolescence, not allowing her to grow up. A Lolita figure, she becomes the lovely, loyal, nonjudgmental daughter of male culture. If she cannot be virginal, she can be recreated by the man, "thawed" from her former state. Using a male myth of motherhood, the men make the star reborn in the image of their desire. Never mind that Madonna's mother gave birth to her in the first place; she has been recreated as a sex goddess by men for the listening and visual pleasure of men. They have taught her how to walk and to talk and to act like a regular virgin.

Popular music is an interpretation of popular culture rooted in the varied musical heritages of the United States. Although they often go unrecorded in official accounts and histories, women significantly influence popular music. From the diversity, common themes emerge. In addition to women's traditional role as muses, or influence on and inspiration to other artists, they are performers in their own rights. They preserve traditions regarding musical styles as well as advocate preservation of the country that nurtures this vast array of music. Along with preserving traditions, women move the music forward by expanding the boundaries of the different categories through innovation, personal style, and crossing over into other genres. Women's involvement in popular music traces women's progress in the twentieth century. No longer are women nonspeaking objects of the turn of the century—nonpersons forbidden to perform in public. Today they are important actors in almost every aspect of popular music.

Although women have taken to the stage in the latter part of this century, they are often painted marionettes with men in control of the strings. Perhaps family ties and oral tradition propel certain genres, such as folk and country music, to be areas in which women performers can occasionally achieve more control or input to other aspects of the production process, such as how songs are performed and distributed. This is not to ignore the fact that country music is big business. Women are exploited there as well as in the other fast lanes of the music business, particularly pop music. Although most are still treated as sex objects, women are now sometimes regarded by male-defined culture as having talents, among which are vibrant voices. Their voices have carried them through a century of popular music, even if their words are often lent to them by men. Women have traditionally been encouraged to use their voices in private, particularly in their role as mother. A woman singing lullabies while rocking a child to sleep is an accepted, even revered, scenario. When modern times allowed that performing in public was not necessarily vulgar or unfeminine, singing was perhaps a natural gateway for female musical expression.

BIBLIOGRAPHY

Ammer, Christine. *Unsung: A History of Women in American Music.* Westport, Conn.: Greenwood Press, 1980.
Bianco, David. *Heat Wave: The Motown Fact Book.* Ann Arbor, Mich.: Pierian, 1988.
Cotton, Lee. *Shake, Rattle, and Roll.* Ann Arbor, Mich.: Pierian, 1989.
Gates, David. "Nashville's New Class," *Newsweek*, August 12, 1985, pp. 58–61.
Lawless, Ray M. *Folksingers and Folksongs in America.* New York: Duell, Sloan and Pearce, 1965.
McCarthy, Albert et al. *Jazz on Record: A Critical Guide to the First 50 Years: 1917–1967.* London: Hanover, 1968.
Whitburn, Joel. *The Billboard Book of Top 40 Hits.* 4th ed. New York: Watson-Guptill, 1989.

23

Lyrical Sexism in Popular Music:
A Quantitative Examination

VIRGINIA W. COOPER

Popular music has been a formidable force in the socialization of attitudes about American women. The impact of song lyrics as a form of public influence is historically evident in the lyrics of various types of music, including war, religious, movement, and protest songs. Music provides listeners with a collective view of the world, a sense of belonging, and a shared identity. It also verbalizes common goals, values, and attitudes. It is reasonable, then, to view the lyrical descriptions of females in popular songs as a significant social phenomenon that communicates standards and values for women. Popular music has been successful in achieving this impact on American culture for two primary reasons: the nature of the lyrics and the nature of tonal music that accompanies the lyrics.

Lyrics generally reflect experiences in a clear, simple, and harmonious manner and are characterized by repetitious phrases, clichés, myths, and stereotypes. The listener is able to comprehend easily the verbal message contained in the song and can remember the key phrases of those songs. The lyrics of popular songs, which are played repeatedly, have the potential to stay in people's memory for many years, even a lifetime.

The impact of popular music on the listener is a function not only of the words but of the tonal melody, which, when added to the lyrics, constitutes a song. Numerous researchers have documented the importance of the tonal or melodic qualities of music. Music that people like reduces physical tension, anxiety, and depression and improves interpersonal relationships. Enjoyed music also causes the listener to evaluate others as more physically attractive. Familiar songs reduce fear in children. Fast music is emotionally arousing, gives people energy, and amplifies their reaction time. Rapid music increases the movement of shoppers and their spending. Other music is sedative and hypnotic. Tranquilizing music even decreases the strength of individuals. Children and adults who associate words and numbers with a certain tone or pitches of music learn them faster and retain more of what they have learned. Given this impressive effect on human emotion, intellect, and behavior, the melodic characteristics of music are truly noteworthy.

The lyrical and melodic qualities of songs make them a more powerful form of communication than any other method of conveying words. Further, popular music accounts for approximately 90 percent of all recording sales within the music industry. It is estimated that 75 percent of these purchases are made by persons in the twelve to twenty age span. Most high school and college students spend between three and five hours a day listening to popular music. It is clear that American youth receive a great deal of exposure to popular music and that the lyrical content of that music is consequential.

Scholars have documented the presence of sexism in song lyrics for a number of years. Sexist lyrics label women as inferior or negative or in a stereotyped manner. Stereotypes are broad cultural generalizations implying that all women possess these attributes. Among the stereotypes found in popular songs are descriptions of women as pretty, heavenly, angels, possessions of men, submissive, hurtful, and loose. The contradictions between some of these stereotypes is also striking. Researchers have found that the descriptions of females vary more than those of males. It is enlightening to examine the changes in predominant stereotypes over time.

Song lyrics can parallel the attitudes of a given period in history, and each decade represents a unique epoch in popular music. This chapter examines the lyrics of popular music during the 1940s, 1950s, 1960s, and 1970s to show that while many of the predominant themes about women presented in music have changed over time, the lyrics of popular music continue to include stereotypical images of women.

To assess the frequency of feminine stereotypes in popular music, the lyrics of 1,164 popular songs about women that appeared in the twelve monthly issues of *Song Hits Magazine* during the years 1946, 1956, 1966, and 1976 were counted. The lyrics published incorporate pop, ballad, folk, rock, country, and soul, since popular music tends to shift in form over time with audience tastes. These songs reflect the top listings in *Cashbox*, *Billboard*, *Record World*, and *Variety*, which were the most played songs on radio and jukeboxes and those having sold the most records.

Eleven female stereotypes were found in these lyrics: (1) passages portraying woman as evil, (2) lyrics focusing on the female body, (3) lyrics depicting woman needing man, (4) words characterizing woman as a possession of man, (5) phrases depicting woman as mother, (6) lyrics portraying woman as a sex object, (7) passages presenting woman as delicate, (8) lyrics describing a woman as childlike, (9) phrases placing woman "on a pedestal, (10) lines depicting woman as attractive, and (11) phrases portraying woman as supernatural. The percentages found for each stereotype across the four decades are displayed in Table 1. Ninety-six percent of the songs from 1946 to 1976 contained at least one of these stereotypes.

Table 1
Percentage of Songs Containing Stereotypes

	1946	1956	1966	1976
Woman as evil	10	17	29	24
Physical attributes	6	12	14	20
Needing man	37	41	20	22
Possession of man	12	18	17	17
Woman as mother	8	9	2	15
Woman as sex object	23	22	15	24
Woman as delicate	15	9	14	13
Woman as childlike	26	26	49	46
Woman on a pedestal	4	5	6	5
Woman as attractive	4	5	8	5
Woman as supernatural	6	4	9	12

The stereotype of woman as evil has origins in the creation stories of both the Judeo-Christian tradition and Greek mythology. The notion that woman, by her very nature, is a tool of the devil and harmful to man was pervasive during the witch craze of the late Middle Ages. Such attitudes toward women by a segment of the American population have continued into the twentieth century. Woman as evil is any reference to a woman as being bad or evil or displaying immoral behavior. Examples of these lyrics include references to a woman lying to a man, tempting a man, seducing a man, causing injury or harm to a man, and being unfaithful to a man.

Using 1946 as the sample year for the 1940s, 10 percent of the popular songs played that year depicted women as being evil or displaying evil behavior. All of the song lyrics examined were written by men, a tendency that would hold fast over the whole sampling. In 1956, 17 percent of the songs characterized women as bad or evil. Perhaps the rise of 7 percent can be explained by examining the changing roles of women during and after World War II. During the war, women worked in factories and were engaged in traditionally masculine activities. When the war ended, women were encouraged or told to abandon their brief freedom and return to their traditional occupation of housewife and mother. Many returned to the home, but many others did not. It is possible that the male writers of song lyrics during this time reflected the fear that women had become too assertive and independent.

As America's women increased their presence outside the home, the tendency to portray them as evil rose higher. During 1966, the instance of lyrics referring to woman as evil rose to 29 percent. Ninety-five percent of these song lyrics were written by men. This sharp increase is most likely correlated to the growth in feminine sexual independence, the American women's movement, and the growing hostility and negative attitudes these "new" women brought out in some men. In 1976 the incidence of woman as evil in popular music dropped to 24 percent. Although this decrease is not significant, there are two possible explanations. One is that 10 percent of these popular songs were written by women; the other is that men had adjusted somewhat to the expanded roles for women and were writing less negative lyrics about them.

The importance of physical appearance for woman in American culture is well documented in all disciplines. Physical attributes have been and remain considerably more important for females than for males in judging the social worth of persons. This value, reflected in popular music, is important because the trend in popular music to emphasize the female body occurred in spite of an increase in female songwriters during the 1960s and 1970s. In examining the same sample years, physical attributes included any mention of any specific part of the female body.

From the 1940s to the 1970s, the tendency for using physical attributes in song lyrics rose by 14 percent. In 1946, 6 percent of the songs written about women included lyrics referring to the female body. The mention of female body parts jumped to 12 percent in 1956. The widespread exposure of most middle-class Americans to television by the mid–1950s, which provided increased visual attention to the female body, may well account for this doubling. Increasingly liberal attitudes toward intimate relationships can also explain this increase. The focus on physical attributes observed in 1966 reached only 14 percent. The slight increase should come as no surprise, as the bulk of the countercultural "free love" themes would come from 1967 through 1971. By 1976, then, the incidence of explicit references to the female body rose to 20 percent, mirroring the changes that had taken place over the past ten years concerning attitudes about portraying the human body.

Woman's need for man has been a predominant feminine image throughout history and can be identified frequently in most popular writings. Examples of this stereotype in popular music include any reference to woman requiring or relying on a man, such as depending on a man, clinging to a man, finding fulfillment in a man, or waiting for a man.

Lyrics describing woman as needing man were fairly common in 1946. Thirty-seven percent of the popular songs played at that time depicted this female dependence on males. The presence of this stereotype in the 1940s represents a dominant societal value for most Americans. Lyrics describing woman's reliance on man rose to their highest point in 1956, at 41 percent. The increase in this stereotype from the previous decade is dramatic. After the war years, when women became a bit more independent, society attempted to reduce the personal freedom they had acquired during the war. The ideology held that working women should return to their homes.

Then, in 1966, there was a dramatic decline in lyrical references to female dependence on men. The frequency had dropped to 20 percent, less than half what it was in the 1950s. This figure clearly represents the renewed freedom asserted during the 1960s and massive efforts by some to alter attitudes about women, including the stereotype that a woman always needs a man. The tendency did not change significantly from the 1960s to the 1970s. In 1976, 22 percent of the popular songs contained this feminine stereotype.

One of the strongest of gender stereotypes is the idea that women belong to men as a sort of possession. In popular music, woman as a possession of man refers to descriptions of woman's being the property of a man—for example, "she belongs to me" and "make her mine" type of lyrics. The incidence of this stereotype remained fairly stable across the four decades examined.

Woman as property of man during 1946 appeared in 12 percent of popular songs. This figure is greater than the 1946 incidence of the portrayal of woman as evil, which was 10 percent, and the 1946 mention of physical attributes, which was 5 percent. Perhaps this implies that male ownership of women was a commonly emphasized stereotype of the 1940s. The 1956 sample revealed that the theme of woman as a possession of a man appeared in 18 percent of popular songs. However, this proportion is significantly lower than the portrayal of woman as needing man in 1956: 41 percent. It may be that the image of woman as man's asset was not as overtly articulated as her needing man because she had demonstrated enough self-worth to warrant some restriction of the property theme. Thus, this motif did not increase significantly. It was more socially acceptable to talk about a less harsh dependency. During 1966, the occurrence of woman as a possession of man remained at the same rate as in 1956: 17 percent. The fact that this theme continued to appear in popular lyrics through the mid–1960s implies that in spite of the emphasis on the women's movement, male ownership of women continued to represent a genuine attitude in American culture. There was little change in the 1970s. Woman as a possession of man appeared in 17 percent of the songs, remaining quite stable across these four decades.

One of the most popular images of woman has her a mother. According to this school of thought, women naturally have the necessary maternal instincts to nurture and raise children. In music, this image holds as well; women are frequently referred to being a mother or exhibiting nurturing, maternal behavior—for example, being the mother of a man's children, taking care of a man, and soothing a man's hurt feelings. In essence, this theme depicts maternal behavior directed to both children and adult men.

Interestingly, woman as mother appeared in 8 percent of the popular song lyrics in 1946 and only 9 percent in 1956. Yet motherhood was the primary feminine role of these decades. During the 1966 sample, the image dropped to only 2 percent, reflecting the growing force of the women's movement and the expanding roles women displayed. In 1976, there was a dramatic swing in the opposite direction, with references to maternal behavior occurring in 15 percent of the popular songs, more than in any previous decade. The change seems to parallel the beginnings of rejection of feminism by many women who saw the goals of some feminists as too radical. Those moving away from feminism feared disapproval of men and saw themselves as being able to have careers and be mothers without the help of feminism.

Perhaps it was difficult for men to write songs about their wives or mothers, but one image that remained high in popular music over these decades was woman as sex object. This refers to any description of a woman being sexually desirable, of a man desiring sex with a woman, or of intimate physical contact between a man and a woman. Examples of this feminine image include "desirable to kiss," "make love," "have my baby," and "getting it on."

Sexual references regarding women was one of the most frequent images portrayed in the lyrics in the first two samples. In 1946, 23 percent of the song lyrics sampled contained images of women as sexual objects, declining to 22 percent in 1956.

Woman as sex object was present in only 15 percent of the songs of 1966, a significant decline. It is likely that the expanded roles publicized by the woman's movement contributed to this decrease. Yet the percentage rose dramatically in the 1976 sample, outdistancing the frequency found in the 1940s to 24 percent, its highest occurrence. The changes in the 1960s and 1970s were not statistically significant, however, indicating no substantial change in the frequency of this image across the four decades.

Other lyrical themes include woman as delicate, which refers to woman as soft or gentle, and woman as childlike. Throughout the four decades, these themes remained high, especially in the latter two samples.

The image of woman as fragile and childlike was frequent in popular lyrics during the 1940s. During 1946, this stereotype was present in 15 percent of the songs. Lyrical portrayals of immature women appeared in 26 percent of popular songs during this year, second only to characterizations of woman's dependency on man. These figures mirror the predominant attitudes toward women of the decade, despite their strong performance as employees filling in for absent men during World War II. Woman as sensitive or tender in song lyrics declined to 9 percent in 1956, while the depiction of women as childlike remained steady at 26 percent.

In 1966 both images rose significantly. Apparently the experiences of World War II had faded from memory, and conceptions of women had returned to a more stereotyped portrayal, a fragility returned to near the

1946 level of 14 percent. The delicate image also may have increased to balance the harsher images being presented by the women's movement. The mid–1960s also saw a formidable change in the representation of women as childlike. During 1966, 49 percent of the popular music that was played contained the image of woman-as-child stereotype. Ten years later, the frequency had changed little; women as delicate remained in 13 percent of the popular song lyrics. The fluctuation of this image indicated little change in this stereotype's presence in popular songs across the forty years. The same held true for the trend of describing women as children, which fell to only 46 percent in 1976. Thus, in the later two decades, the depiction of women as juveniles was at its highest point.

Popular lyrics also depicted women as attractive, supernatural, or on a pedestal. From the 1946 sample on, the image of the woman as physically pleasing remained near 5 percent. Women as mystic or possessing metaphysical powers rose from a low of 4 percent in 1956 to 12 percent in 1976. Popular lyrics that placed women on pedestals also hovered near 5 percent during these years.

Many changes took place in the feminine images expressed in popular music during the four decades examined. These changes are consistent with the trends of societal attitudes toward women and suggest that song lyrics parallel the attitudes of the people who buy the recordings. A few stereotypes remained constant throughout this time period, however, implying the pervasiveness of many feminine images, regardless of the societal changes that have taken place.

Popular music has generated guidelines for the appropriate behavior of woman in American culture, as well as guidelines for men's responses to and relationships with women. At least one of the stereotypes assessed in this inquiry was found in almost every song referring to women that was popular from the 1940s through the 1970s. These stereotyped portrayals are consistent with historical stereotypes, visual media stereotypes, and stereotypes known to exist among the general population. Given the unique nature of music and the level of public exposure, it seems reasonable to conclude that the lyrics of popular music have contributed considerably to American attitudes about women.

BIBLIOGRAPHY

Aldag, R. J., and A. P. Brief. "Some Correlates of Women's Self-Image and Stereotypes of Femininity." *Sex Roles* 5 (1979): 319–28.

Anderson, B., P. Hesbacher, K. P. Etzkorn, and R. S. Denisoff. "Hit Record Trends, 1940–1977." *Journal of Communication* 30 (1980): 31–43.

Bandura, A. "Influence Models: Reinforcement Contingencies on the Acquisition of Imitative Responses." *Journal of Personality and Social Psychology* 1 (1965): 589–95.

Bankart, C. P., and B. B. Bankart. "The Use of Song Lyrics to Alleviate a Child's Fears." *Child and Family Behavior Therapy* 5(1983): 81–83.

Beauvoir, S. *The Second Sex.* Edited and translated by H. M. Parshley. New York: Alfred A. Knopf, 1952.

Booth, M. W. "The Art of Words in Songs." *Quarterly Journal of Speech* 62 (1976): 242–49.

Cooper, V. W. "Women in Popular Music: A Quantitative Analysis of Feminine Images over Time." *Sex Roles* 13 (1985): 523–30.

Denisoff, R. S., and M. H. Levine. "The Popular Protest Song: The Case of the 'Eve of Destruction.' " *Public Opinion Quarterly* 35 (1971): 117–22.

Deutsch, D. "Memory and Attention in Music." In M. Critchley and R. A. Henson, eds., *Music and the Brain: Studies in the Neurology of Music.* London: William Heinemann Medical Books Limited, 1977.

Freudiger, P. "Love Lauded and Love Lamented: Men and Women in Popular Music." *Popular Music and Society* 6 (1978): 1–10.

Freudiger, P., and E. M. Almquist. "Male and Female Roles in the Lyrics of Three Genres of Contemporary Music." *Sex Roles* 4 (1978): 56–65.

Gray, M. "Sexist Songs." *Melody Maker* 49 (1974): 18–19.

Greenburg, B. S., and B. Dervin. *Use of Mass Media by the Urban Poor.* New York: Praeger Publishers, 1970.

Hesbacher, P. "Sound Exposure in Radio." *Popular Music and Society* 3 (1974: 189–201.

Infante, D. A., and C. Berg. "The Impact of Music Modality on the Perception of Communication Situations in Video Sequences." *Communication Monographs* 46 (1976): 135–41.

Hunter, J. E. "Images of Women." *Journal of Social Issues* 32 (1976): 7–17.

May, J. L., and P. A. Hamilton. "Effects of Musically Evoked Affect on Women's Interpersonal Attraction toward and Perceptual Judgments of Physical Attractiveness of Men." *Motivation and Emotion* 4 (1980): 217–28.

Milliman, R. E. "Using Background Music to Affect the Behavior of Supermarket Shoppers." *Journal of Marketing* 46 (3) (1985): 86–91.

Mohrmann, G. P., and F. E. Scott. "Popular Music and World War II: The Rhetoric of Continuation." *Quarterly Journal of Speech* 62 (1976): 145–56.

Neuman, E. *The Great Mother: An Analysis of the Archetype.* Translated by R. Manheim. Princeton, N.J.: Princeton University Press, 1955.

Pearce, K. A. "Effects of Different Types of Music on Physical Strength." *Perceptual and Motor Skills* 53 (1981): 351–52.

Vyatkin, B. A., and L. Y. Dorfmanm. "The Effect of Music on Sensorimotor Behavior as a Function of Neurodynamic Characteristics." *Voprosy Psikhologii* 1 (1981): 94–100.

Wilkinson, M. "Romantic Love: The Great Equalizer? Sexism in Popular Music." *Family Coordinator* 25 (1976): 161–66.

Part VI

Social Context

24

The Ragtime Controversy

DAVID JOYNER

Youth has always had a special relationship with popular music. The teen-aged years are a time of self-assertion, discovery, thrill seeking, and rebellion. It is youth who opens the door of society to new ideas and tastes, indelibly altering the cultural status quo. The rise of rock and roll in the 1950s is often cited as the first fruits of an American youth movement, but as ragtime performer and historian Max Morath outlines, "Ragtime's story, its musical charms aside, is a story of beginnings and of youth. Popular music has always belonged to the kids, and ragtime was arguably America's first popular music."[1] The youth at the beginning of the twentieth century embraced the first, most original, and most pervasive of American popular music forms—ragtime.

Ragtime was popularized without being completely acceptable. It was the rock and roll of its day, considered provocative, naughty stuff. It had the unfettered vigor American youth always desired and never found in the cadre of "safe" formulated products offered by their elders. Its innovative rhythms and perfection of formal design made it the most enduring form of popular music. Ragtime also helped America realize, as it pulled away from its European origins, that its emerging identity was comprised of African-American as well as European-American cultures.

This has never been an easy fact for white Americans to accept. Among other problems, there was always the conflict of aesthetic values between the races concerning styles of artistic and emotional expression. The dominant white culture was at once captivated and repelled by the openness and exuberance of African-American culture. White America struggled between the pressures of its own culture, emphasizing poise and expressive reserve, and individual expressive needs that found fulfillment in the adoption, to whatever extent, of African-American culture.

The post–Civil War era was a period of intense social and economic restructuring. The industrial revolution was on; wealthy entrepreneurs from all regions of the country gravitated to the cities. Among these growing urban centers, New York established itself as the financial and cultural center of America. Vast railroad systems were completed, allowing easier interchange between farms and cities. As a result of immigration, urban transplantation, and general human proliferation, the percentage of urban dwellers in the United States increased from 22 in 1890 to 54 in 1920.

Accompanying the growth of cosmopolitan cities in these years was the rise in the development of symphony orchestras and fine arts support groups. European classical music had a strong voice in the American cultural world, backed by the power of America's wealthy. It was imposed on the often resentful public at large, and the imposition went beyond the concert hall. Music education mandated the exclusive study of European art music from elementary school to the conservatory. Classical music also had the backing of trained music journalists and critics who bombarded the public with Eurocentric music bias. The general public had to conform to the tastes of the wealthy if they hoped to attain similar status. Popular music, particularly American born, was deemed inferior and low class, insinuating that those who openly enjoyed such fare would be viewed in a similar manner.

Yet the same urban social phenomena that brought about the art music contingency also led to an assertion of popular culture in the late nineteenth century. The moral restraint of provincial Victorian culture began to crumble as a freer-thinking and more dynamic urban social style took over. Dominance by class, sex, and race became more ambiguous. Entertainment reflected these changes in both its context and content. Vaudeville, public dance halls, and cabarets were indicative of a more relaxed mode of leisure. New York's Tin Pan Alley, made up largely of lower-class Jews and Italians, brought forth popular music that by the turn of the century began to display the vitality of an American vernacular, replete with colloquialisms, slang, and a more interesting use of rhythm. At the root of this surge of the vernacular was the culture relegated to the bottom rung of the social ladder—the African-American culture.

The African-American cultural component was injected into the mainstream in measured doses over the course of American history. In the 1820s, minstrel theater introduced blackface comedy to the masses, a style of entertainment that enjoyed continued success throughout the nineteenth century. It confirmed white America's fascination with African Americans. Yet minstrelsy was an artificial presentation of black culture and life; neither the actors nor the music was the genuine article. After the Civil War, freed blacks made their way into the entertainment through minstrelsy, effectively competing with white blackface actors for the public's favor. Until the end of the nineteenth century, presentation of black culture in entertainment remained cartoonlike and unrealistic. It seemed doomed never to take a serious role in American culture. By the mid–1890s, however, authentic black dance and music in the form of ragtime managed to work its way to the surface, asserting a powerful influence on the way Americans entertained themselves.

Ragtime made its first public entreé in the theaters as songs. Especially notable in this regard is Ben Harney (1871–1938), a popular singer and pianist at Tony Pastor's Fourteenth Street Theater in New York. Harney wrote and performed ragtime, supposedly music that he had heard from blacks and formally adapted for the stage. Subsequent publication of piano rags and songs with "rag accompaniment" brought the music from its cultural isolation into the limelight.

Another tremendous boon to the rise of ragtime was the technological advances of the late nineteenth and early twentieth centuries. The burgeoning mass production of economical, space-saving upright pianos made the instrument a fixture in the parlor of many homes, a status symbol of the middle class. By 1904, upright player piano technology was perfected, offering piano entertainment for households who had no one to play them. Soon lateral cut phonograph discs and more affordable players came within the financial reach of the general public.

The turning point in instrumental ragtime's rise to popularity came in 1899 when John Stark published Scott Joplin's "Maple Leaf Rag" in Sedalia, Missouri. Thousands of copies ended up on America's pianos, and it is not surprising that its compositional expertise and popularity set the standard for many aspiring amateur and professional rag composers.

The United States and, indeed, the entire world went ragtime mad. From local publishing houses to New York's Tin Pan Alley, the music industry toiled to feed the public's appetite for the music. Piano ragtime was the first instrumental music to be a formidable commercial competitor with the popular song. While Tin Pan Alley had concentrated its energies on the production of songs, it soon recognized the public demand for instrumental ragtime and ultimately was responsible for the majority of piano ragtime that was produced. Under the auspices of publishers such as Remick and Witmark, some of the most polished—if not always the most inspired— ragtime was produced, dominated by white professional composers.

The music stores that sold ragtime sheet music had a motivation beyond mere propagation of a popular style. Ragtime is characterized primarily as piano music, and, before the phonograph and the radio, the piano was the main source of entertainment, in the home and in public. The public demanded ragtime, and to play it, one had to have a piano. Piano retailers and manufacturers quickly recognized the important link between the sale of ragtime and the sale of pianos, both reaching their peak during the years 1897 to 1917.

The primary consumer of ragtime was not just the young but young women. Their upbringing included formal musical training, most often on the piano. Girls laboriously practiced hymns, etudes, and compositions in the European tradition as part of their finishing and were expected to give intimate home recitals and accompany singalongs for family and guests.

Pianos were also a fixture in the American underworld of bars, pool halls, brothels, and other venues of male entertainment. The sexual double standard thrived as men slipped out of their proper Victorian homes and headed for the red-light district to indulge openly in smoking, drinking, gambling, ribald stories and songs, and adventurous sex. The pianos in these establishments were played primarily by itinerant male blacks, performing in the only environment afforded them by the social code of the day. It was in this environment that ragtime was born.

Through vaudeville and the medium of sheet music, this syncopated style of piano eventually made its way from the brothel to the parlor of middle-class white homes. To the amateur home pianist, it offered a lively alternative to the standard bill of fare—sentimental parlor songs, classical and sacred music—and gave her the opportunity to play ragtime for her own enjoyment and the enjoyment of her friends—to be the life of the party. It is one of the great paradoxes in American music that the two groups most conversant with ragtime in its heyday were black male professional musicians and white female amateur musicians.

Ragtime became the first authentic black style to affect American popular music significantly. It quickly became apparent that the popular music industry in general, and ragtime in particular, was posing a serious threat to European art music in America. Most alarming was ragtime's effect on young people, the future supporters of art music, who heartily embraced the exciting new style. The art music community, as powerful as it was, made up only a fraction of the population. Audiences for classical music were never large, and the majority of the support was comprised of women socialites. The suppression of the genuine tastes of the masses could not bear up for long. The tide of the common culture eventually washed over the aristocratic deference to European ways. Heading the onslaught was ragtime. Yet for the duration of its popularity, musicians, educators, clergy, politicians, and businessmen condemned ragtime on a variety of issues.

The major objection to ragtime was that it lowered the tastes of the American public, particularly the youth. A typical comment appeared in *Musician* magazine in 1901: "This cheap, trashy stuff could not elevate even the most degraded minds, nor could it possibly urge any one to greater effort in the acquisition of culture in any phase."[2] At first, the attack on ragtime used the tactic of dismissing it as merely a passing fad. Journalists even attempted to report erroneously ragtime's demise at the height of its popularity. As early as 1901, one writer announced, "Rag-time has passed the zenith of its popularity, musicians say, and they are now anxious to lay out the corpse."[3]

When this deception failed to diminish public enthusiasm for ragtime, stronger measures were taken. In 1901, the American Federation of Musicians declared an official, if impotent, ban on the playing of ragtime. While it was impossible to impose such a ban on the national level, various cities and local organizations did manage to purge ragtime from its theaters and civic events. In Fort Worth, Texas, for instance, the local musicians' union pledged in a 1906 newspaper article never to play ragtime at any concert that included a performance of "The Star Spangled Banner."

Enjoyment of ragtime was viewed by critics as a catalyst for immoral thinking and behavior. Its nature was considered evocative of a physical rather than an intellectual response, running contrary to a Euro-Christian moral code going back several hundred years. As one custodian of American morals declared, "In Christian homes, where purity and morals are stressed, ragtime should find no resting place. Avaunt the ragtime rot!"[4]

Ragtime was seen as a music of excess, particularly in its use of syncopation. "When taken to excess it [syncopation] overstimulates; it irritates," said one critic in 1902,[5] fearing that the musical excess would carry over into society at large. Syncopation seemed to be the key disdainful ingredient in ragtime. One writer noted, "It [ragtime] savors too much of the primeval conception of music, whose basis was a rhythm that appealed to the physical rather than to the mental senses."[6] Another exclaimed, "Ragtime is syncopation gone mad."[7] There were arguments that ragtime's syncopation disrupted normal heart rhythms and the nervous system, adversely affected proper piano technique, and could even potentially induce insanity. Francis Toye wrote in 1913, "The *Valse Lente* might and doubtless did, drive people to conjugal infidelity, but ragtime, I verily believe, drives them to mania."[8]

Moral criticism of ragtime eventually revealed the racial bias of the time— the popular view that blacks were morally limited and of too low a social class to make an acknowledged contribution to American culture at large. "America is falling prey to the collective soul of the negro," wrote Walter Winston Kenilworth in 1913.[9] It was often pointed out that ragtime and the blacks who created it came from the most immoral and reprehensible of settings. This implied that the music and its black creators were inherently evil and that ragtime sheet music was like a carrier of some dreaded disease into the American home. One writer in 1900 cried out, "The counters of the music stores are loaded with this virulent poison which in the form of a malarious epidemic, is finding its way into the homes and the brains of youth."[10]

Opponents of ragtime also included black journalists, who appealed to more high-minded constituents to rid their people of association with the popular syncopated music. Black music critics in turn attacked enterprising white ragtime composers for fanning the ragtime flame. A writer for the *Negro Music Journal* declared in 1902:

White men also perpetuate so-called music under the name "rag-time," representing it to be characteristic of Negro music. This is also a libelous insult. The typical

Negro would blush to own acquaintance with the vicious trash put forth under Ethiopian titles. If the *Negro Music Journal* can only do a little missionary work among us, and help to banish this epidemic it will go down in history as one of the greatest musical benefactors of the age.[11]

One of the earliest objections to ragtime by both blacks and whites was the content of lyrics in ragtime songs. Ragtime songs evolved from the minstrel theater's tradition of racially denigrating lyrics, an abuse that reached its peak with the "coon song" of the 1890s, with titles like "My Coal Black Lady" and "All Coons Look Alike to Me." Black characters in these songs were portrayed as violent, dishonest, lazy, cowardly, and prone to superstition and sexual promiscuity. The songs, sung in Negro dialect, were intended to be comical at the expense of the group they depicted.

Those making objections to this subject matter were not necessarily sympathetic to blacks. They were more opposed to the general vulgarity of the sentiments expressed than how accurately they represented an ethnic group. The lyrics, in fact, were sometimes the only hindrance to the public's acceptance of ragtime. Scott Joplin commented in *New York Age* in 1913 that he had "often heard people say after they have heard a ragtime song, 'I like the music, but I don't like the words.'... So it is the unwholesome words and not the ragtime melodies that many people hate."[12]

Advocates of ragtime were varied in their backgrounds and were as vehement as ragtime's critics in their defense of this unique music. They did not represent only those with a vested interest in the popular music industry. Ragtime charmed and captured the imagination of American critics, as well as European aristocracy and art music composers. Renowned Czech composer Antonin Dvorak told American art music composers to nurture a nationalistic style of composition based on the folk music of African Americans and American Indians. He demonstrated such borrowing in his own "New World" Symphony of 1893, incorporating black American folk spirituals.

What some saw as corrupting and primitive traits, ragtime advocates saw as compelling and exciting. Syncopation, cited as the single most provocative and objectionable aspect of ragtime, was seen by enthusiasts as a powerful and legitimate musical tool. They perceived their own physical response to syncopation as thrilling and positive. Writers marveled, "It [syncopation] has a powerfully stimulating effect, setting the nerves and muscles tingling with excitement"[13] and "You simply can't resist it. ... I felt my blood thumping inside me, my muscles twitching to the rhythm."[14]

One of the most ardent supporters of ragtime was prominent music critic Hiram K. Moderwell (1888–1945), who not only saw ragtime as innovative but as a basis for a national school of composition. On purely technical terms he observed: "It [ragtime] has carried the complexities of the rhythmic subdivision of the measure to a point never before reached in the history of music. . . . It has gone far beyond most other popular music in the freedom of inner voices (yes, I mean polyphony) and of harmonic modulation."[15] In describing ragtime as uniquely American, Moderwell wrote: "As you walk up and down the streets of an American city you feel in its jerk and rattle a personality different from that of any European capital. . . . No European music can or possibly could express this American personality. Ragtime I believe does express it. It is to-day the one true American music."[16] In citing ragtime as the basis for a nationalistic school of composition, he wrote: "But here and nowhere else are the beginnings of American music, if American music is to be anything but a pleasing reflection of Europe. . . . I do know that there will be no great American music so long as American musicians despise ragtime."[17]

Other critics and musicians not only praised ragtime as America's unique contribution to the world but American popular music in general. Russian composer Igor Stravinsky said in a 1916 *New York Tribune* article, "I know little about American music except that of the music halls, but I consider that unrivaled. . . . God forbid that you Americans should compose symphonies and fugues."[18] American composer Olin Downes commented favorably on the popularity of ragtime: "As for 'rag-time,' its wide acceptance by the people can only be accepted as proof that it finds an echo in their hearts. . . . 'Rag-time' in its best estate is for me one of our most precious musical assets."[19]

A critic of ragtime and the most outspoken critic of Moderwell's ragtime defense was Daniel Gregory Mason (1873–1953), an American composer who opposed Moderwell's suggestion of ragtime as a national treasure and a basis for a school of American art music composition. He wrote, "This [ragtime] is not our virtue but our vice, not our strength but our weakness, and that such a picture of us as it presents is not a portrait but a caricature."[20] Mason felt that ragtime was an unsuitable source for American art music and that it only represented an inferior portion of America anyway. Even when he took Dvorak's advice and wrote his *Quartet on Negro Themes*, he held primitive slave songs in higher esteem than ragtime.

A national school of composition based on ragtime never emerged. Perhaps Charles L. Buchanan was correct when he wrote, "Will they never learn that art is a personal matter, that art is only incidentally concerned with nationality, and is in no way, shape or form under obligation to represent the character of a nation?"[21] It was ultimately up to the individual whims of composers to utilize ragtime or not, and few took up the call to do so. The most significant American art music composer to embrace ragtime was Charles Ives (1874–1954). He wrote a series, *Ragtime Dances*, between 1902 and 1904 and sporadically borrowed ragtime elements for his violin sonatas, piano sonatas, and other pieces.

Europeans, meanwhile, helped themselves to the elements of ragtime as resources for their own music. The most notable European products of the ragtime age are Claude Debussy's "Golliwog's Cakewalk" from his piano album *Children's Corner* (1908) and Igor Stravinsky's *Ragtime for Eleven Instruments* (1918).

As ragtime faded in the 1920s, the controversy continued, pitting the guardians of "serious music" and public morality against whatever American popular music was in vogue: New Orleans and Chicago jazz in the 1920s, swing in the 1930s, rhythm and blues in the 1940s, and rock from the 1950s. It is remarkable how consistent the arguments are over the decades, centered around a corrupting African-American rhythmic music threatening to destroy the tastes and values of white American youth.

Today symphony orchestras continue to function in America's cities, supported by wealthy individuals, corporations, and the government. But classical music is practically nonexistent in the music marketplace, comprising only 2 percent of overall record sales. The literary proponents of European art music have a very faint voice in the press. It is now the youth who control much of the musical output of America by virtue of the fact that they spend the most money on the products.

Art music has taken refuge in institutions of higher learning, supposedly immune from commercial pressures and free to exist for its own intrinsic value. In the long run, however, fierce competition will occur within the walls of these sanctuaries as it has on the streets. Schools of music and conservatories are reassessing what forms of music are worthy of serious study. Scholarly research and performance training now include jazz and world music. Serious study of trends in popular music is not far behind. In times of serious federal and state budget cuts, many music schools will be pressured to justify their existence by attracting more students and funding with offerings of studies in popular music, both to prepare young musicians for the business world and to serve the distinctive ethnic and geographic cultural needs of their communities. Art music supporters within the academy will resist these curricular invasions. But perhaps Moderwell, Stravinsky, and others were correct in their observations that America's most significant and unique contribution to world music is its popular music, an entity that was born in the form of ragtime.

NOTES

1. Max Morath, Foreword to Edward A. Berlin, *Reflections and Research on Ragtime* (New York: Institute for Studies in American Music, 1987), p. ix.

2. Weld, "The Invasion of Vulgarity," cited in Edward Berlin, *Ragtime: A Musical and Cultural History* (Berkeley: University of California Press, 1980), p. 43.

3. "Ethics of Ragtime," *Literary Digest*, cited in Berlin, *Ragtime*, p. 41.

4. Leo Oehmler, "Ragtime: A Pernicious Evil and Enemy of True Art," *Musical Observer* 11 (September 1914), cited in Neil Leonard, "The Reactions to Ragtime," *Ragtime: Its History, Composers, and Music*, ed. John Edward Hasse (New York: Schirmer Books, 1985), p. 106.

5. Hubbs, "What Is Ragtime?" cited in Berlin, *Ragtime*, p. 43.
6. Paul G. Carr, "Abuses of Music," *Musician* 6 (October 1901), cited in Berlin, *Ragtime*, p. 43.
7. Edward Baxter Perry, "Ragging Good Music," *Etude* 36 (June 1918), cited in Berlin, *Ragtime*, p. 44.
8. Francis Toye, "Ragtime: The New Tarantism," *English Review* 8 (March 1913), cited in William J. Schafer and Johannes Riedel, *The Art of Ragtime* (Baton Rouge: Louisiana State University Press, 1973), p. 39.
9. Walter Winston Kenilworth, "Demoralizing Ragtime Music," *Musical Courier*, May 21, 1913, cited in Leonard, "The Reactions to Ragtime," p. 107.
10. "Musical Impurity," cited in Berlin, *Ragtime*, p. 44.
11. "What 'the Concert Goer' Says of 'the Negro Music Journal,' " *Negro Music Journal* 1 (September 1914), cited in Berlin, *Ragtime*, p. 42.
12. "Theatrical Comment," *New York Age*, April 3, 1913, cited in Berlin, *Ragtime*, p. 36.
13. "Questions and Answers," *Etude* 16 (October 1898), cited in Berlin, *Ragtime*, p. 46.
14. Kenilworth, "Demoralizing Ragtime Music," p. 46.
15. Hiram K. Moderwell, "Ragtime," *New Republic*, October 16, 1915, cited in Schafer and Riedel, *Art of Ragtime*, p. 41.
16. Moderwell, "Ragtime," cited in Berlin, *Ragtime*, p. 51.
17. Moderwell, "A Modest Proposal," *Seven Arts* 2 (July 1917), cited in Berlin, *Ragtime*, p. 55.
18. Stanley C. Wise, " 'American Music Is True Art,' Says Stravinsky," *New York Tribune*, January 16, 1916, sec. 5, p. 3, cited in Berlin, *Ragtime*, p. 45.
19. Olin Downes, "An American Composer," *Musical Quarterly* 4 (January 1918), cited in Berlin, *Ragtime*, p. 45.
20. Daniel Gregory Mason, "Folk-Song and American Music (A Plea for the Unpopular Point of View)," *Musical Quarterly* 4 (July 1918), cited in Berlin, *Ragtime*, p. 51.
21. Charles L. Buchanan, "Ragtime and American Music," *Opera Magazine*, cited in Berlin, *Ragtime*, p. 52.

BIBLIOGRAPHY

Berlin, Edward. *Ragtime: A Musical and Cultural History*. Berkeley: University of California Press, 1980. This chapter particularly relied on the excellent summary of dialogue on ragtime, pro and con, included in chapter 3 of Berlin's book.
Erenberg, Lewis A. *Steppin' Out: New York Nightlife and the Transformation of American Culture, 1890–1930*. Chicago: University of Chicago Press, 1981.
Leonard, Neil. "The Reactions to Ragtime." In John Edward Hasse, ed., *Ragtime: Its History, Composers, and Music*. New York: Schirmer Books, 1985.
Morath, Max. Foreword to Edward A. Berlin. *Research and Reflection on Ragtime*. New York: Institute for Studies in American Music, 1987.
Schafer, William J., and Johannes Riedel. *The Art of Ragtime*. Baton Rouge: Louisiana State University Press, 1973.

25

Debating with Beethoven: Understanding the Fear of Early Jazz

Kathy J. Ogren

When John R. McMahon, writing in the *Ladies Home Journal* in 1921, observed, "If Beethoven should return to earth and witness the doings of a jazz orchestra, he would thank heaven for his deafness," the author voiced a strong animosity that many Americans felt toward jazz when it first gained popularity in the 1920s.[1] Yet the decade would eventually be known as the jazz age, attesting to the deep significance that the music had for the 1920s. An examination of the fear of jazz illuminates specific social and political anxieties of Americans in the 1920s; it also establishes a context for understanding the symbolic role played by popular music generally in twentieth-century American culture.

Debates about jazz revealed a profound concern about a wide range of changes taking place in American society. Comparing the sounds of the music to howitzers, some critics believed the music evoked the violence and sudden changes that seemed to accompany World War I. Other detractors heard the repetitive grinding of industrial society in the music. Alarmists objected to the locations where jazz was performed or complained about the effects they believed the music was having on young people. Because jazz would be increasingly available to new audiences on phonograph records and radio, some critics were also responding to the growth of these mass cultural mediums—not just to the sounds they transmitted. Some African Americans rejected jazz because they felt the music originated as "devil's music" and was therefore inferior to sacred music. Both enthusiasts and detractors associated jazz with social and cultural changes that seemed to be transforming their lives at an alarming pace. Change itself seemed to be encoded in the lively momentum of the jazz band.

Most objections to jazz were voiced by white Americans who wrote for newspapers and popular and scholarly journals or those who debated cultural values in civic or community organizations. Americans arguing about the meaning of jazz voiced numerous concerns, and their judgments were necessarily shaped by their attitudes toward African-American culture. Any examination of the charges leveled against jazz must begin with a consideration of its musical qualities. Was there something in particular about jazz music itself that antagonized critics like McMahon?

Because jazz opponents typically revered cultural standards that had derived from European elites, they did not appreciate the musical traditions that had nurtured jazz. Jazz evolved from musical traditions that began in Africa and then combined with the European and American sacred and secular music that slaves heard on the plantation in slavery and during Reconstruction. In general, jazz had not been composed by men and women schooled in the conservatory, and it was not performed by musicians in the sedate setting of the concert hall. Jazz was far outside the canon of classical music represented by figures like Beethoven.

By contrast, definitive aspects of jazz, in particular the combined use of syncopation, improvisation, polyrhythms, and blue tonalities, were nurtured in black communities where audience and performer interactions were particularly strong. Jazz musicians emphasized the beats within each musical phrase that had previously been considered weak and played softly in most European-based music. Although syncopation was not unique to African-American music, when it was combined with several rhythmic lines played simultaneously, jazz sounded faster and more rhythmically intense than much of the popular music that preceded it.

In addition, jazz developed in a close relationship to the blues, a vernacular American music that probably originated after slavery when freed men and women developed new songs out of the field cries and hollers, work songs, and laments that they had sung during slavery. Blues music is built around tones that might be considered flat or dissonant to a listener solely familiar with the conventional harmony of European concert music. It is very likely that certain African arrangements of tones, which are not the same as the European diatonic scale, were embodied in blue tonalities. Blues performers often "bent" or "worried" the tones they sang by gliding between the anticipated separations between notes in a song. Although the early blues were typically composed of three lines of words that could be measured out in eight or twelve units of beats per verse, performers elaborated their material at the end of each line or phrase. Jazz musicians often accompanied blues singers and played blues themselves. They incorporated the blues into the evolving improvisational jazz mix.

Improvisation itself, the alteration of melodies, timing, or rhythms, is common to all music. Composers and performers regularly improvise on musical ideas, but early jazz was typically created through improvisation in performance—not by a composer's rewriting music for a later time. Jazzmen in the earliest New Orleans bands, for example, created a heterophonic form of improvisation in which the members of a jazz band played off and against each other as they marched down the street or played dance music from a stage. Other kinds of improvisation developed when soloists or featured sections of a jazz band or orchestra began a musical idea and other musicians took it up and expanded on it.

Improvisation in jazz, when combined with the other central musical characteristics, produced a lively new sound that seemed to violate the expectations of listeners accustomed to slower, more predictable, and less rhythmically complex music. The call-and-response foundations of jazz were a product of participatory performance practices in which not only the individual musicians but also their audiences played an important role in the creation of the music. When early jazz bands marched in parades and festivals of New Orleans, for example, they conducted "cutting contests" on street corners or in dance halls to win business from each other. Listeners cheered on the musicians they preferred. Jazz pianist Willie "The Lion" Smith reported that dancers in saloons would tell him what tempo to use in a song. Both the musical foundation of jazz, as well as the situations in which it was performed, lent it an intriguing, unpredictable quality.

Some music columnists claimed that jazz was simply "not music," and they labeled it mere "dance music" performed by musicians who lacked "professional training." Although many jazz performers took music lessons and some had musical forebears in their families who had played for institutions like the New Orleans Opera, most had learned to play by ear. Novice players apprenticed themselves to more experienced players or learned through improvisation with other players. From the jazz performer's perspective, this method of learning music was certainly as challenging as the more formal education offered by a conservatory. Undoubtedly ear training was more useful for absorbing the improvisational skills required for effective interpretations of material. In any case, elite music education was closed to most aspiring black musicians. The jazz musicians' form of music education was different from that of the conservatory-trained musician yet rigorous in its own way. The ethnocentric orientation and aesthetic prejudices of jazz opponents, however, prevented them from making a favorable comparison.

When jazz first gained national prominence during the 1920s, many white Americans were ignorant of the rich, creative traditions that produced black secular music. White Americans probably had the widest exposure to spirituals and other sacred black music. Some whites might have been exposed to the presentation of black life that had been popularized by the minstrel show, which, until the end of the Civil War, was always performed by white men in black grease paint. Minstrelsy had preserved certain aspects of African-American dance, music, humor, and story-telling, but at the same time, performers often portrayed blacks as simple-minded, foolish, or violent. The presentation of black music—and black people—through the distorting lens of the minstrel show exacerbated negative racial stereotypes across America. Black music was also featured at exhibitions and in some vaudeville shows. By the early twentieth century, an open-minded white listener could enjoy ragtime, stride piano, and other African-American music that did not denigrate black life.

Nevertheless, many white Americans had a limited understanding of and appreciation for African-American music at the time when jazz first became popular. Racist attitudes colored many white interactions with African Americans. This pervasive animosity was most clearly expressed in the continued growth of lynching in the South and by a series of violent attacks on black communities that followed World War I. Race riots exploded in East Saint Louis, Missouri, Charleston, South Carolina, Longview, Texas, Washington, D.C., and Chicago between 1917 and 1919. In all cases, whites attacked black neighborhoods because they resented the increasing numbers of African Americans who were moving to urban areas from the rural South.

Migrating blacks came looking for new jobs, better homes and education, and, they hoped, some freedom from political repression in the South. Instead, they became the scapegoats for white frustrations. White America's widespread acceptance of racist ideas and institutions, particularly when fueled by violence, sustained defenders of the dominant culture in their assertions that African Americans were inferior to whites.

African-American political and intellectual leaders like W.E.B. Du Bois, Alain Locke, James Weldon Johnson, and Marcus Garvey fought back against the upsurge in racism by advocating black pride. The celebration of a militant spirit would eventually be labeled the "New Negro." Justly proud of their distinguished service in World War I, black veterans pointed out that if they had helped to make the world "safe for democracy," as the Allies claimed, then Americans should live up to the same standard.

In New York's Harlem, young black artists and intellectuals like Langston Hughes, Aaron Douglas, Zora Neale Hurston, and Claude McKay advocated a return to African and African-American folk culture for inspiration in black literature and art. This celebration of increased artistic and literary activity became known as the Harlem Renaissance. Jazz and blues served as an important subject and language for these young experimenters.

Jazz rose to national attention against the backdrop of these social, economic, and political debates about race and American life. In retrospect, one cannot separate the hostility or fear of jazz from perceptions about the changes brought about by black migration and increased political activism. The specific locations where jazz was performed also gave it a controversial reputation. Jazz was played in a variety of cities where musicians traveled for work: New Orleans, Chicago, New York, Kansas City, San Francisco, and Los Angeles. In many cities, musical entertainment was concentrated, sometimes by law, in the same vice districts where prostitution, gambling, and other activities deplored by moralists took place. Because jazzmen had occasionally worked in brothels, some opponents claimed erroneously that jazz was a music born of prostitution.

By the 1920s, many vice districts had been abolished, including New Orleans's famed Storyville. In entertainment areas of major cities, the corner saloon or dance hall that primarily attracted a working-class clientele was joined by newly designed nightclubs, which attracted an affluent middle-class audience. Entrepreneurs gave the night spots names like the Plantation Club, the Cotton Club, the Nest, Spider's Webb, the Hole in the Wall, and Bucket of Blood, emphasizing exotic or other-worldly themes to entice patrons through their doors. Large nightclubs featured floor shows, but smaller places often had tables and chairs arranged around the dance floor in a setting that encouraged intimacy and participation by the audience. Although both black and white musicians performed in some of the best-known clubs and ballrooms, most clubs were segregated, with black patrons barred from entrance.

Alcohol was available at many nightclubs, in violation of the national Volstead Act that legislated prohibition. In some cases, the clubs were financed by men associated with organized crime. Moralists concerned about the many—and sometimes illegal—temptations provided in such an environment often claimed that jazz had a debilitating effect in such circumstances. Commentators critical of jazz feared that young men and women might abandon sexual restraint in these clubs as a result of the seductive combination of "primitive" dancing music and alcohol.

Young people, especially college-aged men and women, had declared themselves in hedonistic revolt against the older generation, and many embraced jazz as their favorite music. Young white musicians patterned themselves after black jazzmen. College parties soon moved to the syncopated strains of groups like the Wolverines, composed of young white Chicagoans.

Newspapers and magazines sensationalized the idea that young "flappers" and "sheiks" symbolized an alarming new trend for America's young people. America's adolescents were reputed to smoke and drink to excess, "neck" with abandon, and scorn their parents' staid lives. Rebellious white American intellectuals embraced black entertainment, including jazz, as a form of "primitivism," which they claimed could release them from a materialistic and repressive industrial civilization. Black artists did not necessarily appreciate the patronizing assumptions on which "primitivism" was based, but their objections did not stop its promotion by the avant-garde. Faced with the burgeoning popularity of jazz, parents feared that they had lost control of their children's intellectual and leisure tastes. Jazz was a handy target for their ire.

Jazz developed at the same time as phonograph recordings and, toward the end of the 1920s, the growth of radio broadcasts. These media would eventually disseminate jazz to a much larger audience than the one that could experience jazz live, and broader exposure helped reduce animosity toward the music. Still, some of the negative connotations of jazz were also communicated by the new media. Recordings of black artists were marketed under a race record category separate from the one for white musicians, reinforcing the inferior aura of jazz and blues. Black bands continued to be quite popular, and some performers like Louis Armstrong and Duke Ellington became well known to a white as well as a black audience, but the music first played on radio was typically "symphonic jazz," usually performed by white bands that deemphasized the African-American roots of the music. The fear of jazz dissipated as the process of media popularization promoted what many listeners considered the safest and least improvisational forms of jazz.

Despite calls to ban jazz or regulate it like alcohol, jazz opponents were clearly on the defensive by the end of the 1920s. The attacks on jazz indicated that listeners heard more than mere musical sounds in its notes. To its detractors, the "off-key" sounds of jazz were amplified by its association with African-American culture and politics, red-light and vice districts, invasive media, and rebellious youth.

Interestingly, all of the complaints against jazz testified to its continued power to communicate the unexpected and the challenging—in short, improvisational change. Other styles of American popular music would continue to draw on the same controversial well of participatory creation. When the "older generation" of the 1950s pronounced its antipathy toward rock and roll, John McMahon might have cheered them on. But rock and roll artist Chuck Berry had the final word with the opening line of his 1956 hit: "Roll over Beethoven, and hear them rhythm and blues." Jazz had clearly opened—not closed—American ears to the creative potential of African-American music.

NOTES

1. John R. McMahon, "Back to Pre-War Morals," *Ladies Home Journal* 38 (November 1921): 13.

BIBLIOGRAPHY

Berger, Morroe. "Jazz: Resistance to the Diffusion of a Culture Pattern." *Journal of Negro History* 32 (1974): 461–94.
Erenberg, Lewis A. *Steppin' Out: New York Nightlife and the Transformation of American Culture, 1890–1930.* Chicago: University of Chicago Press, 1981.
Jones, LeRoi. *Blues People: Negro Music in White America.* New York: William Morrow, 1963.
Leonard, Neil. *Jazz and the White Americans: The Acceptance of a New Art Form.* Chicago: University of Chicago Press, 1962.
———. *Jazz: Myth and Religion.* New York: Oxford University Press, 1987.

Nanry, Charles, with Edward Berger. *The Jazz Text.* New York: Van Nostrand Reinhold, 1979.

Ogren, Kathy J. *The Jazz Revolution: Twenties America and the Meaning of Jazz.* New York: Oxford University Press, 1989.

Schuller, Gunther. *Early Jazz: Its Roots and Musical Development.* New York: Oxford University Press, 1968.

Stearns, Marshall. *The Story of Jazz.* New York: Oxford University Press, 1956.

— 26 —

Sounds of Seduction: Sex and Alcohol in Country Music Lyrics

CHARLES JARET AND JACQUELINE BOLES

If you are like most people, this is one of the first chapters you turned to. Why such interest in sex and booze? Maybe you are aware of, and curious about, the fact that so much of what goes on in country music songs (not to mention the lives of country music performers and their associates) revolves around things that happen when alcohol or sex takes over. Perhaps it is simply our fascination with sex and alcohol that accounts for the great appeal these have among country music's songwriters, singers, and audience. Country music is, after all, one of the most "people-friendly" styles we know of, in the sense that it places highest priority on clever, yet accessible lyrics that tell the kind of story many people can relate to. If we are fascinated by the power sexuality and liquor have over our lives, then that is why we so often find these as central themes in the music. Sex and booze sells. Need we say more?

Yes. We think there is another good reason for being interested in how country music treats alcohol and sex. Song lyrics, along with other elements of popular culture, both reinforce our beliefs, values, and attitudes and help to form or guide them. If, for example, song lyrics suggest that drinking is an acceptable way of solving problems, then when faced with a crisis, we are more likely to use alcohol than if we had not been subjected to repeated suggestions that liquor helps in these situations. Studying the lyrics of country songs can help us understand how country fans view using alcohol and sexual relations.

Country music grew out of the music of the Scots, Irish, and English settlers of the Appalachian mountains. Infused into it were elements of bluegrass, African-American gospel, and blues, as well as musical styles from the Southwest. One of country music's most distinctive sounds, the steel guitar, is of Hawaiian origin, and later instruments and styles from rock and pop were incorporated, often despite opposition from country music purists. The first commercial country star was Jimmie Rodgers. He and other early country singers, like the Carter Family and Roy Acuff, sang ballads that featured traditional themes about home, family, religion, and disaster ("Wreck on the Highway"). In the 1950s, Hank Williams and others popularized songs set in bars, honky-tonks, and "juke joints" and vividly described drinking and getting drunk. "Cheating" songs ("Your Cheatin' Heart" by Hank Williams) became important, and frequently drinking and sex were linked in the lyrics.

Back then, country music was most popular in the South and West Central parts of the United States, especially among listeners of rural or blue-collar background. According to Jim Single, a longtime country singer-songwriter, what has made country music special is its honesty: "It's the most honest music there is, except maybe the blues." He adds that "country music developed as country boys went to the cities to work and felt separated from their homes. They weren't real literate, so they expressed themselves in songs, and went to bars in the cities because in the bar they could be around home folks—the lyrics came from broken hearts."[1]

This sort of music, however, was widely dismissed as trite, unsophisticated hillbilly or "hick" music in the Northeast and other urban centers. During the 1970s, a significant shift in audience began as country music radio stations sprang up in urban markets, the highly successful movie *Urban Cowboy* showcased country music, and popular singers from other styles had numerous crossover hits on country charts. It was during this period that a "modern" country sound, which some dub "countrypolitan" crystallized around performers like Barbara Mandrell, Kenny Rogers, and Crystal Gayle; more traditional singers, like Porter Waggoner, had trouble selling records or getting airplay. This development bred a counterreaction among those who felt country music was selling out or losing its soul. First came the "outlaw" rebellion (led by Willie Nelson, Waylon Jennings, Johnny Cash, and Hank Williams, Jr.) and, currently, the more restrained neotraditionalists, like George Strait, Randy Travis, and Clint Black who have returned to their roots by featuring the themes and story format of earlier days.

Despite these and other shifts in style, the audience for country music has continuously grown, expanding far beyond its original base of fans. Although country music accounts for only 10 percent of the records bought in the United States, it is now the most popular radio format (with 60 percent of the American population listening in), and the country music cable television channel (the Nashville Network) is growing faster than any other. A recent survey of purchasers of recorded music found that in terms of income and educational level, people who like country music are almost identical to those who like pop and new age music; they differ only by age, with fewer young and more older people liking country. Despite the broad acceptance of country music, it is still a unique social world and to a large extent remains true to its traditional origins, symbols, and institutions.

Many writers have commented on the way sex and alcohol appear to be inordinately featured in country music. Country song titles often explicitly refer to one or both of them (e.g., "Soft Lips and Hard Liquor," "Red Wine and Blue Memories," "Love in the Hot Afternoon," "She's Actin' Single, I'm Drinking Doubles"), and many are only a little more subtle (e.g., "When Can We Do This Again?" "Heaven's Just a Sin Away").

Although sex and alcoholic drink are prominent themes in country music, these are not the only or main concerns in this musical form. Several writers have identified a host of other themes central to country music, including the values of independence, celebration of home and family, patriotism, and the problems of work, disaster, and prison. In fact, most country music songs do not make reference to drinking and sexual behavior. One study of a random sample of lyrics from *Billboard*'s "Hot Singles" list found that only 30 (or 11 percent) of the 275 songs analyzed mentioned drinking, and another researcher found only 15 percent of the country songs played on the radio made reference to liquor, drinking, bars or honky-tonks.

This same study of country songs played on the radio found that making love (featured in just over 20 percent of the songs) was a little more popular than drinking, and simple romantic kissing was somewhat less frequent (referred to in just over 10 percent of the songs). Thus, country songs typically deal with a number of issues other than sex and liquor. The perception that country music deals primarily with sex and alcohol is an example of stereotyping in which a visible, striking trait that is somewhat common is taken to be typical of the category as a whole.

When drinking is included in a country song, typically the lyrics also mention a bar or honky-tonk saloon. One researcher reported that a bar was the setting for almost three-quarters of the songs that referred to liquor, while motels and hotels were a distant second, and a few songs were set in the home or on the road. The bar is portrayed as a place where the song's protagonist can get into trouble, drown his or her sorrows, or demonstrate his masculinity (or her femininity) through a sexual, physical, psychological, or moral conquest or contest.

Although men are the drinkers most of the time, countrypolitan songs are more likely to portray men and women drinking together than were songs recorded several decades ago, when only "bad girls" went to bars and drank. When the lyrics are about drinking and getting drunk, more often than not the song deals with one of two stages in a romantic relationship: the (usually sad) period after a breakup or the start (or attempted start) of a new one.

In terms of the message or moral conveyed, country lyrics that contain images of liquor and drinking span a broad range. At one extreme are songs that treat alcoholic drink as a serious evil or the Devil's tool. Songs of this type (e.g., "The Letter That Johnny Walker Read," "T-R-O-U-B-L-E") warn that turning to the bottle will take one down the path of ruin by destroying one's reputation or breaking up important ties of love, family, and friendship. Some observers claim this message reflects Calvinist values and fundamentalist religious traditions that were influential in areas where country music first became popular. It is rather rare today, however, to hear song lyrics that depict drinking wholly in this negative manner; more often if this message appears at all, it is intertwined with another one.

The second common way country lyrics present the drinker is as a man (or occasionally a woman) who turns to drink after having a painful experience involving humiliation, failure, or loss (e.g., losing an argument or job, a romantic breakup, death of a loved one). Liquor here is not depicted as the cause of the difficulty but rather as a response or reaction to the personal problem. Alcohol is a means of blocking the pain, a way of temporarily escaping from it, a crutch that enables one to get through it, or a device that may help one avoid responsibility for it. Country songwriters take this image in two directions. The more moralistic approach paints this kind of drinker as a person whom we should feel some sympathy for yet nevertheless is a sad, pathetic, lonely loser whose drinking is the wrong response since it only makes a bad situation worse (e.g., "Bubbles in My Beer," "I've Got a Right to Be Wrong").

The other approach treats turning to liquor in response to personal problems and disappointment more as a socially accepted, even expected, way of coping. It implies the barroom is a good place to let off steam, vent one's anger, or tell one's sad story to others who will listen (e.g., "Bar Wars," "I've Got Friends in Low Places").

The third way that drinking is presented in country lyrics is virtually the polar opposite from the one we discussed first. In many songs, drinking beer, wine, whiskey, or moonshine is treated in a way that says it is an integral part of having a good time, enjoying life, feeling good, loosening one's sexual inhibitions or those of the person one is trying to seduce ("Three Sheets in the Wind," "Love or Something Like It," "After the Fire Is Gone"). Hank Williams, Jr., frequently sings songs of this type. One minute he is complaining that "All My Rowdy Friends Have Settled Down" (nobody wants to go out and have a good old time getting drunk and loud any more); then he is grousing about New York (and the North) because the people up there do not do enough huntin' and fishin' and they do not even drink Jack Daniels whiskey like the folks down South do. In these songs, a positive side of drinking is shown and celebrated: its utility in making people sociable and "happy," its function as a measure of "manliness" (how much can you drink? how well do you handle it?), its symbolic link to particular cherished regions and life-styles.

What is both appealing and fascinating about the use of alcohol and drinking in country music is how a creative songwriter can still work within one or more of these approaches and, after all these years, find something touching and/or original to say. Merle Haggard did a whole album consisting of these types of songs (*Back to the Barrooms*), and the themes we have mentioned are interwoven in many of the cuts.

On a more general level, we agree with George Lewis's suggestion that much of country music's popularity and importance as a form of popular culture comes from its ability to pinpoint and address the tensions and contradictions that exist among widely held American values. This point is especially clear in songs that refer to drinking. What other activity can so easily and realistically be brought in to address the conflicting pulls of home, family, and responsibility, on the one hand, and the open road, "the guys," and freedom, on the other? Alcohol can also be used to play off traditional morality versus the modern view that morality is relative to the situation rather than absolute. In the hands of a good songwriter, images of liquor and drinking can highlight contradictory feelings and behaviors—our alternation between, on the one hand, restraining our impulses, maintaining self-control, or rationally dealing with our everyday troubles, and, on the other hand, getting wild and crazy, living out repressed desires, or retreating from our problems. If most of us did not share these basic contradictory impulses, we doubt drinking alcohol would have such a prominent place in country lyrics.

Just a few years ago, David Frizell had a hit with a song that humorously plays on the tension created among these competing pulls ("I'm Gonna Hire a Wino"). In it, the main character, a long-suffering wife whose husband spends most of his free time in a bar, is so fed up that she threatens to hire a wino to decorate their home. She wants to create the perfect honky-tonk atmosphere (complete with dim lights, a pool table in the living room, signs pointing to the restroom, barroom brawls, and herself decked out in a skimpy bargirl outfit) so her husband will feel happier at home than at the local tavern. The song is sung by the husband (Frizell) in a way that lets listeners imagine some of his ambivalence as he considers his wife's plan— "on the one hand, maybe I'm not such a great husband or dad, and maybe I should shape up; but on the other hand, converting the house into a bar just might be a great idea."

Songs about alcohol in which a woman is the protagonist are fewer in number than songs that feature men. One common image in these is the woman who has taken to drink because of a "bad" man ("Your Good Girl's Gonna Go Bad," "Two More Bottles of Wine"). Because the man is unfaithful, the woman starts hanging out in bars and getting drunk. In this type of song, the woman is usually portrayed sympathetically; the implication is that it is understandable that a woman who has been dumped or abused would become an alcoholic.

"Don't Come Home with Lovin' on Your Mind" illustrates the problem of women whose husbands come home drunk and then expect or demand sex. Again, women are portrayed sympathetically in these songs. Women have to put up with a lot of "grief" from men, but women have a right to expect or demand decent treatment.

In sum, for both men and women, drinking, and drinking to excess, is often portrayed sympathetically in contemporary country songs. We drink to get happy, to celebrate various events, to drown our sorrows, and to free our inhibitions. For country music fans, the lyrics say, "It's okay to drink, to get drunk, and to get crazy." It is not surprising then, that many do just that, sometimes with tragic consequences.

We now take a look at the treatment of sexual themes in country lyrics. We will begin with a note on the variety of sexual behaviors alluded to in country music. In 1978, at a conference on popular culture, Edward G. Armstrong presented a research paper that surprised most listeners. It dealt with the portrayal of sexual issues in country music, and those who thought it would be almost entirely about heterosexual extramarital infidelity were amazed by the variety of sexual issues Armstrong found: autoeroticism, birth control, extramarital sex, frigidity, homosexuality, illegitimacy, impotence, incest, infertility, interracial dating, nymphomania, pornography, premarital sex, prostitution, rape, and voyeurism. To this list he added transvestism and beastiality, for although he did not find songs dealing with these, they were documented by other researchers he was in contact with. Clearly not all of these sexual issues are equally common, and except for premarital and extramarital sex, most of them are rarely, if ever, touched on in the songs that make it on the hit charts and radio station play lists. They are more likely to be heard in an album cut or at a live performance.

Given the diversity of sexual issues in country music, an interesting sociological question is, Why are we so rarely exposed to the more unusual, some would say deviant, sexual themes in country lyrics? Why is there a great predominance of heterosexual extramarital affairs? There are several possible explanations. First, country audiences are older than rock, soul, or pop fans; consequently, most are married or divorced and interested in songs reflecting their experiences and problems. Second, the divorce rate is higher among blue-collar than white-collar couples, and some evidence suggests that blue-collar husbands and wives "cheat" a little more often than do those in the middle class. Finally, fundamentalist religious values are still held by many country fans. Cheating can be viewed simultaneously as sinful yet pleasurable, wrong yet somehow right, and they may feel the other sexual themes are much too immoral or controversial to deal with in popular songs.

In focusing on the ways sexual themes are presented in country music, observers have noted several interesting tendencies. In contrast to other musical genres like blues, rap, or rock, songs that simply treat sex as a pleasurable activity, that is, songs wholly devoted to exclamations of how badly the singer wants sex or songs that emphasize the sheer delight or enjoyment of it, are relatively uncommon in country music. A few such songs do come to mind, such as Gene Watson's "Love in the Hot Afternoon" or "When Can We Do This Again?" by T. G. Sheppard, but they are atypical as far as country lyrics and sex are concerned.

Instead, sex in country lyrics is usually linked to some other aspect of a personal story. Sexual infidelity or lust becomes wrapped up in a tale of marital trouble, either as the cause of a broken relationship or as a response to one that has gone sour. In this vein, DiMaggio et al. indicate that for female characters in country music, their sexual behavior is often a means toward some other end, such as holding together a home, family, or marriage. Many songs suggest that being sexually alluring and pleasing to "their man" was a good tactic for making him stay home and be faithful.

The classic female-to-male exchange of sexual favors in return for psychic and material benefits is frequently found in country lyrics. Much of the surprise and popularity of Loretta Lynn's hit "The Pill" arose because its message on female sexuality cutely, but clearly, played off the well-established pattern of exchanging sex for financial support by proposing that with contraception available, women might become just as free as men to go out looking for sexual pleasure.

Commentators have noted another interesting aspect of country music's treatment of gender and sexuality. They point out how often a female character in a song speaks directly to or about her sexual rival ("the other woman"), in contrast to how rarely males in country songs refer to another man who is either after or has already seduced "his woman." A classic song of this type is Dolly Parton's "Jolene," where the singer pathetically pleads with Jolene (her super-sexy competitor, known to be able to get any man she wishes) not to take her husband from her. More recently, Reba McEntire had a hit with a song telling of her hope for regaining her husband's full love and devotion when an unnamed woman somewhere in New England (where he makes many business trips) gets tired of him. Interestingly, in most of these songs, the other woman, not the husband, is blamed. As in many soap operas, it is as if the man cannot see that the "other woman" is conniving, selfish, and spoiled; he is duped by her but will pay later when she abandons him for another.

Songs about men frequently suggest that a man may have several lovers and/or sexual partners at the same time. Often the song's protagonist is a husband torn between his wife and a girlfriend. For example, in "Holding Her and Loving You," Earl Thomas Conley tells how hard it is for him to hold his wife while actually being in love with another woman. On the other hand, if the song is about a woman, rarely is she described as loving or having sex with more than one man at a time. Several years ago a number of country radio stations refused to play the crossover hit, "Torn between Two Lovers," because male listeners complained about lyrics that would suggest that a woman might have two lovers and be unwilling to decide between them. However, Willie Nelson and Julio Iglesias had a hit with a song describing in vivid detail "The Women I Have Loved." Conversely, in some country songs (like Randy Travis's "On the Other Hand") that describe a man's devotion and fidelity to one woman, despite come-ons from other women, the feeling conveyed is that men get special praise or merit for being faithful, while from women it is expected or taken for granted.

Some gender role researchers have argued that American women are socialized to see other women as potential sexual rivals out to seduce their husbands or lovers. This distrust of other women often prevents female solidarity and means that when a man does cheat, the other woman will usually be blamed. However, male sexual rivalry of another sort can be found in country lyrics. In country, as in other types of popular music, references to sexual liaisons across socioeconomic lines are not uncommon, but in country music they take a fairly predictable turn: a working-class man and a woman of higher social status. Usually it involves some form of flattery of the working-class male's ego (not to mention his libido) by telling how either (1) a higher-status woman, after having sex with a working-class man, prefers the blue-collar guy to her richer but less virile boyfriend or husband or (2) how a woman of working-class origins, who marries a higher-status man, is unhappy with him and longs for her working-class man ("Slide Off Your Satin Sheets").

Songs of this sort have been set on farms, where the farmer's wife finds sexual satisfaction with a hired laborer and in cities, where a rich woman, "out slumming" in fancy, tight-fitting designer jeans, discovers pleasures dancing, drinking, and in bed with a working-class urban cowboy. This theme is sometimes expressed by female singers, as in Jeanne Pruett's "Satin Sheets," where a woman marries a millionaire and has everything money can buy but still is not happy in bed or elsewhere without her less well-to-do former lover, and it also appears in songs by men (Hank Williams's "Mansion on the Hill"). Generally working-class men are portrayed as more virile, sexy, vital, and dangerous than either middle-class or wealthy, dull, soft men. As Waylon Jennings points out, "Ladies Love Outlaws," and much country music testifies to the attraction of cross–social class romance.

Many country songs combine alcohol and sexual themes in the same song. Time and again, the songs tell how wine or some other alcoholic elixir helps to seduce someone ("Barrooms to Bedrooms," "Third Rate Romance"), or if that is not the goal, it helps to sedate one's passion for someone ("Roses in the Wine"), or it may merely be a prop in the pick-up game.

Country songs often contain folk wisdom and insights drawn from personal experiences and observations. Some of these deal with the link between drinking and sex. An example is the hook line of an old country song set in a honky-tonk, "The Women All Get Prettier at Closing Time," which makes the point that when the object is seduction, people get less choosy as the evening wanes. We heard of a student who, inspired by this song, did a term paper on peoples' perceptions of sexual attractiveness and provided evidence that country songwriters know what they are talking about. After comparing men's and women's ratings of each other early in the evening with their ratings after the last call for drinks, the student concluded that after a few drinks and faced with the prospect of spending the rest of the night alone, the ratings rose. Country lyrics tell us that when you mix drinking, a late-night honky-tonk atmosphere, and a potential sexual partner, chances are the level of desire goes up and pickiness about who to choose for the night goes down.

Although country songs often still extol the advantages of country living, most fans now live in metropolitan areas; consequently more and more songs deal with problems of urban life—for example, work problems ("Take This Job and Shove It," "9 to 5") or the difficulties of adjusting to an urban, often northern environment ("Detroit City"). The image of a man or woman being confused, beaten, or frustrated by some aspect of modern life is not uncommon. Quite often country lyrics portray people as turning to alcohol and sex in hopes of overcoming alienation. In other words, characters in country songs frequently use sex and drinking as a haven from a hostile world, as something that will give them a feeling of comfort, stability, strength, and a sense of being someone important. Depending on the songwriter's inclination, the character may find satisfaction in this or may find it leads only to more pain and frustration.

For many it is the latter. Numerous country stars, including Hank Williams, Sr., and, Jr., Freddie Fender, Johnny Paycheck, George Jones, and Waylon Jennings, just to name a few, have fallen victim to alcohol and easy sex. From "The Streets of Baltimore" to "Folsom Prison," country songs reflect the efforts of average Americans' coping with the changing, impersonal world around them. Perhaps the great Kris Kristofferson song, "Help Me Make It through the Night," best expresses a country boy's feelings of loneliness and desperation as he pleads for sex as a substitute for love to help him survive in the harsh world he did not make.

Country music, like any other form of popular culture, must speak to its audience or die. Country music artists probably are less isolated from their fans than artists in other genres. They ride the buses with their band to juke joints, carnival midways, country music clubs, skating rinks, and auditoriums across the country. They sign autographs after the show is over and still make pilgrimages to Nashville to perform at the Grand Ole Opry. Consequently country music continues to reflect the real-life experiences of its fans. For most country fans, life is difficult. Country music may bond them to each other, to home, to country, and to family. On the other hand, it offers easy rationalizations for drinking to excess, hanging out in bars, and engaging in sex with other people's spouses. These kinds of behaviors are dysfunctional; that is, in the long run, sleeping around or getting drunk does not improve one's situation.

By now we hope that people no longer think of country music lyrics as the way to get an inside look at the values and life-styles of "shotguns and pickups," "tobacco roads," or whatever other labels the market segmenters come up with for white working-class Americans, particularly those from the South. Over the past two decades, country music has changed in several directions, one being wider appeal among people in diverse social and demographic categories. This implies that the images of and messages about drinking and sex expressed in country lyrics hit home to a broad range of people, not just the stereotypic blue-collar fan in Dixie. Country songs typically speak to Americans about issues in terms they are familiar with, usually linking personal problems (e.g., those related to alcoholic drink and sexuality) to a personal failing or flaw in their character.

To some critics this is enough to make them frown on country music. The charge against it is like that raised against soap operas: these songs fail to cut through the mist of mystification around us and too rarely raise consciousness. In other words, by usually stressing the personal origin of the common problems we face, country music neglects or obscures the social, political, and economic origins of the problems, focusing instead on some personal defect or weakness of the individual in the song. According to this criticism, the status quo is reinforced rather than challenged. The same mindsets and social structures that produce the problems remain in control.

"Take This Job and Shove It" was hailed by many as an anthem for the working man who finally tells the oppressive, exploitive boss to go to hell. However, the singer/protagonist does not tell his boss off; rather he *wants* to tell his boss off but cannot because he needs the job. We might speculate that when he gets off work, he will go to a bar, get drunk, and try to pick up a woman. Some, perhaps, would prefer country songs that identified the social structures that oppress people rather than described ways of coping with or escaping from them.

How does one respond to this critique of country music (and much of popular culture in general)? We leave this evaluative question with you. Could and should country music deal with the more problematic aspects of drinking and sex in ways that stimulate critical thinking or spark positive social changes? What interests stand in the way of this? Note, for instance, that when singer k. d. lang recently spoke out against eating meat, many stations refused to play her music due to pressure from people in the cattle industry. Could country music have a more politically and socially conscious thrust and still remain commercially popular and profitable? Are there any country artists who already have done or are trying to do this? Would it trivialize important issues into a "social problem of the month" situation? Is there something wrong with music being "just" for fun and entertainment?

Popular culture both reflects the lives of its audiences and influences their values, attitudes, and behaviors. This is true for country music and its fans and for other genres and their fans. The plots of soap operas, situation comedies, and horror movies contain certain themes and behavior patterns common to characters in each. If you note, for example, that in situation comedies, characters continually belittle others, does this not make it easier (lower the threshold) for fans to belittle others, particularly those who are different from themselves?

The study of popular culture is important because it tells us about ourselves. Country music lyrics tell us much about the lives of Americans and also about ourselves, even if we are not big country fans. All of us must cope with rejection, disappointment, loneliness, desperation, and betrayal. Country song lyrics may not offer the best solutions to these problems, but they do let us know that others have faced the same situations and felt the same way. There are few among us who have never felt "I'm So Lonely I Could Cry" or, conversely, the joy of "Rollin' in My Sweet Baby's Arms."

NOTE

1. Jim Single, telephone interview with Jacqueline Boles, November 3, 1990.

BIBLIOGRAPHY

Armstrong, Edward G. "Country Music Sex Songs: An Ethnomusicological Account." *Journal of Sex Research* 22 (3) (1986): 370–78.

Buckley, John. "Country Music and American Values." *Popular Music and Society* 6 (4) (1979): 293–301.

Chalfant, H. Paul, and Robert E. Beckley. "Beguiling and Betrayal: The Image of Alcohol Use in Country Music." *Journal of Studies on Alcohol* 38 (7) (1977): 1428–33.

DiMaggio, Paul, Richard A. Peterson, and Jack Esco. "Country Music: Ballad of the Silent Majority." In R. Serge Denisoff and Richard A. Peterson, eds., *The Sounds of Social Change*, pp. 38–55. Chicago: Rand McNally, 1972.

Jaret, Charles, and Lyn Thaxton. "Bubbles in My Beer Revisited: The Image of Liquor in Country Music." *Popular Music and Society* 7 (4) (1980): 214–22.

Lewis, George H. "Mapping the Fault Lines: The Core Values Trap in Country Music." *Popular Music and Society* 9 (4) (1984): 7–16.

Malone, Bill C. *Country Music, USA*. Rev. ed. Austin, Tex.: American Folklore Society, 1985.

Peterson, Richard A. "The Production of Cultural Changes: The Case of Contemporary Country Music." *Social Research* 45 (2) (1978): 292–314.

Wilgus, D. K. "Country-Western Music and the Urban Hillbilly." *Journal of American Folklore* 83 (1970): 157–84.

27

The Homogenization of Early Rock and Roll

RICHARD AQUILA

One of the most enduring myths in rock music history involves rock and roll's golden era. Many critics and rock historians maintain that the years 1954 through 1958 produced an artistically pure form of rock music, but after 1958 the music began to lose its vitality. Supposedly, by the early 1960s, most rock was mass produced to appeal to middle-of-the-road listeners. This homogenized brand of rock and roll, almost devoid of artistic value, was standardized to make it less threatening than early rock. The watered-down formula rock featured smooth pop vocals, innocuous lyrics, lush orchestral arrangements, and other characteristics generally associated with traditional popular music. Rock and roll allegedly remained in this moribund state until 1964, when the Beatles breathed new life into the music.

This myth concerning the rise and fall of early rock and roll oversimplifies a complex process. Attempts to standardize rock and roll did occur (in fact, as early as 1954), but the homogenization process was never complete. Early 1960s rock and roll remained as diverse and vital as its predecessor. Sometimes the music even benefited from the homogenization process, which introduced new musical ingredients and broadened the base of rock and roll. Contrary to popular belief, rock and roll was still going strong on the eve of the Beatles' arrival.

Rock and roll arrived on the American popular culture scene in the mid–1950s at a time when consensus and conformity were dominant themes in American society and culture. Many Americans, still in the shadow of World War II, lived in the fear of the cold war and the proliferation of nuclear weapons. They were concerned about strange, new forces tugging at the seams of America's social fabric. They watched anxiously as blacks demanded more equality; women struggled over their proper role in life; and baby boomers had social and economic growing pains.

In the midst of this social change, they had to cope with new notions of the good life. The booming postwar economy produced a culture of consumption that washed over America like a tidal wave. The deluge of new products, advertisements, and television shows fed visions of a new, materialistic American dream, which turned into a nightmare for many of those who tried to keep up with the Joneses.

In the 1950s, many Americans sought relief from these anxieties and fears through consensus and conformity. Pledging allegiance to American democracy and capitalism reassured Americans that they and their country were on the right track, and conforming to acceptable behavior, traditional values, and the rules of God and country guaranteed personal and national success. Anything that deviated from this consensus model was viewed as a threat to the American way.

Given this conservative social and political climate, it is not surprising that rock and roll received a cool reception in the 1950s. The new music sounded alien to many Americans accustomed to traditional, Tin Pan Alley–style popular music. Early rock and roll, like the black rhythm and blues music from which it was derived, often featured wild vocals, blues progressions, and loud drums accenting a two-four beat (unlike traditional white pop, which emphasized the first and third beats).

Many Americans, fearing anything new and different, felt threatened by rock and roll. Segregationists and bigots were convinced that the rhythm and blues–based music would lead to integration and miscegenation. Others claimed rock and roll singers like Elvis Presley were destroying American morals and contributing to juvenile delinquency. Rock and roll was linked to almost every social problem imaginable, including drugs, sexual promiscuity, gang warfare, pornography, teenage pregnancy, prostitution, organized crime, and communist subversion.

Anxious and fearful citizens—nervous about the cold war, integration, or anything perceived to be un-American—tried to snuff out rock and roll. Church officials frequently condemned the music as rebellious, satanic, communist inspired, or worse. A Catholic priest in Boston lamented, "There is no doubt that the by-product of rock and roll has left its scar on youth."[1] Occasionally, rock and roll records were destroyed in ceremonies reminiscent of book burnings. One Ohio car dealer promised to smash rock records as a way of increasing his auto sales. In some communities, government officials banned rock and roll parties, and civic leaders tried to dissuade youths from listening to the new music. Even the federal government was concerned. In 1960, a congressional committee investigated alleged corruption in the rock music industry following tips that record companies were paying bribes to disc jockeys to play certain records.

Celebrities also became rock and roll bashers. Mitch Miller denigrated rock and roll records as "the comic books of music." Sammy Davis, Jr., noted, "If rock and roll is here to stay, I might commit suicide." His friend,

Frank Sinatra, was even more abusive. Sinatra told a congressional committee that rock songs had "dirty lyrics" written and sung by "cretinous goons" and concluded that rock and roll was "the most brutal, ugly, desperate, vicious form of expression it has been my misfortune to hear."[2]

To put it mildly, early rock and roll had an image problem, but the new music also had tremendous marketing potential, as evidenced by record sales in 1955 and 1956. Individuals both inside and outside the record industry refused to give up on the music, but they understood that it could not survive or grow, unless more Americans became convinced that the music was neither dangerous nor alien.

This realization contributed to the attempts to standardize rock and roll. The homogenization process, which would be only partly successful, assumed many forms as various interests attempted to mold the new sound to fit their own purposes. Often the music was shaped into a formula designed to broaden its appeal, or it was standardized to conform to acceptable social and cultural norms. In each case, homogenization sought to make the music more acceptable to the masses. In a conservative era, rock and roll could not afford to be too outrageous, too alien sounding, or too revolutionary. It had to be homogenized into a musical form that was uniformly safe, acceptable, and, above all else, marketable.

Record companies led the way in the attempts to homogenize rock and roll. Their primary goal was to produce a marketable product. This was accomplished in a variety of ways. As early as 1954, many major record companies tried to jump on the rock and roll bandwagon through releases that capitalized on the new sound. These "bandwagon records" varied in quality and approach. The only thing they had in common with rock and roll was that their titles and lyrics were also geared to the teenaged market. Some bandwagon records were merely traditional, white pop records, sung by older, traditional, white pop singers. For example, the Chordettes, who started their career as pop singers in the 1940s, made it to the top of the charts in 1954 with the bouncy hit "Mr. Sandman." Pop singer Jodie Sands had a Top 20 hit in 1957, "With All My Heart," a romantic pop song that teenagers could relate to. And in 1958, a husband and wife act named Art and Dotty Todd had a big hit with "Chanson D'Amour," a traditional pop song that became popular on Dick Clark's "American Bandstand," when its refrain, "Chanson D'Amour, ra, ta, ta, ta, ta," caught on with teenagers across the country.

Some bandwagon records aimed more directly at the young audience. In 1955, pop singer Eddie Fisher appealed to youth with his hit, "Dungaree Doll." That same year the Fontane Sisters, another veteran pop act, found similar success with "Seventeen." Kay Starr, a pop singer from the 1940s, made it all the way to the number 1 spot on the charts in 1956 with "Rock and Roll Waltz."

Although most bandwagon records were just contrived imitations, they did allow record companies to capitalize on the rock and roll sound. Their titles and lyrics helped them pass as rock and roll among less discriminating members of the growing rock audience. In the process, they put forth a watered-down version of rock that made the music more acceptable to listeners.

In addition to bandwagon records, major record companies produced cover records as a way to take advantage of the growing rock and roll market. These covers, which featured white pop performers singing versions of songs initially performed by black artists, brought rhythm and blues (R&B) or early rock and roll to the attention of a much broader audience.

The first imitative cover record came in 1954, when Mercury Records signed a white pop group, the Crew Cuts, to record a pop version of the Chords' R&B hit, "Sh-Boom." The Crew Cuts' single zoomed to the top of the charts, overshadowing the Chords' original and establishing a pattern. Every time a black rhythm and blues record (usually released by a small independent record company) began to attract a national audience, it was quickly covered by a white pop performer for a large record company. For example, Pat Boone had a string of hits in 1955 and 1956 covering Fats Domino's "Ain't That a Shame," the El Dorados' "At My Front Door," and Little Richard's "Tutti Frutti" and "Long Tall Sally." The McGuire Sisters found phenomenal success with their cover versions of the Teen Queens' "Eddie My Love," the Spaniels' "Goodnight, Sweetheart, Goodnight," and the Moonglows' "Sincerely." Even Perry Como, the quintessential white pop crooner of the 1950s, got into the act with his cover of Gene and Eunice's "Ko Ko Mo."

Covers were commercial successes for several reasons. Because they were distributed by major record companies with numerous connections to important disc jockeys, radio stations, and record outlets, they had a built-in marketing edge over the originals, which were produced by small, independent labels with little or no marketing clout.

Cover records had other advantages. Many middle-class whites, accustomed to traditional white pop, found bland covers more familiar sounding than the gritty, black, R&B-influenced originals. Due to prejudices and segregation policies, it was also easier for white performers to sell records to the white middle-class audience. Some whites preferred cover versions because they felt black R&B was sexually suggestive. For example, the title of Etta James's 1955 R&B hit, "Roll with Me, Henry" (which used the black slang word *roll* for sexual intercourse), was changed to "Dance with Me, Henry" on Georgia Gibbs's cover record.

Covers also toned down R&B's lyrics to make them less offensive to middle-class whites. The most famous example is Bill Haley and the Comets' version of Big Joe Turner's 1954 R&B classic, "Shake, Rattle, and Roll." Where Turner sings about how his girl teased him with flimsy, low-cut dresses, which he could see through, Bill Haley simply comments about how his girl wore nice dresses but had a heart as cold as ice. Many whites were convinced that cover records were more in line with the moral standards of middle-class America. By homogenizing rock and roll into a safe, familiar sound, covers helped expand the music's audience.

Record companies contributed in other ways to the homogenization of rock and roll. They devised campaigns to portray rock and roll stars in nonthreatening ways through advertising, publicity releases, photos, liner notes, and jacket covers. The basic goal was to create a safer image of the performer and music in order to sell more records. Elvis Presley's manager, Colonel Tom Parker, did all he could to make sure his singer came across as a fine, polite young man. Presley album photos showed him in ties, suits, and sport shirts—perhaps in loud colors but well groomed nonetheless. Elvis was seen in public escorting sweet young starlets and being respectful to his elders. He was signed to movies playing characters who upheld traditional values. The marketing of Elvis as an "All-American Boy" became a cottage industry as Colonel Parker wheeled and dealed to produce Elvis trading cards, lipstick, hats, books, stuffed toys, stationery, and jewelry and clothes. Elvis was a microcosm of what was happening to rock and roll. When he arrived on the scene, Presley had been ridiculed as "Elvis the Pelvis" and decried as a purveyor of smut. But Colonel Parker reshaped Elvis's image to make it acceptable to more Americans. Elvis Presley, like rock and roll in general, was standardized to fit the needs of middle-class Americans.

Other performers followed Elvis's lead, showing that rock and roll was safe for consumption. Male rock and rollers commonly appeared in conservative suits or wore coats, ties, or sweaters on album photos and publicity shots. Female rock stars wore sedate dresses or loose-fitting, high-necked blouses, sweaters, and full skirts. Record jackets reinforced rock and roll's positive image. Many singers were pictured smiling right at the camera. Friendly, informal liner notes spoke directly to the teenaged audience. And album titles often either politely introduced artists or made them seem like old friends: *Presenting Dion and the Belmonts, Rick Nelson Sings for You,* and *Bobby Vee Sings Your Favorites,* for example.

Some album cover art tried consciously to obscure anything that might be objectionable to parents or other adults. One LP from 1957, *Pajama Party,* pictured four white teenaged girls on the cover. Nothing indicated that the music on the record inside featured black R&B rock groups like the Crows, the Cleftones, and the Harptones.

Record companies usually tried to make their product look and sound respectable. They produced soft, pop-rock records, like the Fleetwoods' "Mr. Blue" (1959) or Bobby Vinton's "Roses are Red" (1962), which were closer in spirit to pop than rock. They signed young pop singers like Tommy Sands, Joanie Sommers, and James Darren, whose records could be marketed as rock and roll. They promoted young, clean-cut television actors like Johnny Crawford and Paul Petersen as rock and roll singers. Record companies also used traditional pop arrangers and orchestras to give rock records a more familiar pop sound. For example, ABC-Paramount employed the Artie Singer Orchestra on Danny and the Juniors' hit "At the Hop," and Don Costa's orchestra played on many Paul Anka hits, including "Lonely Boy." Mercury Records used Ralph Marterie's Orchestra and David Carroll to back groups like the Crew Cuts and Diamonds. Cadence Records featured Archie Bleyer's Orchestra behind Johnny Tillotson, the Everly Brothers, and Eddie Hodges. Capitol used Lincoln Mayorga and Nelson Riddle on records by the Four Preps and Tommy Sands. And Liberty Records employed Ernie Freeman's Orchestra and the Johnny Mann Singers on numerous hits by Bobby Vee.

Sometimes specific songs reinforced rock and roll's new, clean-cut image. In 1956, Frankie Lymon and the Teenagers recorded "I Am Not a Juvenile Delinquent." In 1960, Brian Hyland earned a number 1 hit with "Itsy Bitsy Teenie Weenie, Yellow Polka-Dot Bikini," a novelty pop-rock song about a young girl who was embarrassed to come out of the water because her bikini top had fallen off. The following year, Bobby Vee sang about his own shyness on "Bashful Bob." Even the names of many rock stars seemed nonthreatening. There were numerous juvenile-sounding nicknames like Bobby, Frankie, Johnny, and Tommy.

By the late 1950s and early 1960s, some record companies were mass-producing teen idols, whose mainstream sound and appearance were perfect for middle-class tastes. The formula was simple: find a good-looking, white, middle-class teenager. Equip him or her with neat clothes, a nice hairdo, a friendly smile, and a clean-cut appearance. Then have the budding idol record songs aimed at the teenaged audience. A pleasant singing voice was helpful, but almost any youthful-sounding voice would do.

Between 1957 and 1963, numerous teen idols—Ricky Nelson, Frankie Avalon, Fabian, Connie Francis, Bobby Vee, Bobby Rydell, Leslie Gore, and Paul Anka—dominated the rock and roll charts. Bob Marcucci of Chancellor Records in Philadelphia explained: "We now run a school where we indoctrinate artists into show business. We may sign them and spend three months schooling them before they cut their first record. We teach them how to walk, how to talk, and how to act onstage when they're performing. We worked with Frankie Avalon for three months before making 'Dede Dinah.' "[3]

Teen idols played an important role in the homogenization process by making the music more palatable to middle-of-the-road tastes. They often appealed to those who found a Jerry Lee Lewis too wild or a Little Richard too alien sounding. Because the idols and their music were pop oriented and mainstream, they were more acceptable to teenagers and adults alike. As a result, the teen idols' homogenized brand of rock and roll was able to broaden the base of the music.

Along with the record companies, rock and roll performers themselves contributed to the homogenization process. Most young singers accepted the common wisdom that longevity in the record business could be maintained only if their music became more middle of the road and adult oriented. After all, the accepted trajectory for success had always pointed toward the adult pop market. There were no role models to follow other than the Crosbys or Sinatras. Young rock and rollers simply assumed that if they were lucky, pop music, tuxedos, and maybe even a movie career loomed in their future. Very few, if any, expected to be singing rock and roll when they were thirty. Dion, who found success as both the lead singer of Dion and the Belmonts and as a solo artist, explained the reasoning in his autobiography, *The Wanderer*: "No one in the recording business knew how long rock 'n' roll would last.... So they were constantly trying to fit the sound into the safer, more legitimate world of what they called 'good music.' " According to Dion, record executives realized that not all rock and roll singers could make the transition into pop, but those who could were pushed into "a tuxedo mold, like junior league Sinatras and Bennetts. ... It was like a counterfeit of the real thing, a way to tap into some of the popularity, and profits, of teenage music without any of the danger."[4]

Rock and roll stars hoping to become permanent fixtures on the pop music charts recorded middle-of-the-road ballads or pop standards designed to appeal to a wider audience. The records often featured violins and lush orchestral accompaniments. For example, in the late 1950s and early 1960s, Elvis Presley did numerous pop songs, including "It's Now or Never" (a remake of "Oh Solo Mio"), "Witchcraft," and "Viva Las Vegas." Buddy Holly experimented with the pop-influenced "True Love Ways" and "Moondreams" (the latter was a particularly dreadful pop performance, which had Buddy Holly straining to sound like Perry Como, while violins and harps strummed on in the background). Rick Nelson (who dropped the "y" on his first name to show he was growing up) released pop material like "String Along" and "Fools Rush In." And Gene Pitney recorded an entire album of pop standards, including "On the Street Where You Live" and "Rags to Riches." These records undoubtedly convinced many listeners that rock and roll was not much different from traditional pop.

Along with rock performers and record companies, the media did much to homogenize rock and roll. A great deal has been written about media attacks that portrayed rock music as rebellious or evil, but overall the media probably aided the music's image far more than it hurt it.

Most movies—with the obvious exception of *Blackboard Jungle*—treated the music benignly, if not benevolently. Rock and roll films like *Don't Knock the Rock*, *Mr. Rock and Roll*, and *Beach Party* showed that teenagers and rock music were anything but rebellious. Other movies featured rock and rollers like Elvis Presley, Frankie Avalon, Fabian, or Rick Nelson playing "All-American Boy" type characters. Some films, like *Bye Bye Birdie*, poked fun at rock and roll from an adult viewpoint, but even then, the music came across as silly but harmless.

Television portrayed rock in a positive way. Variety shows starring Ed Sullivan, Arthur Murray, or the Dorsey Brothers were among the first to spotlight rock and roll. Usually the adult hosts took a bemused attitude toward the teenagers' new music. Ed Sullivan could be patronizing as he welcomed rockers like Elvis Presley or Buddy Holly. "Hit Parade," a weekly show that reviewed the most popular records in America, further defanged rock and roll. Program regulars, like Snooky Lanson and Giselle McKenzie, served up ludicrous pop renditions of songs like "Hound Dog" or "Peggy Sue." Their attempts, while laughable to the young audience, probably convinced many adult viewers that rock and roll was, at worst, just a frivolous new type of pop music.

Of all the television shows, Dick Clark's "American Bandstand" contributed the most to the homogenization process. Although Clark did play different types of rock and roll, he specialized in middle-of-the-road pop rock. He initiated a dress code for his teenaged dancers and insisted that dance steps be acceptable to home viewers. Clark's own clean-cut appearance and boy scout leader image reassured viewers that rock and roll was safe. Other programs reinforced this homogenized brand of rock and roll. Situation comedies like "Ozzie and Harriet," "The Donna Reed Show," and "My Three Sons" broadcast scenes of well-scrubbed middle-class teenagers enjoying harmless rock music.

Radio showcased rock and roll in a way that made it more acceptable to the masses. Program directors fit rock music into already existing pop music formats, which included disc jockeys, jingles, news, and weather. Most rock stations also played traditional pop music and featured commercials aimed at adults, suggesting that teenagers comprised only one segment of their audience. By plugging rock and roll into established patterns, radio stations made rock music seem more familiar, and therefore more acceptable, to many teenagers and adults in the audience.

Along with movies, television, and radio, the print media contributed to rock and roll's new safe image. By the late 1950s and early 1960s, many books, newspapers, and magazines had convinced readers that rock was not a threat to the American way of life. In 1958, Pat Boone wrote a best-selling book, *'Twixt Twelve and Twenty*, which advised teenagers to be good, love God, and trust in their parents. A few years later, in 1963, Dick Clark had similar success with *To Goof or Not to Goof*, a book that showed teenagers how to cope with the problems of growing up. Magazine articles portrayed rock singers and music in a wholesome way. The January 1958 issue of *Photoplay* contained a story entitled "A Day with Rick Nelson," which described the teen idol as a typical boy who was shy and respectful toward his parents. Rick was quoted saying things like "Gee," and "Good thing Mom can't see me with this hamburger. She's glad I like milk, but she's always after me to eat vegetables." The author explained how Rick's parents made him finish his homework before he could go out, adding, "Ever since Rick could remember, he and Dave had been able to turn to their folks for advice and guidance whenever they needed it."[5]

That same issue of *Photoplay* included a story entitled "What the Home Folks Think of Pat Boone." The answer should not have been surprising to anyone paying attention to rock and roll's new image. Boone came across as a wonderful person—just a regular guy, according to friends and neighbors. His mother agreed, adding, "Pat feels that the Lord has been responsible for his success."[6]

Even Elvis Presley came across as an fine, upstanding young man in a November 1962 article in *Photoplay*. The author asked the king of rock and roll about a woman who was cheating on his friend, noting that Elvis "had been brought up to know right from wrong—nobody had to tell him there wasn't anything worse than a girl who cheats on the boy who's mad for her." The author, moved by Elvis's deep morality, confided to readers, "This was the Elvis who, as a child in a country Sunday school, used to get many a gold star pasted beside his name for correctly reciting memory verses."[7]

Obviously not all media portrayals of rock and roll stars were positive, but by the late 1950s and early 1960s, media coverage was becoming generally more favorable. These positive portrayals contributed greatly to the homogenization of rock into a standardized pop form that was nonthreatening to middle-class Americans.

But the process was not fully successful. Homogenization failed to purge the music of its individuality or its controversial traits. Different rock styles continued to exist after 1959. Various types of R&B-influenced rock thrived due to impressive contributions by James Brown, Ray Charles, the Isley Brothers, Ben E. King, the Shirelles, Mary Wells, Marvin Gaye, and Sam Cooke, to name just a few. Rock and roll influenced by country and western music also flourished, as evidenced by the continued success of the Everly Brothers, Roy Orbison, Conway Twitty, Brenda Lee, Don Gibson, and Marty Robbins. Pop-influenced rock and roll also prospered. It included a variety of sounds, from the West Coast California surf music of the Beach Boys, to the slick, East Coast power pop of Gene Pitney. Other outstanding pop rock was contributed by Del Shannon, Bobby Vee, Rick Nelson, Leslie Gore, Paul Anka, Jan and Dean, the Four Seasons, and Dion.

The homogenization process fared no better in its attempts to disassociate rock and roll from sex. For example, Little Anthony and the Imperials lusted after sexy, native dancing girls on "Shimmy Shimmy Ko Ko Bop" (1959). Intimate, sexually suggestive vocals were featured on the Flamingos' "Mia Amore" (1960), the Paris Sisters' "I Love How You Love Me" (1961), and the Shirelles' "Baby, It's You" (1962). The Mar-keys groaned wickedly on their bump and grind instrumental, "Last Night" (1961). The Kingsmen's hit, "Louie Louie" (1963), was banned on some record stations for its allegedly immoral lyrics. And groups like the Ronettes became notorious for their sexually charged performances.

Many rock and roll hits of the late 1950s and early 1960s also retained the uninhibited quality associated with earlier rock. The Isley Brothers produced wild dance hits like "Shout" (1959) and "Twist and Shout" (1962). Ernie Maresca screamed out his invitation to party on "Shout! Shout! (Knock Yourself Out!)" (1962). Gary U.S. Bonds simulated the revelry of an all-night party on his raucous hit, "Quarter to Three" (1961). And Wanda Jackson unleashed one of the most frenzied vocals in rock history on her hit, "Let's Have a Party" (1960).

The homogenization process also failed to quash rebellious rock and roll. The Coasters ridiculed principals and teachers on their hit, "Charlie Brown" (1959). Roy Orbison railed against authority figures in "Workin' for the Man" (1962). Teenagers disobeyed parents on Dickey Lee's "Patches" (1962), Ray Peterson's "Give Us Your Blessings (Don't Make Us Run Away)" (1963), and Joey Powers's "(Meet Me at) Midnight Mary" (1963). And teenaged rebellion was glorified on other hits like the Crystals' "He's a Rebel" (1962) and the Shangri-las' "Leader of the Pack" (1964).

Even pop rock that was supposed to be homogenized often retained the folk quality of early rock and roll. Rick Nelson plugged into teenaged interests on his hits, "Travelin' Man" (1961) and "Hello, Mary Lou" (1961). Bobby Vee explored the trauma of teenaged romance on well-produced records like "Take Good Care of My Baby" (1961) and "The Night Has a Thousand Eyes" (1963). Little Peggy March's "I Will Follow Him" (1963) reflected teenagers' attitudes toward gender, and Gene Pitney's "Only Love Can Break a Heart" (1962) and "Twenty Four Hours from Tulsa" (1963) authentically captured the feelings of teen angst.

In the end, the attempts to homogenize rock music into a uniformly safe pop form did not succeed. Not only did rock and roll retain its musical diversity and identity, but the sound remained creative and vital. As a result, the late 1950s and early 1960s witnessed some of the greatest hits in rock and roll history.

The homogenization process, despite its shortcomings and failures, was important for several reasons. By presenting safe images and more familiar-sounding forms of rock and roll, homogenization guaranteed rock's survival during a cold war era when anything too different was suspect. It also facilitated the music's growth by broadening its appeal to include a larger middle-class audience. Homogenization made rock more mainstream by introducing new musical ingredients, like pop-style harmonies and orchestral accompaniments, that broadened the style. By the early 1960s, rock and roll's place in American culture was secured.

Attempts to homogenize rock and roll reveal much about the American character in the 1950s and early 1960s. The homogenization process ex-

The Homogenization of Early Rock and Roll 279

emplifies the American quest for consensus and conformity in the immediate post–World War II period, and it demonstrates attempts by a dominant culture to incorporate a threatening subculture. The efforts to homogenize rock into a safe music reflect American anxieties about integration, juvenile delinquency, and the cold war. They might even be viewed as a form of social engineering. Adults inside and outside the music industry were, in effect, trying to standardize rock music into a safe form capable of channeling teenaged energy into socially acceptable behavior. In addition, the homogenization process shows how capitalism operates, co-opting new trends for fun, profit, and survival. It reflects the relationship between pop culture producers and consumers, demonstrating the tension between what people want and what they get.

Furthermore, the homogenization process provides insights about American youth of the 1950s and early 1960s. It suggests that many teenagers shared adult values, and it reveals public attitudes toward the young. The attempts to homogenize rock and roll were based on the belief that youths should think and act like adults. It was assumed that all responsible teenagers looked forward to growing up and would welcome more mature, adult-oriented "good music."

This assumption, like other beliefs that went unchallenged in the 1950s, would come under close scrutiny by the late 1960s as Americans experienced political assassinations, the civil rights movement, the Vietnam War, and the counterculture.

The emergence of the baby boom generation as a dominant force in American society by 1970 brought about a reappraisal of what it means to "grow up." Instead of insisting that teenagers must slide into adulthood, society began to tilt in the baby boomers' direction. More and more people began to realize that they could grow old without acting old. Armed with this belief, aging baby boomers held fast to various elements of their youth culture, including rock and roll. After 1963, British rockers and their American allies would provide a youth-oriented music that adolescents could carry with them into middle age, allowing both the baby boomers and rock and roll to remain "forever young."

In the 1950s and early 1960s, however, both teenagers and their music were still expected to "grow up." It was assumed that eventually all teenagers would gladly trade their Elvis 45s for Sinatra LPs. The notion of a fifty-year-old man like Mick Jagger singing rock and roll was unthinkable. Rock music was still the exclusive domain of the young. The attempts at homogenization indicate how American attitudes toward youth have changed since 1963. Many critics and rock historians look back fondly at rock and roll's first years (1954–1958), referring to them as rock's "golden era." At the same time, they condemn the years between 1959 and 1963 as a time of homogenized "schlock rock." But in reality, both periods produced excellent rock and roll. The years 1959 through 1963 also prepared the way for rock's metamorphosis into the nation's mainstream popular music. The attempts at homogenization have to be viewed in the proper historical context. At the time, they neither replaced nor harmed rock and roll. Given the circumstances, they were a logical—maybe even necessary—phase in the growth of the music. As such, the homogenization of rock and roll and the music of the late 1950s and early 1960s comprise an important chapter in rock music history.

NOTES

1. Bob Marcucci quoted in Ed Ward, Geoffrey Stokes, and Ken Tucker. *Rock of Ages* (New York: Summit, 1986), p. 166.
2. Dion DiMucci with Davin Seay, *The Wanderer: Dion's Story* (New York: William Morrow, 1988), p. 98.
3. Daniel Stern, "A Day with Rick Nelson," *Photoplay* (January 1958): 41, 90.
4. Nancy Anderson, "What the Home Folks Think of Pat Boone," *Photoplay* (January 1958): 27, 72–73.
5. Nancy Anderson, "Cheatin' Woman," *Photoplay* (November 1962): 70–71.
6. Anderson, "What the Home Folks Think of Pat Boone," pp. 27, 72–73.
7. Anderson, "Cheatin' Woman," pp. 70–71.

BIBLIOGRAPHY

Aquila, Richard. *That Old Time Rock and Roll: A Chronicle of an Era.* New York: Schirmer, 1989.
Belz, Carl. *The Story of Rock.* New York: Harper & Row, 1972.
Chapple, Steve, and Reebee Garofalo. *Rock 'n' Roll Is Here to Pay: The History and Politics of the Music Industry.* Chicago: Nelson-Hall, 1977.
Cooper, B. Lee. *Images of American Society in Popular Music.* Chicago: Nelson-Hall, 1982.
Frith, Simon. *Sound Effects: Youth, Leisure, and the Politics of Rock 'n' Roll.* New York: Pantheon, 1981.
Gillett, Charlie. *The Sound of the City: The Rise of Rock and Roll.* New York: Dutton, 1970.
Marcus, Greil. *Mystery Train: Images of America in Rock 'n' Roll Music.* New York: Dutton, 1976.
Miller, Jim, ed. *The Rolling Stone Illustrated History of Rock and Roll.* New York: Random House/Rolling Stone, 1980.
Ward, Ed, Geoffrey Stokes, and Ken Tucker. *Rock of Ages: The Rolling Stone History of Rock and Roll.* New York: Summit, 1986.
Whitburn, Joel. *Top Pop Singles, 1955–1986.* Menomonee Falls, Wis.: Record Research, 1987.

28

Conclusion: The Impact of Popular Music in Society

John Orman

American culture in the 1990s is profoundly influenced by popular music. The role of popular music in American society should be that of popular music in any culture: to allow individuals the opportunity to entertain others and perhaps make some money. When popular music is good, it is entertaining, informative, integrating, invigorating, educational, inspiring, communal, and important. When it is bad, it is boring, insipid, banal, oppressive, useless, exploitative, opulent, indifferent, and insignificant. Most popular music in America exists somewhere in between.

Popular music dominates on television, radio, motion pictures, cassette and compact disc (CD) players, home entertainment centers, videos, elevators, public space, and private businesses. From the ages of six to eighteen, there is more exposure to entertaining pop culture than actual formal schooling time. Popular music provides the glue that holds American popular culture together. Rock music provides the background for the commercials from corporate America that inundate our lives. Popular music provides the backgrounds for political candidates who want to sell images to the voting public. Rock music fills the air in the domed playgrounds of professional sports teams, and popular music is a necessary attraction to sell plays and motion pictures. Finally, popular music dominates on the cable television systems in the United States and throughout much of the rest of the world. Popular music has become more "popular" and omnipresent than popular music of even the 1950s, 1960s, and 1970s. It has become a large multinational corporate undertaking that scores billions of dollars annually for the industry.

American popular music has even had major political and economic impact in some of the profound global changes that have occurred recently. Some analysts have observed that the collapse of the Eastern European bloc countries, and indeed the collapse of the Soviet political economy itself, was not so much the failure of Marxist systems but rather the inability of these systems to deliver Big Macs, Levis, and rock music. Karl Marx in his political theory never anticipated the problem that "I WANT MY MTV" could create for decision makers in socialist countries.

Yet if popular music has acted as a subversive instrument in some socialist states to help bring about more democratic freedoms, ironically in the United States, it has been at the center of controversy for those who want to limit artistic expressions and rights of consumers. Certain rap artists and heavy metal rockers have become the target of morality protectors in the nation who want to forbid certain words or expressions and even to arrest artists on obscenity charges. Citizen groups organize in the 1990s to fight certain forms of popular music, following the tradition established over the past four decades of popular music in America where organized crackdowns against popular music appear about once every ten years.

With the huge success of popular music in America and around the globe in the 1990s, it is time to ask some questions about the impact and consequences of this entertaining pop culture art form. Why is rock music, the core of popular music, still oriented toward prolonging adolescence? With the baby boomers reaching their forties, rock music continues to be their most important form of popular music. Rock did not die, and it is surely here to stay, but it becomes more difficult every year for the aging rock stars like Paul McCartney, Robert Plant, Mick Jagger, Jerry Garcia, Grace Slick, and others to be relevant.

Rock is diverse in the 1990s; it encompasses mainstream pop, oldies and some goodies, heavy metal, rap and hip hop, dance music, urban contemporary, revived psychedelic rock, acoustic, folk, blues, some few soul artists, a little country, and a lot of straight-ahead rock music from the 1960s. The recording buying public consists of those ages seven to fifty-five, with the heaviest music buyers and concert goers coming from those ages fourteen to twenty-nine. This generation is the group that has had the most important consequences on the music industry and on American society.

In the 1980s, with the rise of MTV rock video culture, popular music was robbed of one of its core pleasures. From 1954 to 1980, one could listen to music and conjure up images about what the song was supposed to be about. Every mind had its own image system that would run individual images of a rock song into the listener's consciousness. Now, the video player on television is the image implanted in the imagination whenever the song is played. The video stimulation has become more important in many aspects than the aural importance of the music. Moreover, much of the music has become synthesized, sampled, computerized, and less human.

Rock music lyrics and rock videos still try to communicate with listeners. Most rock music is not political, and the sociopolitical sophistication of the commentary in the very few artists who write songs with social significance is not great. The golden era of political rock was from 1967 to 1971, and even then only about one of every ten artists could in some way be considered "political." Moreover, for these rock politicos, only about one of every ten songs they produced had a social message. The vast majority, about 90 percent of rock in the golden age, was about unrequited love, boy-girl relationships, fun, sugary interaction between lovers, and being with friends. Popular music themes since the 1950s have remained remarkably constant, even in so-called political years.

The 1980s saw an increase in the political and social sophistication of rock stars as a few used their new-found status of celebrity to raise money for causes in which they presumably believed. The concerts and promotions were also designed to raise the consciousness of the audience with respect to a particular issue. In 1985 Bob Geldof organized the global rock satellite hook-up for the Live Aid concert to raise money for starving people in Ethiopia. This came after the efforts of the coalition of British rock artists who had done the Band Aid promotion at Christmas 1984. The phenomenal success of the Live Aid project started a stampede of rock artists trying to better each other as "committed" rock stars.

Concerts were held for Farm Aid, Rock Against Racism, the antinuclear movement, AIDS relief, Save the Rain Forest, Amnesty International, Earth Day, Greenpeace, Nelson Mandela and the struggle against apartheid, El Salvador, Nicaragua, Save the Seals, Dr. M. L. King, Save the Whales, U.S.– U.S.S.R. relations, and many others. Among the most politically important and consistent rock stars were U2, Bruce Springsteen, Jackson Browne, Tracy Chapman, Sting, John Mellencamp, and Midnight Oil, to name a few. These outstanding contributions in the effort to raise consciousness and money for causes by a few rock stars never reached a magnitude so that the industry of popular music could be deemed political and socially conscious. Like the golden era of 1967–1971, the 1980s saw only a few rock stars take a few socially significant stands. Indeed, this was so out of the ordinary for the pop music industry that some critics labeled the 1980s as the return of political rock. It was not the return of political rock. First, there had never really been a political rock, and, second, a few benefit concerts do not make rock political. The vast majority of the pop music industry continued on the course firmly established in the 1950s: to make music in order to entertain people with the hopes of making money.

The few times in its history that rock music has become political were times where rock reflected what was happening in society. Rock rarely influences attitudes but acts to reflect what is already happening somewhere in the United States or around the globe. Rock acts as a regime-maintaining institution and is rarely threatening to the elites in society, even given elite backlashes. Rock is just too entertaining to form a serious indictment of the American political system. Indeed rock music has been used by political elites to communicate, sell candidates, make commercials, and raise money. If citizens actually focused in on societal problems like environmental destruction, nuclear holocaust, world starvation, homelessness, racism, sexism, unemployment, economic ills, and inadequate leaders, then the American political arena would be a much different place. Rock requires the listener to escape, relax, and dream. It makes very few, if any, political or social demands on the listener.

Rock continues to promote a system and a rock popular culture that is opulent, capitalistic, racist, and sexist much of the time. Rock stars are the model of outrageous, consuming life-styles. One would have to search Old Hollywood of the 1930s to 1950s to find similar life-styles. The purpose of rock remains to make plenty of money, and the multinational conglomerates that own the recording industry are succeeding. They want product, and it is difficult for new talent to break in because of the constraints put on rock talent by industry dictates.

Although rappers and hip hoppers have made major mainstream breakthroughs in the 1990s, the rock industry still has an ugly strand of racism running through it. In the 1950s popular music saw white rock artists cover black artists' songs to steal pop profits. In the 1960s soul artists like Sam Cooke, Otis Redding, Aretha Franklin, and the many Motown artists scored huge crossover successes yet the rock industry was controlled by white male executives who dictated policy.

In the 1970s, the few black pride and overtly radical messages that were coming from a few artists in the late 1960s disappeared, to be replaced by popular stars like Stevie Wonder, disco Donna Summer, and a few others. White men still were in charge. In the 1980s Michael Jackson, Whitney Houston, Janet Jackson, and Prince became rock superstars, but for most black artists, the popular charts were for whites only. In fact about the only two places in the 1980s that held onto apartheid were South Africa and the American Top 40 popular music industry. The U.S. recording industry continued its insidious racist practice of having a chart called "black music" or "soul" or "urban contemporary." These segregated charts allowed black artists to exist in the 1980s when the pop music industry conspired to isolate black artists away from the mainstream Top 40. In the 1990s this overtly racist practice continues as pop music is segregated into black playlists and black charts.

In the 1990s rock music continues on its course of being sexist. Two of the dominant forms of popular music, rap and heavy metal, are the most sexist forms of pop music. The brash, macho, swaggering braggadocio of most rap artists makes it clear what they think of women and how they want to relate to women. The heavy metal glamor rockers aim their lifestyle at the fourteen-to-twenty-year-old white male mentality. In this world women are "babes," "chicks," "sluts," or worse. Women serve as sexist props in most heavy metal videos, and the lyrics suggest a misogynist stance. Indeed in the 1990s, the old rock sexual stereotypical life-style of the rock star (male) who had sex with fans in every city seems largely at odds with the 1990s sexual sensibilities that teach that unsafe sex and promiscuity can be deadly.

Some women have prospered in the sexist rock system: Grace Slick and Janis Joplin in the 1960s, Carole King, Carly Simon, and Joni Mitchell in the 1970s, and Tracy Chapman, Bonnie Raitt, and Chrissie Hynde in the 1980s, to name a few. All too often female rock stars and female lead singers are selected by promotional and development men from the record companies on the basis of physical attractiveness, not musical ability. The 1990s rock scene offers little hope that such a quintessential sexist institution as American rock music will change in any major nonsexist way. For every young girl who might want to grow up to be another Bonnie Raitt, there are hundreds who want to grow up to be the next Madonna.

Rock in the 1990s continues to do what it does the best: provide pure, unadulterated pleasure. It inspires people to move and dance. It keeps people from loneliness. It allows others to escape from abusive situations in their family to a fantasy world. It provides the background for social interaction between and among the sexes. It allows close friends the pleasure of charting their life experiences with the charts of popular music. It conveys intrapersonal messages to listeners when songs make deep connections. It can make listeners laugh, cry, empathize, hate, love, and react for a moment while the song is playing. For these reasons and others, popular music is the dominant entertainment form in American popular culture. For these reasons and others, the rock star celebrity is at the top of the list of cultural icons and money makers in America's hierarchical entertainment system.

In the 1990s the most dangerous consequence of this entertaining popular music is that it is so pleasurable and addictive. Young people invest large amounts of time on rock music and, if trends continue, rock culture with its emphasis on the video and the sound will continue to grow at the expense of reading and books. Young people will turn to the visual, aural product in pop culture and stray from ideas in written form. Indeed, one problem of writing a chapter on the role and importance of popular music in society is that no one fourteen to twenty years old will ever read it. If our society continues to be one that places a premium on ideas, it is clear in the 1990s that written words will not have much impact on young people. The poets will be rappers, and the spicy novelists will be the heavy metal rockers. The social scientists will be replaced by the socially concerned rockers, and the creative idea people in the culture will be represented by the rock video makers. Fashion will continue to be dictated by MTV values. Societal role models will continue to be rock stars, and the true hero will be the rock megastar. If the 1980s brought us a decade where a B-grade Hollywood movie actor and former television personality Ronald Reagan became president, can the day be coming when an aging former rock star occupies the White House?

Rock will continue to promote basic rock values in the 1990s. The most important rock value in a capitalistic society is mass consumption. Rock promotes itself, rock promotes artists, rock promotes product, and rock promotes much more in the economy. Rock music on Music Television is in many respects one twenty-four-hour promotion to buy this record or this product or this life-style. Although rock started out with a rebellious streak in the 1950s, the 1990s should see the record industry stuck in safe, predictable patterns. There will be no single performer in the 1990s to dominate popular music as Elvis did in the 1950s or the Beatles in the 1960s. Rock is beyond domination of that level now because it is so diverse. It is so safe now that it is content with recycling old trends from rock music history. Since rock has a definite past and history and since the demographic category of baby boomers is so huge in the U.S. population, rock insiders promote folk artists, rockabilly groups, psychedelic acid rock garage bands, techno-punks, country reggae bands, glamor pop artists, talking beat poets, and others. The decade that is so mythologized appears to be the 1960s. The rock music industry in American pop culture will continue to relive the 1960s in the 1990s. Rock culture used to be antithetical to adult culture in the 1950s and 1960s. In the 1990s, rock culture is now a predigested mix of adult culture and teen culture into one rock society.

Rock in the 1990s will continue to lead the American pop imperialism. We may be behind in automotive engineering and the U.S. may lag behind others in microchip technology, but the dominant popular culture throughout the world is the American rock pop culture. Teenagers around the world are tuned into an American-Euro pop explosion. American pop rock imperialism has even gone so far as to be used as a military weapon. When American troops cornered Manuel Noriega, the Panamanian leader, after the U.S. invasion of Panama, the U.S. soldiers blasted loud rock music toward the Vatican embassy refuge that Noriega used. The idea was to make life uncomfortable for Noriega so that he would surrender. This gave new meaning to the idea of American pop imperialism.

Finally, rock in the 1990s will continue to provide the lure of economic opportunity. Performers will experiment to find their niche within the billion-dollar rock industry with hopes of becoming a well-paid celebrity. As rock progresses into its fifth decade, it has shown an ability to outlast the harshest critics and to provide entertainment for millions of people around the globe.

BIBLIOGRAPHY

Angus, Ian, and Sut Jhally, eds. *Cultural Politics in Contemporary America*. New York: Routledge, Chapman and Hall, 1989.
Frith, Simon, and Andrew Goodwin, eds. *On Record: Rock, Pop and the Written Word*. New York: Pantheon, 1990.

Kaplan, E. Ann. *Rocking around the Clock: Music Television, Postmodernism and Consumer Culture.* New York: Methuen, 1987.

Orman, John. *The Politics of Rock Music.* Chicago: Nelson-Hall, 1984.

Street, John. *Rebel Rock: The Politics of Popular Music.* Oxford: Basil Blackwell, 1986.

Index

Smith, Mamie, 58, 127
Smith, Willie "The Lion," 75, 76, 127, 251
"Smoke on the Water," 34, 36
Smothers Brothers Show, 39
Snow, Valaida, 207–8
Snowden, Elmer, 76
Songs for John Doe, 35
soul music, 14, 20–21, 129
Spector, Phil, 132
Spivey, Victoria, 17
sponsorship deals, 154, 157
Springsteen, Bruce, 10, 41, 83, 87, 158
Stackhouse, Houston, 19
Stacy, Jess, 75
Stark, John, 65
Starkey, James, 19
Starr, Maurice, 137
Stearns, Marshall, 126
Stone, Dave, 177
Stravinsky, Igor, 245, 246
"Summertime Blues," 108
Sun Records, 131, 140
swing: and class, 74, 78; country western swing, 78; cultural/racial integration in, 79–81, 85–93; development of, 73–74, 185–87; and ethnicity, 79–80
"The Swing Era," (Schuller), 73
syncopation, 242, 244, 250

"Take This Job and Shove It," 265 66
Teagarden, Jack, 74, 78–79
teen idols, 274–77
television, and rock music, 92
Terry, Clark, 76
Thirteenth Floor Elevator, 107
Thomas, Henry "Ragtime Texas," 56
Thompson, "Sir" Charles, 76
Tin Pan Alley: development of, 113 20, 138; and motion pictures, 117; prowar songs, 33–36; and ragtime music, 65, 240–41. *See also* music industry
"Tricks Ain't Walking No More," 18
Tubbs, Ernest, 25, 27
Turner, Big Joe, 272

U.S. Decca, 139
union songs. *See* labor songs
"Universal Soldier," 6, 9, 38, 39
U2, 10, 41, 88

vaudeville, 171–72
Vega, Suzanne, 10, 222
Victor Studios, 45
Vietnam War songs, 25, 27, 28, 38 40
Vocalion label, 128, 133
Von Tilzer, Harry, 113, 119

"Waist Deep in the Big Muddy," 39
Walker, Arron "T-Bone," 56, 133
war songs: country music, 23–31; popular music, 23, 33–41; rock music, 85, 96
Warner Brothers, 128, 142, 153
Waters, Muddy, 55, 61, 84, 109, 129
Wells, Kitty, 179, 217, 224
"We're Gonna Have to Slap the Dirty Little Jap," 36
"What's Goin' On?," 39
Wheatstraw, Peetie, 16, 19
"Whip It to a Jelly," 16
White, C. A., 120
Whiteman, Paul, 189
Wilkins, Joe Willie, 19
Will, George, 88
Williams, Hank, 30, 175–83
Williams, Hank, Jr., 30, 46, 48
Williams, J. Mayo, 124
Williams, Martin, 168, 170
Williams, Mary Lou, 128, 208–10
Williamson, John Lee "Sonny Boy," 19, 60, 61
Wills, Bob, 27, 133
Wilson, Teddy, 79, 81
Winterland Productions, 155–56
Witmark, Isidore, 115
Wobblies. *See* International Workers of the World
Wolf, Peter, 151
The Wolverines, 124–25
women: in country music lyrics, 213– 18; as performers in jazz, 205–12; as performers in popular music,

About the Editor and Contributors

KENNETH J. BINDAS is an assistant professor of history at West Georgia College where he teaches courses in American social and cultural history. He has published articles concerning the role of popular music in American society in the *Western Historical Quarterly*, the *Historian*, and other journals.

JAMES E. AKENSON is professor of curriculum and instruction at Tennessee Technological University. He is co-founder of the national Country Music Conference held annually in Meridian, Mississippi, in conjunction with the Jimmie Rodgers Memorial Festival. He is the author of articles, papers, and curriculum materials dealing with the educational applications of country music to curriculum. In 1984 Dr. Akenson received the Handy award from the Blues Foundation for his curriculum materials dealing with Jimmie Rodgers.

RICHARD AQUILA is professor of history and director of American studies at Ball State University. His publications include *The Iroquois Restoration* (1983) and *That Old Time Rock and Roll* (1989). He is currently editing a book, *The Sagebrush Connection: The American West and Popular Culture*.

WILLIAM BARLOW is an associate professor in the School of Communications at Howard University, Washington, D.C. He is the author of *Looking Up at Down: The Emergence of Blues Culture* (1989) and co-author with Jannette Dates of *Split Image: African Americans in the Mass Media* (1990). He is a scholar in residence at the Schomburg Center for Research in Black Culture in New York City.

JACQUELINE BOLES is professor of sociology at Georgia State University. She has published a number of articles on popular culture, focusing on strippers, fortune-tellers, and cartoon humor. She is currently working on an occupational study of entertainers and a research project on prostitution and AIDS.

VIRGINIA W. COOPER is an associate professor in the Department of Speech Communication and Theater Arts at Old Dominion University, Norfolk, Virginia. Her expertise is in interpersonal communication, with emphasis in interpersonal conflict, nonverbal communication, and gender communication. She has published articles in all three areas.

LINDA DAHL is the author of *Stormy Weather: The Music and Lives of a Century of Jazzwomen* (1984, 1989) and has lectured widely on the subject. Her other works include articles for magazines and textbooks on many aspects of Latin American culture. She is completing a novel, *Color-blind*, and preparing a book of short stories.

SCOTT JOHN HAMMOND is assistant professor of political science at James Madison University, Harrisonburg, Virginia. He is working on a defense of Marxian political philosophy.

FRED J. HAY received the Ph.D. from the University of Florida in anthropology and the master's in library and information studies from Florida State University. He has taught at St. Cloud State University, Manhattan Christian College, and Kansas State University and worked in libraries at Kansas State and Florida State universities. He has conducted ethnographic fieldwork in various regions of the U.S. South and in the Caribbean, concentrating on the cultures of the African diaspora. Hay is especially interested in the history and social organization of the blues. Author of *African-American Community Studies* (1991), as well as journal articles and reviews in anthropology, African-American studies, and social science documentation, Dr. Hay is currently employed by the Tozzer Library of Harvard University.

CHARLES JARET is associate professor of sociology at Georgia State University. He has an active interest in urban sociology and racial-ethnic relations and has co-authored several articles on popular music (with Lyn Thaxton). He is writing a textbook on racial-ethnic relations in the United States.

DAVID JOYNER is assistant professor of jazz studies at the University of North Texas, where he teaches jazz history and American popular music studies. He has been researching ragtime composed and published in the southern United States and is working on a textbook, *Jazz and American Popular Music*, and a chapter on ragtime for *Memphis Music*.

WILLIAM HOWLAND KENNEY III is associate professor of history and director of American studies at Kent State University, Kent, Ohio. His articles on the cultural history of jazz have appeared in many scholarly journals, including *American Music, American Studies, American Studies International, Black Perspective in Music,* and *Melus: A Journal of Multi-Ethnic Literature.*

MARTIN LAFORSE is a professor at Ithaca College. He has published articles in the *Journal of Popular Culture, Social Studies,* and *Social Education* and wrote *Popular Culture and American Life* (1981). He presents weekly radio broadcasts of mostly traditional jazz.

JEFFREY C. LIVINGSTON is assistant professor of history at California State University, Chico, where he teaches courses on U.S. foreign relations, twentieth-century America, and politics. He has published book reviews and articles in the fields of American diplomatic, political, and military history, including contributions to *Political Parties and Elections in the United States: An Encyclopedia* (1991). He is working on the history of conservatives' contributions to American globalism through a study of Ohio congressman John M. Vorys and on a book on twentieth-century popular music, war, and politics.

THERESE L. LUECK is an assistant professor of communication at the University of Akron. She received her Ph.D. in American culture from Bowling Green State University in 1989. Since the mid–1970s, she has worked periodically as a professional journalist.

KAREN SAUCIER LUNDY is associate professor and assistant director of the University of Southern Mississippi School of Nursing and holds a graduate appointment in sociology at Delta State University, Cleveland, Mississippi. She has done extensive research in the area of gender role socialization and the family and is the author of *Healers and Heartbreakers: Images of Women and Men in Country Music* (1986). Her current research is a comparative study of the Top 40 country songs of 1981 and 1988 regarding gender role images.

JAMES R. McDONALD is professor of English at Milliken University, Decatur, Illinois. He has taught a literature course on rock lyrics for over thirteen years and is the author of over a dozen articles on rock 'n' roll. He is working on a book on the poetic aspects of rock lyrics.

MELTON A. McLAURIN has been a professor of history at the University of North Carolina, Wilmington, since 1977. He has published several articles and books, most notably *Separate Pasts: Growing Up White in the Segregated South* (1987), and an essay, "Country Music and the Vietnam War," in *Perspectives on the American South* (1985).

CHARLES A. NANRY is a professor of human resource management and sociology at the Rutgers Institute of Management and Labor Relations and executive director of the Rutgers Center for Management Development. Over the last decade, he has served the New Jersey state government as a loaned executive (1984–1985), as the founding director of the senior executive service (1988–1990) and as acting commissioner of personnel (1989–1990). A noted jazz scholar, he has written and lectured on jazz as well as on topics related to personnel management, human resource development, and joint labor/management training programs.

KATHY J. OGREN is an associate professor of history at the University of Redlands. She is the author of articles and reviews concerning the cultural importance of jazz, including *The Jazz Revolution: Twenties America and the Meaning of Jazz* (1989). She is working on a study of jazz autobiographies.

JOHN ORMAN received his Ph.D. from Indiana University in 1979. He is the author of *The Politics of Rock Music* (1984). He teaches a course on the politics of popular culture at Fairfield University in Connecticut and is writing a book on celebrity politics. He is also the author of three books on the American presidency: *Presidential Secrecy and Deception* (1980), *Comparing Presidential Behavior* (1984), and *Presidential Accountability* (1990).

PATRICK R. PARSONS is an assistant professor of communication at the Pennsylvania State University. He received his Ph.D. from the University of Minnesota and has published in a number of journals, including *Journal of Communication*, *Popular Music and Society*, and *Journalism Quarterly*. His research interests include the political economy and organizational sociology of the mass media.

BURTON W. PERETTI is visiting assistant professor of American studies at the University of Kansas. He is the author of articles on music in the American culture since 1865 and a forthcoming book, *The Creation of Jazz: Music, Race, and Culture in Urban America*.

GEORGE M. PLASKETES is an assistant professor of communication at Auburn University. He teaches scriptwriting and other courses in radio, television, and film.

NOLAN PORTERFIELD is the author of *Jimmie Rodgers: The Life and Times of America's Blue Yodeler* (1979). His published work also includes the novel *A Way of Knowing* (1971) and numerous stories and articles in *Harper's*, *North American Review*, *Chicago*, and other magazines. He is at work on a biography of folk song collector John Lomax.

RUDOLF E. RADOCY is professor of art and music education and music therapy at the University of Kansas, where he teaches courses in musical psychology, sociology, and acoustics. He is co-author (with J. David Boyle) of *Measurement and Evaluation of Musical Experiences* (1987) and of two English and two Japanese editions of *Psychological Foundations of Musical Behavior* (1979). Dr. Radocy currently is editor of the *Journal of Research in Music Education*. His research interests include musical perception and preference, the influence of music on human activity, and social roles of music. He holds degrees from the Ohio State University, the University of Michigan, and the Pennsylvania State University.

JEROME RODNITZKY is professor of history at the University of Texas at Arlington, where he specializes in recent American cultural history. He holds a bachelor's and a master's degree from the University of Chicago and a Ph.D. in history from the University of Illinois.

CRAIG H. ROELL is assistant professor of business and cultural history at Georgia Southern University. He has authored a variety of books and articles, including *The Piano in America, 1890–1940* (1989); "Is a Decline in Piano Sales Inevitable? A Historic Analysis," *Music Trades* (February 1990); "John Philip Sousa," in *Great Lives from History* (Frank N. Magill, ed., 1987); *Lyndon B. Johnson: A Bibliography*, vol. 2 (1988); and, with Lewis L. Gould, *William McKinley: A Bibliography* (1988). He is working on a history of the American advertising and public relations industry.

CHARLES R. WARNER is an assistant professor of speech communication studies at East Stroudsburg University of Pennsylvania, where he teaches courses in film study, broadcast management, and popular culture. He is completing a study of the interface of reggae music, Western youth culture, and the music industry.

DEENA WEINSTEIN, professor of sociology at DePaul University, Chicago, is a sociological theorist with special interests in cultural theory and the contemporary cultural scene. She is the author of books, articles, and reviews in the areas of mass media, social organization, sociology of science, and sociological theory. Among her works on rock music are *Heavy Metal: A Cultural Sociology* (1991); *Serious Rock: The Artistic Vision of Modern Society in Pink Floyd, Rush and Bruce Springsteen* (1985); and "Rock: Youth and Its Music," in *Popular Music and Society* 9 (1985): 2–15. She is also a music journalist and reviewer of current metal releases.